1995

ABORTION:
A NEW GENERATION OF
CATHOLIC RESPONSES

CONTRIBUTORS TO THIS VOLUME

Gary M. Atkinson, Ph.D.
Professor of Philosophy
University of St. Thomas
St. Paul, Minnesota

The Reverend Robert Barry, O.P., Ph.D.
Visiting Assistant Professor of Religious Studies
University of Illinois
Champaign-Urbana, Illinois

Richard Berquist, Ph.D.
Associate Professor of Philosophy
University of St. Thomas
St. Paul, Minnesota

Richard J. Connell, Ph.D.
Emeritus Professor of Philosophy
University of St. Thomas
St. Paul, Minnesota

The Reverend Joseph J. Farraher, S.J., S.T.D.
Church of the Visitacion
San Francisco, California

Germain Grisez, Ph.D.
Flynn Chair in Christian Ethics
Mount Saint Mary's College
Emmitsburg, Maryland

James G. Hanink, Ph.D.
Professor of Philosophy
Loyola Marymount University

R. Mary Hayden, Ph.D.
Assistant Professor of Philosophy
University of St. Thomas
St. Paul, Minnesota

Stephen J. Heaney, Ph.D.
Assistant Professor of Philosophy
University of St. Thomas
St. Paul, Minnesota

J.M. Hubbard, Ph.D.
Associate Professor of Philosophy
University of St. Thomas
St. Paul, Minnesota

Mary R. Joyce, M.A.
St. Cloud, Minnesota

Robert E. Joyce, Ph.D.
Associate Professor of Philosophy
St. John's University
Collegeville, Minnesota

The Reverend Ronald D. Lawler, O.F.M., Cap., Ph.D.
Director of Education
Pope John XXIII Medical-Moral Research and Education Center
Braintree, Massachusetts

Patrick Lee, Ph.D.
Professor of Philosophy
Franciscan University of Steubenville
Steubenville, OH

Anne M. Maloney, Ph.D.
Assistant Professor of Philosophy
College of St. Catherine
St. Paul, Minnesota

William E. May, Ph.D.
Michael J. McGivney Professor of Moral Theology
Pope John Paul II Institute for
   Studies on Marriage and Family
Washington, D.C.

Dennis Q. McInerny, Ph.D.
Holy Apostles College and Seminary
Cromwell, Connecticut

Sister Renée Mirkes, O.S.F., M.A.
Department of Theology
Marquette University
Milwaukee, Wisconsin

Charles E. Rice, J.D.
Professor of Law
University of Notre Dame
Notre Dame, Indiana

The Reverend Richard R. Roach, S.J., Ph.D.
Associate Professor of Moral Theology
Marquette University
Milwaukee, Wisconsin

Janet E. Smith, Ph.D.
Assistant Professor of Philosophy
University of Dallas
Dallas, Texas

Mary Catherine Sommers, Ph.D.
Assistant Professor of Philosophy
University of St. Thomas
Houston, Texas

ABORTION:
A NEW
GENERATION OF
CATHOLIC
RESPONSES

Stephen J. Heaney
Editor

THE POPE JOHN CENTER

Nihil Obstat: Rev. James A. O'Donohoe, J.C.D.

Imprimatur: Bernard Cardinal Law   Date: November 20, 1992

The Nihil Obstat and Imprimatur are a declaration that a book or pamphlet is considered to be free from doctrinal or moral error. It is not implied that those who have granted the Nihil Obstat and Imprimatur agree with the contents, opinions or statements expressed.

Copyright 1992
by
The Pope John XXIII Medical-Moral
Research and Education Center
Braintree, Massachusetts 02184

Library of Congress Cataloging-in-Publication Data

Abortion : a new generation of Catholic responses / Stephen J.
    Heaney, editor.
        p.   cm.
    Includes bibliographical references.
    ISBN 0-935372-35-0
    1. Abortion—Religious aspects—Catholic Church.   I. Heaney,
    Stephen J.
    HQ767.3.A24   1992   92-37020
    241'.6976—dc20   CIP

Contents

One recent Sunday, the readings at Mass carried the message of following Christ by acting like Christ: those who followed Christ were those who showed compassion for, those who loved, one another. But in his homily, our priest drew together the elements of these readings with a jolt. Is this in fact how *we* are, he asked? How do we within the Church act toward one another? Are we not rather becoming our own worst enemy?

Intra-church squabbling on a whole range of issues comes across to the rest of the world as so much sniping and backbiting. Spend some time with enough Catholics, or read Catholic books, newspapers, and journals, and one comes to realize that this perception reflects reality. Some who dissent from the authority of the Magisterium spit the names of certain bishops and theologians from their mouths as though they had tasted sewage. Some who defend the Vatican are not only thrilled to see people silenced, or even excommunicated; they seem to hanker after a public flogging as well.

Is this how we Christians love one another?

There is a degree to which such reactions are understandable. Issues such as control of conception, homosexuality, economic structures, the use of deadly force, women's role in the Church, and papal authority touch people in general, but Catholics in particular, in the core of their being, often in a way which is perceived as a threat to their lifestyle or autonomy. This sets off an emotional response which is difficult to rein in. But rein it in we must, for while affective responses are vital to us and not to be ignored, we are still first and foremost creatures of reason and free will. Christ did not say "I hope you all like each other." Rather, he *commanded* us to *love* one another, not to feel certain things, but to *act* in certain ways which show respect for others, which bring about fulfillment of our human nature and lead us to salvation.

The abortion issue has been a severe trial to this commandment, because it brings into question how we act not only as private moral persons, but also as public persons in the legal and political arenas. Abortion stirs up raw emotion in a way no other issue does. Both sides in the debate—Catholics are no exception—are apparently driven by compassion for others. Both sides raise the specters of dead and butchered women, dead and abused children, uncaring men, and unjust societal structures. Ultimately, no one is willing to allow that loved ones, whom they consider "good people," should either be, or be considered, sinners.

The Catholic Church, in her tradition and teaching (if not always in the practice of her representatives) is a Church driven by Christ's commandment to love one another. But the Church's compassion for all human beings does not exist in a vacuum; it is wedded to the truth, the Truth who is Jesus, who is the truth about who we are as human beings, and about how we are to relate to each other, the world, and God. A compassion which steps away from that truth fails in the end even to be compassionate, for it leads people to actions which cannot fulfill them as human beings. The Church has taught from its earliest days that abortion is a grave moral evil, and its performance is an action utterly incompatible with the truth about human nature and God's plan for us. It is a teaching based in both head and heart, in reason and will, in truth and love.

There are those, Catholic and non-Catholic alike, who find the Church to be a model of neither compassion nor consistency. Among these people, many questions have arisen: Is the fetus a person? Might not the sacrifice of the fetus for the mother's health be proper as the lesser of two evils? Does not the Church lack consistency on this point with its other working principles (e.g., double effect, just war theory)? Is the impermissibility of abortion just another way for the Church to repress women? Do we have to be against abortion legally as well as morally? Why not let Catholic politicians actively support legal abortion? Why do Catholics have to obey the Magisterium to begin with?

When it is suggested that abortion is permissible, I generally hear one of two kinds of response. The first kind may be characterized as a direct call to the heart and will. This debate, it is argued, has been going on in this country for over twenty years. Appeals to the intellect have failed. It is time for books and articles, for television and movies which hit us in the gut. We need inspiration. Above all, we need massive amounts of prayer.

My own bent is to the intellect, and so my instinctive response is of the second variety. Prayer and inspiration are utterly necessary, and there are certainly those who have abandoned reason and are resorting to pure emotion and desire. But I have not yet concluded that all those who question Catholic teaching on abortion are blind to reasons. I rather think that the reasons have not yet been fully articulated, and that many reasons already on the table have not been heard by all who question the traditional teaching.

One must be very careful when either questioning or defending the Magisterium through reasoned arguments, for it is easy to slide into intellectual *hubris* and bad faith. For instance, many have called for "dialogue" about issues of dissent, including abortion. Dissenters have occasionally organized "debate anthologies," presenting pieces on both sides of the issue. It is no surprise that such "dialogues" often stretch the use of that term to its breaking point, pitting short, ineffectual essays against lengthy rebuttals in a one-sided debate. To be sure, however, some who support the Vatican's clear message on abortion are equally unwilling or unable to listen to their intellectual opponents. Certainly the arguments against abortion are available, but repeated allusions to the Vatican's "constant teaching" are not satisfying to those who search for reasons.

While some are not really interested in hearing good reasons for a position, many who follow the abortion debate are truly searching: those who are formally non-Catholic, but who look everywhere for well-reasoned arguments on either side; those who have been influenced by dissent, but are not sure of their dissent in their hearts and minds and consciences; and those who remain faithful to the Church, but do not fully understand *why the Church's position makes sense.*

It is for these people that this book was put together. Assembling some of the best minds in the United States, women and men educated both before and after Vatican II, this book sets out to demonstrate with force and detail not simply *what* the Catholic Church teaches on abortion, but *why* it holds this position, and why this is the *only* position that *really makes sense.*

In this volume, the reader will find essays addressing historical misconceptions used to justify abortion, moral methodology and its application to abortion, the personhood of the unborn, pluralism and dissent, feminist issues, public policy and legal responses, and scriptural insights into the Church's understanding of the evil of abortion. Not every argument proposed in support of abortion can be taken up in a limited space, but most have been addressed, dissected, and exposed, and a more logical argument offered in rebuttal.

The authors in this volume write from varying perspectives, and use different philosophical and theological methods. While no one of these methods or perspectives is Church teaching, each author recognizes the truth and authority of Church teaching, and offers support for it. The articles display varying degrees of difficulty and technicality, appropriate to differing topics. Still, each makes its point with rational force.

It would be all too easy to refuse to participate in the dialogue which has been called for, to retreat to the safety of the authority of the Magisterium, to rebuff those who question Church teaching by saying, "The issue has already been settled." Settled the issue may be, but the questioners are not, and so such questioning must be listened to, and answered, in good faith. The authors in this volume will take these questions seriously, yet still defend the traditional position of the Catholic Church: abortion is a grave evil, never to be performed. We will articulate this position rationally and clearly—and passionately. But our passion, we pray, is not contempt; it is rather, we hope, the fire of the Holy Spirit, the fire of the Truth which will set us free.

In the spirit of truth, it is important to acknowledge and thank those who allowed me to follow my passion to bring this volume together. The members of my own department of philosophy at the University of St. Thomas in St. Paul not only allowed my passion, but actively encouraged and participated in it. Several present and former members are contributors, and several others were held back only by pressing responsibilities. Without their participation and guidance, this would have been a very lonely task indeed. To the other contributors, I extend my thanks not only for their insights and erudition, but also for their Job-like patience while waiting for this book to fall into place.

The Pope John Center deserves an enormous hand for picking up this project under less-than-ideal circumstances, and making it work. Especially to be thanked are Daniel O'Brien, M.A., formerly with the Center, who was the first copy editor and editorial advisor; those who gave editorial assistance, Father John A. Leies, S.M., S.T.D., Father Russell E. Smith, S.T.D., and Father Donald G. McCarthy, Ph.D.; and our second copy editor and editorial advisor, Peter J. Cataldo, Ph.D., who brought the book into the light of day through gentle but firm coaxing and lots of hard work. A word of gratitude also goes to the Homeland Foundation and the De Rance Foundation for their generous grants toward the publication of this volume.

On a more personal note, I would like to thank my parents for showing me, by their example, the importance of love for my fellow human beings and for the Truth. Finally, I must thank my wife Anne—the one with whom I am one, in this struggle as in life—who illumines new vistas and challenges me to continue to grow in care and in the Truth.

Stephen J. Heaney
Editor

PART ONE

PERSONHOOD

Chapter 1

WHEN DO PEOPLE BEGIN?

Germain Grisez

"People" here does not refer to God or angels. However, it refers not only to human persons but to beings like E.T., for if such beings arrived on earth, we surely would consider them people like ourselves.

In a 1970 book on abortion, I treated three questions about people's beginnings. When do human individuals begin? In moral reflection, which human individuals should count as persons? And, which for legal purposes? I concluded that most human individuals begin at fertilization and that both morality and law should consider all of

Published in the *Proceedings of the American Catholic Philosophical Association,* Vol. LXIII, 1989, pp. 27–47. Revised and printed here with permission.

them persons.[1] I still think that. But to remedy defects in my treatment and to deal with two decades of development in both embryology and the debate, the questions need fresh treatment, which this paper only sketches out. I hope it will encourage and help someone to write a book on the subject.

To those who are persons, personhood is either accidental or essential. If accidental, it is either bestowed by others or acquired naturally. If essential, persons are either nonbodily substances or bodily. If bodily, either they come to be by substantial change after the biological beginning of new human individuals or every new human individual is a person. And new human individuals come to be either after or at fertilization. Thus, there are six answers to our question.

I. Some think that personhood is a status bestowed by others. On this notion, people begin when others accept them as persons.

II. Others think that personhood is an attribute that some entities develop by a natural process. On this notion, people begin when nonpersonal entities become able to behave as persons.

III. Others think that only certain nonbodily substances—for example, souls or minds—are persons. On this notion, the beginning of a bodily individual need not be the beginning of a person.

IV. Others think that only human bodies with the organic basis for intellectual acts can receive personal souls. On this notion, prepersonal human organisms substantially change into persons.

V. Others think that all whole, human individuals are persons, but that none of them begins until the primitive streak stage. On this notion, people begin two to three weeks after fertilization.

VI. I think that all whole, bodily, substantial individuals of any species having a rational nature are persons, and that most human individuals begin at fertilization. On this notion, most human people begin when a human sperm and ovum fuse.

I shall first dispose of objections against the sixth position by criticizing the other five. Then I shall sketch out the proper rationale of the sixth position.

I. Personhood: A Status Bestowed

Pierre de Locht, a Belgian theologian, having suggested that abortion involves a conflict of rights, formulated one line of argument for the notion that personhood is a status bestowed by others:

> But it seems to me useful to pose a preliminary question: How is one constituted a human person? Is it by a merely biological act? It seems to me astonishing that a spiritual being be constituted by a solely biological act. Does not the fact that the parents *perceive* the fetus as a human person make any difference in its constitution as a human being, as a spiritual being? Is it not necessary that there be established a relation of person to person, a relation of generators with the fetus, for it to become a human person?[2]

On this proposal, parents confer personhood on a fetus by perceiving it as a *thou*, and so giving it a place in the human community.

I suggest arguments along the following lines against this view.

Suppose a pregnant woman does not perceive the fetus as a person, but her husband does. Is that fetus a person or not?

Underlying de Locht's proposal, undoubtedly, is the fact that human meaning-giving constitutes social and cultural realities. But unlike such realities, people are principles of society and culture. So, human meaning-giving presupposes rather than constitutes people.

Also underlying his proposal is the insight that persons are beings who exist only in interpersonal communion. But granting this, one can argue, even without invoking faith, that human individuals are constituted persons not by their parents' perception of them but by God's creative knowledge and love of them.[3]

5

Mary Warnock, who thinks one can handle relevant moral issues without settling the question of personhood, offers another line of argument for the notion that personhood is a status which others bestow:

> The philosopher John Locke understood that, as he put it, the word 'person' (which he distinguished from the word 'man') is not a biological but a *forensic* term. That is as much as to say that whether or not someone, or some corporate body, is to be deemed a person is something that must be *decided.* To settle it, we need to know the criteria that have been established for settling such cases, or else we must establish new criteria for ourselves.[4]

She adds that there can be bad criteria for making such designations, and rejects as not generally applicable a criterion for personhood some apply to neonates, namely, whether they are wanted.

I suggest arguments along the following lines against this view.

Warnock is right in rejecting wantedness as a criterion for personhood. But can she reject it because of its lack of general applicability? To do so is to apply something like the Golden Rule, and to apply such a principle is to presuppose that one can pick out the *others* whom one should do unto as one would be done unto. But Warnock denies that there is any determinate class of relevant others prior to the decision about criteria.

Admittedly, biologists can do without the word "person," and the law does bestow personhood on corporations, seagoing ships, and so on, as well as on some human individuals, while denying it to others. For instance, Chief Standing Bear of the Poncas became a person in April 1879 by a court decision rejecting the U.S. district attorney's contention that the Chief was not a person "within the meaning of the law." The following month, when Standing Bear's brother, Big Snake, tried to leave the reservation, General Sherman pointed out that the decision about Standing Bear applied only to him, and Big Snake was shot to death while resisting arrest.[5] To those who decided criteria for his personhood, Big Snake was not a person, and so the Golden Rule did not apply to him.

The argument I shall sketch out against the second notion of personhood also tells against any version of this first one.

II. Personhood: An Attribute Acquired by Development

Michael Tooley is the leading proponent of this notion of personhood. Like Warnock, he denies that personhood is reducible to membership in the biological species *homo sapiens*[6] and thinks that he can resolve relevant moral issues without settling the definition of "person." But unlike Warnock, Tooley thinks he can settle the definition of "person" by rational inquiry.[7] His strategy is to begin from ethical judgments:

> ... one can first determine what properties, other than potentialities, suffice to endow an entity with a right to life. Then one can define the term 'person' as applying to all and only those things that have at least one of the relevant properties.[8]

To determine what properties suffice to endow an entity with the right to life, Tooley treats rights in general. He assumes that nothing which lacks desires can have rights.[9] On this assumption he argues:

> The non-potential property that makes an individual a person—that is, that makes the destruction of something intrinsically wrong, and seriously so, and that does so independently of the individual's value—is the property of being an enduring subject of non-momentary interests.[10]

Tooley includes the phrase "and that does so independently of the individual's value" to distinguish people from objects such as works of art whose destruction also might be considered intrinsically and seriously wrong.[11] He understands "being an enduring subject of non-momentary interests" in a way that requires "possession, either now or at some time in the past, of a sense of time, of a concept of a continuing subject of mental states, and of a capacity for thought episodes."[12]

Thus, in specifying that personhood be defined by a "non-potential property," Tooley wishes to exclude its definition by an operative potency, such as reason. He does not justify this restriction, but simply stipulates that the defining property may not be potential.[13] He thus excludes not only unborn but newborn babies from personhood.

Tooley also assumes that the morality of acts which bear on others depends on how those acts affect their getting what they want. His metaethics provides no direct support for this ethics; indeed, in discussing metaethics, Tooley claims that he rests nothing important on his view of it.[14] Since he criticizes people who hold ethical theories at odds with his, Tooley perhaps feels that he indirectly establishes his ethical theory. But he does not, because in many cases his criticisms do not concern his opponents' ethical theories. Thus, Tooley provides no grounds, direct or indirect, for accepting the ethical theory he presupposes.[15]

It follows that Tooley's affirmative argument as a whole is question begging against most who disagree with his views on abortion and infanticide.[16]

Against the notion that personhood is an acquired attribute, I suggest the following line of argument.

Both this notion of personhood and the previous one miss what "people" usually means in ordinary language. True, personhood has ethical implications, adult human beings are paradigmatic instances of the concept of *person*, and the word "person" does not mean the same thing as the phrase "member of the species *homo sapiens.*" Still, in ordinary language "person" refers to newborn babies as well as to grown men and women.[17] And we can see why "person" is used in this way precisely by beginning from paradigmatic instances of the concept of *person.*

Adults regularly speak of themselves as persons—for example, when they use personal pronouns—in ways which show that they think of their personhood, not as an acquired trait, but as an aspect of their very being. When one says "I cannot remember that far back; my earliest memory is . . . ," one assumes that one already existed before one had that experience; when one says "I was born at such and such a time and place," one takes the word "I" to refer to the same person one now is.

To put the point in logical language: "person" connotes a *substance sortal.* But a substance sortal is an essential property, which implies that whatever has it necessarily has it and never exists without it: individual persons come to be and become persons at the same time, and they cannot cease to be persons without ceasing to be the individuals they are.[18]

Now, a sound, nonstipulative definition of anything must begin by picking out what is to be defined, and this picking out must employ a concept underlying ordinary language. In forming the definition, one can refine this concept and adjust its extension. But no sound nonstipulative definition can set aside the logic of the concept from which the inquiry began insofar as that logic is evident in the use of the word to refer to the concept's paradigmatic instances. It follows that notions of personhood as a bestowed status or an acquired trait can only be technical notions, and that neither of them can ground a satisfactory answer to the question "When do people begin?" if that question is understood as people in general understand and wonder about it.[19]

III. Personhood: Limited to Nonbodily Substances

If personhood is limited to nonbodily substances, we bodily individuals are persons only because our bodies are associated with the nonbodily entities that we really are. Such a view is dualism, whether cast in terms of soul and body, mind and body, or noumenal self and phenomenal self.

Classical arguments for dualism—for example, those involving the thesis that thought and extension are incompatible properties— were based on the irreducibility to bodily functioning of acts of inquiry, free choice, and purposeful use.[20] Today, hardly anyone argues for dualism, but many assume it. For example, Joseph Fletcher thinks the solution to questions about abortion would be to deny that a fetus is a personal being. He holds that the body is not part of the person, and that persons are to their bodies as artists are to their materials.[21]

Although Tooley mainly defends the second notion of personhood, he also slips into dualism. For example, he says that if a human being irreparably loses cerebral functioning, "it seems plausible to hold that although a human organism lingers on, the conscious individual once associated with that body no longer exists."[22] Again, he argues that a person would be destroyed but no biological organism would be killed if the brain of an adult human were completely reprogrammed with totally different "memories," beliefs, attitudes, and personality traits—for instance, "The pope is reprogrammed, say, on the model of David Hume."[23]

Against the notion of personhood which limits it to nonbodily substances, I know of only the following line of argument.

Every dualism sets out to be a theory of one's personal identity as a unitary and subsisting self—a self always organically living, but only discontinuously conscious, and now and then inquiring, choice-making, and using means to achieve purposes. But every form of dualism renders inexplicable the unit in complexity which we experience in every act we consciously do. For instance, as I write this, I am the unitary subject of *my* fingers hitting the keys, the sensations *I* feel in them, the thought *I* am expressing, *my* commitment to do this paper, and *my* use of the computer to express *myself.* So, in me thought and extension (thinking and moving my fingers) coexist, and dualism starts out to explain me. But every dualism ends by denying that there is any *one* something of which to be the theory. It does not explain me; it tells me about two things, one a nonbodily person and the other a nonpersonal body, neither of which I can recognize as myself. Therefore, whatever persons are, personhood cannot be limited to nonbodily substances.[24]

If the views considered thus far are excluded, it follows that human persons come to be when their personal bodies come to be and cease to be when their personal bodies die.[25]

IV. Personhood: Dependent on Sense Organs and a Brain

Proponents of the theory of delayed hominization reject dualism but hold that an early embryo cannot be a personal body, since, they say, personhood depends on sense organs and a brain. Unlike Tooley, they think that personhood is an essential property. But like him, they think that personhood requires a certain level of organic development. They hold that the early embryo really is a prepersonal entity, which substantially changes into a person when the sense organs and brain develop. Joseph F. Donceel, S. J., argued for this view.[26]

Relying on Aristotle's biology, St. Thomas thought that an active power in semen gradually forms a new living individual out of *non-living* matter (the menstrual blood) and that the developing body is not ready to receive a personal soul until at least forty days after conception. Donceel rejects Aristotle's biology but thinks that modern biology together with the hylemorphic theory still requires delayed hominization.

Donceel's argument for delayed hominization is that since the soul is the substantial form of the body, and a substantial form can exist only in matter able to receive it, the personal soul can exist only in a highly organized body.[27] Donceel notes: "Philosophically speaking, we can be certain that an organism is a human person only from its activities." But that would delay hominization until long after birth. So, he concludes:

> The least we may ask before admitting the presence of a human soul is the availability of these organs: the senses, the nervous system, the brain, and especially the cortex. Since these organs are not ready during early pregnancy, I feel certain that there is no human person until several weeks have elapsed.[28]

In a footnote to this passage, Donceel clearly excludes personhood during the first two or three months after conception.

Against the notion that personhood is delayed until the brain and sense organs develop, I suggest the following line of argument.

Substantial changes are radical, and in typical instances—such as death, digestion of food, and chemical reactions—their occurrence is clearly marked. But nothing in the nervous system's development clearly marks any substantial change. Hence, everything depends on Donceel's interpretation of the hylemorphic theory.

Donceel plainly realizes it would be ludicrous to say that babies substantially change into persons some time after they are born. So he settles for hominization when the brain *first* begins to develop. However, this beginning of the brain's development is not the bodily basis for intellectual activities but only its precursor. Now, if this precursor satisfies the requirement of the hylemorphic theory, there is no reason why earlier precursors should fail to satisfy it. But each embryonic individual has from the outset its specific developmental tendency, which includes the epigenetic primordia of all its organs. Therefore, the hylemorphic theory does not preclude a human zygote's having a personal soul.[29]

It follows that neither the facts nor the theory establishes the substantial change which delayed hominization involves.[30] Thus, that substantial change and the multiplication of entities it involves are unnecessary. Now, entities are not to be multiplied without necessity. Consequently, delayed hominization is to be rejected.[31]

Besides Donceel's argument based on hylemorphism, people sometimes offer other arguments to support a theory somewhat like his.

One is the argument that since brain death is sufficient to mark the death of the person, the onset of brain function is necessary to mark the beginning of the person.[32] This argument fails for two reasons.

First, "brain death" means an irreversible loss of function. But the early embryo only temporarily lacks brain functions. So, the cases are not alike.

Second, "brain death" has two meanings. In one sense, it refers to the irreversible loss of cerebral functions; in another, it refers to the irreversible loss of all functioning of the whole brain. If the argument from brain death is based on the former, it is likely to be question begging, since those who reject delayed hominization generally also deny that a person who loses only cerebral functions is dead. But if the argument is based on the latter, the assumed correspondence between life's beginning and its end does not obtain.

For when the whole brain is dead, nothing remains to integrate the functioning of the organism, and so the organism has ceased to be, and, therefore, the person is dead. By contrast, before the brain develops—even in the zygote—something (some "primary organ" in a broad sense) integrates the whole embryo's organic functioning, and a unified, whole, human individual is developing. As the development of the whole goes on, so does the development of its integrating principles, until, finally, the mature brain integrates the mature individual's functioning.

Another sort of argument for delayed hominization is drawn from common sense. Someone indicates some clear and striking difference between the early embryo and any experientially typical person, even a newborn—for example, "The fertilized egg is much smaller than the period at the end of this sentence," or "It has no eyes, no ears, no mouth, no brain, and like a parasite draws its nourishment from the pregnant woman's blood." Pictures or drawings of very early embryos support such statements, and many people think that this evidence shows that hominization is delayed until the embryo's eighth to twelfth week of development.

Such arguments are rhetorically powerful because they use imagery and directly affect feelings. Usually, in judging whether or not to apply a predicate to an experienced entity, we do not examine it to see whether it meets a set of intelligible criteria. We judge by appearances, using as our guide past experience of individuals of that sort. The early embryo, usually never experienced, falls far outside the range of sensory standards for recognizing people. Images of early embryos do not *fit*; the test of appearances indicates that these strange entities are not persons. The impression is like that of someone who never saw anyone of a different race: those strangers surely are not people.

One can answer this argument only by dealing with its instances: in each case one must point out that while the difference to which attention is called is striking because of our limited experience, entities which are different in that way can meet the intelligible criteria for personhood.[33]

V. Personal Individuals: Formed Two Weeks after Fertilization

This is the view of those who hold that all whole human individuals are persons but maintain that no human individual *ever* begins before the stage of early development after which no individual *can* begin. Norman M. Ford, S.D.B., makes the fullest case I know of for this position.

Ford grants that the zygote "shows all the signs of a single living individual since its activities are all directed from within in an orderly fashion."[34] He also reports the finding of a Royal Commission, which took evidence from "eminent scientists from all over the world. None of them suggested that human life begins at any time other than at conception." Ford adds: "Most embryologists and biologists would appear to agree."[35]

Yet, Ford thinks that persons begin more than two weeks *after* fertilization.[36] Why? Unlike Tooley and others, Ford does not argue that the zygote is only a potential human individual. He acknowledges that the zygote is a real, biologically human individual, but maintains that it is not "ontologically" the same individual as the eventual baby. To prove this, Ford offers arguments to show that there are philosophically significant discontinuities of existence that most scientists overlook.[37]

Ford bases one of his arguments on the fact that, until the primitive streak stage, identical twins can develop from a single zygote. He says that this shows that the zygote has an inherent *active* potentiality to become one or more human beings. And because all the cells into which a zygote divides in the first few cell divisions could, if separated, develop into complete individuals, Ford thinks that every zygote has the capacity for twinning. This leads to a dilemma. If the zygote is a human individual because it can develop into an adult, its openness to becoming one or more adults implies the absurdity that it is at once both one individual and many.[38] But if the zygote *already* is a human individual in its own right, when twinning occurs, that individual either begets its own sibling or ceases to be without dying, leaving behind two new human individuals as its remains. If the former, Ford argues, there would be nothing to determine which twin had been the zygote, since the two would be identical in every way: "Both would be identical indiscernibles, except for their separate concrete existences."[39] But if the latter, both identical twins would be the grandchildren of their putative parents.[40]

Animal experiments also show that genetically distinct embryonic cells or groups of cells can be joined together to develop into one chimeric individual. Ford says that this fact shows that the zygote and the cells into which it divides in the very early stages are too indeterminate to constitute a real ongoing human individual.[41]

Moreover, the zygote's development does not at once differentiate the cells which form the embryo proper from those which form the placenta and other accessory tissues. Ford thinks that this temporary indeterminacy shows that the zygote cannot already be the ontological human individual.[42] He acknowledges that some biologists say that the accessory tissues are an organ of the baby until it is born. But he argues that these tissues cannot be part of the individ-

14

ual: identical twins can share them, fertilization involving only male chromosomes sometimes develops into placental tissue without an embryo (hydatidiform mole), and chimeras can be formed of cells sufficiently differentiated that the embryo proper and the accessory tissues differ genetically from each other.[43]

In some species, ova can develop parthenogenetically— without any sperm. Such development has been induced in mice, but never goes beyond the early stages. Ford thinks that those who hold that the human individual begins before implantation also must hold that a parthenogenetic human embryo would be a human individual.[44]

Ford's main argument—the one he offers for his position that the human individual begins precisely at the primitive streak stage— is that only then does a tiny individual take definite shape with recognizable boundaries, a front and back, a right and left, a head end and lower end. He considers this decisive:

> The unity of the individual human organism would imply a characteristic minimal specific heterogeneity of quantitative parts arranged to provide determinate sites for the coordinated development of structures, tissues and organs along a primordial body axis.[45]

Ford supports this point by invoking the testimony of a biologist, a physician, and two theologians who agree that individuality begins at the primitive streak stage.[46]

Besides his direct arguments, Ford argues for his position indirectly by giving an account of the discontinuity he asserts between the zygote (which he admits is a *biologically* human, new individual) and the "ontologically" human individual which he thinks begins at the primitive streak stage. When the first cell division occurs, he says, the individual which was the zygote ceases to be. From then until the primitive streak stage, each of the multiplying cells is a distinct individual. Thus, the true human individual emerges from "a few thousand" distinct individuals.[47]

Against the notion that personhood never begins until about two weeks after fertilization, I suggest the following line of argument.

Despite the facts about twinning, chimeras, and so on, most unborn babies with their accessory tissues develop from a single zygote and are alone in developing from that zygote. Unless the facts support Ford's theory that the baby is formed at the primitive streak stage from a few thousand distinct individuals (the "mass" of cells), in most cases individuality will have to be admitted *to appear* to be continuous, and there will be no reason to deny it, unless the arguments from twinning, chimeras, and so on *by themselves* plainly show that a substantial change is absolutely required—for example, at the primitive streak stage.[48]

Now, the evidence does not support Ford's theory that cell division gives rise to really distinct individuals until a small army of them form the true human individual. It would be interesting to review the facts. But it is enough to notice that if they supported Ford's theory, most biologists would not think: "Fertilization in mammals normally represents the beginning of life for a new individual."[49]

Ford tries to minimize the evidence for the functional unity of the developing "mass" of cells.[50] He also argues that to use this evidence to establish individuality is to beg the question, because distinct individuals—the male and female, and also the sperm and ovum—likewise function toward a common end. Of course, Ford is right that groups of individuals can function toward one end, but he ignores a fact about such a group which prevents us from regarding it as an individual: it is not even a *physical* whole, undivided in itself.

Moreover, the coordinated functioning of male and female, sperm and ovum, can be explained, but Ford has trouble explaining why a few thousand distinct individuals work together in embryogenesis to make themselves into one individual. Finally, he says:

> Prior to this [primitive streak] stage we do not have a living individual human body, but a mass of pre-programmed loosely organized developing cells and heterogeneous tissues until their 'clock' mechanisms become synchronized and triggered to harmoniously organize, differentiate and grow as heterogeneous parts of a single whole human organism.[51]

However, Ford's own summary of the scientific literature indicates that the synchronization and triggering essential to his account are a construct that he imposes on the data. For he says that embryologists

... suggest that the timing of early differentiation at the blastocyst stage is governed by some 'clock' mechanism inbuilt into the DNA of the chromosomes of each cell of the embryo. It seems to be set from the time of fertilization, with each cell's 'clock' running in dependence on, and in co-ordination with, what is happening in its surrounding cells.[52]

If so, the cells and tissues do not need to have their "clock" mechanisms synchronized and triggered, because they always are working together harmoniously, which is to be expected if they are, not a mass of distinct individuals, but integral parts of one developing *individual.*

It follows that most unborn babies with their accessory tissues appear to be individuals continuous with the biologically human, new individuals formed at fertilization. Thus, the question is: Do twinning and so on *by themselves* show that the "ontological" human individual comes to be by a substantial change at the primitive streak stage?

The phenomena of twinning and chimeras do not. Even Ford does not suggest that all zygotes have an active tendency to become parts of chimeras. If all zygotes had an active potentiality to become twins, they would do so unless some accident prevented it. Thus, contrary to what Ford asserts (without argument), in those zygotes which develop continuously as individuals, the facts do not evidence an *active* potentiality to develop otherwise. Rather, at most the facts show that all early embryos could *passively* undergo division or combination.

Nor is it evidence of substantial change that the zygote will develop not only into the embryo proper but into the accessory tissues which will be discarded as afterbirth. The accessory tissues are an organ of the unborn baby. Identical twins can share this organ until birth just as Siamese twins can share other organs at birth. Hydatidiform mole, an abnormal development, will be considered below. That chimeras can be formed with accessory tissues from one contributor and an embryo proper from another does not show that the accessory tissues are not an organ of the embryo, for chimeras also can be formed in which the embryo proper includes genetically different contributions.

Nor does the fact that the embryo proper first becomes recognizable at the primitive streak stage show that a substantial change brings the person into being at this stage. For once one sets aside Ford's hypothesis that many distinct individuals form one individual, his main argument comes down to an appeal to common sense: all the people we know have at least a recognizable, definitely shaped body; prior to the primitive streak stage there is no recog izable embryo proper; so, prior to this stage there is no "ontological" human individual. Like all appeals to common sense, this argument is based on appearances. It does not show that a substantial change occurs at the primitive streak stage, for it does not show that either new individuals or the epigenetic primordia of a developed human person come to be only at this stage.

A hydatidiform mole is a new organic individual, genetically both human and unique, but it is not a new human being. Why not? A sperm and an ovum are two distinct organisms, each an individual cell with its own membrane. A sperm loses its membrane when it enters the ovum; the ovum quickly reacts; the two cells fuse into one, and the process of development begins.[53] The sperm and the ovum no longer exist as distinct entities; the activated ovum is a new, biologically human individual.[54] If it has in itself the epigenetic primordia of a human body normal enough to be the organic basis of at least some intellectual act, this new individual is a person. But the activated ovum lacks these epigenetic primordia if it includes *in itself* anything which predetermines it, genetically or otherwise, to develop only into accessory tissues. That is the case with the activated ovum which develops into a hydatidiform mole.[55]

There are no logical or biological problems if identical twins come about by the division of a previous individual and if chimeric individuals are formed from previously distinct individuals.[56] Ford virtually admits as much when he is reduced to saying that such an account "has little appeal" and that "it would be more plausible to argue that an ontological human individual had not yet begun to exist."[57] It does offend common sense to say that a couple's identical twins are really their grandchildren. But common sense simply cannot be trusted when the subject matter is unfamiliar. Moreover, the twins are not grandchildren in the familiar sense, but descendants mediated in an unfamiliar way.[58]

In sum, Ford's supposedly inductive philosophical reasoning actually proceeds from judgments of common sense, based on appearances. None of his arguments shows that scientists overlook philosophically significant discontinuities in development.

Many, especially of a theological bent, deny the personhood of the zygote with an argument which Ford satisfactorily answers. Donceel, for example, cites a theological opinion which questions basing moral norms on the supposition that hominization occurs at conception, inasmuch as "50% of the 'human beings'—real human beings with an 'immortal' soul and an eternal destiny—do not, from the very start, get beyond this first stage of a human existence."[59] As Ford points out, many natural pregnancy losses are due to severe chromosomal defects (and so as explained above are not losses of human beings). Moreover, for most of human history the infant mortality rate was very high. And, theologically, the argument is presumptuous, since we know nothing about how God provides for those who never come to the use of reason.[60]

VI. Persons: All Whole, Bodily Individuals with a Rational Nature

According to this notion, what is necessary and sufficient to be a human person is to be a whole, bodily individual with a human nature. On this notion, if a human activated ovum has in itself the epigenetic primordia of a human body normal enough to be the organic basis of some intellectual act, that activated ovum is a person.[61] But some activated ova are too abnormal to be people, and some people, including some or all identical twins, never were activated ova. Thus, most human persons begin at fertilization, although some begin during the next two or three weeks by others' dividing and perhaps also by others' combining.

The argument that a normal human zygote is a person is *not* that it is a *potential* person, which will develop into an actual person if all goes well. The argument, rather, is that the activated ovum which has suitable epigenetic primordia is an *actual* human individual which—unless he or she ceases to be, which can happen to anyone—will remain the same individual while developing continuously into a grown man or woman. Now, whatever, remaining the same individual, will develop into a paradigmatic instance of a substantial kind already is an actual instance of that kind.

Thus, to deny that the activated ovum is a person is either to deny that any bodily human individual is a person or to posit a substantial change between the zygote and the adult. Arguments against the fourth and fifth notions of personhood exclude substantial change, and the argument against dualism excludes denying personhood to bodily individuals.

A unique, human genome is neither necessary nor sufficient to constitute a person. It is not necessary, since someone like E.T. would be a person without a human genome and identical twins are persons with the same genome. It is not sufficient, since a unique, human genome is present in tissues surviving from people who have died as well as in hydatidiform moles and other biologically human entities which lack the epigenetic primordia that make normal human zygotes persons.

Persons are whole bodily individuals. The human body is personal through and through: if others harm my body, they harm me, for my body is I. Yet persons are more than their bodies; we subsist in our bodies but transcend them. So, although I am my body, I am not my body in the *same sense* that my body is I. I am the subject of my bodily properties, processes, sensations, and feelings, but I also am the subject of my non-bodily intellectual knowledge and choices, and my more-than-bodily use of things to achieve my purposes.

Tooley raises an important question: How can personhood defined in terms of *rational nature* account for the ethical significance that each individual's personhood has for others' moral responsibilities?[62] For instance, why should newborn babies' personhood require their parents and others not to kill them? The answer is that all moral responsibilities toward others arise, not from their desires and interests, as Tooley assumes, but from moral truth, beginning with the first principles of practical reason, which direct deliberation and freely chosen acts toward the fulfillment of persons—of the agent and of others as well—in interpersonal communion. Precisely because the goods which are objects of these principles are aspects of what unborn and newborn babies *can* be as persons, these goods generate responsibilities toward these persons, not on the basis of anything actual about them beyond their being persons, but precisely on the basis of their potentialities and needs, whose fulfillment depends as much on the love and care of their parents and others as on their own eventual desires for goods and efforts to attain them.[63]

Tooley's work also shows that if one defends the sixth notion of the person, one must carefully handle the metaphysical and logical concepts involved. One must explain and defend *substance, individual,* and so on.[64]

If the preceding lines of argument were developed fully, would there remain any room for questions about whether normal human zygotes are people? Perhaps room for theoretical questions—which always can be raised—but not for practical doubt. There is a very strong factual and theoretical ground for thinking that almost all of us once were zygotes. The counterpositions are weak. To be willing to kill what for all one knows is a person is to be willing to kill a person. Hence, in making moral judgments the unborn should be considered persons from the beginning—their lives instances of innocent human life.[65]

Some argue that a notion of personhood like Warnock's is sufficient at least for legal purposes. I still consider sound the case I made against that position in my book on abortion. That case is complex, but its central idea is simple:

> The law with all its fictions and devices exists to serve persons, to protect them, to guide them in fulfilling their duties, to assist them in vindicating their rights. People are not for the law; the law is for people. Thus the person in a sense stands outside the legal system and above it. Hence the law cannot dispose of persons by its own fiat, any more than action upon a stage can make non-entities of the producer, the stage crew, and the audience.[66]

Thus, when fundamental rights are at stake, just law may not stipulate who are persons but must recognize as persons all who really are persons.

NOTES

1. *Abortion: The Myths, the Realities, and the Arguments* (New York: Corpus, 1970), 11–33, 273–307, 361–410.

2. Pierre de Locht, "Discussion," in *L'Avortement: Actes du Xème Colloque International de Sexologie* (Louvain: Centre International Cardinal Suenens, 1968), 2:155 (my translation). Also see: Louis Beirnaert, S.J., "L'avortement: est-il un infanticide?" *Études*, 333 (1970), 520–23.

3. Stanislaw Grygiel developed this argument in a lecture, "The Identity of the Unborn Human Person," at a conference, *Marriage and Family in Modern Culture*, 17–20 March 1988, Franciscan University of Steubenville (Ohio). Dr. Grygiel's address: John Paul II Institute for Studies on Marriage and Family; Pontifical Lateran University; Piazza S. Giovanni in Laterano, 4; 00120 Vatican City.

4. "Do Human Cells Have Rights?" *Bioethics*, (1987), 2.

5. Dee Brown, *Bury My Heart at Wounded Knee* (New York: Holt, Rinehart and Winston, 1970), 351–66.

6. Tooley argues this point at length: *Abortion and Infanticide* (Oxford: Clarendon Press, 1983), 50–86.

7. Ibid., 33–39.

8. Ibid., 35. Tooley here states his strategy only in a provisional way; he later dispenses with "right to life" and finally holds (419) "that it is being a subject of non-momentary interests that makes something a person." My criticism will not depend on the difference between his formulations.

9. See ibid., 95–123, where Tooley undertakes to argue for this view, but begs the question by assuming what he needs to prove (101). A telling critique of this element of Tooley's position: Michael Wreen, "Whatever Happened to Baby Jane?" *Nous*, forthcoming.

10. Ibid., 303.

11. Ibid., 53–54.

12. Ibid., 419–20.

13. Ibid., 34–35. Because normal adults are paradigmatic instances of the concept of *person* and because Tooley argues at length against restricting personhood to human beings, his stipulation might seem to him reasonable. But granting those points, one can hold a principle such as Jane Beer Blumenfeld proposes: "It is morally wrong to intentionally kill an innocent individual belonging to a species whose members typically are rational beings, unless at least one of the following conditions obtains:... " But Tooley also rejects (ibid., 69–72) this proposal, and in doing so he simply assumes that individuals who have not manifested rationality can at most have a potentiality for it (rather than have it as a capacity which will be exercised under suitable conditions).

14. Ibid., 24.

15. That ethical theory—which is consequentialist—is shared by many others who defend this notion of personhood. For example, Daniel Callahan, *Abortion: Law, Choice and Morality* (New York: Macmillan, 1970), embraces it (although without facing its implications for infanticide): "Abortion is an act of killing, the violent, direct destruction of potential human life, already in the process of development. That fact should not be disguised, or glossed over by euphemism and circumlocution. It is not the destruction of a human person—for at no stage of its development does the conceptus fulfill the definition of a person, which implies a developed capacity for reasoning, willing, desiring and relating to others—but it is the destruction of an important and valuable form of human life" (497–98; cf. 384–89, where he first adopts the "developmental" notion of personhood). Callahan likes this view partly for the precise reason that it "provides a way of weighing the comparative value of the lives at stake" (396). As usual, the consequentialist who provides the scales determines the outcome of the weighing: the "body-life" of the potential person is easily outweighed by the "person-life" of the pregnant woman in "a huge number of situations" (496; cf. 398, 498). Like Tooley, Callahan gives no argument whatever for adopting the ethical theory he assumes.

16. Tooley considers some arguments involving other notions of personhood when he deals with potential persons; he also criticizes a "metaphysical" argument (which he constructs but insinuates is Thomistic) for the personhood of neonates: op. cit, 169–241 and 332–347. Rosalind Hursthouse, *Beginning Lives* (Oxford: Basil Blackwell/Open University, 1987), 107–17, also criticizes the circularity of Tooley's argument.

17. Both *Weber's Third New International Dictionary* and the *Oxford English Dictionary* say that a standard use of "person" is to refer to a *living, human individual.*

18. To develop this argument: David Wiggins, "Locke, Butler and the Stream of Consciousness: and Men as a Natural Kind," *Philosophy,* 51 (1976), 131–58, and the works Wiggins cites in his note 33; James W. Anderson, "Three Abortion Theorists: A Critical Appraisal" (Ph.D. diss., Georgetown University, 1985), 176–201; Michael Lockwood, "Warnock versus Powell (and Harradine): When Does Potentiality Count?" *Bioethics,* 2 (1988), 187–213, "Hare on Potentiality: A Rejoinder," *Bioethics,* 2 (1988), 343–52.

19. Stephen D. Schwarz, *The Moral Question of Abortion* (forthcoming), chapter seven, develops some other promising lines of argument against a position like Tooley's. One of them is based on the implications of using for personhood criteria which are subject to degree. On this, also see Germain Grisez and Joseph M. Boyle, Jr., *Life and Death with Liberty and Justice* (Notre Dame, Ind.: University of Notre Dame, 1979), 229–36. Two criticisms of the earlier version of Tooley's argument will repay study: James G. Hanink, "Persons, Rights, and the Problem of Abortion" (Ph.D. diss., Michigan State University, 1975), 42–172; Gary M. Atkinson, "Persons in the Whole Sense," *American Journal of Jurisprudence,* 22 (1977), 86–117.

20. A nondualistic theory can account for the irreducibility to bodily functioning of spiritual acts: Germain Grisez, *Beyond the New Theism: A Philosophy of Religion* (Notre Dame, Ind.: University of Notre Dame Press, 1975), 343–53.

21. *Morals and Medicine* (Boston: Beacon Press, 1954), 152, 211–13.

22. Op. cit., 64.

23. Ibid., 103. Tooley often uses this notion of person-as-software (see 154–55, 163–64, 175–76); he even asks (130) "whether the desires before and after reprogramming belong to the same mental substance."

24. Some articulations of this line of argument: B. A. O. Williams, "Are Persons Bodies?" in *The Philosophy of the Body: Rejections of Cartesian Dualism,* ed. Stuart F. Spicker (New York: Quadrangle/New York Times Books, 1970), 137–56; Gabriel Marcel, *The Mystery of Being,* vol. 1, *Reflection and Mystery* (Chicago: Henry Regnery, 1960), 127–53; Grisez and Boyle, *Life and Death with Liberty and Justice,* 70–71, 375–79, 402; J. M. Cameron, "Bodily Existence," *Proceedings of the American Catholic Philosophical Association,* 53 (1979), 59–70. On Kant's form of dualism and some related theories: Joseph M. Boyle, Jr., Germain Grisez, and Olaf Tollefsen, *Free Choice: A Self-Referential Argument* (Notre Dame: University of Notre Dame Press, 1976), 110–21. If no dualism can explain me, much less can the sorts of dualism usually assumed today explain people with amnesia and other abnormal mental states: Kathleen V. Wilkes, *Real People: Personal Identity without Thought Experiments* (Oxford: Clarendon Press, 1988), 100–131.

25. When human persons die, there may be not only bodily but spiritual remains: St. Thomas, *Super primam epistolam and Corinthios lectura,* XV, lec. ii: "We naturally desire salvation for our very selves, but since the soul is part of the human body, it is not the whole person; therefore, even if the soul attains salvation in another life, still I am not saved, nor anyone else."

26. "Immediate Animation and Delayed Hominization," *Theological Studies,* 31 (1970), 76–105.

27. Ibid., 79–83.

28. Ibid., 101.

29. Benedict Ashley, O.P., makes a cogent case against delayed hominization: "A Critique of the Theory of Delayed Hominization," in *An Ethical Evaluation of Fetal Experimentation: An Interdisciplinary Study,* ed. Donald G. McCarthy and Albert S. Moraczewski, O.P. (St. Louis, Missouri: Pope John XXIII Medical-Moral Research and Education Center, 1976), 113–33. Ashley points out that Donceel drastically understates the case when he says that St. Thomas knew well that the early embryo was not yet a fully organized body. In fact, following Aristotle, Thomas thought that life originates from the semen and the menstrual blood, that neither is alive, and that the very limited, active instrumental power in the semen only gradually organizes the blood into a body which can begin to grow and nourish itself. But Thomas also held that God's infinite power accomplished instantaneously in the conception of Jesus what the semen's power normally takes forty or eighty days to do. Thus, it seems that Thomas accepted Aristotle's theory of hominization, not because he thought that matter cannot receive a personal soul until it has the *organs* required for the sensory basis of spiritual activities, but only because he thought that the semen does not bring about the epigenetic *primordium* of the personal body until forty or eighty days.

30. Moreover, to maintain this hypothesis, Donceel is forced to add another. He stresses (op. cit., 85) that the soul, as form, cannot be the efficient cause of the development of the embryo; rather, the soul is the term of the generative process. St. Thomas thought that the father imparted instrumental efficacy to the semen, and that it remained present as the active principle of development. Since that hypothesis plainly is mistaken, Donceel offers another: Somewhat as in evolutionary development of humans from lower forms of life, God is the proper efficient cause of embryonic development, creatively transforming the parents' contributions until the material is ready to receive a personal soul, which he then also creates.

31. Donceel also claims (ibid., 92–96) that historical evidence shows that delayed hominization was given up under the influence both of the erroneous biological theory of preformation and of Cartesian dualism. On this, see my *Abortion,* 171–72.

32. The clearest statement of this argument I know of: Robert M. Veatch, "Definitions of Life and Death: Should There Be Consistency?" in *Defining Human Life: Medical, Legal, and Ethical Implications,* ed. Margery W. Shaw and A. Edward Doudera (Ann Arbor, Michigan: AUPHA Press, 1983), 99–113.

33. Stephen D. Schwartz, *The Moral Question of Abortion* (forthcoming), chapter six, skillfully treats numerous versions of the common sense argument, and in doing so provides an excellent model for treating many others.

34. *When Did I Begin? Conception of the human individual in history, philosophy and science* (Cambridge: Cambridge University Press, 1988), 108.

35. Ibid., 115.

36. Ibid., 168–70.

37. Ibid., 129.

38. Ibid., 119–20; cf. 121–22, 135, 170–72.

39. Ibid., 122. Sentences like this make it hard to interpret Ford's argument in a way that allows it coherence and plausibility. But I have done my best.

40. Ibid., 136.

41. Ibid., 139–45.

42. Ibid., 124; cf. 117–18, 133, 157.

43. Ibid., 133, 159. He also relies heavily on arguments based on common sense, e.g. (157): "But the placenta has no nerves, is insentient and has always been regarded as extraembryonic tissue. While respect and grief have traditionally been expressed for the still-born fetus, at times giving it a burial, this has not been so for the placenta."

44. Ibid., 149–51; cf. 107, 119, 132.

45. Ibid., 162; cf. 170–77.

46. Ibid., 174–77. The biologist, Anne McLaren, recounts her journey to this view ("Prelude to Embryogenesis," in *Human Embryo Research: Yes or No?* [Ciba Foundation], ed. Gregory Bock and Maeve O'Connor [London: Tavistock, 1986], 14–15), acknowledging that after an initial insight: "It has taken a further ten years *and some pressure from outside the scientific community* for this distinction to result in a suggested change of terminology to eliminate the ambiguity of the term 'embryo' [emphasis added]." Already at a 1964 international biomedical conference on the IUD, Christopher Tietze urged that a consensus be developed that "pregnancy, and therefore life, begins at implantation" (see my *Abortion,* 111–12).

47. Op. cit., 175; cf. 118, 137–38, 162, 170. Ford deserves credit for *trying* to give an account of the discontinuity he posits. Most who share his view simply ignore the problem: Is it an individual all along or not? If so, why not the same individual? If not, what is it until it becomes an individual?

48. Gabriel Pastrana, O.P., "Personhood and the Beginning of Human Life," *Thomist,* 41 (1977), 247–94, who criticizes (252–53) my attempt—which I admit was not entirely satisfactory—in *Abortion* to show that the human individual begins at fertilization, thinks hominization occurs by a substantial change at the primitive streak stage. But he does not show (274–84) that the facts require that hypothesis, and Ashley's argument against Donceel also tells against Pastrana's understanding of the implications of the hylemorphic theory.

49. The quoted sentence opens a recent, magisterial, fifty-page summary of what is currently known about mammalian fertilization: R. Yanagimachi, "Mammalian Fertilization," in *The Physiology of Reproduction,* ed. E. Knobil, J. Neill, et al. (New York: Raven Press, 1988), 135.

50. Op. cit., 149; cf. 117, 133, where he suggests that the cells formed by early divisions are identical, whereas in reality they begin at once to differ (although at first not so much that each could not develop as a separate individual), which is why not all embryonic individuals have precisely either 2, or 4, or 8, or 16, or . . . cells; see a work that Ford himself often cites: Anne McLaren, "The Embryo," in *Reproduction in Mammals,* book 2, *Embryonic and Fetal Development,* ed. C. R. Austin and R. V. Short, 2nd ed. (Cambridge: University Press, 1982), 2–3: "Embryos with 2 and 4 cells are much more often encountered than those with 3 and 5 cells; the following day, 8-cell stages predominate, but the scatter is wider; after four or five successive cleavage divisions, little synchrony remains. The first cell to divide from the 2-cell stage mouse embryo has recently been shown by Chris Graham and his colleagues in Oxford to contribute a disproportionately larger number of progeny to the inner cell mass of the blastocyst, and fewer to the outer trophectoderm." Also, Ford, op. cit., 137–38, describes the blastomeres as if they were marbles in a bag, forgetting that in this case the bag (the zona pellucida) also is an organic *part* of the reality and that the blastomeres interact; see, for example, D. J. Hill, A. J. Strain, and R. D. G. Milner, "Growth Factors in Embryogenesis," in *Oxford Reviews of Reproductive Biology,* 9 (1987), ed. J. R. Clarke (Oxford: Clarendon Press, 1987), esp. 403–4 and 411, for evidence that the early embryo's cells are in constant and intense interaction, and that until implantation "the early embryo is self-sufficient with regard to the expression of intercellular messengers" (411).

51. Op. cit., 175.

52. Ibid., 155. Ford's note to this passage (n. 36, p. 206) refers to two works on embryology; neither supports Ford's fanciful notion (175) that distinct, individual cells' " 'clock' mechanisms become synchronized and triggered" to form them into one new individual.

53. See ibid., 102–8. Antoine Suarez, "Hydatidiform Moles and Teratomas Confirm the Human Identity of the Preimplantation Embryo," *Journal of Medicine and Philosophy,* 15 (1990), 629, describes the origin of such moles: "Hydatidiform moles of the complete type (CHM) arise from androgenetic eggs (i.e., from eggs with two paternal nuclei). Most CHM arise from fusion of an egg and sperm followed by duplication of the sperm genome and loss

153, 238

25

of the female nucleus. A smaller number of CHM arise by dispermy (two sperms enter into the egg) and loss of the female nucleus." In support he refers to three articles: S. D. Lawler and R. A. Fisher, "Genetic Studies in Hydatidiform Mole with Clinical Correlations," *Placenta,* 8 (1987), 77–88; R. A. Fisher, *et al,* "Frequency of Heterozygous Complete Hydatidiform Moles, Estimated by Locus-specific Minisatellite and Y Chromosome-specific Probes," *Human Genetics,* 82 (1989), 259–63; M. Plachot *et al,* "Cytogenetic Analysis and Developmental Capacity of Normal and Abnormal Embryos after IVF," *Human Reproduction,* 4 (1989), 99–103. A factual description of the fusion of sperm and ovum and the normal initial development of the new individual: R. G. Edwards, *Conception in the Human Female* (London: Academic Press, 1980), 593–605.

54. For a detailed defense of the position that the new individual begins at this point, not at syngamy, see: St. Vincent's Bioethics Centre Working Party, "Identifying the Origin of a Human Life: The Search for a Marker Event for the Origin of Human Life," *St. Vincent's Bioethics Centre Newsletter,* 5:1 (March 1987), 4–6; T. V. Daly, S.J., "Individuals, Syngamy and the Origin of Human Life: A Reply to Buckle and Dawson," *St. Vincent Bioethics Centre Newsletter,* 6:4 (December 1988), 1–7. The address of the St. Vincent's Bioethics Centre: St. Vincent's Hospital; 41 Victoria Parade; Melbourne, Victoria 3065; Australia.

55. An analogous account, presumably, can be given of an ovum developing parthenogenetically. However, if some parthenogenetically developing human ovum had in itself the necessary epigenetic primordia, it too would be a person. What about an anencephalic baby? In most cases the cause of anencephaly is unknown, and cases vary greatly: D. Alan Shewmon, "Anencephaly: Selected Medical Aspects," *Hastings Center Report,* 18:5 (October/November 1988), 11–19. Even if such a baby now lacks (but previously had the primordium of) the bodily basis of some intellectual act, he or she is a brain-damaged person, just as is the adult whose higher brain functions are irreparably lost.

56. The fact that individual plants remain individuals although they *could be* divided and grafted shows that there is nothing logically or biologically absurd in an organism remaining substantially the same although it could have been divided into two or more individuals of the same sort or combined with another or others. On this and other facts which Ford and others use to argue against beginning at fertilization, see Thomas V. Daly, S.J., "The Status of Embryonic Human Life: A Crucial Issue in Genetic Counseling," in *Health Care Priorities in Australia: 1085 Conference Proceedings,* ed. Nicholas Tonti-Filippini (Melbourne, Australia: St. Vincent's Bioethics Centre, 1985), 45–57.

57. Op. cit., 120, 136.

58. Ford offers two other arguments. First, he says (118) that until the two-cell and perhaps the four-cell stage, the messenger RNA already in the ovum before fertilization controls events, and argues that the new human individual "could hardly be said to exist before the embryonic genome, including the paternal genes, is switched on. If the embryo's own genome is not activated or expressed, or if it is suppressed, no human individual or offspring results." But granting the factual supposition, the conclusion does not follow. For, since the ovum with its maternal RNA does nothing until the sperm penetrates it, and at that point a biologically new individual begins to be, the switching on of the embryonic genome is not necessary for the zygote's individuation. (The nonexpression or suppression of the new individual's genome can be understood as resulting in his or her early death.) Second, Ford points out (168) that circulation begins around the end of the third week and argues (170) that this is sufficient to show that the new individual has begun, since it is now a living body with the primordium of at least one organ formed for the benefit of the whole organism. Ford does not use this argument to deny individuality at the slightly earlier primitive streak stage. In this context, however, Ford denies (170) that "the DNA of the genes of the zygote could be taken as the equivalent of an organ of a human being. The genetic instructions for the formation of the

whole human being and its organs must not be confused with the actual human being and its organs." His implicit conclusion is that the zygote has no organ whatsoever, and so has no vital function at all, and therefore is not an organic individual. Both the argument based on the beginning of circulation and the assumption that the zygote has no functioning organ can be answered with the same answer: once Ford's denial that there is a continuously developing biological individual is set aside, it is clear that the individual is functioning from the start in one respect: it is growing, not in the sense of gaining mass but in the sense of multiplying and differentiating its cells. *Something* in the individual (not necessarily only the DNA) controls this process; that something is the individual's functioning organ, and the individual's development is that organ's function.

59. Op. cit., 100; the opinion is quoted from Karl Rahner, but many others propose the same argument.

60. Ford, op. cit., 180–81.

61. "Activated ovum" refers to the organic individual constituted at the very beginning of the process of conception, when a sperm has entered the ovum and the ovum has reacted so that other sperms are prevented from entering. The union of the paternal and maternal genomes has not yet occurred, but the new individual already had begun to exist (see note 54, above). Whether it is appropriate to call the new individual a "zygote" at this early stage is a terminological question of no real importance.

62. Op. cit., 61–77, 231–41.

63. For the most recent refinement of several elements of this theory: Germain Grisez, Joseph Boyle, and John Finnis, "Practical Principles, Moral Truth, and Ultimate Ends," *American Journal of Jurisprudence,* 32 (1987), 99–151. We always have talked about basic *human* goods. But the principles, having been disengaged by abstraction from the specific content of human experience, actually point to the goods of bodily persons (who are the only sort of beings whose acts can be directed by these principles), whether or not of the human species. Thus, the goodness of life for bodily persons and the wrongness of choosing to violate any basic personal good entail that it would be wrong to choose to kill E.T., but do not entail that it is wrong to slaughter steers or use chimpanzees for medical experimentation.

64. See Tooley, op. cit., 77–86, 146–64, 333–46. For significant help toward doing the necessary work, see Francis C. Wade, S.J., "Potentiality in the Abortion Discussion," *Review of Metaphysics,* 29:2 (December 1975), 239–55; John Gallagher, C.S.B., *Is the Human Embryo a Person? A Philosophical Investigation* (Toronto: Human Life Research Institute, 1985). The Human Life Research Institute's address: 240 Church Street, Toronto, Ontario M5B 1Z2.

65. While Tooley and others think otherwise, it is wrong to try to answer the question about how to treat individuals that might or might not be people before answering the question about when people begin. For if one does not answer the latter question first, one is likely to treat some individuals that should be considered persons as nonpersons—a grave injustice if they are in fact persons.

66. *Abortion,* 407, to be read in the context of 361–429. See also, Germain Grisez and Joseph M. Boyle, Jr., *Life and Death with Liberty and Justice,* 68–71, 229–41, 298–313.

Chapter 2

THE HUMAN ZYGOTE IS A PERSON

Robert E. Joyce

Many supporters of protection for all human life from the moment of conception would argue that abortion is a grave crime, even if an individual human person is not present until later in the pregnancy. According to this view, the willingness to deprive a potential human person the zygotic and embryonic base of his or her existence reveals gross unconcern—and even contempt—for every person *as a person*. At the very least, the argument would say that no one has proven beyond a shadow of a doubt that the human zygote is *not* essentially a person, and that, in the absence of such proof, reasonable people must act as if it were a person.

Published in *The New Scholasticism*, 52, 1 (Winter 1978), pp. 97–109. Revised and printed here with permission.

This perspective gives "the benefit of the doubt to life" and is worthy of serious consideration. Moreover, the Catholic faith apparently does not require one to believe that abortion at an early stage is murder—the deliberate killing of an innocent person—even though it does require belief that abortion is a grave moral wrong. But I would argue that we can be reasonably certain that the *human conceptus* is essentially a human person. This conclusion is, moreover, not a matter of probability, but of considerable certitude.

I claim that the human zygote is just as specifically and truly a person as you or I, though less developed. Through a properly philosophical interpretation of the increasing scientific data, we are brought to know that conception or fertilization is the definite beginning of at least *one* whole individual person—possibly more. I will attempt to show that it is unreasonable to hold that there is such a thing as "potential human life" and that it is quite reasonable to hold that at conception an individual human person "in the whole sense" is present physically in the space-time world as we naturally and normally perceive this world.

The outline of my argument might be stated simply: Every living individual being with the natural potential, as a whole, for knowing, willing, desiring, and relating to others in a self-reflective way is a person. But the human zygote is a living individual (or more than one such individual) with the natural potential, as a whole, to act in these ways. Therefore the human zygote is an actual person with great potential, and not at all a potential person.

In the 20th century, until the mid-sixties, the vast weight of medical and legal opinion leaned toward the view that the life which started in the human being as the result of fertilization was worthy of serious moral and legal protection. What has happened in recent decades? Why have many jurists, scientists and other intellectuals attempted to deny essential personhood to the unborn, or at least tried to redefine conception? What new scientific evidence or philosophical insight can justify this shift? I claim that there is none. The evidence mounts inexorably on the side of the humanity of the prenatal individual.

Yet the judgment about whether this or that entity is a human person "in the full sense"—whether the entity in question is Caucasian or Negro, Aryan or Jewish, born or preborn—is decisively philosophical, not scientific. Scientific evidence is differentiated physical evidence, but the judgment about what constitutes human personhood and which entities are instances of it is specifically philosophical. Necessary help can and must come from both scientific and religious sources: but the normal question of personhood and its application is centrally philosophical.

The philosophical tradition most closely united with Catholic faith traditionally has been characterized as reflective common sense. In what follows, I will try to suggest that we need and can obtain greater philosophical understanding of the good common sense notion that a human person can be a tiny one-celled creature.

First, I offer a definition of "person" and some comments by way of clarification. Second, a brief descriptive interpretation of the conception event is presented. Third, responses are given to some significant objections. And in conclusion, I mention a couple of major implications of the idea that the person exists at conception.

I. The Person

The first element of a sound interpretation of what occurs in human conception seems to be a definition of person. Person can be defined as a whole individual being which has the natural potential to know, love, desire, and relate to self and others in a self-reflective way. There are many alternate ways of phrasing the definition, depending upon different needs of emphasis. But it would seem to be crucial that we recognize a person as a natural being, and not simply as a functional being.

A person is a being that has the natural, but not necessarily the functional, ability to know and love in a trans-sensible or immaterial way. As soon as one would require a person to have the functional ability for this kind of activity, he or she would seem to be slipping into a subjectivistic elitism such that the comatose, senile, and retarded—even the sleeping—would not be regarded necessarily as persons. This is an unrealistic position that seems to be out of touch with the human condition.

If nature has no essential value in our knowing and judging who or what is a person, independent of accepted functional abilities, then there is little hope for recognition of an objective nature transcending the limits of our personal consciousness in *anything* else.

31

We who judge *are* persons. If we cannot attain an objective, though partial, grasp of our own nature and definitely distinguish it from other natures, our discourse about any serious subject is invalidated.

In recent times, some philosophers have adopted what has been called the "developmentalist" interpretation of the beginning of a human person. Daniel Callahan views it this way. "(Abortion) is not the destruction of a human person—for at no stage of its development does the conceptus fulfill the definition of a person, which implies a developed capacity for reasoning, willing, desiring, and relating to others—but is the destruction of an important and valuable form of human life."[1] The language of the Supreme Court in *Roe v. Wade* is harmonious with this perspective.

But I would claim that a person is *not* an individual with a *developed* capacity for reasoning, willing, desiring, and relating to others. A person is an individual with a *natural* capacity for these activities and relationships, whether this natural capacity is ever developed or not—i.e., whether he or she ever attains the functional capacity or not.

Individuals of a rational, volitional, self-conscious *nature* may never attain or may lose the functional capacity for fulfilling this nature to any appreciable extent. But this inability to fulfill their nature does not negate or destroy the nature itself, even though it may, for us, render that nature more difficult to appreciate and love. The difficulty of love and care would seem to be a challenge for *us*, precisely as persons, more than it is for them.[2]

Neither a human embryo nor a rabbit embryo has the functional capacity to think, will, desire, and self-consciously relate to others. The radical difference, even at the beginning of development, is that the human embryo *actually* has the *natural capacity* to act in these ways, whereas the rabbit embryo does not have and never will have it. For all its concern about potentialities, the developmentalist approach fails to see the actuality upon which these potentialities are based.

Every potentiality is itself an actuality. A person's potential to walk across the street is an actuality that the tree beside him does not have. A woman's potential to give birth to a baby is an actuality that a man does not have. The potential of a human *conceptus* to think and talk is an actuality. This *actual potential*—not mere logical possibility—would seem to be a much more reasonable ground for affirming personhood than a kind of neo-angelic notion of personhood which requires actual performance of subjectively recognized spiritual activity.[3]

II. Conception: A Descriptive Interpretation

If the person is an individual entity with the natural, though not necessarily functioning, power to think, will, and relate self-reflectively, then when does such an individual actually begin to exist in the world of space and time? There would seem to be but one reasonable point at which to acknowledge the existence of a new individual person in this world.

Conception is the moment when the so-called "fertilization" process is complete. From then on, a genetically and physically unique individual is present and growing. In the following description of the conception event, I wish to challenge or correct a few common misunderstandings: common to scientists, philosophers, and laypersons.

Before a sperm penetrates an ovum, these two cells are clearly individual cells and are parts of the bodies of the man and woman respectively. They are not whole-body cells as is the zygote cell which they crucially help to cause. They are body-part cells.

The zygote is a single cell that is a whole body in itself. From within it, all the rest of the individual comes to exist, including the strictly intra-uterine functional organs of the placenta, amnion, and chorion, as well as the rest of the body that is naturally destined for extra-uterine life.

The sperm and ovum are not potential life. They are potential *causes* of individual human life. They do not, even together, become a new human life. In the fertilization process, they become *causes* of the new human life.

Fertilization is a process. The process may take twenty minutes or several hours. But it has a definite conclusion. The moment at which this process terminates in the resulting zygote can be called the conception event. The sperm and ovum are specific, instrumental causes of the new human being. The man and woman are the main agents of this procreative effect. They cause an actual, not a potential, existence of a person in the space-time world. They do not cause a person to exist as a person (any more than they cause the person to exist as a body)—human persons in this world as persons cause artifacts and developments of nature (e.g., relationships), but do not cause other bodies or other souls, as such. But they do cause (in an important, if partial, way) a bodily person to exist in this world.

Parental bodily matter (the sperm and ovum) is a crucial element of procreative-causing on behalf of the new being, but is not the stuff (the material cause) out of which this unique bodily being is adequately constituted. The bodily matter of the zygote comes into existence *by means of* the bodily matter of the parents but does *not* come *from* their bodies. It only looks that way to the unphilosophical mind.

The matter of the new person proper is constitutively different matter. The chromosomal uniqueness of the zygote is sufficient testimony to the radical difference of both form and matter in this new being. The unique matter of the zygote has traits similar to, but in no way identical to, those of the parents. With the perspective of an evolutionist, who once said that the evolution from non-life to life was a "leap from zero to everything," we might say that the transition from parent body to offspring is a leap from zero self to all of self.[4]

Moreover, the so-called fertilization process is not as passive as the terminology would suggest. The nuclei of the sperm and ovum dynamically interact. In so doing they both cease to be. One might say they die together. They really should not be said to unite. That suggests that they remain and form a larger whole. But the new single-celled individual is not an in-tandem combo of the two parent sex cells.

In their interaction and mutual causation of the new being—by the testimony of biological observation—we see that the sperm and ovum are self-sacrificial. Their nuclei are the quasi-subject of the fertilization process; the zygote is the result of this process. There is neither sperm nor ovum once the process of interaction is completed, even though cytoplasmic matter from the ovum remains. It is really a misleading figure of speech to say of the ovum that it is "fertilized" by the sperm, passively as a farmer's field is fertilized. It is proper rather to speak of the sperm-ovum interaction process. There is no such thing as a "fertilized ovum." And the sperm and ovum do not "unite."

Obviously the new individual's growth is ever a process. But neither its coming into existence nor its final exit is a process. We need to be paradoxical in our thinking, not simple-minded and reductionistic, if we are going to appreciate both the process and the non-process factors involved. In contemporary philosophy, when process is valued on a par with substance, the dignity of person and nature are served and enhanced. But when process is enthroned above substance, such that, in effect, the process itself is the only substance, we are engaged in a self-deception fraught with epistemological and moral chaos.

At any given moment, a whole living substance—be it a peach tree, a rabbit, or a human person—either is or is not. Once a living substance such as these is (and is thus alive), it is *wholly* there as this particular *actual* being—even though it is only partially there as a *developed* actuality. There is no such thing as a potentially living organism. Every living thing is thoroughly actual, with more or less potential: actually itself; potentially more or less expressive of itself.

A one-celled person at conception is an actual person with great potential for development and self-expression. That single-celled individual is just as actually a person as you or I, though the actual personhood and personality of the new individual are, as yet, much less functionally expressed.[5]

In fact, the new personality is so little developed that we are not yet able to recognize it functionally, unless we are willing to go beyond the vision of the eyeballs. Many are not willing. As one life scientist remarked, in speaking of the users of the IUD: " . . . Ignorance is bliss, for the blastocyst is only a little larger than the egg to begin with, and its passage through the womb is unknown and undetectable."[6]

The issue thus becomes whether we are prepared to acknowledge the *natural roots* of the individual's personality within this largely, though not entirely, undifferentiated stage. The genetic differentiation of a zygote or a blastocyst, however, must be reasonably acknowledged as the natural roots of a *personality,* not of a "dogality" or of a "rabbitality." The human zygote is a member of a unique species of creature. It is not a genus, to which a species is gradually

35

attached. Such a process of attachment can occur in the mind of the observer, but not in the reality of the observed.

No individual living body can "become" a person unless it already is a person. No living being can become anything other than what it already essentially is. From the perspective of the beginning of a living thing, for such a being to *become* something essentially other—say, for a "subpersonal human animal"[7] to become a person—it would have to be a person before it was a person, so that *it* could be said to *become.*

Moreover, from the point of view of an adult, if, at this moment, I do not simply *have* a body, but in some radically natural sense I *am* my body, then, it is likewise perceptive to say or reasonable to conclude that I did not simply *get* a body at some point, but *was* that whole body naturally and radically at every point of *its* time as well as *its* space. Otherwise, I could never properly say such things as, "When I was conceived...."

III. Objections and Response

A. A first objection comes from the idea of the human person as an individual. Many theologians have argued in this way. "The human *conceptus* is not necessarily an individual. But individuality is essential to personhood. Therefore, the *conceptus* cannot be reasonably regarded as a person."

Proponents of this argument cite as evidence the fact of so-called "identical" twins and other multiple births resulting from the causality of a single ovum and sperm. They rightly insist that the living zygote which divides in half cannot be viewed as one, identical human being dividing into two.

But the evidence would seem to indicate *not* that there is *no* individual present at conception, but there is *at least one,* and possibly more. Geneticist Jerome Lejeune of Paris, for instance, has indicated that individuality may be fully existent at the point of fertilization, but that thus far we do not have the technical capacity to discern how many individuals are present at that point[8]. Moreover, it seems to me that at this very early stage of human development there may occur, at times, a process of generation similar to that common in other species. In that case, we could say that one of

36

the twins would be the parent of the other. The original zygote could be regarded as the parent of the second, even though we may never know which one was parthenogenically the parent.[9]

There is also the disputed evidence that in the first days of life, twins or triplets sometimes "recombine" into a single individual.[10] Actually, this could readily mean that one individual's body absorbs the body of the other, resulting in the latter's death at this particularly vulnerable stage in life.

The individuality of the human person must be affirmed on the basis of scientific evidence and a philosophy of reflective common sense. In determining the individuality of human personhood at conception, just because we do not know the number of individuals at that point, it would be irrational to conclude that there is not at least one. From not knowing how many, we cannot conclude that there are not any.

B. The major type of objection to personhood at conception involves some kind of developmentalism, such as gradual ensoulment. Developmentalists claim to take into account life potential as well as life actual, and thereby to give a more reasonable interpretation to the beginning of human personhood.

But this approach fails on at least three counts. It tends to confuse process in the collective with process in the individual. It makes a typically utilitarian projection of mechanistic potential onto organic potential. And it seems to suffer from the misleading, yet popular, notion that man is a rational "animal."

The first problem is that this gradualist approach does not distinguish sufficiently two kinds of process.

There is the process of the cosmos, as it might be called, within which living substances exist, and which causes these individuals to exist in space and time. The individuals themselves are not the subject of the process nor are they the cause of it. This grand process of the whole of physical nature would seem to employ individual substances, such as parents and their gametic cells, in the causation of new individual substances.

But there is another distinctive process, one that occurs within the living individual entities themselves and one which they themselves cause. It is the process of their own unique life and growth. This process is primarily caused by the individuals; not by the environment and the whole process of Nature. The individual in the womb of his or her mother is in charge of the pregnancy, just as every individual in the womb of "Mother Nature" is in charge of its own life and growth, even while being thoroughly conditioned by its environment.

Second, in their call for attention to potential life, gradualists have really confused two different kinds of potency. The *potency to cause* something to come into existence is improperly identified with the *potency* for this new being *to become* fully what it *is*.

This latter kind of potency applies only to living beings, since only these can grow or become manifestly themselves. The zygote especially exemplifies this growth kind of potency—the *potency* of an existing being *to become* more expressly what it already is. The ovum and sperm particularly exemplify the first kind of potency—the *potency to cause* something to come into existence.

One of the important sources of confusion regarding these radically different kinds of potency is that they interweave and interact. The potency to cause something to come into existence—which is proper to the ovum, for instance—also entails the latent function of disposing the newly caused being (the zygote) to become fully what it is, once it is. And once the zygote is, its potency to become fully itself (growth potency) also entails the latent function of internally causing (cause potency) its own stages of organization and development. But the potency to cause something (within self or within another) is radically different from the potency to become developed (to grow).

The gametic and zygotic cells primarily illustrate this difference and this confluence of potencies. The ovum, for instance, besides having the potency to cause, together with the sperm, something else (the zygote) to come into existence, also has the potency to become fully itself once *it* is. And, as with all organic potencies, the potency is attained at the beginning of the ovum's existence (even though it is simply a body-part existence).

The potency of an ovum to become fully itself, as an ovum, includes its capacity for containing 23 chromosomes, as well as its capacity for causing, together with a sperm cell, a new human being. Moreover, the new human individual, as a zygote, has its own radically different potency for becoming what it *is*, once it is. And within its potency for becoming what it *is*, is potency for causing embryonic, fetal, infant, child, adolescent, and adult stages of development,

38

as well as the potency for causing new human beings through the instrumentality of its gametes.

In this age of the electron microscope, we now know that the matter of a zygote is essentially of the same structure as the matter of an adult. Even a hylomorphic theory, then, demands an acknowledgment that the zygote and the adult have the same formal cause.[11] Only the soul of a *human person* could serve the zygote and embryo as an internal final cause of the development of a specifically human brain or of a specifically human anything. No part of a person can be rationally understood as being developed through the internal direction of a plant or an animal soul.[12]

A second major flaw in the gradualist approach is its subtle or not so subtle projection of a mechanistic model of development onto an organically developing reality. It fails to distinguish between natural process and artifactual process.

Only artifacts, such as clocks and spaceships, come into existence part by part. Living beings come into existence all at once and then gradually unfold, to themselves and to the world, what they already, but only incipiently, *are.* Some developmentalists use the analogy of a blueprint in characterizing the zygote. But a blueprint never becomes part of a house, unless it is used, say, to paper the walls.

Moreover, the human zygote is much more than a genetic package. It is a living being that *has* genes. We do not think that an adult is a package of organs, muscles, and bones, but that he or she *is* a being who *has* these structures. The whole of a living being is always, at every stage, much more than the sum of its parts.

A third major weakness in the gradualist approach is the implicit or explicit notion that a human person is a rational animal. But a person is not a rational animal any more than an animal is a sentient plant. Persons are animal-like, plant-like, rock-like and God-like in many ways. We fall like rocks when dropped. We digest food like animals. And in our contemplative moments we act *like* God. Essentially, we are a wholly unique kind of *material* entity; even more different from animals than animals are from plants.

The latent idea that a human person is an "incarnate spirit" also seems to be at work in many who have a developmentalist approach. One's own body and biology are regarded as thoroughly subject to the superior and inevitably imperious judgments of mind and the commands of will. The body is not valued as a vitally identifiable and intrinsic part of our person, but as an alien animal to be civilized by socialization and technology, or as a high class pet, to be tamed and trained to do one's bidding and give one pleasure. By implication, then, one's own body is not regarded as an intrinsic revelation of person, but as a sophisticated instrument for personal use and eventual discard. The utilitarian society—well known for its tin cans, paper cups, disposable babies, *et al.*—can find in the "developmental school" the heart of its rationale.[13]

In this view, nature is not a friend to be known and loved, but an alien, massive and impersonal monster ultimately to be outwitted and subdued. Thus the most immediately threatening and most symbolic part of this monster is one's body. One should not claim ownership of this body until one is sure he or she can handle it: until one is functionally capable of reasoning, desiring, and willing. These are the minimal criteria for a meaningful bodily existence, conferred by the person whose self-concept represents a refusal to be essentially (not exclusively) identified with body and biology. Such is the Cartesian legacy of the gradualist approach.[14]

Conclusion

The point in time when an individual person begins to exist in the spatio-temporal world is one of the most crucial metaphysical and social issues of our age. Induced abortion is a massive enterprise in both the East and West. A recent U.N. estimate cites a conservative figure of fifty million per year. Highly industrialized and presumably progressive nations, such as Japan and the U.S.A., account for more than a million legal abortions in each nation per year. Philosophers on both sides of the Pacific are being challenged anew to make sense of human life beginnings.

In this country, the present movement for Human Life Amendment, protecting all human life from conception until unneglectful natural death, underscores the need for distinctive philosophical contribution to the issue itself. Prebirth individuals are now being dehumanized-by-definition through quasi-scientific and erroneous philosophical endeavors. The more subtle form of this dehumanization is the attempt to redefine conception in order to justify newer forms of chemical birth control that do not prevent ovulation but rather, systematically induce early abortion.[15] This sexual utilitarianism gravely obfuscates critical discernment of the metaphysical features of incipient personhood.

In order to put the issue of personhood and conception into its truest perspective, philosophers are being challenged to represent, clarify, and deepen our understanding of the value of the person in himself or herself. Because this value is, as it were, a seamless robe, our thinking must be woven from the natural substantive, and non-functional levels of meaning. Otherwise, "quality of life" ethics becomes the "survival of the fittest," of the most functional; and the ethic itself becomes a non-ethic.

I think we need an ethics sensitive to a deeper and richer vision of our dignity even as adults, who are dependently developing persons in the environment of space and time. Without appreciable insight into the inexhaustible process of personhood development, we will not be prepared to respect and protect the prenatal person.

Finally, there is hope that we will come to realize how we can learn from the prebirth child concerning the meaning of human existence. Eventually, people could come to see, within the studies of fetology and ontology, many points of convergence and mutual respource.[16] And through cooperative endeavors in these and other disciplines, we could grow in wisdom through the careful study of our prenatal brothers and sisters, as we ourselves continue to gestate within the premortal womb of space and time.

NOTES

1. D. Callahan, *Abortion, Law, Choice and Morality* (New York, 1970), pp. 497–498.

2. The recognition of a person involves, in part, a moral decision. This point is made effectively by John Noonan in the booklet *How to Argue about Abortion* (New York, 1974), p. 10.

3. Even the potential to receive actuation ("passive potency") is itself an actuality that is not had by something lacking it. There are subtle ways to overlook the actuality of potentiality in the case of personhood. E.g., Louis Dupre does so by using equivocally "person" and "personal" in his essay, "A New Approach to the Abortion Problem," *Theological Studies* (1973), 481–488.

4. In accord with the Aristotelian principle that *motus* (motion) is always *in* the *patient* (the thing undergoing motion) and not in the agent (the cause acting upon it), we can say that the new nature or essence or living form (of the zygote) comes to be *out of* prime matter, but

by the activity of the agent causes—in this case the ovum and sperm. Thus the zygote comes *from* or *out of* primary matter, not from or out of the gametes of the parents. The zygote comes *by the interactivity* of the sperm and ovum, in and out of the prime matter common to them and the new zygote itself. In interacting with each other, the sperm and ovum co-act upon prime matter to cause the substantial change from no-zygote to zygote.

5. Cf. Robert and Mary Joyce, *Let Us Be Born* (Chicago, 1970), pp. 21–24.

6. N. Berrill, *Person in the Womb* (New York, 1968), p. 32.

7. An expression used by H. Tristram Engelhardt, Jr. in "The Ontology of Abortion," *Ethics* (April, 1974), p. 217 *per passim.*

8. J. Lejeune, "The Beginning of a Human Being," a paper presented to the *Academie des Sciences Morales et Politiques,* Paris, Oct. 1, 1973.

9. This kind of explanation is likewise recognized in the position paper of Scientists For Life, "The Position of Modern Science on the Beginning of Human Life" (Fredericksburg, Virginia, 1975), p. 18.

10. This phenomenon is alleged by Andre Hellegers, M.D. in an article, "Fetal Development," *Theological Studies* (March, 1970), p. 4. Thomas Hilgers, M.D. *et al.* dispute it. Cf. T. Hilgers, "Human Reproduction: Three Issues for the Moral Theologian," *International Review of Natural Family Planning,* I (1977), 115–116. Germain Grisez deals deftly with this issue and similar ones in his survey of argumentation on "When Do People Begin," in Chapter 1 of this volume.

11. Thomas Aquinas would be the first to admit it. His minimal conditions are underscored in places such as *Q. D. De Anima,* 2 ad 2; and 10 ad 1.

12. For St. Thomas, not only is the soul an internal final cause (as a formal cause) of the body; but it is also united with the body as an efficient cause. Cf. *Q. D. De Anima,* 9 and 10. In the light of contemporary genetic evidence, the entrancing and exciting of souls logically required for the mediate-animation interpretation would seem to degrade hylomorphic theory as an integrative theory of natural identity.

13. An excellent critique of utilitarian ethics is given by G. Grisez, *Abortion: the Myths, the Realities, Arguments* (New York, 1970), p. 317 *et passim.*

14. Cf. D. Demarco, *Abortion in Perspective* (Cincinnati, 1974), *passim.*

15. E.g., note the attempt of J. Diamond, M.D., "Abortion, Animation, and Biological Hominization," *Theological Studies* (1975), 305–324.

16. In fetology, A. M. Liley is perhaps foremost in the world. Cf., e.g., "The Foetus as a Personality," *The Australia-New Zealand Journal of Psychiatry,* VI (1972), 99–105. Or, e.g., J. Lejeune, "On the Nature of Man," *American Journal of Human Genetics* (March, 1970), 119–128.

Chapter 3

AQUINAS AND THE PRESENCE
OF THE HUMAN RATIONAL SOUL
IN THE EARLY EMBRYO

Stephen J. Heaney

First in relation to evolution and more recently in relation to abortion, there has been a recurrence of Thomas Aquinas's arguments for the thesis that the human rational soul is not present in the human body immediately upon conception. Since soul and body must be proportioned to each other, it is argued, a rational soul cannot be present until the human body is formed enough to support it,

Published in *The Thomist*, 56, 1, (January 1992), pp. 19–48. Reprinted here with permission.

i.e., until there are organs in place through which the rational soul can begin to exercise its proper powers.

The question of this paper is: Given modern embryological knowledge, would Aquinas be likely to come to the same conclusion? In regards to such a question Rudolph Gerber has made the following observation:

> Some scholastic philosophers and theologians insist that it is simply impossible to determine exactly when rational animation occurs. This belief, however, has deterred few prophets in either camp from stating their positions with dogmatic certainty.[1]

The authors whose interpretations we will be encountering in this paper have generally been less than dogmatic, but they have been insistent on the rectitude of their respective positions. I will attempt to do likewise: I am in no position to be dogmatic (after all, how will we test the thesis?), but I believe I have good grounds for the conclusion I have reached.

We begin with certain positions which both sides in the debate agree upon: the human intellectual soul is produced immediately by God and not through another agency since, as immaterial, it cannot come from a change in matter;[2] further, the human soul is infused, that is, produced directly in a body as the body's natural perfection.[3] As we shall see in the texts, Aquinas argues that this latter position requires that, while the embryo is alive, it is alive first through the power of a vegetative soul, then a sensitive soul, and finally, when the body is organized enough to be able to perform the functions demanded of it, by a rational soul, this ultimate form replacing the previous one.

This theory of delayed animation—or, more to the point of this paper, the view that Aquinas would today still hold such a theory—has several contemporary proponents. The most prominent spokesman is Joseph Donceel, S.J. He has presented his arguments in a pair of articles[4] which we will now review.

In the earlier article, Donceel blames a latent Cartesianism for the proliferation of supporters of immediate hominization. If you hold, with Descartes, that the soul and body are two separate substances, that the soul is *not* the *form* of the body, then there is "no longer any reason for rejecting the presence of a real human soul in a virtual human body,"[5] i.e., in matter that has the potential to be a human body (with human shape) but is not one yet. Thus, the soul could act as the efficient cause of the body, molding the matter into the organs proper to human beings. This, however, is not Aquinas's view, Donceel argues: "he did not admit that an *actual* human soul could be coupled with a *virtual* human body,"[6] because "a substantial form can exist only in and with a human body."[7] If we accept the Cartesian explanation, we would be equating the soul with the architect or builders of a building. These, however, are not the building's form; that exists only in the finished building. Rather, Donceel says that the soul is related to the body as sphericity to a ball. An embryo is like a deflated ball; it cannot contain the form of ball until it is actually spherical.[8]

For these reasons, Donceel approves of the arguments of Henri de Dorlodot, who says the following:

> One would have to be extremely ignorant of embryology not to know that... a fertilised ovum, a morula, a fetus which has reached the stage resembling a gastrula, and even an embryo in the first period of its existence, do not possess the organisation of a specifically human body. And the seat of the imagination and the *vis cogitativa* does not exist so long as the brain itself does not exist, and indeed as long as there are not present the first rudiments of the structure of a human brain. We might perhaps add that it is very probable that the organization necessary in order that the brain may be said to be human is completed only during the third month after conception, and in fact nearer the end of the month than the beginning.[9]

It is in the later article that Donceel lines up some texts from Aquinas and Aristotle in support of this position. We will consider all the relevant texts a little bit later. For now, let us quote from Donceel this summary of his position.

> To my mind, these statements of St. Thomas contain a mixture of erroneous biological information and sound philosophy. If this philosophy were derived from the biology, we

would have to drop it. Likewise, if Thomas had reached his conclusions only by subsuming his scientific mistakes under his sound philosophical principles, we would have to question them. But it is my contention that these conclusions have been reached, or could have been reached, on the basis of sound philosophical principles and of the common-sense-knowledge which was available to Thomas and his contemporaries.

The main philosophical principles are as follows. The soul is the substantial form of man. A substantial form can exist only in matter capable of receiving it. In the case of man's soul this means: the human soul can exist only in a highly organized body. Now these philosophical principles owe nothing to primitive medieval biology. They represent Thomas' hylomorphic conception of man. This conception continues to make sense even today, at least for him who understands it. Without it we are steadily in danger of slipping into some kind of Platonic or Cartesian dualism.[10]

In Donceel's understanding of the situation, Aquinas's conclusion of delayed animation is as sound today as it was in medieval times, because a) the philosophical principle is sound, and b) both medieval and modern embryology agree on "the following undeniable fact, of which Aquinas was fully aware: at the start of pregnancy there is not yet a fully organized human body."[11] What we have instead is "potentially, virtually, a human body."[12] For ensoulment, for the presence of a human rational soul, we must have the organs necessary for the activities proper to human beings, i.e., we need a brain and sense organs.[13]

If form and matter are strictly complementary, as hylomorphism holds, there can be an actual human soul only in a body endowed with organs required for the spiritual activities of man. We know that the brain, and especially the cortex, are the main organs of those highest sense activities without which no spiritual activity is possible.[14]

Quoting authors who suggest that the soul, in its role as form of the body, shapes and organizes the body, Donceel argues that such

46

an understanding is erroneous. Such a formative principle could not be a substantial form, for, as Aquinas says: "Every substantial generation precedes and does not follow the substantial form."[15]

Difficulties in Donceel's Interpretation

Donceel makes a number of very good points here, but there are also some difficulties in interpretation that need to be dealt with. Obviously, the big questions will be whether Donceel is correct in his assertion that the human body must have such a high degree of organization before the soul can be present and to what extent Aquinas's conclusion was rooted in biology. But there are a few lesser, but instructive, points to be raised first.

For one thing, it is begging the question to assert that the "body at the moment of conception is obviously virtual."[16] To say that immediate animation requires a rational soul to be joined to a virtual or potential human body misses the fact that, when a rational soul *is* joined to matter, you no longer have a potential human body but rather an *actual* human body with potential, potential to develop in certain ways. Thus, Donceel's use of Aquinas's statement, "Every substantial generation precedes and does not follow the substantial form," is misplaced. Donceel seems to think that, by joining a rational soul as form to a body as yet unorganized (i.e., not having organs), we would have generation (the coming-to-be of a substance) *after* the form is in place. Obviously, however, when the substantial form is in place, substantial generation is complete, and all further changes would be developments of the substance. We can only say that the embryo body is a potential human body *once we have established* that there is no rational soul present. This remains to be seen.

A second point of interest is Donceel's analogy of a building to the human body. He suggests that the form of the building is only present in the finished building and that the human soul is similarly present in an organized human body. But this analogy is somewhat off base. As Aquinas notes in *De Anima,* the "form" of a house is artificial; a building does not have a substantial unity as a human body does.[17] The body is one because it is perfected by one form.[18] The building is an aggregate or composite; it is, if you will, only analog-

47

ically one. Donceel's comparisons of the soul to the form of a ball or of a statue are somewhat more apt. There is a sense in which the form of ball is not present until it attains a spherical shape; a statue needs to be molded in clay or chipped from the stone before it is a statue. There is, on the other hand, still a basic artificiality to these forms. Does the ball, for instance, have to be perfectly spherical to be a ball? Can it not be a fair or poor ball rather than only a potential ball? How many chips in the stone does it take to make a statue?

The uniqueness of the forms of living things as compared to man-made objects is an interesting topic in itself but takes us away from our main point. The question remains to be answered: Is it possible that there is a human intellectual soul in the embryo from conception, or must there be time enough for the development of the body before God infuses such a soul? The only way to answer such a question is to go directly to the texts of Aquinas in which he lays out his theory of human generation and of the proper proportionality of soul to body.

The Thomistic Texts

Donceel relies heavily for his interpretation of Aquinas on the following definition of the soul, which is taken from Aristotle: "The soul is the act of a physical organic body which has life potentially."[19] Since "organic" in this context means "having organs," Donceel interprets this statement as saying that all the organs necessary for the proper operations of the human soul must be in place for a human rational soul to be infused in the body. There are other texts throughout Aquinas's works to support this understanding.

In the *De Anima,* for instance, Aquinas says that

> form gives an act of existing and species to matter according as matter is disposed for the operations of the form, and because the body, which is capable of being perfected by the soul, requires diversity in its parts in order that it may be disposed for the different operations of the soul.[20]

Similarly, in the *Summa Contra Gentiles,* Aquinas says the following:

[S]ince the intellective soul is the most perfect of souls and its power the highest, its proper perfectible [subject] is a body having great diversity in its organs through which the multiplicity of its operations can be carried out ... [21]

Clearly, however, the embryo is alive, even from conception. But if the embryo is not informed by a human rational soul, what sort of form does it have? Today's thinkers in favor of mediate animation turn again to Aquinas's texts, where the answer is available. Agreeing with Aristotle that the embryo is an animal before it is a man,[22] Aquinas says: "The embryo has first of all a soul which is merely sensitive, and when this is removed, it is supplanted by a more perfect soul, which is both sensitive and intellectual."[23] In order to stay with his understanding of the higher soul as containing within it the operations of the lower forms,[24] he explains further:

And therefore it is said that since the generation of one thing is the corruption of another, it is necessary to say that, both in man and in other animals, when the more perfect form comes, the prior is corrupted, in such a way that the subsequent form has whatever the first had, and even more. And so through many generations and corruptions it arrives at the ultimate substantial form, both in man and in other animals. And this is apparent to the senses in animals generated from putrefaction. Thus it is said that the intellectual soul, which is simultaneously both sensitive and nutritive, is created by God at the end of human generation, the preexisting forms being corrupted.[25]

Clearly, then, Aquinas believes that there is a succession of souls, nutritive and sensitive, before the body is finally in a position to be informed by its ultimate form, the human rational soul. How can this change take place?

Given that what comes into being is brought into being by something already existing (reduction from potentiality to act by what is already in act), we need to find the part or being that does the moving or changing in this situation. There is a suggestion in the *Summa Contra Gentiles* that it is the soul which is responsible for the change.

That which is configured to something is constituted from the action of that to which it is configured: the wax which is configured by the seal receives this configuration from the impression of the seal. Now one sees the bodies of men and other animals to be configured to the proper soul: for the disposition of the organs is such that it suits the operations of the soul exercised through them. The body therefore is formed by the action of the soul; and that is why Aristotle says (*De Anima* II) that the soul is the efficient cause of the body.[26]

Aquinas concurs in this,[27] insofar as it makes sense to say that a soul is responsible for the formation of the human body.

Could it be that each successive soul, in some way, manages to transcend itself—that is, to produce by its own power a body capable of receiving a higher form? In this scenario, the original vegetative soul produces a body with the organs necessary for the sensitive soul, which in turn produces a body capable of receiving an intellectual soul. No; such a production is impossible and is not what is indicated by the argument of wax and seal. There is a lack of due proportion of producer to what is produced; a cause cannot be the cause of what is greater than itself. Thus a lower soul, which itself is incapable of higher operations, could not be responsible for the production of organs of higher operations. Nor could it be the case that a lower soul upon further perfection *becomes* the higher soul, for this would mean: a) that a substantial form is susceptible of degrees, and b) that a rational soul is corruptible, since it would thus be founded in a vegetative and sentient substance.[28]

It would seem, then, that a rational soul must be responsible. Granting for the sake of argument that a rational soul is the informing principle of the embryo, Aquinas goes through its powers one by one. The power to organize the body cannot come from the embryo's generative powers, for these are operative only in adults and for the purpose of generating *others*. It cannot be the embryo soul's nutritive power at work here, for in this process nourishment is not assimilated but nutritive material in the mother is brought together to form organs. The power of growth is not responsible, Aquinas claims, because its function is to produce change in quantity, not form. Obviously, the sensitive and intellective powers are inappropriate to such a formation.[29]

What is Aquinas left with?

It remains therefore that the formation of the body, especially concerning its primary and principal parts, is not from the soul of the thing generated, nor from a formative power acting by virtue of the generated thing, but from [a formative power] acting by virtue of the generative soul of the father, the work of which is to make something like the generating thing according to its species.[30]

It is thus apparent that, for Aquinas, it is the soul of a parent that is responsible for the development of the embryo body until it is capable of supporting a rational soul.

In Aristotelian physics, whenever we speak of change or movement, there is that which acts and that which is acted upon, i.e., something passive. The same holds true for Aristotelian biology, which Aquinas accepted completely as authoritative. In the abstract, it would serve perfectly well if the active part were donated by the mother, and the passive part by the father. This is not the case, however, according to this early theory of generation. Each parent donates a particular element: the female provides the menstrual blood, the father the semen. From a practical perspective, it makes some sense that the fetal matter be provided by the female, simply in terms of mass. This is precisely what Aquinas says is the case: the female provides the passive element.[31] If this is so, however, then the father provides the *active* element. This means it is the *father's* soul which is responsible for the development of a human body in the embryo. Yet this seems to put us in the awkward position of saying either a) the soul is transmitted in the semen, or b) the action of the father's soul must take place at a distance.

Aquinas devotes a chapter in *Summa Contra Gentiles* to laying out arguments favoring the transmission of the soul in, or the forming of the soul from, the semen; he spends the next chapter showing how this is impossible.[32] We have already seen how the soul cannot develop through its stages on its own account. It is equally impossible that the soul be transmitted in the semen, for thus we would have the form before the generation.[33] It is possible, however, for the father's soul to act at a distance, not directly, but through a medium. The generative power of the soul is at work in the instrument of the semen,[34] rather as the power of the hunter would be in the arrow which strikes an animal at a distance.[35] "This active force, which is in the semen, and which is derived from the soul of the generator, is, as it were, a certain movement of the generator's soul itself.... "[36] The semen contains a "formative power" which is based "on the vital spirit which the semen contains as a kind of froth."[37] The semen contains an active "spirit," rather like an active gas or heat or electrical charge, which explains the frothy whiteness of the semen. When this comes in contact with the matter being carried in the female, the menstrual blood, the semen goes to work transmuting this blood, organizing it into a body. For the animal, this transmutation by the semen takes place until the body is disposed to activation by the sensitive soul.

> Afterwards, however, through the power of the active principle which was in the semen, the sensitive soul was produced in the thing generated in respect to some principal part, then already the very sensitive soul of the offspring begins to work to the completion of its own body through nutrition and augmentation.[38]

Only then does the semen, as the instrumental agent, dissipate. This is an important point. Since the species of the subject formed changes, passing from semen to pure blood and on further until it receives the ultimate form of a rational soul, it is necessary that the formative power remain the same throughout the process, from the beginning of the body's formation until the end (when it can support a rational soul). Thus one power is at work through many generations and corruptions.[39]

Arguments against Mediate Animation

Donceel believes that, even in the context of contemporary embryology, Aquinas would still today hold for some theory of delayed hominization; the body would be seen to develop step by step, through vegetative and sensitive stages, until it is developed enough to have organs, or at least the beginnings of organs, capable of performing the tasks demanded of the body by an intellectual soul. Donceel's claim is that Aquinas's conceptualization of a succession of souls is valid regardless of the facts of generation. But this claim rests completely on an understanding of the relationship between soul and body which prohibits the soul's presence unless the body has reached a sufficient degree of organization.

We must take issue with Donceel's claim. Aquinas's acceptance of Aristotle's theory of a succession of souls is, in fact, totally dependent on his acceptance of the corresponding theory of generation. But what if generation does not take place in the manner described? In order to explain the succession of souls, which are not themselves responsible for the formation of the body, there must be an active power, the semen, at work on the passive matter, organizing the body *throughout* the succession of souls. Without this organizing power, there is no way to explain the formation of the body.

Clearly, the semen—or, in modern terms, the sperm—does not perform such a task. It *appears* that the development of the organs is an activity *internal* to the embryo, not one being performed by an extrinsic power. At the very least, we can definitely say that the semen does not have an active power or spirit in the sense that Aquinas understood the term. Such spirits, as I said earlier, were "like hot, energetic gases (or even like our idea of electricity)."[40] Thus the seminal spirit contained the quality of heat necessary for the refinement of the menstrual blood and the consequent proper disposition of a living body as something with both natural heat and natural moisture.[41] Obviously, neither the semen nor the sperm have such properties as this, nor do they continue to exist in themselves after conception. The sperm that do not penetrate the ovum die shortly thereafter. The semen that is not used as nutrient by the sperm is absorbed or otherwise dissolved in the maternal body.

One might suggest that the genetic material carried by the sperm (and, for that matter, by the ovum) performs this formative function, thus organizing a human being by the power of the soul of the begetter rather than of the begotten. This seems implausible, however, given the apparent character of the embryo. Genetic material from the sperm does not work independently, any more than does that from the mother; it is only when they come together that there is any development in the direction of the maturity of the individual. Conversely, *whenever* they come together, such a tendency toward a mature individual is the result. Genetic material, being essentially chemical, operates by the same basic properties as any chemical compound: the parts may have one set of characteristics, but, with their joining, they each cease their former existence, and a new set of characteristics becomes manifest. (In Thomistic terms, a new form manifests itself.) Sodium and chlorine, for instance, are both poisonous to human beings, but as the chemical compound sodium chloride ($NaCl$) they become common table salt. Such, analogously, is the case with human genetic material. The ovum carries twenty-three chromosomes, bearing the generative power of the mother; the sperm's twenty-three chromosomes bring the generative power of the father. When they meet at fertilization, however, the combination takes on a new set of characteristics specific to this embryo.

We are thus without a way for the soul of the parents to provide the power, either immediately or mediately, to organize the body of the embryo. Without the power of the soul of the begetter, Aquinas clearly would have nowhere else to turn but to the soul of the begotten to explain this development.

This seems to put us between a rock and a hard place. We are forced to say that the power must be in the soul of the embryo, since the soul of the parent has been ruled out. Aquinas, however, has already said how it is *not* a power in the embryo. How do we get around this difficulty? First of all, I think it would be fair to say that Aquinas worked through his theory with such consistency, coming to the conclusions he did, because he was never faced with the possibility that generation might take place in a way he had never even considered. Aquinas was a philosopher interested in metaphysical principles not so much in themselves but rather as proper explanations of the facts of the world. The "known facts" of his day included this primitive theory of generation and embryology. Faced with the facts as *we* know them, however, he probably would have worked out a different theory to explain human development.

Naturally, we do not want to abandon any metaphysical principles or ideas needlessly. Perhaps there is a way out of this difficulty, based on principles drawn from within this philosophy.

54

Arguments for Immediate Animation by the Rational Soul

The first thing that needs to be explained is how the soul of the embryo can be responsible for the development of a human body capable of exercising the operations proper to the intellectual soul. We have ruled out the possibility of the vegetative or sensitive souls *of themselves* being responsible for such development. Donceel offers a modified version of this idea. Borrowing from Rahner and Teilhard de Chardin, he suggests that "God [as primary cause] enables the secondary causes to transcend their own virtualities, inserting, as it were, His divine causality within their own causality, without becoming a constitutive element of their being."[42] Such a theory, while interesting and arguable, is not Aquinas. Since we are trying to sort out how Aquinas would answer the question, it is best to leave this theory aside.

Given that neither a vegetative nor a sensitive soul is capable of producing a human body, we are left with something of Aquinas's answer but with an important difference: a human rational soul must be responsible, not the soul of the begetter, however, but the soul of the begotten, of the embryo. Of course, we have yet to explain how it is possible to say that the matter of the embryo is sufficiently disposed to receive such a form.

Let us return for a moment to the analogy of soul to body as impress of seal to wax. Aquinas seems to have some feeling for this analogy and for its implications, for he says the following in another work: "a soul is said to be in a body through a definite shape, not in the sense that the shape is the cause of its being in the body, *but rather the shape of the body results from the soul. . . .*"[43] Thus, he is following closely Aristotle's explanation of the soul as cause.

> The soul is the cause or source of the living body. The terms cause and source have many senses. But the soul is the cause of its body alike in all three senses which we explicitly recognize. It is a) the source or origin of movement, it is b) the end, and it is c) the essence of the whole living body.[44]

We have already recognized the soul as the essence or ground of a living thing's being, as the substantial form. For now, the point of interest is the soul as end or final cause. Nature does what it does, notes Aristotle, for the sake of something. All natural bodies are organs of the soul and exist for the sake of the soul.[45] In other words, we need a soul even simply to have the organs we do, and we need a rational soul. As we have seen, it cannot be the rational soul of anyone but the embryo.

Lest it be said that I have been unfair to the text of Aquinas, let us continue for a moment with a passage quoted above. In a line which once again appears to support mediate animation, he says the following: " ... and hence where there is no shape suited to 'this soul', 'this soul' cannot actually be."[46] Now if this is taken to mean that, the human soul cannot be if the complete human organism is not present, with all the organs necessary for the operations of the soul, then we must contest this statement. For one thing, this conclusion not only does not follow from the premises; it is, in fact, contrary to the premises. It also appears to be empirically falsifiable. If I am missing my arms or my eyes or if I have an artificial heart, am I less a person simply because I do not have the right shape? The real point here is that we have a *natural tendency* toward certain limits of shape.

It seems to me that these natural tendencies are precisely how it is that we define a thing and decide what sort of form it has. Natural potentialities are due to the form, in this case, the soul. Francis Wade talks about them in this way:

> Between natural potentialities and their action there is nothing needed except usable matter and this latter is from the side of the patient, not the agent. The agent's constitution is ready and prepared to act when conditions permit. This will, of itself, supposing usable matter, develop all that is needed to become what it will be.... However one accounts for this process, no one would say that the plants and animals in fact do not do their own self-developing from resources in their constitution....
>
> [To summarize.] The potentiality of the fetus to become an adult is not a passive potency [like the ability to get a good suntan], which is neutral to the future; nor a specifiable active potentiality [such as the potential to learn geometry], which is a very "iffy" promise; but is an

56

active natural potentiality or tendency, which is a guarantee of the future as far as the agent is concerned.[47]

Rudolph Gerber argues that the whole point of the term "organic" or the phrase "having organs" is to indicate "specifically human structure." The genotype is sufficient to give us this structure;[48] through the DNA, the entity is determined to develop in a specifically human way, toward becoming an adult human, with all the organs necessary to perform the operations of a rational soul. Wade concurs:

> Now, I would like to suggest . . . that the natural tendency to think and to choose is basic to the being of the fetus, and the biological tendencies (the ones most clearly active in the genotype) are only specifications of the radical tendency to become a thinking being.[49]

Some suggest, however, that while it may be true that the rational soul might be present, it is necessary for it to have an *organ* by which it might perform the formation of the rest of the organs necessary for its functions. Without a first primary organ, one might argue, the whole will never even get started. Benedict Ashley takes this objection particularly seriously and looks for something that could be considered such a primary organ in the one-celled conceptus. His answer is the nucleus of the cell. The nucleus contains the specifying genetic material. Following this, the nuclei of the daughter cells can be considered the primary organs, until the appearance of the "primary organizer" and the beginning of cell differentiation. Soon, there appears the primitive streak, the primordial central nervous system, which from its beginning exhibits a polarity indicating at which end the brain will be formed. From this point on, we have the beginnings of the primary organ in the human being.[50] Ashley argues that the nucleus in the one-celled conceptus "is epigenetically and substantially identical with the primordial central nervous system manifested in the primitive streak."[51] He goes on to say that this means that

> an existential and dynamic continuity can be traced from the nucleus of the zygote to the cortex of the human infant.

There is at all times a central organ maintaining life and producing development and differentiation, and this constitutes epigenetic identity.[52]

It could be argued, however, that a nucleus is not an organ in the sense that Aquinas meant the term, and thus we are left without the properly disposed matter to move the rest of the matter of the zygote into the proper human shape. There is an answer to this objection available in Aquinas. In describing the whole process of generation in question 118 of the First Part of the *Summa Theologiae,* Aquinas makes these two statements.

[T]his active power in the semen, which is derived from the generating soul, is as it were a certain movement of the generating soul itself. . . . Therefore *it is not necessary that this active power have some organ in act. . . .* [53]

[T]he fetal matter is provided by the female. In this matter there is already from the beginning a vegetative soul, not according to second act, but according to first act, like the sensitive soul in one who is sleeping. When, however, it begins to take in nourishment, then it already operates in act.[54]

The significance of these lines must not be lost. The first is saying that the formative power does not need an organ to be operative. If this is true of a power of a soul working at a distance, how much more must it be true of a soul immediately present.

The second is saying that it is possible for a soul to be present *even though there are no actual organs present.* When the organs develop, then the soul begins to operate. Aquinas is saying this of the nutritive soul, but a rational soul, which also contains the powers of nutrition *and* sensation, is equally capable of informing such matter. Gerber makes this point forcefully.

In the first place, one might question the validity of the mediate animists' attempt to interpret the Aristotelian-Thomistic definition of the soul as the rigid requirement for the time of the soul's infusion. With the exception of the words *actus primus,* that definition is an operative account of the soul. The soul itself is the first or vivifying, substantial act; its operations are second acts, and it was from the diversity of these operations that Thomas concluded that the subject of the soul needed a diversity of organs.... But the soul itself is first act independently of its operations, which are second acts. In order to account for the required perfections of matter, it does not seem necessary to posit additional substantial forms as preparatives of the matter of the soul. Rather, it would suffice to consider the soul as a causally complex form which itself prepares matter for those operations. Since the human soul as substantial form contains the vegetative and sentient faculties within its own influence, it could by these functions progressively inform the embryo to the operative intellectual stage.[55]

Aquinas himself seems to be making this same point in the following passage.

Aristotle does not say that the soul is merely the act of a body, but the act of a physical organic body having life potentially; and that this potentiality *does not reject the soul.* Thus it is manifest that in this the soul is called the act such that the soul itself is included, in the same way of speaking that we say that heat is the act of what is hot, and light of what is lit; not that separately there be a lit thing without light, but because it is a lit thing through the light. And similarly we say that the soul is the act of a body, etc., through which soul it is both a body, and organic, and has potential life [i.e., is capable of performing living operations]. But the first act is said to be in potency in respect to the second act, which is operation; for such potency is not rejecting—that is, not excluding—the soul.[56]

It is important not to rely too heavily on the phrase "organic" or "having organs" in discussing the relationship of soul to body and what constitutes a properly disposed body. The human body must have a diversity of organs to be properly disposed for the *operations* of the soul, that is, for second act. A one-celled conceptus with the specific human genotype, on the other hand, is matter well enough disposed to be the proper subject of the human intellectual soul in regard to first act, to be the matter for which such a soul is the substantial form.

In summation, I hope to have shown several things: a) that Aquinas's theory of the succession of souls is dependent on his theory of generation, based in an outmoded biology; b) as a result, there is no power other than the embryo's own soul which can perform the formation of the organs necessary for the operations of the soul; c) that soul must be a human intellectual soul from the beginning of the embryo's being; and d) from the time of fertilization the conceptus is matter properly disposed to be the subject of such a form as the rational soul. Thus, it is reasonable to say that infusion of this soul by God takes place at conception and that we are from conception human persons.

Postscript: More Recent Opinions

Views similar to Donceel's are expressed in an article by William A. Wallace, O.P., entitled "Nature and Human Nature as the Norm in Medical Ethics."[57] This article contains some very interesting attempts to cast substantial form and prime matter in the light of contemporary physics, chemistry, and biology, but with regard to our problem here Wallace presents the following arguments:

> Is the transient form that is becoming a chimpanzee really a chimpanzee from the first moment of formation of the zygote? Alternatively, is the radioactive neptunium that is breaking down into lead really lead from the first moment of its radioactive decay? Invoking the *agere sequitur esse* axiom, one would think that, just as an element with the properties of neptunium should be regarded as neptunium and not as lead, even though it will eventually become lead, so a transient nature that exhibits only vegetative activities should be regarded as a plant and not as an animal, even though the term of its growth is a stable animal nature.[58]

The case is similar for humans. Wallace concludes that

a Thomistic natural philosophy, updated to incorporate the findings of modern science, can influence the decision between the two alternatives, and would probably favor delayed over immediate hominization on the basis that the former is more consonant with nature's other operations.[59]

For Wallace, the theory of immediate hominization "misconstrues how nature itself operates as a cause in the eduction of forms, and would bring God into a natural process at a stage where his action is not required."[60]

Wallace's analysis in this area misses the mark on several key points. 1) "Nature" is not something above and beyond the substantial forms that make it up. Each individual nature is what it is because of its substantial form, i.e., the substantial form gives the thing its nature. (In the material world, it must be coupled with matter to be a complete nature.) 2) An effect cannot be greater than the cause. Demanding, however, that lower forms be responsible for the shaping of the material, such that a higher form is educed, in effect demands that a lower form produce what is greater than itself. The analogy between the movement from neptunium to lead and that from "transient-" or "plant-chimpanzee" to "animal-chimpanzee" is not valid. A shift in form on the same level might be possible due to the power inherent in the first forms. A "downgrading" of form—say, from sensitive to vegetative—might also be possible, due to the fact that a higher form contains within itself the powers of the lower forms. An "upgrade," however, violates the principle of the effect not being greater than the cause. 3) Aquinas escapes this dilemma by saying that the soul (the substantial form) of the parent has produced a body ready for infusion of a new soul by God. As we have seen, this is not the case. Thus, we are left with only one conclusion: there must be a human soul from fertilization to account for human development. The argument Wallace notes regarding historical and functional identity[61] is *not* an account of biology which *demands* infusion at fertilization but rather an *explanation* of how such infusion—*already* demanded by causal concerns—is possible.

Norman M. Ford, S.D.B., (of the Catholic Theological College in Melbourne, Australia) has put together one of the most thorough treatments of this topic in *When Did I Begin?*.[62] This book is impressive not only because it presents a depth of scientific research and explanation but also because it takes so seriously the argument for immediate animation and the Aristotelian-Thomistic principles involved, before deciding in favor of delayed animation. Indeed, once one reads the section on immediate animation, one is hard-pressed to figure how *anyone* could find fault with such a position—and yet Ford does. Unfortunately, it seems to this writer that he comes to his conclusion by misappropriating the very principles he seemed to understand so clearly earlier on.

For Ford, it is true that the fertilized ovum has a "biological human nature",[63] but this does not mean that a human person, with a human soul as form of the body, is present. Rather, he argues that a *genetic* human being is present but not an ontological human being. The latter does not seem to be present until the primitive streak stage.[64] A person is "a distinct on-going ontological individual with a biological human nature."[65]

Ford argues that the possibility of twinning and recombination indicates that such an on-going individual is not present. If, for instance, one cell divides into two, neither is said to be the original cell—neither of the two new individuals is the first individual. Similarly, recombining cells would destroy the identity of the recombined cells, with a new entity—the combination—being a new individual. Ford is also concerned with the fact that both the embryo and placenta come from the same cell mass at differentiation, even though one is the individual and the other is not. Since there is no guarantee prior to cell differentiation that twinning or recombination will not occur nor that any particular cell will differentiate into embryonic vs. non-embryonic cells, Ford is unwilling to say that there is an ontological human individual (a person) prior to the appearance of the primitive streak. Like Donceel, Ford waits until an actual organ (of sorts) appears before conceding that a human soul is present in this matter.

There are several problems with Ford's analysis, despite the care he takes. 1) In Thomistic terms, what would it mean to say that something has a "biological human nature" without thereby having a human form? Ford claims to be fighting against dualism,[66] but this is a very dualistic notion. 2) Just because it is not *this* human individual person does not mean that it is not a human individual person. Ford has not adequately dispelled the argument that at least one individual *could* continue through twinning or recombination—a position which he is careful to spell out.[67] Even if it were true, however, that the coming to be of two individuals from one, or of one from two, entails the death of the prior individual(s), it does not entail that there was *no* ontological individual at all. In fact, Ford's own definition—"a human person begins as a living individual with the inherent active potential to develop towards adulthood without ceasing to be the same ontological individual"[68]—applies equally to the one-celled zygote as to the blastocyst. The conceptus *has* this inherent active potential; the fact that some might not realize this potential does not argue against their being ontological individuals. The problem here seems to be a confusion of material with formal causality. To say that one individual may give rise to two is true but only materially. The form either ceases to be in this matter or continues in one of the material bodies. It seems to me that Ford ultimately makes the same mistake that Donceel and many philosophers make in this area: he is searching for material conditions rather than looking to see what operations are being performed that *require the presence of the human soul.*

Two other articles which appeared recently seem to put the same metaphysical cart before the horse.[69] The first article appeared in *Theological Studies* in December of 1990. Entitled "Reflections on the Moral Status of the Pre-Embryo," it was authored by Thomas Shannon and Allan B. Wolter, O.F.M. The second piece, "Who or What is the Preembryo?" by Richard McCormick, S.J., led off the inaugural issue of the *Kennedy Institute of Ethics Journal* in March 1991.

Essentially, McCormick asks the question: What is necessary for personhood? His answer is developmental individuality. Even genetic individuality is not enough. In taking on the arguments of the Congregation for the Doctrine of the Faith expressed in *Donum vitae,* McCormick says this document seems unaware that in the preembryo's earliest stages the constituent cells are only "loosely associated."[70] Thus:

> For the CDF, if the preembryo is genetically individualized,
> it is individualized in the most radical sense. Thus it asks:
> "How could a human individual not be a human person?" A

possible, and in my judgment sufficient, response to this question is: "by not yet being a human individual (developmentally single)."[71]

Ultimately, however, the question is rather: What is necessary for development toward a physically discernable individual at the primitive streak stage? I suggest Aquinas's answer (and mine) would be that it is the presence of a human rational soul. McCormick's own observation seems to indicate this.

> Under favorable circumstances, the fertilized ovum will move through developmental individuality then progressively through functional, behavioral, psychic, and social individuality. In viewing the first stage, one cannot afford to blot out subsequent stages.[72]

How is such development possible at all without the presence of a human rational soul?

Shannon and Wolter's errors are similar. Concentrating on the question of human individuality, they assert that "a determinate and irreversible individuality is a necessary, if not a sufficient, condition for it to be a human person."[73] Further, this individuality, i.e., being properly speaking a "human individual," cannot eventuate until after the process of restriction and determination.[74] Until that time, the possibility of twinning and the totipotentiality of cells in the zygote indicates that "the organism is not necessarily single."[75] In other words, the zygote is more correctly a loosely bound aggregation of individuals.

Again, though, the issue arises: while immediate animation can explain the facts of twinning and totipotency, how can the mediate animation theory explain the fact that most zygotes do *not* divide—or, for that matter, that *any* do not divide? that the totipotent cells are loosely bound in *this particular way,* and not in a variety of ways? that they all develop according to the same process? For Aquinas, if effect is not to be greater than cause, a human soul must be responsible. Since for us the soul of one of the parents cannot be the cause, the cause must be the human rational soul of the zygote, right from the moment genetic uniqueness is established.

Furthermore, one is struck by the somewhat dualistic characterization of the relationship between soul and body in this account of the human person. Dualism could be seen in Norman Ford's explanation, but it is much more evident here. For instance, Shannon and Wolter opt for the terms "immaterial individuality" and "immaterial selfhood" instead of "soul."[76] This sounds more Platonic than Aristotelian / Thomistic. For Aquinas, there is no human immaterial individual or self apart from the composite of body and soul. While the soul may survive death, it is incomplete in its nature, not fully a self or particular individual.[77] A second instance of this dualism occurs where they examine the definition of personhood used in Catholic moral theory: an individual substance of a rational nature. When is such a rational nature present? they ask: at the primitive streak stage, or the completion of simple neural circuits, or at the appearance of an integrated nervous system?[78] Of course, the Thomistic answer to the question is: there is a rational nature when the material being is informed by a rational soul. The soul is the form of the body and so makes it to be, to be a body, and to be this kind of body (living and rational). "Nature" is not limited to material things. Angels and God are considered persons because they are complete individual substances of a rational nature, yet they are non-bodily.

In the third instance of dualism, and using an argument much like William Wallace's, Shannon and Wolter reach back to Wolter's own 1960 article, "Chemical Substance."[79]

> Philosophically speaking, we have every reason to believe that the dynamic properties of the organic matter—the elements of the fully formed zygote—owe their existence to their organizational form or the system. Important to note is that "where there are only material powers—that is, the ability to form material systems—, there is only a material nature or substance." Thus the material system or form of the developing body can explain its own activity. We conclude that there is no cogent reason, either from a philosophical or still less from a theological viewpoint, why we should assert, for instance, that the human soul is either necessary or directly responsible for the architectonic chemical behavior of nucleo-proteins in the human body.[80]

The mistake here, it seems to me, is precisely the same as Wallace's: the argument fails to respect the utterly foundational axiom that an effect cannot be greater than its cause. Yes, form can be educed from the potency of matter, but *only if* there is a sufficient cause, equal to or greater than the form educed, which is responsible for bringing the matter to that potentiality. Aquinas would hold that the human soul *is* directly responsible for the behavior of proteins in the human body. Otherwise, we must say there is more than one form, more than one soul, in the human being, and this in turn would mean we are *not one being,* but several—which Aquinas emphatically denies.[81]

Finally, although the passage and footnote are fairly brief, Shannon and Wolter seem particularly concerned about the problem of embryonic wastage. The fact that about 55% of fertilizations come to a quick end in miscarriage "intuitively argues against the creation of a principle of immaterial individuality at conception."[82] This is, indeed a jarring statistic, and perhaps one day we will have a full explanation of why this might be the case. Still, our job as philosophers is to explain how all the facts are possible. This the theory of immediate animation does; the theory of mediate animation cannot. We should not be deterred from accepting the explanation simply because the corollaries make us uncomfortable.[83]

There is one small item in Shannon and Wolter's article which sent me searching for more information. In discussing the physiological status and development of the preembryo, they quoted an article by Carlos A. Bedate and Robert C. Cefalo, entitled "The Zygote: To Be or Not to Be a Person."[84] What was most significant there was the claim that, for the zygote to become an embryo, "further essential and supplementary genetic information to what can be found in the zygote itself is required."[85] In other words, the zygote appears not to be self-sufficient for further development. Could it be that Aristotle was right—that, at least in the earliest stages, the body *is* still being formed by the power of the parent? If so, it would not be necessary to posit the existence of a human rational soul from the time of the combination of genetic material.

In their very short article, Bedate and Cefalo come at the personhood of the zygote from a completely different (and particularly challenging) angle. As their introductory paragraph states:

Many of the philosophical and moral-theological arguments against very early abortion or manipulation of the preembryo presuppose that the zygote contains all the information necessary to produce the specific biological character of the future adult. . . . In such arguments the zygote is accorded a special status because of the claim that the biological uniqueness of the future adult is determined at the moment of conception. Such philosophical and theological positions that depend on this empirical presupposition must be radically revised if that presupposition can be shown to be false.[86]

Bedate and Celafo's argument runs essentially as follows: 1) The fact of differentiation cannot be explained simply by reference to genetic information already in the zygote; for 2) a hydaditiform mole can be produced from a healthy zygote; therefore 3) not all genetic information necessary for becoming an embryo is present in the zygote, so 4) it must come from interaction with the mother.

If the authors are correct about 2), this would *indicate* that the personal soul is not present at this stage but would not prove it. It would be still possible that this zygote was subject to a genetic defect or other malady which killed it as a person. The fact is, however, that Bedate and Cefalo's information has simply been superseded. An article by Donald DeMarco in the January 1991 issue of *Ethics and Medics*[87] cites Jerome Lejeune's testimony in the Tennessee frozen embryo case from August of 1989. Lejeune has proven that the hydaditiform mole is formed not from a healthy zygote but from a "pseudo-zygote" formed by two male gametes, two sets of male chromosomes.[88]

In like manner, differentiation may *indicate* lack of sufficient material in the zygote, but it does not prove it. As Bedate and Cefalo argue:

It seems that extrazygotic information is not necessary during the first division of the zygote. . . . However, at a certain moment this information for producing more blastocysts is lost, since the division stops and another completely different process (differentiation) begins. Where does the information necessary for this other process come from? Some type of interaction between molecules of the zygote and extra-zygotic molecules must occur, because a stage develops at which the blastocyst is established in the uterus with absolute physiological dependence on the mother. At this point the process of embryonic differentiation begins.[89]

Since our knowledge of the coding and workings of genetic information is far from complete, it is certainly not *necessary* that the information triggering differentiation be extra-zygotic. The coincidental evidence, however, is striking. Let us grant, for the sake of argument, that interaction with molecules outside the zygote provides the last piece of information which sets off the differentiation process. What *metaphysical* significance does this have? Does it mean that a human rational soul—hence, a person—is not present? Is a power of the parent still at work, *forming* the body of this individual?

The evidence suggests a more likely scenario. A parental power may be at work, but its power is only instrumental, not formative. Take this passage, for instance: "At most, the zygote possesses the molecules that have the potential to acquire informing capacity."[90] What seems to be going on here is that the maternal molecules supplying the necessary bits for the beginning of differentiation simply *enable* the zygote to do its *own* work of formation. The human soul of the zygote can do this work alone, even though, for a while, certain necessary physical conditions must be supplied from outside the zygote. The power of differentiation at a certain stage is a power of the thing, hence derived from its soul, but it is a passive power, requiring certain triggering events. An analogy might serve as an illustration. We have powers of sensation, but these powers do not act all by themselves. They require an external stimulus to begin their operation. Without a sound, the power of hearing is useless. This does not mean sound is part of the power of hearing, but it is a necessary condition for it. Likewise, the power of formation into the embryo stage is already present in the zygote, awaiting the necessary conditions for beginning its operation.

Under this latter scenario, the better explanation of the personhood of the zygote and embryo would be that the same soul, the human rational soul, is present in the zygote and embryo, and it alone is properly responsible for the formation of the body from the combination of male and female chromosomal material. The power of the parents in the formation of the zygote and embryo, necessary in

Aristotle's and Aquinas's understanding of fetal development—in fact, necessary to *any* theory of mediate animation under Thomistic metaphysical principles—is simply not present.

Each of these authors under scrutiny has missed the mark by approaching the issue from the perspective of material conditions rather than what operations require the human soul. They suggest that we must *have* a human ontological individual before the soul comes. But it is, in fact, the soul which *makes* this matter to be a human ontological individual.

NOTES

1. Rudolph Gerber, "When Is the Human Soul Infused?" *Laval théologique et philosophique* 22 (1966): 235.

2. *S. Th.* I, 90, 3, corp.

3. *S. Th.* I, 90, 4, corp.

4. Joseph Donceel, S.J., "Abortion: Mediate v. Intermediate Animation," *Continuum* 5 (1967): 167–71; "Immediate Animation and Delayed Hominization," *Theological Studies* 31 (1970): 76–105.

5. Donceel, "Abortion," p. 169.

6. Ibid., p. 168.

7. Ibid.

8. Ibid., p. 169.

9. Canon Henri de Dorlodot, "A Vindication of the Mediate Animation Theory," in E. C. Messenger, ed., *Theology and Evolution* (London: Sands and Co., Ltd., 1949), p. 260. Cf. Donceel, "Abortion," pp. 169–70.

10. Donceel, "Immediate Animation," p. 79.

11. Ibid., p. 80.

12. Ibid.

13. Ibid.

14. Ibid., p. 83.

15. *S.C.G.* II, 89, in Donceel, "Immediate Animation," p. 94.

16. Thomas Wassmer, S.J., "Questions About Questions," *Commonweal* 86 (1976): 417.

17. *De Anima* X, ad 16.

18. *De Anima* X, corp.

19. *S. Th.* I, 76, 4, ad 1; cf. Aristotle, *De Anima* II, 1.

20. *De Anima* X, ad 2.

21. *S.C.G.* II, 86, 4.

22. Aristotle, *De Gen. Anim.* II, 3.

23. *S. Th.* I, 76, 3, ad 3; cf. *S.C.G.* II, 89, 9; *De Spir. Crea.* III, ad 13.

24. *S. Th.* I, 76, 3, corp.; 4, corp.

25. *S. Th.* I, 118, 2, ad 2.

26. *S.C.G.* II, 88, 11.

27. *S.C.G.* II, 89, 21.

28. *De Spir. Crea.* II, ad 13; *S.C.G.* II, 89, 6 and 7.

29. *S.C.G.* II, 89, 8.

30. *S.C.G.* II, 8; cf 89, 21.

31. *S. Th.* I, 118, 1, ad 4.

32. *S.C.G.* II, 88 and 89.

33. *S.C.G.* II, 89, 4 and 5.

34. *S. Th.* I, 118, 1, ad 4.

35. *De An.* II, ad 2.

36. *S. Th.* I, 118, 1, ad 3; cf. *S.C.G.* II, 89, 8.

37. *S.C.G.* II, 89, 8.

38. *S. Th.* I, 118, 1, ad 4.

39. *S.C.G.* II, 89, 9.

40. Benedict Ashley, "A Critique of the Theory of Delayed Hominization" in D. G. McCarthy and A. S. Moraczewski, ed., *An Ethical Evaluation of Fetal Experimentation: An Interdisciplinary Study* (St. Louis: Pope John XXIII Medical-Moral Research and Education Center, 1976), Appendix I, p. 119; cf. *Generation of Animals,* ed. A. L. Peck (Cambridge, Mass.: Loeb Library, 1953) Appendix B, pp. 576–93, for a discussion of the semen and *pneuma.*

41. *De An.* IX, ad. 16.

42. Donceel, "Immediate Animation," p. 85.

43. *De Spir. Crea.* IV, ad 9 (my emphasis).

44. *De Anima* II, 4 (415b 9–10).

45. *De Anima* II, 4 (415b 15–20).

46. *De Spir. Crea.* IV, ad 9.

47. Francis Wade, S.J., "Potentiality in the Abortion Discussion," *Review of Metaphysics 29* (1975): 239–55.

48. Gerber, p. 245–6.

49. Wade, "Potentiality," p. 254.

50. Ashley, pp. 123–4.

51. Ibid., p. 125.

52. Ibid.

53. *S. Th.* I, 118, 1, ad 3 (my emphasis).

54. *S. Th.* I, 118, 1, ad 4.

55. Gerber, "Soul Infused," p. 244.

56. *S. Th.* I 76, 4, ad 1; cf. Aristotle, *De Anima* II, 1 (412b 25ff.).

57. William A. Wallace, O.P., "Nature and Human Nature as the Norm in Medical Ethics," in *Catholic Perspectives on Medical Morals,* ed. Edmund D. Pelligrino (Dordrecht, Netherlands: Kluwer, 1989), pp. 23–52.

58. Ibid., p. 47.

59. Ibid., p. 48.

60. Ibid., p. 50.

61. Ibid., p. 49.

62. Norman M. Ford, S.D.B., *When Did I Begin?* (New York: Cambridge University Press, 1988).

63. Ibid., p. 128.

64. Ibid., pp. 168–77.

65. Ibid., p. 128.

66. Ibid., p. 130.

67. Ibid., pp. 112–16.

68. Ibid., p. 85.

69. This may be due to the fact that they rely so heavily on some of these same authors.

70. Richard McCormick, S.J., "Who or What is the Preembryo?" *Kennedy Institute of Ethics Journal,* March 1991, pp. 7–8.

71. Ibid., p. 8.

72. Ibid., p. 12.

73. Thomas Shannon and Allan B. Wolter, O.F.M., "Reflections on the Moral Status of the Pre-embryo," *Theological Studies* 51 (1990): 613.

74. Ibid., p. 614.

75. Ibid., p. 613.

76. Ibid., p. 615.

77. See *S. Th.* I, 75 art. 2 and 4.

78. Shannon and Wolter, p. 620.

79. Allan B. Wolter, "Chemical Substance," in *Philosophy of Science* (Jamaica, N.Y.: St. John's University, 1960), originally titled "The Problem of Substance."

80. Shannon and Wolter, pp. 620–621.

81. See *Summa Theologiae I,* Q. 76, art 1, 3, and 4.

82. Shannon and Wolter, p. 619.

83. I find it far more disturbing that the authors are willing to suggest that the claim of immediate animation is "not only irrational but blasphemous" (p. 618). In footnote 60 (p. 618), they say, "To ascribe such bungling of the conceptual process to an all-wise creator would seem almost sacreligious." It seems to this writer that our job is to discover and explain what is happening and not to set about blaming God for his apparent inefficiency. The blasphemy occurs when we try to hold God to our far from wise standards.

84. Carlos A. Bedate and Robert C. Cefalo, "The Zygote: To Be or Not to Be a Person," *Journal of Medicine and Philosophy* 14 (1966): 641–645.

85. Shannon and Wolter, p. 608.

86. Bedate and Cefalo, p. 641.

87. Donald DeMarco, "Zygotes, Persons, and Genetics," *Ethics and Medics,* January 1991, pp. 3–4. The Lejeune testimony is published in *Child and Family* 21 (1989/90): 7–52.

88. Demarco, p. 4. Similarly, a demoid cyst occurs from division of an unfertilized ovum.

89. Bedate and Cefalo, p. 643. It should be noted that the authors do not seem intent on proving this conclusion beyond any doubt. The argument is qualified at several key points with phrases such as "It is likely..." and "It seems that...."

90. Bedate and Celafo, p. 642.

Chapter 4

SELF-CONSCIOUSNESS AND THE RIGHT TO LIFE

Patrick Lee

One way of trying to justify abortion is to argue that what is killed in abortion is not a person. Although in popular and political circles it is still often denied that the embryo or fetus is a human being, this denial is contrary to the biological facts, and so in philosophical circles is rarely made. Instead, in those circles, proponents of abortion often claim that the human fetus is a human being but not a *person*.[1] In this article I reply to two common arguments for this position, and also present a positive argument for the position that unborn human beings have basic moral rights.

I. Ways of Begging the Question

Before examining this position further, I would like to clarify a bit the question expressed by, "Are unborn human beings persons?" The use of the word "person" can sometimes be a way of begging the question whether unborn human beings have basic moral rights. Clearly, if one argued that human fetuses do not have a right to life because they are not persons, and by "person" one merely meant an entity that has basic moral rights, one would beg the question.

But one also begs the question if, like Mary Anne Warren, one argues that fetuses are not persons because they lack characteristics which, *according to the conventions of our language,* a thing must have in order to be called a person.[2] For, whatever the linguistic conventions of our culture are—although I think, as a matter of fact according to those linguistic conventions unborn human beings *do* qualify as bearers of the name "person"—one could always doubt whether those conventions are morally correct. This is not to say that every argument relying on the use of the word or concept "person" is unsound, but it is to say that the claim that unborn human beings differ from us *in such a way* that they lack basic moral rights, is a substantive moral claim, and therefore requires evidence. The argument that unborn human beings are not persons must show, not only that they lack some characteristic associated with entities which have rights, but also why having these characteristics is a necessary condition for having basic moral rights. Most authors who deny the personhood of unborn human beings do not even attempt to establish this crucial step in their argument.[3]

It is worth noting, also, that if there were a time in conception-gestation in which it was not clear whether what exists is a human being or human person yet, it still would not follow that the question of when there is a human person must be settled by convention. If A's are treated radically differently from B's, and there are some situations where it is not clear whether what exists is an A or a B, it simply does not follow that there is no clear-cut difference between A's and B's nor that how individuals in those types of situation should be treated is a matter of convention. Thus, when Joan Callahan claims that, "deciding when to classify a developing human being as a person is like when to call a shoot a tree,"[4] and concludes that therefore one must simply *decide* or settle by *convention* when to mark the distinction between person and nonperson,[5] she makes two mistakes. First, she assumes without argument that there are no radical breaks in the conception-gestation process. But there is a radical break: at conception. Second, she infers from this alleged uncertainty as to when the distinction occurs (between what is not a whole human person and what is) to the claim that the distinction is not objective—an unsound inference.

II. Potentialities for Higher Mental Functions

The most common reason given for the position that unborn human beings are not persons is that they lack such characteristics as self-consciousness, self-motivated activity, and other higher mental functions.[6] Joan Callahan refers to such characteristics when she claims that a conceptus has none of the characteristics that would compel us to recognize it as a person or a being with moral rights.[7]

It is sometimes pointed out, in illustrating this position, that an unborn human being does not behave differently at all from an unborn or born member of another species, such as a kitten or a chimpanzee. It is then argued that just as it is not wrong to kill (under certain circumstances) kittens or chimpanzees, therefore it cannot be wrong to kill (under certain circumstances) unborn human beings.[8] This is only the application of the general argument that a thing must exhibit higher mental functions to qualify for a right to life.

Yet, in terms of what a thing actually does, a chimpanzee is not very different from a sleeping person, or a person in a temporary coma either. Therefore the quality of one's *actual* mental state cannot be the feature which unborn human beings lack and which a thing must have to have a right to life.

So, to avoid saying that sleeping people also lack a right to life, proponents of this position must allow that the *potentiality* or the *capacity* for higher mental acts suffices to bestow a right to life on an individual. Yet, if "capacity" or "potentiality" is construed broadly, one will have to say that unborn human beings as well as sleeping people have the capacity for higher mental functions, and thus the position will not constitute a defense of abortion. So, the position we are examining must distinguish between the kind of potentiality a

75

sleeping person has for higher mental functions and the kind that an unborn human being has. Then, it will have to say that only entities with the first sort of potentiality have a right to life; those with the second sort have no right to life.

Michael Tooley, for example, makes such a distinction by calling the first sort "capacities" and the second sort "potentialities." To say that a thing has a potentiality is to say, "at least that there is a change it could undergo, involving more than the mere elimination of factors blocking the exercise of a capacity, that would result in its having the property it now potentially has."[9] In turn, he distinguishes between two sorts of capacities, immediately exercisable and blocked: "To attribute an immediately exercisable capacity to something is to make a statement about how the thing would be behaving, or what properties it would have, if it were now to be in certain circumstances, or in a certain condition."[10] In a blocked capacity everything positive on the part of the agent is present, but there is some negative factor blocking its actualization, as opposed to the agent lacking something positive in its constitution, such a lack being characteristic of a potentiality. Since an unborn human being must undergo changes in her constitution before she has mental functions, Tooley denies that an unborn human being has the capacity for higher mental functions. Rather, she has only the potentiality for them.[11]

So, using Tooley's language, one might argue: one must have a *capacity* for higher mental functions in order to have a right to life; those entities which have only the potentiality for such acts do not have a right to life.[12]

One reason against this position, as Tooley discovered, is that there are counter-examples to it. Unlike the person who is asleep, the person who is in a temporary coma will not exercise consciousness in response to any stimulus. To say, as Tooley does at one point, that the individual in a coma does have the capacity for self-consciousness, but that it is blocked, that there is some other factor present blocking the actualization of that capacity, is simply not true of all persons in comas. Often the brain tissue itself is damaged and requires self-repair or external correction (and hence a change in the thing's constitution).

A second reason against this position concerns the nature of potentiality. The distinction between the kind of potentiality for higher mental functions that a sleeping person has and the kind of potentiality for such functions that an unborn human being has is scarcely as momentuous as this position requires it to be. In fact, it is difficult to see why the distinction should be viewed as *morally* significant at all.

The potentiality for higher mental acts which an unborn human being has is, first of all, an *active* potentiality.[13] An active potentiality is the ability to *do* something; a passive potentiality is the ability to undergo a certain change from another. For example, the ability of fire to burn is an active potentiality, while the ability of wood to be burnt is a passive potentiality. The potentialities specific to living things are active potentialities. Moreover, they are potentialities of an organism to act on itself, instead of acting on another: in nourishment, growth, and self-motion, the object of the act, in the sense of what is developed or perfected by the action, is the same as the thing that performs the action. Typically, in such acts some external material is required that is used by the agent in its self-perfective action. In nourishment, for example, the object of the act is the organism itself, and the material used is food.

The unborn human being is a living being and so he has active potentialities that distinguish him from non-living beings. Now, there is certainly a sense in which the unborn human being does *not* have an active potentiality to perform higher mental acts. Just as the unborn human being cannot breathe before he grows lungs, so he cannot perform higher mental acts before the development of the brain. But there is also a real and important sense in which the unborn human being *does* have the active potentiality to perform such acts. The human embryo or fetus is not in the same condition as, say, a canine embryo or fetus, which never will perform such acts, and does not have within itself the positive reality required for actively developing itself to the point where such activities will be performed. The living thing is dynamic, and it has within itself the source of what it will become. True, it needs food, a certain type of atmosphere, and so on. But, given these materials, it actively develops itself to its mature size and structure.

The situation of the unborn human being is this: it is possible that this entity perform a certain action, z, but to do that she must first do x and y, and she is in the process of doing x. Does such an entity have the potentiality to do z or not? I think the answer must be that in one sense she does not, but in another, perhaps more fundamental, sense, she does. Nor is this just to say that she *will* have that potentiality. Rather, there is that about this entity here and now which makes her quite different from those not actively developing themselves to the point where a more proximate potentiality is possessed. If one asks, "Does Jones have the potentiality (or capacity) to run a marathon?" it is perfectly natural to reply, "Yes, with a good night's sleep behind her she certainly can do it." And the point of the reply is that she is now in that sort of condition. Still, if one insists on calling this positive reality by a different term or phrase, the terminology is unimportant. What matters is that the difference between the kind of potentiality an unborn human being has and the kind that a sleeping person has cannot carry the moral weight which the proponents of this position need it to.

The important dividing line is that between the passive potentiality of the sperm or ovum on the one hand, and the active potentiality of the embryo on the other hand. And we can see this point if we ask *why* higher mental functions or the capacity or potentiality for higher mental functions should be a trait which bestows value on those who have it. There are two views one could take. One could say that a capacity for such functions bestows value in the sense that the entities which have such functions and capacities are carriers or recipients for what actually has value. In that case the organisms in which the higher mental functions inhere are not intrinsically valuable, but rather the mental functions and states themselves are valuable and the organisms are instrumentally valuable. The other view is that having a potentiality or capacity for higher mental states (of whatever sort) means that those entities themselves are intrinsically valuable.

It will not do, however, to say that only the mental states are intrinsically valuable and the entities which have a potentiality for them are instrumentally valuable because of their relation to those mental states. If that were the case then the basic moral rule would be simply to maximize higher mental states. It would not be morally wrong to kill a child, no matter what age, if doing so enabled one to have two children in the future, to "replace" the one carrier of intrinsic value with two. But this is surely mistaken. So, potentialities for higher mental states are of ethical significance not because they themselves are the only intrinsic values but because entities which have such potentialities are of intrinsic value.[14]

If the entity itself is what has value, then it is hard to see why it would not have value from the moment that it exists. That is, it is hard to see how a thing could come to be at one time, but acquire intrinsic value, and hence basic rights, at another time.

And so it becomes clear that the important distinction is that between active and passive potentialities rather than that between capacities and potentialities. When an active potentiality is actualized the result is the achievement of a higher level of development or perfection by the entity whose potentiality is actualized. Thus the thing whose active potentiality is actualized remains intact as a distinct, whole entity. In the actualization of a passive potentiality, on the other hand, the result is often that the entity, or some components of the entity, enter(s) into the constitution of a larger entity, and so the original entity does not exist after the change.

In the relevant case, when the sperm and the ovum fuse to become a zygote, which is a distinct organism, the sperm and the ovum do not survive as distinct and whole entities. Rather, the genetic material in each enters into the constitution of the larger entity, the new organism which comes to be through their fusion. Thus, a sperm has no active potentiality to develop any of the traits of mature human beings; it has only the passive potentiality to surrender its material into the constitution of that same human being. The zygote, on the other hand, the new embryo, is a distinct organism which actively develops himself in a continuous fashion until he reaches the mature stage of his development. Thus the fact that he has the active potentiality for the traits of a mature human being also means that the actualization of his potentiality does not produce a distinct entity but rather the maturation of the same entity which has existed since conception. Since this entity is identical with the entity two years later which indisputably has intrinsic value, it is most reasonable to hold that this entity now has intrinsic value.

III. Dualism

There is a second way in which one could argue that unborn human beings are not persons, i.e, do not have basic moral rights. One might grant, at least implicitly, that entities which have intrinsic value acquire intrinsic value at the time they come to be, and also grant that human organisms come to be at conception, but deny that what has intrinsic value is, at any time, identical with a human organism. That is, one could hold a dualist position on the human person.

Michael Tooley's later position is an example of this position. He argues that a thing has a right to continued existence (a right to life, if it is a living thing) only if it is an enduring subject of conscious experiences and other mental states. He denies that unborn human beings, and infants also, are such subjects. According to Tooley, the human physical organism comes to be at one time, but the subject of consciousness and other mental states comes to be only later. He also holds that the subject of consciousness can be destroyed and the human organism continue to exist. Clearly, he presupposes that the person, what has intrinsic value, is a subject of experiences and other mental states *associated with* a physical organism, but not identical with it.[15]

However, dualism is mistaken. When walking I am directly aware that I am *walking* and that I am *thinking*. True, I do not intuit the self, myself, separate from or independently of any property.[16] Yet, on the other hand, I am not aware of the properties of walking and thinking as independent properties, but as properties of a thing, I or me. I am aware of myself as that of which these different properties are properties, and, what is important here, I am also aware that the thing which has the property of walking is not a different thing than the thing which has the property of thinking. I am aware of this not through some middle term or common property, but directly. That is, I am directly aware that I am both walking and thinking. One might ask: is unity a property that is intuited? My answer is no, it is the *lack of division*. One might object: but then how can one be directly aware of an indivision? My answer is, I do not notice any division, and I also am aware that I *would* notice division in this area if there were any, just as I see that there is no elephant in this room. I am aware that I am walking and that I am thinking; I move smoothly from one thought to the other with no awareness of any shift in reference for the two "I's". But if the I's in the two cases *were* different, surely the movement from one to the other would not be so smooth.

But walking is a material property, and thinking is a higher mental function. A thing which walks is a physical organism. Therefore the thing which thinks is a physical organism. And this thing—the subject of the walking and thinking, is what is referred to as "I" or "me". Therefore the "I" or "me" is a physical organism.

The word "person" refers to the same thing that the word "I" or "me" does. The person is the "I", but the "I" is a physical organism. Therefore the human person is a physical organism.[17]

IV. Conclusion

In short, there are two ways of holding that an unborn human being is not a person and therefore lacks a right to life. One way, criticized in section II above, is to say that (1) the human physical organism is, eventually, the subject of those capacities or acts which confer rights, but (2) the human organism comes to be at one time, but acquires rights only when it acquires the capacity for higher mental acts (as opposed to the potentiality for them). Against that position I argued: (a) that there are counterexamples to it, (b) that the distinction between capacities and potentialities cannot be of such moral significance as this position claims, and (c) that the capacities or potentialities of a thing are important because they show that the thing itself is (or is not) inherently valuable, and so the time that the *thing* (which perhaps only at a later time possesses the relevant capacities) comes to be is also the time that it begins to have inherent value. This argument shows that the thing which has basic moral rights acquires them whenever it comes to be.

In the second way of holding that an unborn human being is not a person, one can grant that the distinction between potentialities and capacities is not the crucial point, and one can grant that the thing which has basic moral rights has them as soon as it comes to be, but one holds that the basic rights belong to a subject of consciousness distinct from the human physical organism. This position I criticized in section III. The criticism there shows that the human person is identical with the human physical organism.

So, putting these points together, we can say the following: (1) the thing which has basic rights acquires them at the time at which it comes to be; (2) the thing which has basic rights is the human organism. Now, let us add another point, which I am convinced is true although I have not argued for it here: (3) the time at which the human organism comes to be is conception. Then, the conclusion is: (4) human beings acquire basic rights at conception.

A different way of expressing the argument is as follows. It is agreed that: Killing adult human organisms is (at least prima facie) wrong. Now to argue convincingly that killing unborn human organisms is not wrong, one would have to determine what feature it is present in the killing of adult human organisms that makes it wrong, and then show that it is not also present in the killing of unborn human organisms. In this article I have examined two proposed features. First, some hold that killing adult human organisms is wrong because they have a capacity, not to be confused with a mere potentiality, for higher mental functions. Section II argued against that position. Secondly, some hold that killing adult human organisms is wrong because the continued existence of those organisms is a means for the realization of higher mental functions by subjects of consciousness associated with those physical organisms. Section III argued against that position.

I have not in this article argued for a specific criterion for having basic moral rights, that is, I have not tried to establish what it is about killing human beings that makes it wrong. But I have argued that the criterion for having moral rights, whatever it is, concerns a general area or category with respect to which mature human beings and unborn human beings do not differ (viz., a type of thing or substance as opposed to a property of a thing). Put otherwise, without establishing what it is about entities which qualifies them for moral rights, I have argued that the respects in which unborn human beings and mature human beings do differ are morally irrelevant.

Notes

1. In "The Fetus and Fundamental Rights," (in *Abortion and Catholicism, the American Debate,* ed. P. Jung and T. Shannon, New York: Crossroads, 1988, p. 219), Joan Callahan argues that opponents of abortion simply muddy the issue by couching the question in terms of the beginning of human life, as if the moral issue of abortion could be settled by a biologist. "What we *really* want to know <she says> is whether the living human fetus should be recognized as a bearer of the same range of fundamental moral rights that you and I have.... "<219>

Pro-life people do often argue that unborn embryos and fetuses should not be killed because they are human beings. But this is because the major premise of this argument (Human beings should not be directly killed) has been, generally, at least in theory, up until recently agreed upon in this country. Callahan simply concedes what has in popular circles been the main bone of contention, namely, the minor premise. She next says that what we *really* want to know is whether what is stated in the major premise is true, and then accuses the proponents of this argument of begging the question of not zeroing in on their major premise. Compare: "Yes, I grant that Socrates is human, but what we *really* want to know is whether all humans are mortal."

As to what question belongs to biology and what belongs to philosophy or some other discipline, the answer is simple. The major premise is ethical, and the minor premise is biological. The entire issue is clearly mixed.

2. Mary Anne Warren, "On the Moral and Legal Status of Abortion," in Joel Feinberg, ed., *The Problem of Abortion,* 2nd ed. (Belmont, California: Wadsworth, 1984), 102–119.

3. Joan Callahan writes: "And you and I *are* significantly different from a conceptus, which has *none* of the characteristics which morally compel us to recognize it as a being with rights. It will not do simply to deny that there are significant changes between the time of conception and the time when we have a being which we simply *must* recognize as a bearer of rights." In "The Fetus and Fundamental Rights," in *Abortion and Catholicism,* p. 223.

No one denies that there are significant differences between a conceptus or embryo and a mature human being. But, of course, everyone must also grant that there are significant *similarities* as well. The question is: are the differences *morally* relevant? Are the similarities morally relevant? One needs an argument to distinguish the morally relevant from the morally irrelevant. Without that, one's concentrating on the differences rather than on the similarities is likely to be merely another typical case of prejudice or unjust discrimination.

As to Callahan's first claim—that the conceptus has none of the characteristics which morally compel us to recognize her as a being with rights—she nowhere argues for it. I argue below, pp. 7–15, against it. For another approach to the question of what trait a thing must have to have rights, and why it must have this trait (viz., a rational, free agent, i.e., a thing with the basic potentiality to act rationally and freely) see: Patrick Lee, "Personhood, the Moral Standing of the Unborn, and Abortion," in *Linacre Quarterly* 57 (May, 1990), pp. 80–89, the last third of the article.

4. Joan Callahan, *op. cit.,* p. 221.

5. *Ibid.*

6. Mary Anne Warren, work cited in note 1; also Jane English, "Abortion and the Concept of a Person," in Joel Feinberg, work cited in note 2, p. 151–160.

7. Joan Callahan, *op. cit.,* p. 221.

8. Cf. Laura Purdy and Michael Tooley, "Is Abortion Murder?" in Robert Perkins, ed., *Abortion* (Cambridge, Mass.: Schenkman, 1974), p. 141.

9. Michael Tooley, *Abortion and Infanticide* (Oxford: Clarendon, 1983), p. 150.

10. *Ibid,* p. 149.

11. *Ibid,* p. 150.

12. Tooley held this position in earlier articles (see the article cited in note 8, and his "Abortion and Infanticide," *Philosophy and Public Affairs* 2 (1972), pp. 37–65). However, he abandoned it in his book of 1983, cited in note 9.

13. Tooley defines "active potentiality" as a condition of having all of the positive factors present, on the side of the thing with the potentiality, that are necessary for the exercise of the potentiality—lacking only the appropriate circumstances. However, with this definition, one would never have the active potentiality to nourish oneself, or to paint, or to perform any activity that requires outside objects as instruments or material.

14. In the article cited above in note 3 I argue for this point from the proposition that what is intrinsically valuable for a thing is its fulfillment, arguing that it is incoherent to hold that the fulfillment of a thing is intrinsically valuable but not the thing itself. I argue there also against the main view which competes with this position, hedonism, which holds that only the experiences of a thing are intrinsically valuable.

15. Cf. Tooley, *Abortion and Infanticide,* pp. 118–120; 97–103.

16. And this, really, is the only reason Kant and Hume had against the notion of a direct awareness of the self, but it is spurious. Cf. Roderick Chisolm, *Person and Object: A Metaphysical Study* (London: Allen and Unwin, Ltd., 1976).

17. The person, the I or me, is *essentially* a physical organism. That is, a physical organism is the (general) kind of thing which a human person is. Therefore, the time at which the physical organism comes to be is also the time at which the human I, or the human person, comes to be. Since the human organism comes to be at conception, the human person comes to be at conception also.

PART TWO

MORAL METHODOLOGY AND APPLICATIONS

Chapter 5

DIVINE REVELATION AND ABORTION

The Reverend Richard R. Roach, S.J.

Abortion is not simply a moral issue which can be isolated from Christian faith; it has to do with the very content of Christian faith. In other words, two persons may not agree to disagree about whether it ever is licit directly to procure an abortion while continuing to agree as Christian believers. If they are conscious of the implications of their differing stands on abortion, they must recognize that they profess two different faiths, only one of which is Christian. Such would not be the case if, for example, they agreed to disagree about relative or practical pacifism, which objects to particular wars or forms of war.[1] In so disagreeing neither party holds that Jesus the Christ forbade the use of all potentially or actually deadly force, which he did not do. They both agree that the use of such force must be limited. They disagree over only the limits. No fundamental principle of faith or morality is at stake. Neither ascribes a fundamental principle to Jesus Our Lord as teacher which contradicts the fundamental principle the other ascribes to him. They disagree over the application of the same principles.

Such also would be the case if they agreed to disagree over whether civil disobedience made for good or bad tactics in an effort to protect innocent human life and to reinstate the protection of the law for such innocent human life. One might hold that rescues (sit-ins which disrupt the running of an abortion mill and which lead to the arrest of demonstrators) are good tactics; the other, that they turn people of good will against the pro-life movement. In this case too, both agree that killing innocent human life is wrong, which Jesus taught. They disagree only over prudential matters, i.e., how best to defend innocent human life from slaughter. Both may be genuine believers.

But if two people disagree as to whether such slaughter is licit or not, they do not share the same faith.

I am sure that the intelligent reader senses immediately that my claim about the inviolability of innocent human life being essential to Christian faith is very serious indeed. Because it is so serious, I am obliged to set forth the fundamental reasons in clear order. First, God has revealed himself in Jesus the Christ. "The most intimate truth which this revelation gives us about God and the salvation of man shines forth in Christ, who is himself both the mediator and the sum total of Revelation."[2]

Secondly, we see what shines forth in Christ primarily through the Church he founded. It was that organized People of God, i.e., the Church, which recognized the inspired character of the writings that make up the sacred Scriptures of the Christian faith. Nor do we find all that shines forth in Christ explicit in these privileged writings which we call sacred Scripture or the Bible. Sacred Tradition completes them and provides the key to interpreting them rightly;[3] just as at the beginning of the Church sacred Tradition served to select the writings which make up the sacred Scripture and to select only those writings from a host of others: "By means of the same Tradition the full canon of the sacred books is known to the Church and the holy Scriptures themselves are more thoroughly understood and constantly actualized in the Church."[4] When our separated brethren in the 16th century broke away from the Catholic Church, they defended their fundamental doctrine of justification by faith alone with a further doctrine whereby they claimed that the sacred Scriptures alone are authority for belief. As a consequence they in principle could no longer look to sacred tradition for the canon. Finding another justification for the canon resulted in reducing the Christian Old Testament to the rabbinical canon for the Hebrew Scriptures which the rabbis had settled on by the end of the first or the beginning of the second century of our era. Some of the rejected writings contain significant doctrinal matter which the Protestant reformers also rejected, such as Purgatory and the intercession of the saints. For a period Martin Luther even questioned a number of books in the New Testament (Hebrews, Jude, 2nd Peter, Revelation [Apocalypse]), and dismissed James as "a straw epistle."[5]

"Sacred Tradition and sacred Scripture make up a single sacred deposit of the Word of God, which is entrusted to the Church."[6] "But the task of giving an authentic interpretation of the Word of God, whether in its written form or in the form of Tradition, has been entrusted to the living teaching office of the Church alone. Its authority in this matter is exercised in the name of Jesus Christ."[7]

I believe that if one meditates upon the vicissitudes of history during the nearly two thousand years which separate us from Jesus when he walked the earth, then one begins to realize that only through an organized people guided by God Himself could we have access to the mind of a man who lived without Roman citizenship approximately two thousand years ago in an obscure part of the ancient Roman empire. Furthermore, Jesus was a man who wrote nothing and who did nothing of the sort that would have made his mark in ordinary history. We know something of Julius Caesar, who lived but a short time before Jesus, only because he chronicled his own wars and made himself emperor before he was assassinated. These sorts of activities may leave a trace in ordinary history as they did in the case of Julius. Jesus, on the other hand, wrote nothing, taught a little, and suffered the capital punishment reserved for non-citizens and slaves. How many others of the thousands ancient Rome crucified do we know anything about? Jesus would be among the most obscure of the lot if he were just a man and not also God, as he claimed to be. And even though he is God, memory of him as the obscure man he chose to become would have been lost in human history if he had not founded the Church and empowered her to preserve his memory. This is to say that even if he had been exactly as I believe him to have been, namely, a man who also is God and who as man died and rose from the dead, because he chose to live and die as an obscure human being, we would have no coherent, non-contradictory knowledge of the mind of this humanly speaking obscure individual man if, when he rose from the dead, he had not sent the Holy Spirit to the organization which he had founded in order to make his mind known to us until he comes again. If God chose to be as obscure as Jesus was and if he had not founded the Church, he would still be our Lord, but we would know next to nothing for sure about him. There is a choice here. If we recognize that Jesus the Christ wanted us to know his mind, then we must accept the instrument, namely, the Church, which he fashioned to make his mind known.

I believe Jesus is Our Lord and that as such he has a consistent mind which he has revealed through the sacred Scriptures and through his Church (both in sacred Tradition and through the living teaching office often called the Magisterium). He has not revealed his mind about everything, but about those matters which are important to our salvation. As I said, I believe I have access to that mind through the Church he founded. Quite evidently, then, if in his name his Church has consistently proscribed directly procured abortion, as she has, Jesus himself condemns abortion.

As Jesus is the revelation of God, by reflecting on this fact we can come to see why he condemns directly procured abortion. All reality divides into two parts: God, who always was, always is, and always will be, and everything else which he created. To use the term 'God' to refer to any being other than the uncreated Being who created everything else that actually exists is simply to leave the Christian faith completely. If Jesus were the revelation of some other kind of 'god', he would not be at all remarkable. If Jesus were divine in some sense in which divinity meant something other than the Being who always is, was, and will be, and which created everything else that actually exists, he would be most uninteresting. Perhaps a Hindu avatar. But, as he is the Word of God in the proper sense, we can come to see why he condemns directly procured abortion, for God alone has sovereignty over human life.

Faith in Christ results in the following profession of faith: "We believe in one only God, Father, Son, and Holy Spirit, creator of things visible such as this world in which our transient life passes, of things invisible such as the pure spirits which are also called angels, and creator in each man of his spiritual and immortal soul."[8] Because God is the only creator in the fullest sense of the word, the only Being that brings other beings into existence from nothing, the proper name for human reproduction is procreation, which signifies sharing in God's creating. Each new human life is the special creation of Almighty God. It follows simply that unless the human life has done something to disqualify itself, it belongs immediately to God. We may not dispose as we may wish of such innocent human life without in practice denying God's sovereignty over it as its creator. Directly procured abortion, therefore, is practical atheism. By denying the creator's rights over his creation, we deny the creator who is the only living God.

We express practical atheism in a number of ways, for it usually means no more than that 'I' claim there is no God in 'my' case. Practical atheism comes down to believing that there is nothing relevant from or about God binding upon me in the decisions I make. Such a false claim can take a number of forms, so God's revelation tries to hedge in practical atheism in a number of ways. The first hedge turns out to be the first of the Ten Commandments.

We express our faith in God not simply by professing it or avowing it. We express our faith in God by obeying him. Yet the obedience we give God is unique. Obeying him is unlike obeying any other authority. We distinguish obeying God from submission to any other authority in that we rightly submit to God without qualification, without reserve, without limit or restriction. Furthermore, our deepest motive for obeying him should be love. We obey God unqualifiedly; we should so obey no other authority. Therefore, in obeying God we must acknowledge him alone as God, and we do so by the way we obey him. If we obey anyone else, including ourselves, as if this other authority were God, we thereby violate the first commandment, which is: "I, the Lord, am your God. You shall not have other gods besides me."[9] The adult catechism simply summarizes Exodus 20:1–6 and Deuteronomy 5:6–10. What, then, is the link between this commandment and the practice of abortion?

I think that the story of Cain and Abel reveals the link. (Gn 4:1–16.) We recall that Cain killed his brother Abel because God preferred Abel's sacrifice to his own. Cain pits himself against God's sovereign and free choice. To do so, he kills the innocent life whose sacrifice God had chosen. The New Jerusalem Bible notes: "... : after the revolt against God we now have fratricidal strife; against these two evils is directed the double command that sums up the whole Law—the love of God and of neighbour, Mt 22:40."[10] The first of the ten commandments begins the Law which Our Lord summed up. In this story of Cain and Abel set in a time before God gave the Law through Moses, Cain, who rebelled against God's choice by killing his brother, violated *practically* the sovereignty which God would claim for himself in the first commandment. We today violate the commandment in the same way any time we choose to kill one whom God has chosen to create.

Of course, the practice of abortion more clearly violates the fifth commandment: "You shall not kill."[11] Again the catechism simply proclaims what we read in Exodus 20:13 and Deuteronomy 5:17. And both the catechism and we must recover the context which makes precise what God proclaimed in the fifth commandment. For example, in the 21st chapter of Exodus, following almost immediately upon the Ten Commandments, we find provision in the Law for capital punishment—e.g., Ex 21:12–17. Therefore, the fifth commandment, understood in its context, does not forbid all killing of human beings, but most fundamentally does prohibit all killing of innocent human beings. Nor did Our Lord change this understanding of the fifth commandment. In his condemnation of hypocrites who misuse the Law, he endorses the provision for capital punishment found in Ex 21:17, which the scribes and Pharisees whom he calls hypocrites have succeed in evading. (Mt 15:4; Mk 7:10.) Since human life before it is born is innocent, the fifth commandment patently prohibits killing it. Such killing offends God.

I trust the reader noticed that Our Lord's interpretation of the fifth commandment involves our understanding that the commandment does not prohibit all killing, but only human life which has done or is doing no harm (innocent is from the Latin for not harming). By contextualizing the commandment Our Lord understood it to have a somewhat narrower meaning that it might have had if it were rightly understood out of context. But this 'narrowing' can be taken too far; it can be taken to the point where it simply falsifies the commandment. Two sets of arguments brought against my reading of the commandment illustrate this excessive 'narrowing' which falsifies the commandment. Both sets identify the killing which the commandment prohibits with a narrow definition of murder. The narrow definitions (and there are a variety) do not include abortion as a murderous act. Therefore, so those who argue in this way claim, the fifth commandment does not prohibit abortion.

The first set of arguments start from penalties imposed in Church law and other law under Christian influence against those who procure abortions. The penalties have ordinarily been less than for murder. Therefore, it is reasoned that abortion is not murderous. Quite frankly, I find it amazing that otherwise intelligent and educated people can be taken in by such arguments, or worse, propose them. First, it should be clear that there is a gap which cannot be completely bridged between the moral law and positive law such as the civil and criminal law of the state. A similar gap is affixed between the moral law and the canon law of the Church. Positive law in all forms merely approximates the moral law. It may never licitly proscribe contrary to the moral law, but it cannot simply embody the moral law. On the other hand, the Ten Commandments give voice to the moral law. Still one of the ten is strictly positive law, although divine positive law: i.e., the third commandment, "Remember to keep holy the Sabbath day."[12] Because it is strictly a positive law, this commandment has to be interpreted and applied differently from the way the moral law is. We see this throughout the New Testament and the life of the Church. How to comply with God's intent in the third commandment differs remarkably from how to comply with, for example, God's intent in prohibiting adultery. The latter requires no complicated interpretations, and Jesus never said of the prohibition of adultery what he said of the Sabbath: " 'The Sabbath was made for man, not man for the Sabbath; so the Son of man is master even of the Sabbath.' " (Mk 2:27) God did not make adultery; God so made man that adultery always is wrong for him. Adultery and abortion are not at all the same as the Sabbath. Of adultery Our Lord, after forgiving her, said to the woman caught in it: "Go away, and from this moment sin no more." (Jn 8:11)

In its effort to approximate the moral law when assessing murderous deeds, the criminal law, because it is positive law, has to take a number of things into consideration. Premeditation is but one. How could a human criminal court sort out those abortions which fulfilled all the conditions of true murder from miscarriages that might have been induced, from abortions chosen without malice or free consent to the evil done, and so forth? Through this all is the realization that the mother who aborts her child is often a victim as well as the child she aborts. It is very unlikely that criminal proceedings could fairly sort out this kind of thing. So, the law draws a general minimum penalty. And I would note that good law punishes those who perform abortions more than it does the mothers. Although some may freely procure them with true murderous intent, many others may merely submit to them while the true guilt lies elsewhere.

Nevertheless, when it comes to the moral law, which God adjudicates, an abortion may truly be murderous in the fullest sense. Just as a man may be judged guilty by a criminal court merely of manslaughter and therefore punished very lightly, when morally speaking he is guilty of murder in the fullest sense, so also one may procure an abortion with all the requisites of murder in the eyes of God. It is human eyes which cannot see clearly, and positive law (as distinct from the moral law) must reflect that limitation.

A perfect example of this kind of argument which would try to exempt abortion from the fifth commandment has its starting point in the 21st chapter of the Book of Exodus, the chapter wherein one may learn that the fifth commandment does not prohibit all killing of human beings. In the 21st chapter just before, and connected to, the *lex talionis*, we read: "If people, when brawling, hurt a pregnant woman and she suffers a miscarriage but no further harm is done, the person responsible will pay compensation as fixed by the woman's master, paying as much as the judge decides." (Ex 21:22) If harm greater than just the miscarriage has been done, then the *lex talionis*, which regulates and limits vengeance, should be applied. (Ex 21:23–25) The argument points out that the law provides a much more severe penalty for accidentally killing a human being than for this miscarriage. For example, " 'Anyone who by violence causes a death must be put to death. If, however, he has not planned to do it, but it comes from God by his hand, he can take refuge in a place which I shall appoint for you." (Ex 21:12–13) They then conclude that the law does not consider the unborn child, a human being, or it would have provided a comparable penalty for accidentally bringing about a miscarriage.

But, the precise difference is not that between a human being who has already been born and an unborn child; the precise difference consists in the quality of violence. The blow, for example, which would bring about a miscarriage in a pregnant woman without further damage, is not likely a blow which would kill a man standing on his own two feet. The blow which would not only bring about a miscarriage, but would also wound the mother (break her leg or crack her skull) might well kill a man standing on his own two feet, and the Old Testament provided for that difference. In this latter case, the full force of the *lex talionis* came into play: "If further harm is done, however, you will award life for life, eye for eye, tooth for tooth, hand for hand, foot for foot, burn for burn, wound for wound, stroke for stroke." (Ex 21:23–25)

The fundamental point remains that a person could kill, and the criminal law (as given, for example, in the 21st chapter of Exodus) would only be able to punish him as one who killed accidentally (what today might be called criminal negligence). Nothing more could be proved. He might still be guilty of murder in the eyes of God who voiced his moral law in the Ten Commandments.

Although there is the gap between the moral law and all merely positive law, this gap does not mean that the positive law, especially that found in the Old Testament, teaches us nothing about the moral law. We have seen that we understand the meaning of the fifth commandment in part from the positive law which follows it. Since the positive law of the Old Testament was legislated under divine inspiration, it does not contradict the moral law even when it falls below the moral law, as when God dispensed, as it were, from the moral law.[13] Since the positive law of the Old Testament does not contradict the moral law, we may learn from it how to read the moral law. It is because of the privileged character of the positive law found in the Old Testament that it can help us in this way—e.g., show us that the fifth commandment does not prohibit all killing of human beings, as I have made clear above. But from the more sophisticated point we have just discussed we learn not an exception from the fifth commandment, but that the positive law cannot possibly capture all sin. If we do not see this, we can use the positive law to excuse ourselves from the moral law, as many in the United States today are using the Supreme Court decision to exempt abortion for the criminal code as an excuse for thinking that abortion can be moral. In this way positive law leads us to misinterpret the moral law. Positive law can even be used to undermine the moral law. The fact that not even the positive law in the Old Testament could capture all fully murderous abortions does not mean that abortion fails to violate the fifth commandment. It does. Merely because 'Christian' legal codes have not punished abortion as murder does not mean that directly procured abortion does not always gravely violate the moral law. It does.

The second argument has a philosophical or theological tone about it. It goes as follows: We do not know for sure when a human life becomes a human person. The ancients used to think that human life became a person when the foetus began to look like a human being. Today we emphasize something subjective like human consciousness rather than something objective like form. So, in the late twentieth century we are inclined by our prejudices to think that human life does not become personal until it can show signs of consciousness, particularly by relating to other beings. Infants in the womb, at least in the early stages of development, do not show signs of consciousness and do not seem to relate to other beings; so, we are inclined to decide that they are not yet human persons. Then, we re-interpret the moral law to the effect that it prohibits killing only (innocent) human *persons*. So, having decided to doubt that the unborn baby is a human person, we feel free to kill it. I am disturbed by this line of argument. (Since there is no reasonable doubt but that the unborn baby is innocent of wrong-doing, I am not dwelling on that issue.)

I am disturbed by this line of argument, but not because I think the question whether human life is personal from the moment of biological conception until natural death is settled. I do not think that question has been settled and the Church recognizes that it is open. I am disturbed because I know that a muddle has led some into thinking that the speculative question about when a new human life becomes a person has something to do with the morality of abortion. Abortion is a procedure for directly killing innocent human lives. Whether the lives are personal in some philosophical or theological sense, or any other sense, has nothing to do with it. They are distinct human lives. This we know for sure; the rest will always be speculation. I fear that use of this speculation to justify abortion hides an unacknowledged atheism, as I hope to show.

With regard to the question of when a human life becomes a human person, I follow the ancient and intelligible definition of person received from Boethius: "an individual substance of a rational nature." This definition, of course, can fit angels and the persons of the Trinity as well as human beings. To make it refer only to human persons, one must add that the individual substance of a rational nature, which is in question, is an animal. Note that Jesus, who is human, is not a human person. Before becoming man, he already is "an individual substance of a rational nature" as the Second Person of the Blessed Trinity. He could not lose that identity by becoming a man. He could not be two persons. Instead he expresses himself, a divine person, through his humanity which has all that makes up a human person without becoming a second person: i.e., Jesus lives and expresses who he is, a divine person, as a man. If this second argument were followed—namely, that we are forbidden only to kill innocent human life when we are sure it is a human person—then the judicial murder of Jesus (his crucifixion) would have been licit. After all, he is a divine, not a human, person.

Since I am not an atheist, but rather one who believes that God is the Creator of everything else, particularly human beings, I am not inclined to think of 'person' simply in terms of consciousness and/or the expressed ability to relate to other beings. Therefore, I am not impressed with contemporary notions of personhood. Nevertheless, following the definition which Boethius gave, I have my doubts that a new human life is a person from the moment of biological conception. An individual substance of a rational nature cannot divide into two or more such substances. Yet, the phenomenon of twinning can and does take place after biological conception. So, I would not think it certain that a new human life had become a human person— I would not be sure that a person had fully come into being—until after the possibility of twinning had passed. Even if I am right, a position which the Church considers possible and not one I hold very strongly, it would still be wrong to invade the woman and deliberately kill the zygote (the human life at an early stage). God's commandment protects innocent human life; his protection does not hinge upon our ability to determine whether the life in question is or is not truly a person. We need know only that it is a distinct human life as a new human life is genetically distinct from its mother. If we do not kill it or something untoward does not happen to it, the new human life certainly will become a human person; and as such, even if still only in the process of becoming a person, the new human life is what God protects with his moral law from our ability directly to kill it. The new human life belongs to him and we sin against God if we violate it.

For this reason the Church has authoritatively declared: *"The human being must be respected—as a person—from the very first instant of his existence."* The same document states: "The Magisterium has not expressly committed itself to an affirmation of a philosophical nature, but it constantly reaffirms the moral condemnation of any kind of procured abortion. This teaching has not changed and is unchangeable."[14]

With regard to the beginning of human life, I do not find it surprising that some would think that God's creation of the soul does not take place in an instant, but rather over time concomitant with physical development. The same, I suspect, may be true of dying. The soul may not depart in an instant, but slowly. Reflecting on this probability, I find a profound reason why we are forbidden to kill the unborn. Killing the unborn is like 'killing' God at work. At least, it is like killing his work while it is in his hands and still unfinished. While he is creating a soul, that is, turning a new human life into a person, we kill what he is working on. If we look at things this way, we see why the question of when a human life becomes a person may not rightly be used to regard at least some abortions as licit.

I suspect that there is, in fact, an atheism hidden in the effort to justify abortion by using the notion that personhood develops much later than biological conception. How do such people think personhood comes about? Some who use the alleged delay to justify abortion seem to think that personhood is conferred solely by relating to, or through communication with, other human persons. They do not consider the new human life's relationship with God. If the relationship between the new human life and God is not considered, then any further speculation about how human beings become persons would make human persons the sole creators of other human beings. This view is atheistic at least in the sense that it denies an essential aspect of our relationship to God, the creator. Those who know that God is the creator of everything else know that a new human life is primarily related to God, only secondarily related even to his or her parents. How God goes about producing a person is in a sense his business. If he does so sometime after biological conception, that too is his business. The new human life has been related directly to him from the moment of conception. The life belongs to God whether a person as yet or not. It is no wonder that the Church says, *"The human being must be respected—as a person—from the first moment of his existence."*

In revealing himself God has asked for our faith. St. Paul used a pregnant phrase to say what God asks of us when he asks for our faith. The phrase is "the obedience of faith." We do not really believe in God unless we offer him this obedience. What he asks of us all in some detail we know through the sacred Scriptures, sacred Tradition and the living teaching office of the Church he founded. Nothing he might ask through personal inspiration of anyone of us would ever contradict what he asks generally of us all. He asks that we all obey him in faith:

> "The obedience of faith" (Rm 16:26; cf. Rm 1:5, 2 Co 10:5–6) must be given to God as he reveals himself. By faith man freely commits his entire self to God, making "the full submission of his intellect and will to God who reveals" (DS 3008), and willing assenting to the Revelation given by him. Before this faith can be exercised, man must have the grace of God to move and assist him; he must have the interior helps of the Holy Spirit, who moves the heart and converts it to God, who opens the eyes of the mind and "makes it easy for all to accept and believe the truth." (DS 3010) The same Holy Spirit constantly perfects faith by his gifts, so that Revelation may be more and more profoundly understood.[15]

Obviously I believe that divine revelation entails the respect for human life which proscribes directly procured abortion. Therefore, if one considers directly procured abortion licit, one does not offer this obedience of faith, thereby rejecting divine revelation.

NOTES

1. Cf., Roach, "A flaw in the Bishops' Pastoral," in *The Dynamic Character of Christian Culture: Essays on Dawsonian Themes,* edited by Peter J. Cataldo (Lanham, MD: University Press of America, 1984), pp. 179–216.

2. "Dogmatic Constitution on Divine Revelation (*Dei Verbum*)", *Vatican Council II: The Conciliar and Post-Conciliar Documents*, general editor, Austin Flannery, O.P. (Northport, NY: Costello Publishing Co., 1975), section #2; henceforth, *DV* and section number.

3. *Ibid.*, #7ff.

4. *Ibid.*, #8.

5. Schroeder, Bible III, 3: "History of New Testament Canon," in *New Catholic Encyclopedia:* Vol. II (New York: McGraw Hill, 1967), p. 395, 2nd column.

6. *DV* #10.

7. *Ibid.*

8. Pope Paul VI, Profession of Faith (The 'Credo' of the People of God), June 30, 1968.

9. *The Teaching of Christ: A Catholic Catechism for Adults* (2nd edition), eds. Lawler, Wuerl, and Lawler (Huntington, IN: Our Sunday Visitor, 1983), p. 276.

10. *The New Jerusalem Bible* (Doubleday, 1985), Gn 4, footnote a.

11. *The Teaching of Christ*, p. 276.

12. *Ibid.*; cf. Ex 20:8–11; Dt 5:12–15.

13. Cf., Mt 19:7–9; Our Lord abrogating the "dispensation" in the Old Law which provided for divorce.

14. Congregation for the Doctrine of the Faith, "Instruction on Respect for Human Life in its Origin and on the Dignity of Procreation," in *L'Osservatore Romano* (English Edition), n. 11 (979) 16 March 1987, Part I, section #1, p. 3.

15. *DV* #5. For a more complete analysis of the "obedience of faith" and its nuances, see William E. May's, "Abortion, Moral Absolutes, and Dissent form Magisterial Teaching," in this volume.

Chapter 6

THE CHURCH'S CONDEMNATION OF PROCURED ABORTION: A PHILOSOPHICAL DEFENSE

Gary Atkinson

I. Introduction

The Sacred Congregation for the Doctrine of the Faith's 1974 "Declaration on Procured Abortion" accorded equal moral protection to all members of the species *Homo sapiens,* particularly those at the earliest stages of membership. This paper is a philosophical defense of the Church's traditional position.

The central thesis of this paper is that **the right to life is possessed by all members of the human species.** I begin by spelling out what is involved in the view that a particular individual possesses a right to life (Section II). I then examine possible reasons that might be offered for holding that some individuals possess a right to life (Section III).

I take it as an agreed-upon starting-point that you my reader and I both possess the right to life as defined. I then turn to the question of who in addition to ourselves possesses the right to life. I develop the notion of what it is to be a "non-thing," an individual over whom it is impermissible to assume a stance of domination by deliberate killing, and I employ that notion to deal with forms of killing other than abortion (Section IV).

With a sketch of an over-all theory of killing in hand, I then examine directly the topic of abortion. I argue that if you and I possess the right to life, that right must be traced back in time as far as there are members of the species *Homo sapiens* who are identical with the members of the human species we now are. Although I admit some uncertainty about this question, I argue that the identity of membership is traceable at least to some point very near the time of fertilization (Section V).

I next examine difficulties with the appeal to personhood as a means of blocking this argument against abortion (Section VI), and I conclude by showing how a denial of my analysis of what it is to be a "non-thing" necessarily undermines respect for others (Section VII).

II. The Content of the Right to Life

It is customary when discussing rights to distinguish between negative and positive rights. If we define a right as a justified claim on someone's behavior, then a negative right is a justified claim on someone that he **not** act in a specified way, and a positive right is a justified claim that he **do** act in a specified way. The specific action or non-action is a necessary component of any right and it is sometimes called the right's **content.**

Rights may have both negative and positive content, and this seems true of the right to life. The right to life has at least two negative features—the right not to be deliberately killed or grievously harmed and the right not to have one's life or physical integrity recklessly endangered. A speeder who barrels down my residential street doing seventy violates my and my family's right to life even if no one is in fact killed or harmed.

Although some will dispute this point, it is difficult to avoid recognizing a positive component to the right to life. If I watch you drown in a swimming pool simply because I am too lazy to throw you a life preserver, I have violated your right to life even though I didn't do anything. It is precisely because I didn't do what I was obliged to do that I violated your right.

In addition to a right's content, every right also possesses a determinate **strength,** the conditions under which the right's claim may be overridden without wrongdoing. For instance, we may ask whether a harmless individual who otherwise possesses a right to life may be deliberately but rightfully killed under conditions of extreme necessity, and how extreme must those conditions be?

Setting aside questions of the strength of the right to life, we can say that the content of the right involves at least three distinguishable components: the right not to be deliberately killed or grievously harmed, the right not to have one's life or health recklessly endangered, and the right to some minimal assistance in preserving one's life.

III. Inadequate Bases For the Right to Life

I assume that you and I both believe each of us possesses a right to life. What would be the warrant for that belief? Two answers commonly are given to this question, but neither is adequate to capture our fundamental moral convictions.

A. UTILITARIANISM

What is the basis for saying that anyone has a right to anything? One answer is the answer of utilitarianism: if we accord certain individuals rights to certain things, then doing so will maximize net expected utility. We consider all the possible sets of rights we could recognize (including the null set of recognizing no rights), consider the consequences of the recognition of each, discern which set of rights is likely to produce the most good by its recognition, and thereby justify that set of rights.

We would then defend the contention that you and I each possess the right to life by claiming that the recognition of our possession of that right belongs to the set of rights whose joint recognition can be expected to maximize total net utility as measured by pleasure or happiness or whatever.

There are two radical shortcomings with this utilitarian answer. In the first place, even if this utilitarian answer rests on a truth, it is only a contingent truth. It may in fact be true that the way to maximize total utility is to recognize our right to life, but that it is not a necessary truth. It has to be argued for on the basis of the actual consequences in this our actual situation. If our situation were different, recognizing our right to life might not in fact maximize social utility, and then we would not under those circumstances possess the right to life.

Utilitarianism can provide only a contingent ground for justifying the possession of the right to life, or any right for that matter. This is an irredeemable defect in the utilitarian theory. You and I who possess the right to life do so necessarily. It may be that we can forfeit that right or waive it, but it cannot be that we just happen to possess the right to life and aren't we lucky we do. The right to life belongs to us in virtue of the kinds of beings we are and not in virtue of the kinds of situations we happen to inhabit. (These considerations receive more development in the next section.)

In the second place, the contingent nature of the right to life in a utilitarian theory shows that the right to life is not accorded the individual for his own sake. If it were, if the right to life were possessed by the individual for the sake of that individual's own good, then it would make no sense to condition the possession of a right to life on its maximizing net social utility. The **collective** of such individuals might be valued for **its** own sake, but as every logic student who has studied the fallacy of division knows, what is true of the whole collective is not necessarily true of any of its parts. A utilitarian cannot accord the right to life to individuals for their own sake, otherwise he would not accord that right only on the utilitarian condition.

104

B. Capacity for Self-Awareness

What the utilitarian position entirely misses is the notion that you and I possess value for our own sakes. It may be useful to others that your and my right to life be recognized, but that is not the most basic reason why you and I should be accorded a right to life. The basic reason is that we are **worth** it. There is something about you and me that makes our lives worthy of being protected by a right to life. But what is this feature of ours that makes us worthy?

One possible answer to this question is that you and I have the capacity to value our own existences. We have value in ourselves because we find value in ourselves. We are glad that we are alive and wish to continue in this state for the future.[1]

You and I are different in this respect from other animals of other species (though there is some uncertainty perhaps about chimpanzees and dolphins). Animals in point of fact do not possess the capacity to value their own existences because they are unaware of their own existences. They are not self-conscious, not self-aware. They have no true selves because they are unable to objectify themselves, cannot view themselves as objects, and so cannot view themselves as beings whose continued existence they desire.

In short, the basis of ascribing to you a right to life is your capacity to find value in yourself, and this presupposes a more fundamental capacity to be aware of yourself as a self whose continued existence you value.

The principal shortcoming with this approach is that it has an unpleasant consequence. It follows necessarily from this position that you had no value in yourself when you were a child of one or two. You were no doubt valued a great deal by your parents, but you had no value in yourself because you lacked self-awareness.

But this contradicts the way you and I view ourselves. We think that each of us was a being of inherent worth prior to the time that you or I acquired the capacity for reflective self-awareness sometime during the second year of life.

It may very well be that the special worth we attribute to ourselves in some way depends upon our capacity for self-awareness. But it does not follow that the possession of such worth demands the actualization or exercise of that capacity. Explaining why that is so is the subject of the next section.

IV. The Scope of the Right to Life

In addition to content and strength, every right has a **subject,** a possessor of whatever is the justified claim. I have assumed that you and I each recognizes himself and the other to possess the right to life. We recognize both of ourselves as subjects of that right. Who else do we recognize as the right's subjects?

To answer this question, we must begin by noting a point of logic. If we adopt some feature X as the basis for any particular right, then we are committed simply as a matter of logic to recognizing as possessors of that right anyone who shares feature X. If the basis of the right to life is the capacity for self-awareness, then you and I must recognize as possessing the right to life all other beings with this capacity. Thus, you and I must recognize all other normal human beings above the age of two or so as possessing that right along with ourselves. (I set aside for now the complicating question whether the right to life may be forfeited or waived.)

What are we to say of the irreversibly comatose and the mentally retarded who will never possess the developed capacity for self-awareness? Even if the comatose have irreversibly lost this capacity, it does not follow that killing would be appropriate, that the comatose individual has lost the status that makes killing wrong. The reason for this is that to kill an individual is to assume a stance of mastery or domination over the individual killed. This is what is implied by any justification of our killing plants and non-human animals. I call this stance of domination "attributing to the individual the status of **thinghood.**" The status of **non-thinghood,** then, is the status that renders illegitimate the stance of domination inherent in any act of killing.

The status of non-thinghood, once acquired, is a status that cannot be lost as long as the individual continues to exist. (If it cannot be lost, it cannot be waived or surrendered either, so that suicide and voluntary euthanasia would be wrongful expressions of the stance of domination even over oneself. Whether the status can be forfeited by a criminal act so as to permit capital punishment is a separate question I need not go into here.) Once we have become non-things, we continue to remain non-things as long as we continue to exist. Non-thinghood does not have a terminus short of the subject's ceasing to exist. Non-thinghood is permanent. Impermanent non-thinghood is a contradiction in terms. Therefore, the right to life, particularly the negative component forbidding killing, is possessed by the irreversibly comatose who once possessed the capacity of self-awareness.

The question of the mentally retarded is more closely connected with the status of infants and fetuses. By "mentally retarded" I mean here an individual who has never attained the capacity for self-awareness and, owing to the severity of the retardation, will never do so. By "infant" I mean a born individual otherwise normal who has not yet exercised the capacity for self-awareness but could be expected to do so in the ordinary course of events. You and I were once infants. By definition, you and I were never mentally retarded and will never be.

The argument for the right to life of the mentally retarded runs as follows. You and I are not mentally retarded, but we could have been. (I postpone to Section VI raising and dealing with an obvious objection.) It is only owing to our good luck that we are not mentally retarded. It is only owing to their bad luck that they are. Now the possession of the status of non-thinghood is not a matter of luck. The fortunate or lucky possession of the status of non-thinghood is a contradiction in terms. Luck, like impermanence, is contrary to the notion I have been trying to capture with the language of "non-thinghood." If you possess the status of non-thinghood, it cannot be a matter of luck that you possess it, any more than it can be something you might lose in the future. Thus, even if it is true that the special status or worth involved in the possession of the right to life is dependent on the capacity for self-awareness, this is not a status whose possession is a matter of impermanence or luck. Thus, the mentally retarded possess the right to life.

A fortiori, if the mentally retarded possess the right to life, so do infants. As I defined the terms, the mentally retarded will never possess the capacity for self-awareness whereas infants will. That they are still infants and not possessors of the exercised capacity for self-awareness is a matter of time, and thus from their perspective a matter of luck.

What if I decide to kill the infant before it can acquire the exercised capacity? For me, the infant's lack of exercised capacity is not a matter of luck. The answer is that you and I possess the status of non-thinghood. No one could have prevented our acquisition of that status. The status of non-thinghood is not something that can be stolen or whose acquisition can be prevented. Preventing the acquisition of the status of non-thinghood is a contradiction in terms.

I can prevent the coming into existence of an individual who, if it existed, would possess the status of non-thinghood. What cannot be done is to prevent a being who already exists from acquiring that status. (I examine this point in more detail in Section VII.)

You and I exist. We possess the special status of having the right to life, a status of not being a mere thing to be dominated by killing. That status we possess cannot be lost, is not temporary, is not a matter of luck or accident, and is not something someone could have prevented us from acquiring. Therefore, infants possess the right to life.

V. The Right to Life of the Fetus as a Member of the Species *Homo Sapiens*

If the status of non-thinghood cannot be lost, and if you and I possess that status, then we will continue to possess that status as long as we continue to exist. And if the status is not a matter of luck and cannot be prevented from being acquired, then we can trace that status as far back in time as we have existed.

If time is an accident or matter of luck, so is the condition of being born. Whether a viable fetus is or is not born is a matter of luck, so the viable fetus is a non-thing and possesses the right to life. But whether a fetus is or is not viable is a matter of luck, so a non-viable fetus is a non-thing possessing the right to life. What is the problem here?

The lurking difficulty can be gotten at by this question: just how far back can we go? And have we already gone too far? Does a sperm or an ovum have a right to life? We would say that they do not, because you and I were never either sperm nor ova. But were we ever fertilized ova, one-celled beings called zygotes? If you were born, let us say, some thirty years ago, were you not conceived some nine months before that, give or take a week or two?

Although it is natural for us to talk about the date of your birth, it is much less natural for us to talk about your once having been a zygote. Although there is a distinct spatio-temporal continuity stretching from "your" conception as a zygote through your birth as an infant on up to you as an adult, we find it much more difficult to think of you as once a single-celled fertilized ovum. There seems to be too great a discontinuity not in space or time but in form and function.

But the problem is more than just one of appearance. When the one-celled zygote divides, it becomes a two-celled and then (after subsequent cell divisions) an n-celled organism called a "morula" (from the Latin for "mulberry"). And we know that natural twins result when cells from the morula split off before implantation occurs about two weeks after conception.

The problem is that the morula looks very much like an aggregate of cells. By "aggregate" I mean a mere collection of individual things, much like a heap of marbles. The morula seems to be a heap of cells, each cell acting on its own, ceasing to exist when it divides into its two daughter cells, they in turn ceasing to exist when they divide into the four granddaughter cells, and so on.

But you and I do not see ourselves or one another as mere aggregates, as mere collections of cells. We each view ourself and the other as fundamentally one thing, fundamentally a unity, a substance, though a substance with parts. Now if you are a substance and the morula is not a substance but a collection of substances, then you cannot have been a morula. And if you were never a morula, then you were never a zygote either. Rather, it may seem more plausible to suggest that the substance that was the zygote ceased to exist when it divided into two cells, which in turn ceased to exist when they divided into four cells, and so on.

On this view, you can be traced back only as far as there ceases to be a mere aggregate of cells and there comes to be a thing fundamentally one which we call a substance. This stage would have to be fairly early, say around the time of implantation in the second or third week. After that point, cell division would of course continue, but it would be the growth of a continuing substance. I call that point "the point at which there comes to be an individual member of the species *Homo sapiens.*"

What are the zygote and morula, then? On this view, they would not be individual members of the species *Homo sapiens.* They are distinctively human, of course, as are human sperm and ova, any haploid or diploid cell of a human body, distinctively human owing to their DNA. On this view, the zygote and the morula would be said to be "incomplete in species"—human, but not a complete member of the human species. In this respect, they would be like a human hand or foot, distinctively human and belonging to no other species, but not a complete or individually existing member of the species *Homo sapiens,* a substance complete in itself.

On this view, the right to life grounded on the status of non-thinghood would extend as far back as back as there begins to be a member of the species *Homo sapiens,* a substance (and not a mere aggregate of cells) complete in its kind.

There are those who deny that you or I are substances. A mechanistic approach to living beings holds that they are simply complex machines having no substantial unity. If this view is sound and you and I are aggregates and not substances, then there is no reason why you and I were not once morulas and therefore zygotes. If no members of the species *Homo sapiens* are substances, then we have no reason to deny that morulas and zygotes are members of the species *Homo sapiens* on the ground that zygotes and morulas are mere aggregates.

One recently offered variation on this theme admits (at least implicitly) that both adult humans and zygotes are mere aggregates, but denies that the aggregate that is now an adult can be identified with the aggregate that was then a zygote.[2] The two aggregates do not resemble each other in any way, except for a spatio-temporal continuity between them. The identity of two aggregates is then a function of the similarity between them. This means that there are degrees of identity between two aggregates linked by spatio-temporal continuity. Aggregates that closely resemble each other have a high degree of identity, those that remotely resemble each other have a low degree.

On this view, we should begin with the point when a desire for continued existence first comes to be. Call the individual (or aggregate) with such a desire **A**. Killing **A** will be wrong because of that desire. Call any prior stage in the development process **N**. Now the degree of wrongfulness of killing **N** will be a function of the degree of identity between **A** and **N**. The more remote the similarity between **A** and **N**, the less wrong it is to kill **N**. On such a view, aggregates that are members of the human species are divided into two classes, those that can (or do) possess a desire to continue living and those that cannot. Members of the first class possess a right to life and killing them (at least without their consent) would be (absolutely?) wrong. Members of the second class do not possess an absolute right to life. The wrongfulness of killing them would be a function of the degree of their similarity to members of the first class. Thus, infanticide would be more wrong than early abortion because the newborn is more similar to (and therefore possesses a higher degree of identity with) a young child with a desire to live.

Although this position yields the moral conclusion desired by those who favor abortion, it has absurd theoretical implications. According to it, all members of the human species are aggregates, and the identity of aggregates is on a sliding scale of more-or-less. Thus, statements about such aggregates made regarding the past or future take on the odd feature of possessing a sliding scale of truth or falsity.

To illustrate. Imagine yourself a seventy-year-old man. You had breakfast this morning, and yesterday morning, and ten years ago, and twenty, and thirty, etc. Are these statements equally true? Not on this view, because *you* refers to the aggregate you now are, and the farther back in time we go, and the less similar you-then are to you-now, the less identical are the two you's. You-now (the being or aggregate that you now are) gradually fades into non-existence both toward the past and toward the future as the aggregate ceases to resemble the you-now. It will be straightforwardly true that you ate breakfast yesterday because of the perfect similarity between you-now and you-yesterday. But it will not be strictly true that you-now got married forty years ago because of the greatly increased dissimilarity between the two you's. It will be even less true that you-now entered college fifty years ago, and still less that you-now entered grammar school sixty-five years ago. It becomes almost impossible to talk of when and where you-now were born. Even less can we talk about the stages of your-now embryological development. As we regard the future, this theory entails that most newborns will never die, since the aggregate that is the eighty-year-old resembles the newborn so slightly. Clearly, this variation on the theme of members of the human species as mere aggregates radically distorts how we view ourselves as beings with a fundamental, substantial continuity over time.

If we avoid thinking in terms of aggregates and think instead in terms of substances, but yet maintain that the zygote is not fully complete in species, we must nonetheless admit that the zygote cannot be incomplete in the way in which a sperm or an ovum or any other cell or collection of cells (e.g., a hand) is incomplete. For the zygote is not a part of any individual member of the species *Homo sapiens,* nor does it fuse with anything else to become an individual member. The spatio-temporal continuity between the aggregate that was the zygote and the aggregate that is now you would be sufficient to identify you with the zygote you once were.

My own view is that the zygote is complete in species, that it is an individual member of the species *Homo sapiens,* that you and I are the substances that were once zygotes, and that therefore the status of non-thinghood and the right to life are to be accorded zygotes. The morula, on this view, is not an accidental but a substantial unity. Should splitting off of cells from the morula occur and twinning results, then either the substance that was the morula ceases to exist and two new substances come into being,—two new individual members of the species *Homo sapiens* come into being, or the old substance continues in existence and an additional one comes to be.

I do not wish to argue, though, regarding the status of the zygote and morula. I acknowledge the uncertainty about whether they are complete in species, individual members of the species *Homo sapiens.* But whatever their status, uncertainty on this point must not deflect attraction from the principal thesis of this paper.

Furthermore, as the 1974 "Declaration on Procured Abortion" makes clear (footnote #19), the wrongfulness of killing does not require knowledge of the being's possession of a human soul (or membership in the human species). It is sufficient that ensoulment (or membership) be supportable by plausible argument for the killing of such a being to be morally wrong. The readiness to kill what-for-all-we-know-is a member of the human species cannot be distinguished morally from the readiness to kill known members.

You and I are individually existing members of the species *Homo sapiens* possessing the status of non-thinghood whose possession is not a matter of accident or luck. Therefore, although I admit some uncertainty regarding the precise stage, that status which we now possess can be traced back as far as there are individual members of the species *Homo sapiens,* the point at which there comes to be individual members of the species *Homo sapiens.* And the right to life grounded on this status would also be possessed by all individual members complete in species.

112

One possible objection that initially appears preposterous is to (a) admit that complete membership in the species *Homo sapiens* comes to be, let us say, at fertilization or at some point two or three weeks later, but (b) deny that the members of the species who you and I now are were ever identical with those early members. This view requires holding that there are two types of members of the species *Homo sapiens,* I call them "primary" and "secondary" members. (For sake of simplicity I ignore the possibility of "tertiary" etc. membership.)

On this view, primary members of the species *Homo sapiens* come to be at an early stage, but cease to exist at some later stage to be replaced by secondary members. You and I are secondary members of the species *Homo sapiens.* You and I possess the status of non-thinghood and the consequent right to life. As long as we are, we possess this status. But we were never primary members of the species *Homo sapiens.* Those primary members ceased to be when we came to be. Therefore, although the primary members are members of the species *Homo sapiens,* they do not possess the status of non-thinghood and the right to life.

This is not only a possible position to take, but it has actually been adopted by Lawrence C. Becker who maintains that an organism becomes fully human only when it has acquired the complete set of bones, muscles, tissues, and organs around the twenty-eighth week of fetal development.[3] Becker does not use the terminology of primary and secondary membership in the species *Homo sapiens* because he does not name the species to which the early fetus belongs. But if "membership in the species *Homo sapiens*" be taken as a genetically grounded category, then Becker's position would have to be expressed in something like the language of primary and secondary membership.

The problem with this position is that it is sheer question-begging, lacking any empirical support whatsoever. There is no empirical basis for the belief that the organism (member of the species *Homo sapiens*) which is now the infant is not identical with the organism which was once the fetus at three months. No one would start with an investigation of the empirical data and arrive at this conclusion.

On the contrary, Becker's position is an implicit recognition of the force of the argument of this section. Becker's position (really, it cannot be called an argument) is manifestly tendentious, adopted solely to avoid recognizing the status of non-thinghood in the unborn.

There is no empirical basis for dividing *Homo sapiens* into two or more subgroups, the members of one of which cease to be or die when members of the other come to be. Thus, the status of non-thinghood and the right to life are possessed by all members of the species *Homo sapiens.*

VI. Personhood

In Section IV I pointed out that although you and I are not mentally retarded, we might have been. It seems somewhat a matter of our good luck that we were not conceived with a serious abnormality or suffered some grievous accident after conception which rendered us incapable of ever acquiring the exercised capacity of self-awareness. This seems such an obvious point, but there are those who will deny it.

The reason given is that *you* and *I* are personal terms and refer only to persons, to those with the developed or exercised capacity for self-awareness. If this is so, then you and I logically could not have been mentally retarded (i.e., individuals who can never acquire that capacity). Nor were you or I ever infants, because infants do not possess that developed capacity whereas you and I exist only when we do possess that capacity.

On this view, one could agree with everything said thus far about the status of non-thinghood, that its possession is permanent and not a matter of accident or luck, and that a being already existing cannot be prevented from acquiring its possession. But, it will be said, the status of non-thinghood belongs only to persons, and to be a person one must possess the actualized capacity for self-awareness.

I discussed a variant of this position in Section III and noted the implication that infants have no worth in themselves. But that view maintained that although we once were infants, we had no worth (i.e., we were things and not non-things). Here I am presenting the view that we were never infants.

What are we to make of this possibility? I assume that the born infant is an individually existing member of the species *Homo sapi-*

114

ens. Now the interesting question is—Are **we** (the referents of the terms *you* and *I*) individually existing members of the species *Homo sapiens?* Yes or no.

If yes, then either you and I are identical with the members of the species that once were infants, or you and I are not identical with those members. The position we are considering here cannot adopt the former alternative for that would be self-contradictory. An individual which necessarily possesses the exercised capacity for self-awareness (a person) would be identical with an individual which by definition does not possess that actualized capacity (an infant). So the position must adopt the latter alternative, which is nothing other than the unempirical doubling of members of the species we noted at the close of the last section.

So, the most plausible alternative for the defenders of this position is to deny that you and I are members of the species *Homo sapiens.* Or, to speak more strictly, the defenders must hold that *you* and *I* are personal terms and refer only to persons who are beings possessing the exercised capacity for self-awareness. And the right to life would be a personal and not a human right.

Let us back up a bit and note the possibility of only four positions that agree in holding that you and I possess the status of non-thinghood and the right to life. First, you and I are members of the species *Homo sapiens* but the fetus or infant is not a member and so does not possess the right to life. Second, the fetus or infant as well as you and I are all members of the species *Homo sapiens,* but we are all different members, and so only you and I possess the right to life. Both of these possibilities lack empirical plausibility. Third, you and I are members of the species *Homo sapiens* and are identical with the members that once were fetuses and infants, so that fetuses and infants possess the status of non-thinghood and the right to life. Fourth, although fetuses and infants are members of the species *Homo sapiens,* you and I are not, so that members of the species *Homo sapiens* do not possess the right to life but only persons like you and me.

This fourth position seems intolerable, but one is driven to it by the conjunction of four considerations: (1) the need to avoid the unempirical postulation of primary and secondary members of the species *Homo sapiens;* (2) the desire to recognize the right to life of individuals like you and me; (3) the desire to deny the right to life of human fetuses; and (4) the recognition that the status of non-thinghood is not a status acquired sometime after the being who possesses it has come into existence.

This position is driven to one of two options. Either a bearer or subject of the right to life is a spiritual substance (immaterial thing) in some way united to a body that belongs to the species *Homo sapiens,* or the bearer is not a substance at all but a set of qualities or actualized powers rooted in a substance that is a member of the species *Homo sapiens.*

Both of these options show how tendentious, question-begging, and *ad hoc* is the position that would recognize the right to life of you and me but deny it to the unborn offspring of the species *Homo sapiens.* To take the second alternative first, no one has ever been so mad as to suppose that a set of powers can be the bearer of rights rather than the substance that is the subject or possessor of those powers. Metaphysically it represents a kind of epiphenomenalism. Morally it reduces to the position that would reduce the status of non-thinghood to a matter of impermanence, luck, and preventability.

The first alternative is a form of dualism. It is interesting to note how this position frequently is adopted by those who are otherwise materialistic or reductivistic in their understanding of the universe. Moves that implicitly rely on dualistic assumptions are made in an *ad hoc* fashion solely to avoid the force of the argument against abortion. Their implications are then conveniently ignored in the development of an over-all view of the world.

The principal problem with both options, though, is not any inherent inconsistency or *ad hoc* character but their lack of empirical support, their disregard of the evidence of a fundamental unity of physical and psychical powers of the human subject.

VII. The Threat to the Status of Non-Thinghood

In Section IV I argued that if the status of non-thinghood attaches to an individual at any single stage of its existence, it must attach to that individual at all stages of its existence. That view is entailed by what it means to be a "non-thing," an individual possessing worth in itself whom it is impermissible to assume an attitude of domination over by deliberate killing. The only moral uncertainty arises over whether the individual in question has begun to exist or has ceased to exist. It is this necessary feature of non-thinghood which drives supporters of abortion into the odd metaphysical positions delineated in Sections V and VI.

One can, of course, avoid these metaphysical implausibilities while accepting abortion by implicitly or explicitly denying this view of what it means to be a non-thing. I suspect that most proponents of abortion, whether they realize it or not, in fact adopt this alternative. Let us see what this comes to.

You, I have acknowledged, possess the right to life. You are a non-thing over whom it would be impermissible to adopt a stance of domination by deliberate killing. But your being a non-thing is not necessarily connected with your existence. That you are a non-thing is a matter of luck, time, development, the acquisition of a quality. There was a period of time when you existed but were only a thing, and there may be a period of time in the future when you continue to exist but become a mere thing once again. Furthermore, it would have been perfectly appropriate for me to have prevented your acquiring that status.

By what means may I have prevented you from acquiring the special quality, self-awareness or whatever? By killing you, certainly, but also by preventing you from acquiring that quality without killing you. That is, if you were a mere thing at birth and I could have killed you, I may just as well have rendered you permanently mentally retarded, forever incapable of acquiring the capacity for self-awareness. That I could have no plausible motive for doing so is beside the point. The issue concerns what is and is not morally permitted on the assumption of the impermanence of non-thinghood.

What you are to imagine, then, is the possibility that I might have prevented you from developing the capacity for self-awareness without killing you. (This possibility is much like that imagined in Aldous Huxley's *Brave New World*, where prenatal development is variously affected to yield alphas, betas, and gammas.) In theory, there would seem to be nothing morally I could not do to you, assuming I treat you no worse than I would an animal and have the consent of other self-conscious humans. Of course, you would not be aware of any basis for complaint. But what is more important, you would in truth have no basis for complaint. It is not as if I were to sneak up on you after you had acquired the capacity for self-awareness and without your realization kill you or render you mindless. Doing that would violate your rights because it goes against your desires. But the case you are to imagine is one in which I act before you have ever been able to acquire such desires.

Now the position that there is nothing wrong in my so acting is first of all absurd. No one in his right mind seriously entertains it. But we need to see the implications for someone not in his right mind in this regard, someone who seriously maintains that acting in this way would be morally permissible.

Suppose you know me to take this position seriously. Is such knowledge a matter of indifference to you, or is it certain to affect your attitude toward, your confidence in, me? For myself, I know that I could not bring myself to trust anyone who viewed me in that manner. Such an individual's respect for me is contingent on my possession of certain features, and conditioned respect is not the kind of respect I want for myself.

My claim here is not that anyone who views me with conditioned respect is necessarily more likely to act in a wrongful way toward me when subjected to pressures of whatever kind to do so. People's psyches are too variable to admit of any universal statement. But the *fear* in any given case is eminently reasonable. If it is only a matter of *accident* that you are a non-thing, only something incidental to your being that you are worth anything at all, that belief is of its very nature capable of reducing respect. Conditioned respect is not necessarily lessened respect. But it necessarily contains the threat of lessened respect.

This is why legitimized abortion poses such a threat to the rest of us, and why abortifacient societies historically have not been high on the list of societies respectful of human beings. It also explains why societies (like ours) that become increasingly abortifacient display marks of increasing brutalization in other areas of human life. Systematically to deny the status of moral personhood (non-thinghood) to any class of members of the human species is to separate that status from the being that possesses it. Such a separation necessarily weakens the connection between the status and its possessor, and necessarily poses a threat under the right circumstances to those whose protected status had hitherto been non-problematic. The Catholic Church's traditional, adamant opposition to abortion

118

even in the face of acknowledged uncertainty regarding ensoulment is a testimony to her wisdom, and in particular to her recognition of the close bonds that tie all of us human beings together in a web of mutual dependence and respect.

NOTES

1. This is the answer of Michael Tooley whose argument first appeared in "Abortion and Infanticide," *Philosophy and Public Affairs*, 1972/3.

2. Clement Dore, "Abortion, Some Slippery Slope Arguments and Identity Over Time," *Philosophical Studies* (Holland), 1988/9.

3. "Human Being: the Boundaries of the Concept," *Philosophy and Public Affairs*, 1974/5.

Chapter 7

ABORTION AND THE RIGHT TO LIFE
BEFORE PERSONHOOD

Richard Berquist

Introduction

Does the intentional destruction of a human embryo or fetus constitute a violation of the right to life? This is the most fundamental question in the abortion debate.

I shall argue in this paper that abortion is a violation of the right to life from the moment of fertilization. I shall not assume, however, that an early embryo is an *actual person*. On the contrary, I shall assume that the embryo becomes an actual person only after a certain period of development. How long this period might be is not relevant to the argument I intend to propose.

This does not mean that I reject the theory of "immediate animation"—i.e., that the human soul, the life principle by which each of us becomes an actual person, is present at fertilization. Actually, I am inclined to favor this theory, although I am not certain about it. I am assuming "mediate animation" for the sake of argument. I shall argue that abortion is always a violation of the right to life, whether the aborted embryo is an actual person yet or not.

The argument is difficult and will require us to go more deeply into the foundation of human rights than is usual in discussions of abortion. We shall first examine the traditional principle that all and only persons have rights. I shall argue that this principle, properly understood, is true. We shall then consider the further question of whether only *existing* persons have rights. Finally, we shall ask specifically whether persons who are coming into existence through a process of embryonic and fetal development possess the right to life even before this process has terminated in actual existence.

Whether All and Only Persons Have Rights.

In the following discussion, the word "right" is used in its strongest sense to designate that which is categorically or unqualifiedly due to an individual from others. Rights, understood in this sense, cannot be overridden, although the validity of some rights may depend on circumstances. By the "right to life," at least in the sense of the "right of the innocent not to be killed," I understand a right which cannot be overridden and which, moreover, is independent of circumstances. The existence of such a right will appear from our analysis of the foundation of rights.

The view that all and only persons have rights seems common sense. We identify ourselves as persons and we recognize our obligation to respect all other persons. But we do not consider animals (still less plants) to be persons and we do not perceive them as having rights. We use them as slaves; we experiment on them; we mutilate and kill them for our benefit. Clearly, then, we think of rights as essentially connected to personhood.

But is this common sense view correct? Is there an essential connection between rights and personhood such that all and only persons have rights?

122

This question may be approached by assuming at the outset that the concept of personhood is, at least in part, a "moral concept."[1] The world can be divided into "persons" and "things." Persons are beings that have rights; things are beings that do not have rights. The statement that all and only persons have rights is then true by definition.

By itself alone, however, this concept of personhood does not enable us to identify any particular beings or kinds of beings as persons. Without further specification, we have no way of knowing whether all human beings are persons, or whether any are, or whether perhaps some animals are persons. By what criterion can we distinguish persons from things?

According to a theory frequently proposed, a being can have rights only if it has or is *capable* of having conscious desires or "interests."[2] As stated, this criterion gives us no more than a necessary condition for the possession of rights. It states that a being cannot have rights without conscious desires or the capacity for them, but it does not state or imply that these are *enough* to endow a being with rights.[3] Therefore, if by "person" we understand a being that not only is capable of possessing rights but actually does possess them, then this criterion is not sufficient to define personhood.

In spite of its incompleteness, this criterion is of great importance for the question of the right to life of human embryos and fetuses. Such beings, at least during the early stages of their development, do not seem to be aware—or *proximately* capable of being aware—of the desirability of continued existence. It follows that they are not persons and that they do not have a right to life. At most, they might have the right not to have pain inflicted on them.

Leaving aside, for the moment, the question of an adequate definition of personhood, let us ask to what extent it makes sense to found rights on a "conscious desires" criterion.

There are, first of all, questions of clarification. Are rights founded precisely on *actual* conscious desires? Or is the *capacity* for such desires the decisive element in the criterion? Must the desires or interests in question be *rational*—i.e., based on an explicit understanding of ends and means? Or do the instinctive desires of animals also count? Is there a distinction between good and bad desires? If so, are rights founded on both sorts of desires or only on good desires?[4]

However these questions may be answered, it seems plainly impossible to found rights on actual desires or on the capacity for such desires *per se*. No one believes that the mere fact that I want something or am capable of wanting it or have an interest in obtaining it gives me a right to it. A desire cannot have the character of a right unless it has a certain status, a status such that we are obligated to respect it. A criterion based merely on desires does not give us the slightest hint as to why some desires (but perhaps not others) have moral status.

Why, then, do at least some desires or interests have the status of rights? Is social or legal recognition an essential element? Or are there natural rights which are valid whether they are recognized or not? If there are no natural rights, why should society recognize or (more precisely) confer any rights at all? Are the reasons entirely pragmatic, dependent on the interests of those who have the power to influence public opinion or legislation? Is it ultimately a matter of enlightened self interest or of the psychological dispositions of the people in a given culture? If, on the other hand, there are natural rights, what is the basis of these rights and of the corresponding obligation to respect them?

The "conscious desires" approach to the foundation of rights is inadequate because it does not ask the most important question: what is the source of our strict moral obligation to recognize, respect and even promote the good of another being?[5] When the question is thus posed, the sort of answer we require is readily apparent. Beings that possess rights are beings that have a certain kind of value, a value such that in and of themselves such beings are worthy of respect.

What sort of value could this be? Clearly not utility value. Objects of utility have their ultimate value in relation to the good of other beings; they are not, strictly speaking, valuable in themselves. There remains, then, the value we call "intrinsic value" or "dignity." Dignity is the value of a being which exists ultimately for its own good. It is evident that a being which exists for its own good is, by that very fact, worthy of respect. We may conclude that all and only beings with intrinsic value or dignity have rights.

Let us now return to our original question: whether all and only persons have rights. We could, at this point, simply define persons as "beings with dignity" and then attempt to identify which beings have this kind of value. I prefer, however, an older and more common sense approach. I shall define person in the traditional way as an "individual rational substance" (including but not necessarily limited to human beings) and then argue that persons, so defined, possess dignity by their very nature.

In the following argument, I shall refer to human persons or human beings rather than to persons in general. This will make the discussion more concrete. However the logic of the argument is such that it applies to all persons, human or not.

The dignity of human beings is a consequence of their rationality. Because they are rational, they understand their own good as an ultimate end and freely direct their lives toward that end. In this they differ from animals which lack reason and are therefore unaware of their ultimate purpose. The lives of animals are directed by natural instinct (and by experience as interpreted by instinct) and not by their own understanding. This is why they never react *per se* to their status as objects of utility. Human beings, however, normally refuse to accept this kind of status even when they are well treated.

The fact that human beings naturally seek their own good and refuse to be a mere means to the good of others shows us their value. It shows us that human beings are naturally oriented to their own good as an ultimate end. They possess an inherent value or dignity by nature. Note, however, that their dignity does not depend on their level of development or on the degree to which they are capable of exercising their rational faculties. Immature, retarded, senile and unconscious human beings possess dignity simply because they are human beings naturally oriented toward a rationally directed life even when they cannot attain it. A being's dignity depends on what it is meant for, not on the degree to which its natural purpose is realized.

This concept of dignity together with an understanding of the human good in its various dimensions (e.g., life, physical integrity, emotional and spiritual development, etc.) provides the foundation for the system of natural rights. We are concerned here only with the most basic right, the right to life. If humans exist for their own good as an ultimate end and if life is a prerequisite for the attainment of any further good, it is clear that human beings have the right to life.

Let us summarize the foregoing discussion and see what remains to be considered. The most important point is that human rights are a consequence of the dignity of the human person and therefore do not necessarily presuppose conscious desires. Nor do they presuppose the *proximate* capacity for conscious desires. They *do,* however, presuppose the power of reason, but only insofar as this power is inherent in human nature. It is not necessary that reason have yet attained or be presently capable of attaining the concepts of life, physical integrity and other human goods.

Some rights, of course, do presuppose conscious desires—for example, the rights that arise from contracts. Such rights flow from human dignity only through the mediation of explicit agreements. But the most basic human rights, including the right to life, follow from human dignity immediately.

Even if all this be granted, however, we have not yet resolved the abortion problem. Our previous discussion has shown that a developed capacity for rational desires is not necessary for personhood. The *rational nature,* however, must be present. Does an early embryo possess a rational nature? If so, it is a person and possesses the right to life. If not—and this is the assumption I have been making in this paper—then further argument is required.

Whether Only Existing Persons Have Rights.

As a first step, we must consider whether it is possible for persons who do not exist to have rights. For if only persons have rights and if (by assumption) the embryo is not yet a person, then the right to life cannot belong to the embryo *per se.* The right bearer must be the person who is coming-to-be through the process of embryonic development. But this person does not yet exist—at least not in full actuality. Therefore, in order to argue that abortion is always a violation of the right to life, we must first show that even persons who do not exist can have rights.

Persons who do not exist are either (a) those who do not yet exist or (b) those who have existed and are now dead.

(I am assuming—again for the sake of argument—that a dead person no longer exists. A discussion of whether the person is to be identified with the soul and of whether the human soul is immortal would carry us too far from our main concern. The important question for our purposes is this: supposing that a dead person does not exist, could he or she still have rights?)

It is easy enough to see that a dead person can have rights. Consider, for example, a person's will concerning the disposition of his or her property after death. If we unjustly violate the terms of the will, we violate the dead person's rights. The same may be said about the dead person's previously expressed directions regarding funeral and burial. It is impossible, however, to violate a right unless it exists. Therefore, a dead person can possess rights.

The right to have one's will respected flows from human dignity through the medium of an explicit declaration previously made. But not all of a dead person's rights presuppose conscious acts of will. Dead persons have the right to their good name and reputation. To ruin a dead person's reputation by lies is to violate that person's right, even if he or she, while alive, never thought about the matter.

Nevertheless, the rights of dead persons to respect for their reputations and for the provisions of their wills depend essentially on previous existence. What of persons who do not yet exist? Can such persons have rights?

Persons who do not yet exist would seem to have some rights. One example is the right to inherit property. Imagine a case in which a thief steals an inheritance intended for a person who is still in the process of coming into existence. The thief violates that person's right at the time of the theft and therefore before he or she actually exists. Another example is the right to health and bodily integrity. A mother who takes drugs during pregnancy may inflict serious injury on an embryo or fetus before actual personhood. Like the thief, she violates the rights of a person who is coming to be before the person exists. It is clear, then, that a person who does not yet exist possesses rights.

Although they may precede existence, the rights to bodily integrity and inherited wealth are, nevertheless, essentially related to future existence. For the objects of these rights are of value to persons precisely insofar as their future existence is anticipated. Logically, then, though not temporally, these rights presuppose existence and are contingent upon it. They presuppose that the person *will* actually exist at some time in the future or, at least, that he or she has a *right* to exist.

But what of the right to existence itself, the right to life? Can this right belong to a person who does not yet exist? To this, our final question, we must now turn.

Whether Persons Who Are Coming into Existence Possess the Right to Life.

I shall now propose three arguments intended to show that persons who do not yet exist but are coming into existence through the process of embryonic development possess the right to life. From these arguments it follows that abortion is intrinsically wrong, i.e., that abortion is a violation of human dignity *per se* from the moment of fertilization.

The first argument is based on the fact that embryonic development is naturally ordained to the life (existence) of the new person. To approach this argument, let us briefly consider the foundation of the right to life in existing persons.

When we try to explain to ourselves or others why we think that existing persons have a right to life, we almost always begin, I think, from the conviction that each person's life is his or her own and does not belong to others. Life is not "owned," of course, in the way that property is owned. Property ownership depends on human agreement and tradition whereas life belongs to each person by nature.

The fact that each person's life is his or her own by nature does not, by itself alone, imply the right to life. An animal's life—or even a plant's life—is its own by nature, and yet most people do not think that an animal has the right to life. As we have seen, the system of human rights is founded on the principle of human dignity according to which human beings exist for their own good. On the basis of this principle, we can say that the life given to each person by nature is for the sake of that person and may not be disposed of by others in the furtherance of their interests.

Let us now consider whether a person can possess the right to life by nature before he or she actually exists. In other words, can existence be due to a person before it is received. In general, something is due to a person either because it is legitimately possessed by that person or because it is intended to be possessed. The critical question, then, is whether life can be naturally meant for or intended for a person before he or she actually acquires it.

Once again, a precise posing of the question leads quickly to the answer. The process of embryonic and fetal development which precedes the existence of each person is naturally ordained to the existence of that person. Therefore, from the very beginning of that process at fertilization, life is naturally intended for and therefore naturally due to the new person. From this fact, together with the principle of human dignity, it follows that the right to life of every human person begins at fertilization.

The following analogy, though imperfect, may help to clarify the argument. Imagine a father who has willed an inheritance to his son. The will is irrevocable and the father is dying. A thief steals the inheritance before the father dies. Is it not true that the son's right to the inheritance has been violated, even though he has not yet received it? In the same way the abortionist deprives a new human person of the inheritance of life which he or she was naturally meant to receive.

Before turning to the second argument, we may consider briefly two possible objections. The first is this: why should the right to life begin at fertilization rather than earlier? Sperm and ova are naturally ordained to the existence of new human beings. Therefore, wouldn't each person have a right to the union of the particular sperm and ovum which would begin the process of his or her coming into existence?

I would reply that no particular sperm is naturally ordained to fertilize a particular ovum and no particular ovum is meant to be fertilized by a particular sperm. This objection would be valid only if *this* sperm and *this* ovum from which *this* individual person would emerge had some kind of specific natural claim on each other—an absurd supposition.

The second objection concerns twinning and the formation of chimeras, phenomena which are possible for about two weeks after fertilization. (Twinning occurs when a single early embryo gives rise to identical twins; chimeras are formed when two or more early embryos coalesce to form a single individual.) The occurrence of these phenomena during this period raises the question of whether "individuation," the formation of a unique human organism, has yet taken place. If it has not, then how could the right to life of some definite person begin at fertilization?

But is it so certain that a unique human organism cannot exist during the period when twinning is possible? Some worms can be divided into parts, each of which develops into a new individual. Yet the original worm was surely one individual worm. Regarding the

129

formation of chimeras, there seems to be no reason, in principle, why one early embryo, originally destined to develop into a particular person, might not be absorbed, lose its independent identity and become part of another early embryo, destined to become a different person.

The main point is that each early embryo, so far as we can tell, is naturally ordained to become a particular person. This original ordination is not affected by the fact that a particular early embryo subsequently ceases to exist as an independent being (chimera formation) or gives rise to another early embryo (twinning). The occurrence of these phenomena, therefore, does not refute the existence of a right to life from fertilization.

My second argument begins from the premise that whatever exists in any way for the sake of the person shares, proportionately, in the dignity of the person. Private property, for example, because it is ordered to the welfare of the person who owns it, shares to some extent in the inviolability of the person. We are obligated to *respect* private property. To an even greater degree, we are obligated to respect the parts of a person's body. These exist by nature for the sake of the person and belong to his or her very substance.

The embryo or fetus is related to the person who is coming to be in the most intimate way of all. It is destined, precisely, to *become* the person. Hence it shares even more in the dignity of the person for whose sake it exists than do the parts of the body. The destruction of a part of the body (other than a vital organ) deprives a person of a useful instrument; but the destruction of an embryo deprives an emerging person of life itself. If, then, it is a violation of human dignity to mutilate a person's body, it is an even greater violation to destroy a developing embryo or fetus.

The third argument is derived from a consideration of the kind of value that belongs to a being which is developing into something more excellent than itself. Such is the human embryo (assuming that it is not already a human person), for its sole reason for being is to become a person. But, surely, that which is moving from a lesser to a greater perfection should be evaluated primarily according to the greater perfection toward which it is tending. Therefore, the value of the embryo must be understood primarily in terms of the dignity or intrinsic value of the emerging person, and, for the sake of that person, must be accorded respect.

130

Consider this analogy. The world was shocked some years ago when a vandal attacked and defaced Michelangelo's Pietà. What if something similar had happened while the Pietà was being sculpted? What if someone had attempted to destroy the emerging work of art under Michelangelo's very hands so that it could never be completed? Surely this would have been more like the destruction of the Pietà than like the destruction of a block of marble. Similarly, the destruction of a developing embryo is more like the destruction of a person than of a sperm and ovum. Indeed, the argument is even stronger for the developing embryo, since it tends towards the person of its very nature, whereas the block of marble is ordained to the Pietà only through Michelangelo's creative intention.

Conclusion

It is often said that the abortion question is complicated. While this is true with respect to the many practical problems involved, it is not true of the central moral question: whether the developing embryo or fetus has a right to life. It is, nevertheless, a very difficult question, for it requires a clear understanding of the foundation of rights in human dignity and a careful analysis of the consequences of this principle.

In this brief paper, I have tried to outline a series of arguments which have led me to believe that abortion is a violation of the right to life, from the moment of conception, whether the early embryo is an actually existing person or not. Because the present discussion is so brief and the arguments so fundamental and so difficult to state adequately, I would welcome the reader's comments and criticisms.

NOTES

1. Mary Ann Warren states that the concept of a person is in part a moral concept and that it implies the right to be treated as a member of the moral community. Mary Ann Warren, "On the Moral and Legal Status of Abortion," *The Monist* 57:1 (1973), p. 56.

Michael Tooley stipulates that he will treat the concept of a person as a purely moral one so that the sentence "x is a person" is synonymous with the sentence "x has a (serious) moral right to life." Michael Tooley, "Abortion and Infanticide," *Philosophy and Public Affairs* 2:1 (1972), p. 40.

Joel Feinberg distinguishes between "normative" and "descriptive" personhood and states that normative personhood implies such moral qualities as rights and duties. Joel Feinberg, "Abortion," in Tom Regan, ed., *Matters of Life and Death,* 2nd ed. (New York: Random House, 1980), p. 258–59.

2. The authors cited above all accept the capacity for conscious desires as a necessary condition of personhood. They also make the criterion more precise.

Mary Ann Warren lists five traits as central to the concept of personhood: consciousness, developed reasoning capacity, self-motivated activity, extensive capacity to communicate, the presence of self-concepts and self awareness. However, she does not insist that all of these are necessary for personhood. Warren, "On the Moral and Legal Status of Abortion," p. 55.

Referring specifically to the right to life, Laura Purdy and Michael Tooley write " ... an organism can have the right to life only if it now possesses or possessed at some time in the past, the capacity to have a desire for continued existence." Laura Purdy and Michael Tooley, "Is Abortion Murder," in Robert Perkins, ed., *Abortion: Pro and Con* (Cambridge, Mass.: Schenkman, 1974), p. 144. Some of Purdy and Tooley's further discussion suggests that it is not so much the capacity for desires as the actual existence of desires (past, present or future) that is the foundation for rights. Ibid., p. 145.

Feinberg favors what he calls the "actual possession" criterion of personhood which he specifies at some length. He writes: "It is because people are conscious; have a sense of their personal identities; have plans, goals and projects; are liable to pain, anxieties, and frustration, can reason and bargain, and so on—it is because of these attributes that people have value and interests, desires and expectations of their own, including a stake in their own futures, and personal well-being of a sort we cannot ascribe to unconscious or nonrational beings. ... Only because of their sense of self, their life plans, their value hierarchies, and their stakes in their own futures can they be ascribed fundamental rights." Feinberg, "Abortion," p. 270.

3. Feinberg discusses what he calls the "interest principle" according to which " ... the sorts of beings who *can* have rights are those who have (or can have) interests." Joel Feinberg, "The Rights of Animals and Unborn Generations" in William T. Blackstone, ed., *Philosophy and Environmental Crisis* (University of Georgia Press: Athens, Georgia, 1974), p. 51. The concept of an interest, for Feinberg, implies conscious desire. Ibid., p. 49. A propos of the rights of fetuses, he writes: "It is important to reemphasize here that the question of whether fetuses do or ought to have rights are substantive questions of law and morals open to argument and decision. The prior question of whether fetuses are the kind of beings that can have rights, however, is a conceptual, not a moral question, amenable only to what is called 'logical analysis,' and irrelevant to moral judgment." Ibid., p. 64.

Tooley states that the 'interest principle' discussed by Feinberg is a necessary but not sufficient condition for possessing a right to life. Michael Tooley, "In Defense of Abortion and Infanticide," in Joel Feinberg, ed., *The Problem of Abortion,* 2nd ed. (Belmont, CA: Wadsworth, 1984), p. 124. See also, in the same volume, the essay "Abortion, Infanticide, and Respect for Persons" by S. I. Benn.

4. I do not mean to imply that the authors I have been citing give no attention to any of these questions. But space does not permit a satisfactory discussion of this topic here.

5. S. I. Benn touches on this problem very explicitly. He writes: " ... the fact that someone happens to have, or is capable of having, desires of any kind is not *obviously* a reason for anyone else to recognize such a one as having any claim on him whatsoever." Benn, "Abortion, Infanticide, and Respect for Persons," p. 141. His solution, however, does not seem to me to get to the root of the problem. Ibid., p. 141.

Chapter 8

THE ABORTIFACIENT RU 486

Richard J. Connell

A. Introduction

RU 486 is a drug that has two types of use, one as an antiglucocorticoid that blocks the effects of adrenal hormones such as cortisone, and it has, for example, been used successfully to treat Cushing's syndrome, which is caused by excessive cortisone production. Its second use is as an antiprogesterone, which is the action by means of which it functions as an abortifacient. Progesterone is a hormone that makes the lining of the uterus able to support a developing embryo. The hormone estrogen stimulates the growth of the uterine smooth muscle and also the glandular epithelium, the endometrium, which is the lining of the inner surface of the uterus. Progesterone acts upon the endometrium that estrogen has prepared and makes it an actively secreting tissue. "The glands become coiled and filled with secreted glycogen; the blood vessels become spiral and more numerous; various enzymes accumulate in the glands and connective tissue of the lining. All these changes are ideally suited to provide a hospitable environment for implantation of a fertilized ovum."[1] Now because RU 486 can function as an antiprogesterone, it is responsible for the endometrium breaking down and subsequently being expelled, which means that if a fertilized egg has been implanted on the uterine wall, it also is expelled. In short, during the early stages of pregnancy, RU 486 functions as an abortifacient either by preventing the fertilized ovum from being implanted or by causing it to be expelled with the endometrium. Furthermore, the usual procedure followed by a woman who takes RU 486 to prevent or interrupt implantation is to return to the physician shortly after taking the drug in order to receive an injection of prostaglandin, which causes uterine contractions, ensuring thereby that the abortion is complete. So briefly described, that is how the drug works.

The introduction of RU 486 was received enthusiastically by those who favor abortion as a means of birth regulation. For the woman undergoing it, the procedure is considered to be a simple and convenient method to use, one that is less traumatic than other means. However, the aim of this paper is not to focus on the technical characteristics of this abortifacient; rather it is to discuss the notion of *control* and what control implies about the use of drugs in preventing births. Underlying the use of every method of abortion is the claim that "a woman has a right to control her own body," and those who do procure abortions claim that they are exercising that right. To be sure, one could raise the issue of "rights" and what a *right* is, but that is neither desirable nor necessary here. Instead we shall attempt to show that the use of RU 486 violates a fundamental moral principle that is accepted by the medical profession in its treatment of disease, a principle that is also accepted by those who seek to preserve the natural environment from pollutants and which means that to be consistent, environmentalists must be anti-abortion. The general principle that we shall focus on has not been articulated in the way in which we shall present it, and that, we think, will be our contribution to the debate on this issue.

To make our case we shall first have to consider the kind of control that we have over ourselves and how that control is limited, after

134

which we may examine the moral principle itself. Compared to some of the "reasons" offered to justify abortion—emotional stress for the mother, financial hardship, etc.—the claim to be exercising the right to control one's own body is abstract, and the notion of control requires that we look at certain aspects of the causality which we exercise over our own activities. In sum, we shall do the following: 1) examine two main kinds of activity; 2) look at the general moral limitations of medical practice; 3) look at the moral limitations on our use of the environment; 4) examine the general moral principles underlying the limitations in both of these areas; 5) judge the moral issue in the use of RU 486.

B. Two Kinds of Activities

Obviously we are born into a world not of our own making. We and everything else in nature originate from causes other than the human will. Furthermore, nature constitutes an integrated whole, exhibiting an order of mutual dependence and interrelationship among the biological species, together with the inanimate environment, a state of affairs that ecologists have been pointing out to us for some time. As a part of nature, as a natural entity, man is not the cause of himself. He is not the designer or the producer of his bodily organs, their functions, and the physico-chemical activities that are subordinated to the principal operations: all of these he has received and which is plain to every one of us. So when we speak of the control we exercise over ourselves, we are of course not speaking about a control over the design and commensurate function with which our bodily parts are endowed. Such a state of affairs serves, however, to point up wherein our control does lie, namely in the use of operational capacities already constituted.[2] There are, however, two main kinds of activities that nature manifests, and the contrast between them is an important one; so to it we shall now turn our attention.

If we use the term "activity" or "action" in its broadest sense to signify any movement, behavior, or operation whatsoever of living and non-living things alike, then we may distinguish two kinds of action found in nature: 1) those that are goal-directed, and 2) those that are random. The first kind is characterized by the determinate end-state or thing toward which the action is antecedently oriented, while the second is characterized by the absence of any such determinate orientation. The difference is important; so we shall elaborate upon it in order to make its sense as plain as possible.

That goals are necessary for human actions is understood by all. In order to do something, we must first desire a goal and then plan the activities that lead to its realization. If I wish to go to a baseball game, I must drive to the ball park, buy a ticket, walk in through the gate, and take a seat, all of which are actions that are preliminary to enjoying the game. What is important here is that the goal has a twofold effect upon the agent: 1) it turns the action, which is a means, on and off; that is, by moving someone to desire, the goal brings an action into existence; 2) the goal also is the principle according to which we decide what action, what means, will lead to the end. Thus the goal is cause of our actions by initiating them and by being responsible for their character.

But human actions are not the only ones that are goal-directed, for the actions of plants and animals are too (albeit not consciously in the human sense), a statement that is well-illustrated by the egg-laying activities of birds. A particular species of bird will lay a number of eggs that constitutes a normal clutch, the size of the clutch representing the number of offspring for which the parents (or parent) are able to care at one time. We ought not to be surprised, then, to learn that clutch size plays a role in determining how long the egg-laying continues. Normally the female will produce eggs until the appropriate number is reached, at which time she ceases to lay; and farmers know that by gathering the eggs they will prevent the normal clutch from being reached and keep the hen laying. Yet once the normal clutch number is reached the laying stops. Interfering with the goal's attainment keeps the hen laying; allowing the action to proceed uninhibited brings it to an end. So we see that the exercise or non-exercise of the act of laying depends upon the presence or absence of the goal; in other words the presence or absence of the goal is responsible for the activity's existence or non-existence and is therefore clearly causal in character.

Other ordinary activities such as nest-building by birds, dam-building by beavers, predatory attacks on prey also indicate the goal-directedness of animal activities, and of course we could point to the behavior of plants in healing wounds, etc. as further illustrations.

136

And once again we see that the goal to be achieved determines the action-means by which the goal is to be achieved. Thus without the goal the actions would neither exist nor be determined in kind. The activities make sense and find their reason for existing in the goal.

The same relationship exists between purely physiological activities and their goals, as the production of red blood cells within the mammalian body shows. If bleeding occurs, diminishing the number of red cells, the body immediately begins to produce new ones, continuing the production until a number within the normal limits of the count is reached. On the other hand, if a transfusion is given very quickly after the hemorrhage starts, then little or no production of cells takes place; and if more red cells are introduced than are needed, a destructive process known as phagocytosis brings the number down within normal limits. Thus what we said above about the principal, observable actions of animals we may also say about their physiological counterparts: they exist in order to bring about a determinate end-state or goal that is beneficial to the organism; they constitute goods for that organism, and that is their reason for being. Now, however, let us look at another kind of activity, namely the random.

We are all aware that molecules or atoms within a substance are said to move randomly, a state of affairs that facilitates the changes the stuff can undergo. The motion that is imparted to them is random because it is not *antecedently determined by some pattern either innate or extrinsically imposed.* Instead a molecule undergoes a change of momentum solely from a chance encounter with some other molecule. No one molecule is determinately foreordained to strike another particular molecule. Of course the randomness of the parts of a substance does not imply that the whole acts or moves in a random way. The movement or movements of individual parts is not the movement or operation of the whole. Nor does this mean that randomness *as such* has a purpose. The random as such is first distinguished by the fact that it is unlike that which is clearly goal directed: individual atoms and molecules do not have a foreordained orientation to move in one direction rather than another; that is hardly open to dispute.

There is, of course, a sort of indetermination in natural causes that gives rise to a certain random activity. Plants produce more

137

seeds than actually germinate, and this is fortunate, for otherwise many species would cease to exist. But the proliferation of a super-abundance of seeds is not random even though the germination of the individual seeds is a matter of chance. The plant produces the seeds but does not have within itself a system of distribution; consequently the germination of daughter plants is to some extent the result of random activity. In short, the profligate reproduction of seeds is foreordained by the plant's constitution precisely because the distribution system is subject to chance.

Nonetheless in the biological realm there is some genuine randomness, which is illustrated by the growth of cancerous tissue, for the reproduction of such cells (cells are by their nature parts) is without a determinate goal, that is, they are not parts of a distinct organ or operational bodily part, which is precisely why they are said to be cancerous. Tumors are pathological bodies; how, then, can they be goal-directed? Once again, then, random, cancerous growth is not programmed to bring about a determinate end-state possessed of a function that contributes to the welfare of the whole organism and for that reason is not goal-directed and may be said to be random.

The role of the goal is perhaps made most manifest by the words of E. S. Russell when he compares the actions of organisms to those that belong to inanimate things:

> Coming to a definite end or terminus is not *per se* distinctive of directive activity, for inorganic processes also move towards a natural terminus; the moving stone rolls down the hill till it reaches the bottom, or is stopped by some obstacle; the unstable system moves toward a stable equilibrium; the same stable equilibrium may even be reached from different starting points. What *is* distinctive is the active persistence of directive activity towards its goal, the use of alternative means towards the same end, the achievement of results in the face of difficulties.[3]

Russell's point is clear: being goal-directed is not peculiar to the animate. What it clearly does show, however, is the causal role that the end-state or goal plays both with respect to the occurrence of activities and with respect to their kind. Clearly only certain actions can produce an offspring, repair tissue, etc. Digestion requires certain actions, reproduction different actions, and self-defense still others that are different from both of the first two kinds. In fact, the end is that which determines not only the exercise but also the character of the operation by requiring that it be proportioned to bringing about the end or goal itself, which as Russell says[4], responds to a need. Thus once again: without the end, the organism will not attain those goods which it requires. But we need not multiply our comments further, for we have said enough to make our main point: the exercise and persistence of biological actions depend upon need, upon the absence of the end-state or entity which is to come about through the operations, upon the absence of a benefit or good; and once a goal is reached, the activity that leads to it ceases.

We need to stress that where goal-directed activities occur an orientation or pattern or "program" must exist within the organism by means of which the complex of activities is adapted or proportioned to achieving the end in question, a pattern that includes the set of relations between the parts which make up the whole. Moreover, the regularity which is characteristic of animals other than man indicates that however complex the organism's performance, its set of operations is directed by instincts. All beavers have the same "occupation," that is, they behave the same way, as do leopards, moles, rabbits, etc., and the regularity of animal activities allows us to infer that those which make up the animal's "good life" are directed by patterns that are inborn, patterns by means of which the organism pursues benefits and avoids evils. In other words, the patterns take their character from the primary good to which the organism's life is directed, namely its preservation and more importantly the preservation of the species. That, in fact, is what "adaptive" means.

Man, on the other hand, does not act instinctively; his mode of living is voluntary, and the variety of occupations that make up human life is nearly endless. Human occupations vary from one individual to another and from one historical period to another, and this great variety allows us to infer that no set of instinctive behavioral patterns exists that directs human occupations. Of course we do have internal experience of making our own decisions and choices, but the external evidence alone suffices to make our point: the mode of living proper to the human species is varied and therefore voluntary. Man is cause of his own operations, determining not only their exercise but also the particular kinds to be elicited, depending, of course, on the goal for which he has chosen to act. More particularly, man is cause of his actions insofar as he directs and moderates the desires or drives that incline him to actions of one kind or another that he perceives to be beneficial. The pattern of our actions, patterns of pursuing some good or avoiding some evil: that is what we are primarily causes of—as everyone knows.

But as we have said, if we are the cause of the relations or order among our operations, it is certainly true that we are not causes of the *kinds* of operational powers that we possess and the subordinate physiological activities which they include. On the contrary, operations are present in us as a consequence of a conception and development that is not in any way our own doing, which means that our bodily functions are good independently of us and that our causality over ourselves is limited to determining the exercise of operations which nature has provided and to directing them toward various goals according to the circumstances in which we find ourselves.

We must emphasize, too, that in addition to the actions that we do control, other actions occur in us that we do not control. We cannot *directly* control our digestion, the production of red blood cells, the osmotic processes by which fluids enter cells and the blood stream, etc. These physiological processes are controlled by chemical and physical activities in ways that are not directly voluntary; they are, however, presupposed to and necessary for all those actions that we do control. To sum up, then, we may say that some actions are controlled by volition, while others are controlled by non-voluntary, physical and chemical causes.

Having said these things, we may now move on to look at the therapeutic, medical arts and their relation to human self control. It is, of course, under the aegis of medicine, its surgical and drug-administering practices, that the issue of abortion has come to be discussed.

C. Medical Practice and the Human Good

Medicine, the ministrations of surgeons and physicians, are necessary for the existence and well being of most of us. We become sick, injured, need operations to restore us to normal activity, etc., all of which is obvious. But who would allow that the physician or surgeon can treat us without being subject to limitations and restrictions? Certainly the large number of malpractice suits imply that we regard the medical profession to have certain responsibilities and to be subject to certain limitations. No one will knowingly permit himself to be the object of capricious medical practice. The limitations to which a physician is subject can be seen best if we begin by noting the general character of bodily ills: physiological activities or bodily functions are defective either by reason of an excess or deficiency stemming from the body itself, or by reason of foreign, destructive substances of either a chemical or biological character that have entered the body. A gland supplying hormones, for example, may reproduce too much or too little. If the latter happens, the physician seeks to stimulate the gland or substitute for its lack of production; if the former, he attempts to inhibit the production, or at least to counteract the excess. If a destructive foreign substance or organism is present he seeks to remove it or offset its effect, and to do so he may introduce some other foreign substance the direct effect of which is restorative. Should the drug have secondary, side-effects which are harmful, the physician must of course take them into account; but as long as the primary effect that is the object of his intention is restorative or therapeutic, he may employ the drug as long as the (uncontrollable) side-effects do not offset the benefits to be gained.

The surgeon, too, is limited by nature. He may repair a part that is defective or remove one that by its malfunction or disease attacks the whole person, but it goes without saying that he may not deliberately mutilate or remove a healthy and normally operating organ; and in general, the medical profession attempts to observe those limitations on its functions.

The fundamental point, however, is that medicine takes as a starting point a norm or standard which is established by investigation into what the body caused by nature actually does; it takes as a standard a norm or state of affairs that is established by nature. In other words, that which is normal or healthy and therefore beneficial or good is determined by causes other than man; and the *objective* determination of what is humanly beneficial sets the limits to medical practice and therapy. To repeat: what is naturally beneficial and good in the human body does not depend upon, and is not the result of, human causality; therefore the relation between the medical art and the natural body implies certain moral restrictions. It is clear that to stimulate or inhibit bodily functions beyond normal limits, to injure, poison, or remove a healthy, normally functioning bodily part is immoral; and the courts of law recognize that fact when they permit lawsuits for malpractice on the part of physicians and surgeons. The physician may inhibit what is excessive and stimulate what is deficient; the surgeon may operate to restore an organ to a normal or as nearly normal a state as is possible, or he may remove a part that is diseased or in some way a threat to the whole organism; but he may not do more. To attack a healthy organ is to attack an activity that is naturally and thus inherently beneficial, introducing thereby a state or condition that is inherently bad, and certainly we are not at liberty to destroy the goods which nature provides us. Who would permit a physician to stop a normal thyroid gland from secreting, to inhibit a normal pancreas, to impede the functioning of healthy lungs, heart, liver, etc.? On the other hand, since a diseased organ threatens the existence of the whole, the body benefits from the removal—when that is the only remedy—of the afflicted part, and such a practice is clearly licit. Few would deny that in removing an evil one brings about a good; so it would seem clear that every therapeutic art ministers to nature and therefore must be regulated by it. Once again: the good which medicine intends to bring about is antecedently established by nature, not by man, and therefore it is a measure of what a ministerial action of a physician may or may not do.

At this point it ought to be evident that the limitations described above do not involve introducing principles that are new. On the contrary, they are as old as the systematic discussion of ethical problems and are also recognized by the ordinary man. They lead, however, to a discussion of still more general principles under which the moral limitations discussed above fall as particularizations. In other words, the limitations that bind the medical art are the consequence of applying a very common principle that in the past two or three decades has come to be applied by ecologists and environmentalists to nature as a whole. The nature of species and the order among them is a benefit, a good, not only for them but for all of mankind, and interference with the order of nature ordinarily—far too often it seems—brings nature to a state of "sickness," so to speak.

Nature is not to be conquered, as Mill tells us, but instead is a whole to which we must accommodate our actions, point that many have made. So let us look a bit at the issue of pollution, for it reveals the conception of nature that motivates the environmentalists.

D. Pollution and the Environment

For more than two decades now the United States and the international community have been concerned about the deterioration of the natural environment and its ecosystem, a deterioration that has been brought about by pollutants and by the destruction of natural species of plants and animals. We have all heard about the depletion of the ozone layer over the antarctic, the increasing amount of carbon dioxide in the atmosphere, the polluting of water supplies, etc. And we have seen laws enacted to protect endangered species and programs begun to restore their populations. The airing of such issues has made us all aware of the fact that the physical environment together with the biological community constitute an ordered whole that in an important way is analogous to the human body. Every individual animal organism, especially the more sophisticated, is a complex whole made of heterogeneous parts which have determinate relations to one another. The simultaneous physiological functioning of the parts involves a kind of integration and balance among them that the biologist calls "homeostasis." In a similar way the activities of the plants and animals that constitute the whole ecosystem are ordered and balanced with respect to one another so as to provide a kind of ecological homeostasis, and we are all aware of the many television programs that describe in detail the delicate balance of species and environment that goes to make the whole to be stable. But our point is this: limiting by legislative means both what may be cast into the environment and the destruction of animal and plant populations presupposes that the order of natural entities in a community is a good not only for them but most of all for man, a good, that is, of which we are not the cause and which is presupposed to the pursuit of the good human life. Indeed, we may well say that man is socially dependent not only in a political way, he is also socially dependent in a more extended sense insofar as he is dependent on other biological species and the environment for his continued general well being, both physical and mental.

To repeat our point, the environment together with the ecosystem is an ordered whole that is not caused by man, and the benefits which it provides, like the parts of the body, are not of human origin. And so the environment and the ecosystem represent an order among species and inanimate nature that is beneficial antecedently to man's action upon them. Therefore the character of the natural community must be respected *as it is given,* just as the character of the human body must be respected as it too is given. Of course we may treat nature in the same way that a physician treats the human body: we may restore to normal the deficient and we may remove what is excessive, provided we can clearly establish exactly what that is. What we may legitimately do to nature is limited by the relationships among the species and the environmental habitats which they occupy. Can we, for the sake of increasing industrial profits and consequently our short term convenience dump toxins into streams, lakes, the oceans, and the atmosphere? Or can we attack the natural processes of the human body for the sake of our pleasure or convenience? It would seem, then, that in relation to the environment and its ecosystem man is subject to the kind of moral restraints that regulate the practice of medicine: he may inhibit (harvest) what is excessive and promote what is deficient in the natural community, but to destroy or pollute deliberately an important part of the system is analogous to attacking a healthy organ.[5] Man has to take the natural community according to its constitution and respect its activities as benefits not determined by human decisions. And so, anticipating a bit, it would seem that to be consistent an environmentalist cannot both promote abortion and demand the preservation of the environment together with its ecosystems. But having said these things, we may now take up the general principles to which we referred earlier.

E. The General Principles

Not only professional moralists but the public at large has often heard that "The end does not justify the means," a proposition which tells us first of all that a means that is bad cannot be used to pursue an end. Still, at first sight such a statement does seem false, for the end is the whole reason for the means. Every means is selected, rightly or wrongly, because it is thought to bring about the end; and so it appears that the end is precisely that which does justify the means. What reason other than its suitability for the end enters into our selection of materials and tools when we set out to make something? Yet despite this sort of objection, we all understand that what our first statement means is that the end does not justify any means whatsoever but only some. The understood restriction, however, leads us to ask what it is about a means that precludes its being used to attain an end or goal.

To be sure, the answer is plain enough, for in many cases a means is good or evil independently of its order to some goal of human choosing; and that is precisely the condition of the goods and benefits that are of natural origin, whether those of the body and its parts or those of the natural environment. Such entities and activities are good antecedently to and independently of their being ordered by us to some goal that we have in mind, on account of which using their destruction as a means to an end, as a means to some "convenience," is morally evil; that is the effect of the limitations that nature imposes on what we do. To violate them is to claim that the end justifies *any* means, a principle whose universal acceptance would destroy every moral rule we might adopt.

Human operational powers are subject to voluntary control; we are self-determining insofar as we direct the application of operational powers already constituted, but we do not determine the nature of our operational capacities. We are not the cause of the eye having a lens, vitreous fluid, retina, etc., nor are we the cause of a vibrating diaphragm in the ear. All that we are able to do is to direct the application, the use of the powers that we already have. As a consequence we may not morally attempt to alter their character and their function—except therapeutically—in place of disciplining ourselves to their controlled use. But let us elaborate.

The kind of alteration that is at issue is one that promotes pleasure and avoids pain. That is to say, abortion is practiced as a means of last resort to avoid an unwanted forthcoming birth even though the sexual activity that brings about the pregnancy was exercised. Abortion kills a human being in order to escape the natural end, the child, to which reproductive actions are ordered for the good of the species, at the same time allowing the participants to enjoy sexual pleasures and satisfactions.[6] Of course one must concede at once that the pleasures which accompany natural physical operations are ends; we may pursue pleasure as an end provided it is not separated from the action which it ordinarily accompanies. At the least we would probably be undernourished were eating not pleasurable, and the race would not be reproduced were sexual activities likewise not enjoyable. Furthermore, pleasure does serve to restore our spirits when we are fatigued from our labors, and therefore one cannot deny the role it plays in human life. Sexual relations do promote the mutual love of husband and wife and so constitute a legitimate goal by themselves. But one is now faced with a contention as old as the study of morals, namely that pleasure can be separated from the actions it accompanies, which is to say, pleasure is good no matter what the action and their goals that gives rise to it. Only under such a "principle" can one consider sodomy as no more than "an alternative life style."[7]

What all this means is that one may not alter in a physical way a natural activity, a natural means in order to frustrate the natural goal to which the pleasure is attached. To do so is tantamount to attempting to alter the character of the operational capacity, and in so doing one removes the end and the good to which a cause other than ourselves has directed the operation.[8] Thus to alter functions by drugs or surgery beyond their normal use in order to prevent the attaining of the natural goal is to attack the voluntary character of human nature; it is to reduce activities subject to voluntary control to the status of those that are purely physico-chemical and that must therefore can be corrected by physical or chemical means. As we have repeatedly said, unlike other animals that act under the direction of instinctive behavioral patterns, man is a voluntary animal; he controls the use and non-use of his operations, and the habitual right use of them makes him disciplined. Man's first moral obligation is to operate voluntarily according to a well-formed judgment, and that is what sets him apart from other species.

F. The Abortifacient RU 486

Whether the use of RU 486 is moral or immoral can now be judged by the principles that we have discussed, principles which regulate not only medical practice but the use of drugs generally by members of the human species, as well as pollution of the environment. First let us note that the exercise of the acts which lead to reproduction are among those that are subject to voluntary control and are to be managed by self-discipline. That is what "control of one's own body" entails. The use of physical and chemical means to control what is innately voluntary is, as we said above, contrary to human nature and therefore out of order. What should we say about someone who is unafflicted with some disorder but who seeks to "control" his excessive eating through a surgical bypass that prevents what he eats from being absorbed? Is there any moral difference between him and the one who vomits out his food in order to go back to the table? Of course the bypass will allow him to stay alive and may in some sense be "convenient," but is human life worth living when it is gained at the expense of moral behavior? The entire moral tradition of the West says no to that question.

Because RU 486 introduces a pathological condition, its use is immoral, whatever the "benefit" the end might be expected to provide. That it produces a pathological condition in the woman who takes it is not open to genuine challenge, for the drug interferes with the normal reproductive process by introducing menstruation and destroying the normal habitat of the fertilized egg; and since this contravenes what nature does, since it interferes with the attaining of the goal or end to which all the physiological processes are ordered, it attacks what is naturally good, bringing about a pathological condition which is by definition evil and so makes the action immoral. The fact that menstruation is at the proper time and under the proper conditions a natural process does not make the use of RU 486 a "natural" method; for RU 486 acts to produce menstruation at a time when it naturally would not occur, that is, when the uterus has received or is prepared to receive a fertilized ovum. The order among natural actions is formal to their being both natural parts of a whole—of the body as an integral unit—and of their being beneficial. Suppose, for example, that sweating were to occur after one had been exposed to prolonged cold; would it be good for man? Moreover, adultery as a physical act is not evil; only its improper order or use makes it immoral. Therefore *the way we order one act to another or to a goal formally determines whether our actions are moral or immoral.* The same holds true of our relation to nature as an integrated ecological and environmental whole: we may use

147

other natural species provided we do not do so in a "pathological"— if I may extend the word—manner.

Were the pathological state introduced by RU 486 to affect the user directly in the sense that it interfered with a goal directly related to her own welfare, neither she nor her male partner would tolerate it. But because reproduction is an activity that is directed to another, to someone other than the sexual partners, because it may not introduce pain into the woman's body, the users do not find damage to the reproductive operation subjectively distressing beyond what is regularly experienced, except by reason of side-effects, which alone directly affect the woman.

The abortion of offspring by man stands in sharp contrast to the behavior of non-human animals, which are willing to surrender their lives for the welfare of their young. The human species alone is willing to sacrifice the lives of its young on the altar of venereal pleasure, all because of the difficulty of self-discipline, the rejection of which actually amounts to the abandonment of the "control of our own bodies."

Finally we would note once again that the environmentalists who seek to protect the ecosystem and its species are not consistent in their position if they promote abortion. We can only hope that they come to see that such is the case.

NOTES

1. Arthur J. Vander, James H. Sherman, Dorothy S. Luciano, *Human Physiology* (New York: McGraw-Hill Book Company, 1975), p. 446.

2. We ought to note that physiological activities that are part of the operational power that is being used are not under direct voluntary control, a point that is plain enough.

3. E. S. Russell, *The Directiveness of Organic Activities* (Cambridge: At the University Press, 1946), p. 144. In my judgment, this is a very well done work, very much worth the attention of philosophers.

4. Op. cit.

5. Obviously the moral principles which regulate the practice of medicine are often difficult to apply, and one cannot expect the application of similar principles to the whole of nature to be less difficult. Coping with environmental problems requires a prudential judgment and scientific sagacity that in many ways exceeds that which must be brought to bear on medical issues.

We must note too that in a sense nature produces excessive amounts of plants (forests, for example) and animals (herds), the harvesting of which is beneficial to man. Agriculture of course amounts to the production of surpluses by voluntary efforts. Yet we have learned that agriculture must respect the environment, and that we cannot, for example, devastate our forests. We have had to learn the hard way that we are a part of nature; as physical entities we do not transcend it.

6. Animals engage in sexual activity only when the female is fertile and when she indicates her state by being in heat. In the human species, however, sexual activity exists not only for the continued welfare of the species but also for the intimacy and mutual love of husband and wife, whose union is necessary, constituting them as a single cause for the begetting and rearing of children. Nor ought we to forget that the union, whether children issue from it or not, is an end in itself. One must, however, always keep in mind the words of *Gaudium et Spes* (par. 50): " . . . while not making the other purposes of matrimony of less account, the true practice of conjugal love, and the whole meaning of the family life which result from it, have this aim: that the couple be ready with stout hearts to cooperate with the love of the Creator and the Savior, who through them will enlarge and enrich His own family day by day." It is universally true that what God has joined, we may not separate. Husband and wife constitute one cause, and unless there is a union of minds, wills, and bodies their causality cannot be realized as it ought.

7. Of course no one who aborts a fetus states outright that his or her reason is to engage in intercourse without the encumbrance of rearing a child. Instead we hear pleas to the effect that the pregnancy will be stressful, impose economic hardship, etc. Unfortunately one seldom sees the principles articulated that are necessary for such arguments to conclude. Consider: this child may be destroyed because this child will cause psychological stress. The unstated premise is, "Whoever causes psychological stress may be destroyed." The same kind of principle obtains in other examples; for instance, "Whoever causes economic hardship may be destroyed." No one, of course, is unaware of these premises, but seldom do the discussions address them explicitly.

8. Of course one could in principle alter the constitution of an organ for the sake of improving its operation, not only as the operation is constituted in itself but also insofar as it is subordinate to man's voluntary, intellectual mode of existence. Such an alternation, however, is not at all the sort of alteration that is attempted by abortifacient drugs.

Chapter 9

ABORTION AND PROBABILISM

The Reverend Joseph J. Farraher, S.J.

I. What is Probabilism?

In the ongoing discussion among Catholics about abortion, some have tried to defend abortion, at least in some cases, by appealing to the principle of Probabilism. Probabilism has been a well known and well accepted system of resolving doubts about morality for several centuries, when used properly. However, it is the intent of this chapter to show that the system has been misused in trying to defend abortion. The basic principle on which Probabilism rests is that a truly doubtful law does not oblige; or, that a doubtful obligation is no obligation. Probabilists combine this principle with the further argument that a solidly probable opinion that an obligation does not exist, renders it doubtful. Probabilism therefore concludes that one may follow a solidly probable opinion for freedom under certain conditions: 1) that no higher law obliges one to follow the safer course of action, as in matters concerning necessary means for salvation, or concerning the validity of a sacrament, or for the protection of basic rights of others; and, 2) that the supreme Magisterium of the Church has not settled the question. This last condition is based on the presumption that the supreme magisterium (i.e., the pope personally or through one of his Roman Congregations, or an ecumenical council) teaches the truth even when not solemnly defining a matter as *de fide*. This presumption, in turn, is based on our Lord's commission to Peter and to the Church until the end of time. As a presumption when not an infallible declaration, it can be overcome by sufficient proof, but merely questioning the teaching or not understanding the reasons involved does not destroy the presumption.

Another way of achieving probability, known as extrinsic probability, is by the testimony of theologians. To consider an opinion solidly probable merely on the authority of one or a number of moral theologians, without grasping the force of their reasons (or without knowing their reasons) should be based on another presumption: that the authorities in question would not hold such an opinion without good, solid reasons. Very few theologians have regularly been considered as sufficient individually to constitute a reasonable presumption of solid enough reasons because of the honor in which their writings have been held in the Church. St. Thomas Aquinas and St. Alphonsus Ligouri are such theologians. Otherwise, for an expert to judge an opinion solidly probable without seeing the reasoning or its force, one should be able to cite at least five or six *auctores probati* who hold the opinion. And the term, *auctores probati* (approved authors or authorities), has generally been taken to mean experts in the field of moral theology recognized as such by the Magisterium or by most other experts in the same field. And in all of these cases, the presumption can be overcome by a decision of the supreme Magisterium or by proof that the experts were guilty of false reasoning or false premises. And, of course, even Thomas and Alphonsus may not be considered to prevail over subsequent declarations of the Magisterium.

II. Proper Application of Probabilism

How does all this apply to the matter of abortion? Apparently no Catholic moralist has gone so far as to allow abortion on demand. To quote one dissenter:

> Perhaps one of the most significant facts about current Roman Catholic moral theology is that it has consistently insisted on the moral evil of abortion, in spite of the pluralism that has entered into so many other aspects of moral theology.[1]

This should not be too surprising, granted the constant teaching of the Church that the deliberate destruction of innocent human life, before or after birth, is a serious offense against the law of God, culminating in modern times in the "Declaration on Abortion," issued by the Congregation for the Doctrine of the Faith on November 18, 1974.[2]

However, several neo-modernist Catholic theologians have suggested that early abortion for a victim of rape might be justified since there is solid probability that the rational human soul is not infused until implantation of the fertilized ovum in the uterus. They base the probability on the biological evidence that, in the first days after fertilization of the ovum and before implantation, twinning can occur with the one fertilized ovum dividing and forming two distinct individual beings; and a soul is indivisible. However, as the CDF Declaration points out, in footnote n.19 at n.13, this does not prove that there could not be a human soul at the moment of the union of ovum and sperm, and it will never be able to be proven. So, on the basis even of a mere probability that a fully human life is not present, one may not invoke probabilism to justify attacking what may be a human life. And that the recent constant statements of Pope John Paul II and the CDF on the respect due to human life from the first moment of conception refer to the period before implantation can be seen from the context of the statements in several instances: e.g., the "Instruction on Respect for Human Life in Origin and the Dignity of Procreation," issued by the CDF on February 22, 1987 towards the end of n.1 where it says:

Certainly no experimental datum can be in itself sufficient to bring us to the recognition of a spiritual soul; nevertheless the conclusions of science regarding the human embryo provide a valuable indication for discerning by the use of reason a personal presence at the moment of this first appearance of a human life: How could a human individual not be a human person? The Magisterium has not expressly committed itself to an affirmation of a philosophical nature, but it constantly reaffirms the moral condemnation of any kind of procured abortion. This teaching has not been changed and is unchangeable.

Thus the fruit of human generation from the first moment of its existence, that is to say, from the moment the zygote has formed, demands the unconditional respect that is morally due to the human being in his bodily and spiritual totality. The human being is to be respected and treated as a person from the moment of conception, and therefore from that same moment his rights as a person must be recognized, among which in the first place is the inviolable right of every innocent human being to life.[3]

This explicit teaching of the Congregation for the Doctrine of the Faith should indicate that there is no room for the application of probabilism on the basis of a doubt about the presence of a human soul before implantation. It is true that the phenomenon of twinning does cause philosophical problems concerning the human soul. There are two souls when twins form from what was one being before the cleavage. So far we have no way of knowing whether God infuses a second soul in one of the twins and leaves the original soul in the other, or just what does happen. But to try to cite St. Thomas and others who held that the human soul could not be present until the matter is sufficiently organized to support a substantial form in the Thomistic hylomorphic sense is not a valid argument. The existence of the female ovum and the male sperm were not discovered until centuries later. With our present knowledge of biology, we can say that once the ovum and sperm unite to form a new being, the matter is so arranged that it will naturally develop into a complete human being. And throughout the history of the Church it was always held that it was gravely immoral to interfere in the process of

154

the beginning of new human life, even when it was thought that there was not yet rational human life.

III. Some Historical Notes

This latter argument appears in two sixteenth century papal documents, to which I would never have adverted, except for an experience in an abortion debate with an Episcopalian priest, who claimed that Pope Gregory XIV had allowed abortion in a formal papal "constitution." I felt sure that he was misquoting that pope, but determined to find out what led this cleric to make such a statement. What I found was that Pope Gregory XIV in his constitution, *Sedes Apostolicae* of May 31, 1591, reduced the severe restrictions on absolution of the excommunication declared on those guilty of the crimes of abortion or sterilization and of those who aid or abet those crimes, so that, instead of being reserved to the pope personally, as Sixtus V had decreed in his constitution, *Effrenatum,* of 1588, any approved confessor could absolve those guilty of such crimes, but only in the forum of the sacrament of penance. At the same time, Pope Gregory called such acts very serious crimes ("gravissimi sceleris") of those "who procure the aborting of a fetus, whether ensouled or not [tam animati quam inanimati] and also of those who impede the fecundity of women, and offer sterility potions or medicaments [sterilitatis potiones, seu venena]." Furthermore, the classical moral theologians before the discovery of the ovum also deemed aborting of the products of conception a grave sin, whether animated or not, whether in human form or not.

John T. Noonan, Jr., in the book he edited on *The Morality of Abortion,* in his own chapter, "An Almost Absolute Value in History," develops the idea that the terms *pharmakeia* in Greek and *venena* in Latin and their cognates, in the writings of St. Paul (Gal 5:19–20) and St. John (Apoc 9:21; 21:8; 22:15) referred to preparations or medicaments which included abortifacients and contraceptives. He also argues that the *Didache* (2:2) and other early writings did the same. If I may be permitted a personal note, I had often wondered why St. John in the Apocalypse or Revelation, at 9:21, had included sorcery in his list of serious sins between murder and fornication, since he seemed otherwise to be following the order of the Ten Commandments. When I heard Noonan's explanation of the use of "*venena*" as including medicaments or preparations which might cause abortion or sterility, I studied the matter more fully. Both the Douay and King James versions of the Bible had translated the "venena" of St. Jerome's translation as "sorcery," I had thought that *venena* might mean potions supposed to be magic and so superstitious. But on further study of the words, I learned that sorcery was one possible translation but that they could also signify any medicament or preparation meant to cause some effect, and that they could well mean preparations to cause sterility or abortion. That would fit perfectly for the term's use between murder and fornication: abortion is a form of murder, and contraception is an abuse of the proper use of sex, mandated by what we number as the sixth commandment. And the next sin mentioned in that verse is theft.

As noted above, Pope Gregory XIV in his apostolic constitution, *Sedes Apostolicae* of May 31, 1596, used the term *venena* in this same sense, as did his predecessor, Sixtus V, in his apostolic constitution, *Effrenatum*.

IV. A Current Controversy

In the volume *Abortion and Catholicism: The American Debate*, the application of traditional probabilism is treated by Carol A. Tauer, a professor of philosophy at The College of St. Catherine in St. Paul, Minnesota, pages 54–84, with the title, "The Tradition of Probabilism and the Moral Status of the Early Embryo."[4] Professor Tauer gives a reasonably good description of traditional probabilism. In expressing one of the limitations she says: "when some doubts of fact are included, those which involve questions of human life and justice are not; in these situations, what moralists call the safer course must be followed, not the course favoring liberty." However, she then cites cases that might seem exceptions to this limitation, allowing actions which might be harmful to life, citing especially two cases offered by Thomas Wassmer, S.J., in *Commonweal* in 1967, one dealing with measures considered licit after rape to try to remove the rapist's sperm, the other with removing life-supports from a comatose patient when there is a chance that the person might regain consciousness.[5] Under the conditions in which these matters were treated by orthodox Catholic moralists, neither was an application of probabilism. The first was an application of the principle of the indirect voluntary (or, "double effect"), the latter an application of the principle concerning the obligation to use extraordinary means to prolong life or health. When orthodox Catholic theologians treated the question of what could be done to prevent conception after rape, they always insisted that means should not be used which would cause the ejection of a fertilized ovum. Knowledge of medical and biological facts hindered the moralists' treatment at times, but they always insisted that one may never intend the abortion of a new human being. If it might happen, it would be an unintended side effect.[6] As to the second case, orthodox Catholic moralists would not allow a comatose patient's heart to be removed for a transplant until it had been established that the patient was dead. The probability of the return to consciousness of a comatose patient would undoubtedly be a factor in a decision whether or not to continue life-support systems, such as artificial respiration and intravenous feeding. However, whatever means were being used to keep the patient alive could be removed by the consent of the proper person as long as they were truly disproportionate to the hope of recovery or were too expensive or burdensome.[7]

Professor Tauer uses a strange argument to try to show that a doubt about the existence of a rational human soul in the early embryo is not a doubt of *fact* in the sense in which traditional moralists use that term. She found that the examples given by the authors she consulted concerned doubts about the presence of human life in "empirically verifiable" situations. From this she concludes that, since the presence of a human soul in the early embryo is not empirically verifiable, that its presence or absence is not a doubt of fact in traditional moral theology.[8] This is definitely a misunderstanding of traditional moralists. Not being empiricists, they believed in many truths that were not empirically verifiable, and would certainly understand the word "fact" to apply to any reality.

From what has been said so far, it should be clear that traditional probabilism cannot be legitimately applied to allow the abortion of an early embryo, since this would clearly contradict both of the limitations of traditional probabilism as explained in the beginning of this article: there is a higher law which obliges one to follow the safer course where following the more liberal opinion could result in violating the basic right to life of an innocent human being; and the supreme Magisterium of the Church has pronounced formally on the matter. To paraphrase St. Augustine, *Roma locuta est; causa finita est.*[9]

V. Whence the Dissent?

If the case is closed, why do so many Catholic theologians and other Catholics refuse to accept the teaching of the Magisterium? Does the number that do contradict the teaching of the Magisterium constitute some kind of extrinsic probability to the denial of the teaching of the supreme Magisterium? Professor Tauer quotes Karl Rahner, S.J., as claiming that the fact that the dissent of so many Catholic moral theologians from Magisterial teaching is tolerated by the Magisterium shows the inadequacy of n.25 in Vatican II's "Dogmatic Constitution on the Church" (*Lumen gentium*).[10] Of course, the Magisterium has not "tolerated" such dissent, but has spoken out repeatedly against it and has taken action in removing teachers like Fr. Charles E. Curran and Fr. Hans Küng from their teaching positions as Catholic Theologians in spite of the grave difficulty in pursuing such cases. Still, why have so many dissented? Let me suggest an answer, using what I have said about this in "Questions answered" in the *Homiletic & Pastoral Review* with some editing.[11] Here I will touch summarily on two major factors: false philosophies and the contraception controversy.

Existentialism and allied "philosophies" denied all absolutes. Of course, a statement that there can be no absolutes is self-contradictory, since it is given as an absolute. One of the major influences in the spread of such ideas was Jean-Paul Sartre, a self-professed atheist. I have treated the various ways in which such philosophies have influenced, first, Protestant religious thought, then, Catholic thinking, in two articles in the *New Catholic Encyclopedia,* a little over ten years apart: Volume 9 of the original 15-volume set, under the title of "Moral Theology, History of (Contemporary Trends)"; then, in the 17th volume (an updating volume), under the same title. Unfortunately, misunderstandings of some statements of Vatican II contributed to the spread of these philosophies. Vatican II urged us to "read the signs of the times" and especially urged seminary professors to study the new philosophies. The purpose of both such exhortations was that well-educated Catholics should be aware of what is going on in the world and be prepared to point out the falsity of many modern attitudes and thoughts. Many also have taken Vatican II's "Declaration on Religious Freedom" as a vindication of freedom of conscience, when the import of the document was that governments should not force persons to go contrary to their religion or to their informed consciences or to hinder them from doing what, by their religion, they feel bound to do. The declaration also indicated that the conscience in the matter should be an informed conscience; and that the common good and rights of other individuals may necessitate some limitation to do what they think they are obliged to do. It did not mean, as some took it, that everyone is morally free to do whatever he or she feels is good. The word for conscience in Latin, *conscientia*, can mean either what one *feels* is good or, in the traditional Catholic theological sense, what one judges to be morally good, bad or indifferent, using what sources one has for knowing the truth.

The history of the contraception controversy is modern history, too; having mainly begun in this century, especially with Margaret Sanger's Planned Parenthood campaign to achieve women's equality with men with regard to casual sex: a man could have casual sex with many women and not have to worry about becoming pregnant. Women should have the same freedom. Hence, the advocacy of contraception, and of abortion as a follow-up in case the contraception failed. Opposition from New England Protestants helped to induce her to campaign in England. Those who accepted her teaching brought enough pressure on Church-of-England divines that the Lambeth Conference in 1930 passed, with a majority but not unanimous vote, an article which seemed to allow exceptions to the previous unanimous teaching of that church for couples in hardship cases. This evoked the very strong statement of Pope Pius XI at the end of 1930 in his encyclical on Christian marriage, *Casti connubii*, condemning contraception even in hardship cases.[12] Ex-Catholic Anglican Bishop James Pike was active in getting a subsequent Lambeth Conference to give wider approval to contraception. Some other non-Catholic faiths followed suit. At first, this did not have much effect on Catholics.

Among factors influencing Catholic thought toward the more liberal thinking on contraception was an article by a Fr. Louis Janssens of Louvain in the periodical, *Ephemerides Theologicae Lovanienses,* in its issue of April-June, 1958. In that article Fr. Janssens defended the licitness of using the contraceptive pills to alleviate fears of pregnancy, saying that their use was licit for the medicinal purpose of alleviating stress and fear by application of the traditional principle of the "double effect." I proposed his argumentation to our first-year theology students in a year-end examination. If any would have failed to see the fallacy in Father's reasoning, I would have flunked them. But everyone saw the flaw. He was clearly violating one of the conditions of the principle of "double effect," which is more properly called the principle of the indirect voluntary. By his argumentation, he was allowing the direct willing of the contraception to achieve what he proposed as a good end, the alleviation of grave fears of pregnancy.

However, outside of theological circles, that article would undoubtedly have been unnoticed in this country had not an ex-Jesuit, R. B. Piser, later known as R. B. Kiser, been tipped off about it, and, as part of the TIME Magazine staff for religious matters, mentioned it in TIME Magazine. (He, himself, had not yet begun his formal theological studies in the Jesuits.)

Undoubtedly the single most important factor for the spread of false doctrine on the morality of contraception in this country, especially even among priests, was Fr. Charles Curran, as a professor at the Catholic University of America. He had been giving false advice on the matter even before he was given the position at C.U. When he first came up for tenure there, the board of trustees, at that time all bishops since it was their university, voted to deny him tenure. His political expertise, plus a persuasive personality, were such that he got the faculty and students to strike in protest against the decision. Apparently fearing that the University might have to close, the bishops reversed their decision and gave him tenure. For almost 20 years thereafter he has been teaching that contraception is all right for some couples. When Pope Paul VI finally issued his encyclical, *Humanae vitae,* Fr. Curran managed to get a large number of theologians to sign a protest letter against the encyclical before copies were available in the U.S. And, of course, he influenced many future theology professors by his classes.

Another factor which aided such widespread dissent was the leaking to the press of the majority report of the Commission appointed by Pope John XXIII and enlarged by Pope Paul VI to study the question of contraception, especially the anovulant pill, and advise the Pope. That was published in France, and a translation was published in this country by the *National Catholic Reporter,* along with the statement by the opposing minority. Apparently that led many priests to think that the Pope would accept the advice of that majority, and so they began to act accordingly in advice to penitents and other questioners. Added to that was the earliest prediction of Fr. Bernard Häring, C.Ss.R., that the Pope would make changes in the doctrine. When asked about the majority report, I tried to point out that the Pope had specially chosen some who had spoken against the Church's teaching, such as Fr. Janssens, mentioned above, to see whether they could find any legitimate reasons for a change. They didn't! So, of course, the Pope could not in conscience accept their advice, but rather followed the advice of the minority members who pointed out the flaws of the majority report.

Still another factor that influenced many U.S. Catholics was John T. Noonan, Jr.'s book: *Contraception: A History of its Treatment by the Catholic Theologians and Canonists,* in 1965. The book was quite scholarly in gathering a great deal of history of the Church's attitude towards contraception, but Noonan's interpretation of the gathered data was faulty. (The same could be said of his books on usury and even on abortion, although at least he ended up on the right side in the latter, and gave me an idea on the term *venena* mentioned above.)

The opposition to the Church's teaching on contraception, especially the encyclical *Humanae vitae,* has caused a loss of a proper acceptance of the teaching authority of the pope. True Catholic teaching holds that we should accept what the pope teaches as pope, even though not *ex cathedra,* unless one is *certain* that he is in error; a mere feeling that he might be wrong, or even a probability that he is wrong does not excuse. This seems to be the spirit of the often cited n.25 of the *Dogmatic Constitution on the Church (Lumen gentium)* of Vatican II.

Another factor that may seem minor, but real, is that dissenting Catholic theologians regularly get more publicity than the more orthodox. Perhaps it is a good sign that news reporters consider dissent from papal teaching more newsworthy than acceptance of it. At any rate, the ordinary magisterium of the Church from the beginning of the Christian era to the present has universally and constantly taught that direct abortion is always seriously wrong even when it was thought that the human soul was not present until some time after the beginning of pregnancy, and this teaching should be accepted by all who accept the teaching authority instituted by Jesus Christ.

NOTES

1. *Sexual Morality: A Catholic Perspective* by Philip S. Keane, S.S. (New York: Paulist Press, 1977), pp. 134f.

2. *Acta Apostolicae Sedis* 66 (1974) 730–747 in the original Latin; in the English translation in *The Pope Speaks*, 19, 3, (1974), 250–262, and in *Origins*, 4 (1974–1975), 385–392.

3. *TPS*, 32, 2 (1987), p. 142. For the whole text see, *AAS* 80 (1987) 70–102; English, *TPS* 32, 2 (1987), 137–156.

4. New York: Crossroad, 1988, pp. 54–84. Originally published in *Theological Studies* 45 (March 1984), 3–33.

5. "Questions about Questions," *Commonweal*, June 30, 1967, pp. 416–418.

6. Cf. Farraher, "What Can be Done to Prevent Conception After Rape?" *Homiletic & Pastoral Review*, 85 (March 1985), p. 70.

7. Cf. CDF, "Declaration on Euthanasia," *AAS* 72 (1980), 542–552; *TPS* 25, 4, (1980), 286–296.

8. Tauer, p. 70.

9. Sermon 131, *Enchiridion Patristicum*, n. 1507.

10. Tauer, p. 61; Rahner, in *Stimmen der Zeit* 198 (1980) p. 373.

11. April 1988, pp. 69–71.

12. Cf. "Is *Humanae vitae* infallible?" *HPR* (October 1984) pp. 63–64.

Chapter 10

THOMSON AND ABORTION

The Reverend Robert Barry, O.P.

Probably the strongest arguments in behalf of the morality of abortion have been proposed by the M.I.T. philosopher, Judith Jarvis Thomson, for her comparisons are the most lively and her analogies most imaginative. In her famous articles, "A Defense of Abortion" and "Rights and Abortion," Thomson makes a number of claims in defense of abortion that have not been directly and successfully challenged to date, and that is perhaps one reason why many seem to be coming to the view that there is nothing morally objectionable with abortion.[1]

She bases her arguments on the morality of abortion assuming that unborn human life is personal and still finds that there is room for morally permissible abortion. Thomson contends that the conceptus is not a person, anymore than an acorn is an oak tree, but we cannot be entirely sure of this for there are a number of notable differences between an acorn and the conceptus.[2] A conceptus is in the process of becoming a fully mature human being, and it would be more proper to compare it to an acorn that is sprouting into a full-grown oak tree. As we would probably consider such an acorn to be an oak tree and not just an acorn, we should also consider the conceptus to be a person.

Thomson defends withdrawal of "maternal support" from babies, and not the killing of unborn babies and she contends there is no right to a dead baby.[3] She argues that classical morality requires a mother to be not just a "minimally decent Samaritan" to the unborn child but a "splendid Samaritan" and to bear far more burdens for the child than she would have to bear for others.[4] She also claims that this withdrawal of maternal support is not culpable killing and is not the withdrawal of a morally obligatory form of care.[5]

She claims that no one has the right to use a woman's body unless she grants that right and that the mother has a right to deny protection to a baby who is not wanted.[6] This is doubtful because the maternal organs are teleologically directed toward both the needs of the child as well as those of the mother. Because of this teleological orientation, the mother is not simply "letting the child use her body," for the child has some sort of rightful claim to use organs which are naturally directed toward the gestation of the child. Maternal organs are unique in that they have this dual teleology ordered toward mother's and baby's needs. What she says would be true of organ donations, but it is not entirely true for pregnancy because one loses use of organs temporarily in pregnancy, but in organ donation one permanently loses them and gives them away.

Thomson also justifies abortion by denying that direct killing is morally impermissible in some cases.[7] She argues that direct killing is not always and everywhere wrong and that the innocence of the victim is often irrelevant to the morality of actions.[8] To support this, she argues that it would be permitted to directly kill children in a missile silo who could accidentally launch the missile, even though they would be innocent of deliberately threatening others.[9] This is disputable, however, for it would be permissible to attack the missiles and only indirectly threaten the children, assuming they launched the missiles unintentionally. Deliberately killing them in this instance would not be permissible, but deliberately attacking the missiles while indirectly threatening the children would not be unjust.

She justifies abortion by invoking the situation where an older brother is given a box of chocolates and does not share them with his younger brother. Thomson claims that he is not being unjust to him, but only callous and selfish.[10] Similarly, a woman who does not grant use of her body to the baby is not unjust, but merely callous. This characterization however does not accurately portray the structure of rights in an abortion, for it suggests that the younger brother had no preexisting right to the chocolates. This comparison implies that the right to life is entirely dependent on its recognition by others, just as the right of the younger brother to the chocolates is entirely dependent on recognition by the older brother.

But the anti-abortion claim is that the right to life preexists the claims of others, and I think even Thomson would agree that the right to life is prior to such claims and assertions. The rights structure of abortion is better illustrated by a situation where the older brother takes chocolates away from his younger brother that had been given him or that he had bought for himself. This comparison not only expresses Thomson's belief that there is a right to life that preexists others' claims, but it also expresses the preexistent character of this right in a way Thomson's comparison does not. Unfortunately for her, this comparison argues rather forcefully against permitting abortion.

In what follows, I would like to give further critical consideration to her claims about the morality of abortion.

A. Abortion and Aggression Against the Mother

1. Most of Thomson's arguments in support of abortion are grounded on the assertion that the baby is some form of an unjust aggressor, but it is not quite clear just what type of aggressor the preborn child is.[11] Thomson does not state explicitly that the unborn child is a formal, intentional and deliberate aggressor because she knows that the baby is incapable of such an intentional and deliberate action. She therefore has to indirectly infer (without close scrutiny) that the baby is a type of material aggressor that can be deliberately killed "as if" it were a formal aggressor. But if the baby

were an intentional and deliberate aggressor, there would be no moral problem with abortion, for the baby could simply be killed as a threat to the mother. If the baby were a threat to the mother, the worst it could be would be a material threat because the baby is incapable of intentional, deliberate and willful action.

But it is even hard to see how the baby could be a material aggressor because the baby is quite isolated from the mother and because most of the life-threatening conditions suffered by the mother result either from the condition of pregnancy itself or from deficiencies or weaknesses in the mother and not the baby *per se*. However, even if the child was a material aggressor, that would not necessarily mean that it could be deliberately, willfully and directly killed. For if a child was playing in a car on a grade and accidentally caused the car to roll down the hill at a pedestrian, that would not mean that the child could be shot by another bystander simply because it was posing a material threat to the pedestrian.

2. Thomson's favorite comparison to demonstrate fetal aggression involves a world famous violinist who is hooked up to a woman that the Society of Music Lovers kidnaps and forces to remain in bed for nine months in order to use her kidneys to save his life.[12] She concludes that because the violinist is an aggressor and can be disconnected by the woman so also can the baby be "disconnected" by the mother. This is her strongest argument for the morality of abortion but in itself it is not entirely persuasive.

This comparison is flawed because the Society of Music Lovers is a deliberate and intentional aggressor against the woman, and she has a moral right to protect herself from that aggression. But a baby is not a formal and intentional aggressor as is the Society of Music Lovers. The violinist was connected to the mother by deceit and fraud without the knowledge or consent of the woman, and after having his life saved, the violinist apparently abandons the woman altogether. With the exception of rape, pregnancy does not usually involve the profound deceit or fraud her hypothetical case does. This situation is also quite unlike a mother-child relationship, for that relationship is a more enduring and complicated one. This dissimilarity calls the authenticity of this comparison into serious doubt. Just as the woman would have the right to disconnect herself and not support the violinist, Thomson contends that a woman has a right to an abortion. She asserts that the baby is an aggressor, that the burdens of pregnancy can justify abortions and that the mother is protecting her rights to her organs for which the baby is competing by abortion.

The violinist suffers from a clinically diagnosable medical treatment that apparently can only be treated by another assuming an extreme and radical burden: being immobilized for nine months. The fetus ordinarily does not suffer from a diagnosable pathological condition that requires the therapeutic "medical treatment" of abortion. Thomson compares abortion to withdrawal of medical treatment, but if abortion is comparable to any action, it would be more comparable to the woman reaching over and strangling or decapitating the violinist to whom she is connected than to withdrawal of "medical treatment."[13] Disconnecting the violinist is a withdrawal of a therapeutic treatment that is burdensome for the woman, and it is quite clear that the Society of Music Lovers or the violinist have no right to invade the woman and use her body against her will. But that does not give the woman the right to reach over and stab or poison the violinist which is morally equivalent to what a mother permits in abortion.

The physical action undertaken to remove the violinist is also quite different from the physical action of ending the life of the fetus. When the woman disconnects the violinist, she physically removes a medical treatment and her action only indirectly and remotely impinges on the violinist. But when the baby is "removed" from the mother in an abortion, the action has the unborn child as its immediate physical object and is a bloody, violent action that immediately, proximately and directly kills the child. When the unborn child suffers withdrawal of "maternal support" or the "medical treatments" given the violinist, the baby suffers horrors such as decapitation, dismemberment, saline burning or suffocation, which are not inflicted on the violinist. Not all babies would die if medical treatments like those given the violinist were withdrawn. And all fetuses would die if they were subjected to the actions Thomson calls "withdrawing maternal support" which strangely resemble butchery and savagery when done to extra-uterine life. Thomson wants these actions to be compared to "withdrawing maternal support," but that simply cannot stand and the actions used to "remove" the baby are more like brutally torturing a person to death.

By holding that abortion is a withdrawal of medical treatment which supports the baby's life, Thomson implies that a baby is a

167

pathological force in the woman, which is doubtfully the case. But when an abortion is performed the child does not die from an omission of a treatment and an underlying pathological condition, but from a death-dealing positive action, which is unlike what prevails with the violinist. Unplugging the violinist is more like disconnecting a respirator from a gravely or terminally ill patient. But this is not what happens to an unborn child, for ordinarily such children can live indefinitely with "maternal support." The unborn child usually does not need "medical treatment" to continue growing. Rather, what the child usually needs are measures that can be more properly classified as "normal care," and for the mother to refrain from certainly lethal positive actions.[14]

Interestingly, she holds that the woman should be allowed to kill the child if it poses a lethal threat to her, but she will not let the child have the mother killed if she poses a threat to the baby.[15] Thomson does not allow the converse to apply, for it is doubtful that she would allow the mother to be killed if the child's head could not pass through the birth canal. Thomson also justifies abortion by asserting that the child dies from removal of "maternal support" which she compares to removing the "medical treatments" from the mother.[16] One must wonder about this comparison, for if abortion is simply comparable to withdrawing support like that given the violinist, why is there such controversy about that even though hardly anyone would object to the woman's action with the violinist?

3. She draws a number of other comparisons to argue that the baby is an aggressor that can be killed by the mother. She contends, for example, that pregnancy is analogous to that of a housewife finding her home inundated with "people-seeds" which enter her home when she opens her windows.[17] Just as the woman would be morally permissible to sweep them away as unwanted aggressors, she asserts that a woman would be justified in removing the unborn child as an unjust aggressor against her.

This is not a terribly apt comparison for it implies that this poor housewife had no role whatsoever in the entrance of the "people-seeds" into her house, which is quite different from a woman who becomes pregnant by engaging in intercourse. This example also implies that the baby has a hostile intention and has willfully imposed itself on the woman when it was free not to do so, both of which are not true.

168

4. She also compares pregnancy to a woman who is trapped in a house with a baby who is growing so rapidly that it will kill her if she does not kill it, and she concludes that the woman could kill the baby in self-defense.[18] But a little reflection about this example would make one wonder if Thomson really believes this argument. If the baby was threatened by a rapidly growing mother in a small house, would she not permit the baby to kill the mother, and thus she would deny the baby rights she would accord to the mother. If the woman would be permitted to kill the child, would it be permissible for the child to have the mother killed if the child were to be threatened by her in morally similar circumstances? She bolsters her contention by claiming that to deny the woman the right to abort would be to deprive her of the rights of a person that are being imputed to the fetus.[19]

Thomson fails to see that the baby itself can pose no deliberate and formal threat to the mother, and for equity to prevail, the mother should pose no threats to the baby. The condition of pregnancy poses threats to both, and she permits the mother to kill the baby in such a situation but does not allow the mother to be killed in order to save the baby. Most of the threats to the mother come from defects in her that are made present in the pregnant condition, and there is no way to eliminate that condition without directly killing either the mother or the baby.

I would suggest there is a better example than this one of the moral structure of the pregnancy relationship in the comparison of a woman and a baby trapped in a house that is falling in on them. Just as it would be unjust to kill the baby because the house is collapsing, I would suggest that it would be unjust to kill the baby when a woman's life is threatened by pregnancy. This is what it is like when the mother's life is threatened by pregnancy, for it is not the baby who is the threat to her but her inability to deal with the pregnancy that is the true threat to her health.

5. Thomson compares the condition of pregnancy to that of a woman whose bedroom is invaded by a burglar who sneaks through the bars put in place by the woman.[20] And just as a woman would have a right to slay such a burglar, she also asserts that a woman would have a right to slay an unborn child. The difference between these two cases, however, is quite great, for the burglar is obviously intending to harm the woman, in a free, direct, deliberate, willful and

knowledgeable manner. However, the unborn child does not intend such harm against the mother.

But she denies that one could kill an innocent person who inadvertently stumbled through bars into the woman's bedroom.[21] Thus, she affirms that the woman's right to kill intruders depends on whether the one who intruded upon the woman was guilty (the burglar) or was innocent (the innocent bumbler). This would seem to confirm that a woman would not have the right to abort an unplanned and unexpected pregnancy. But one would wish to extend this comparison and ask if it would be legitimate to kill an innocent person who was forced through the bars of a woman's bedroom by an aggressor? I suspect she would say that one could not kill such a person because the person is the victim of the aggressor as is the woman. Her judgments about this would argue against her justifications of abortion unless she could conclusively show that the fetus was a formal aggressor. Another difference is that the woman has only imposed a partial barrier to the burglar, for she could take further measures to protect herself. This case is much like a woman who has sexual relations while using contraceptives, for she too could take further measures to protect herself from pregnancy, namely abstinence.

6. She claims that the baby and mother are like Smith and Jones fighting for the same overcoat in freezing weather.[22] This view assumes that if either Jones or Smith gain the coat the other will die if they do not acquire the overcoat, and that does not necessarily apply to abortion. Thomson hints that Smith or Jones are morally permitted to directly kill each other to possess the coat, but this is not true, for one cannot directly kill an individual not guilty of formal aggression to save one's life. Similarly, the mother is not permitted to directly kill the unborn child if she should find herself in some situation comparable to that of Smith and Jones.

Abortion is also justified by Thomson because the mother and the baby compete for maternal organs.[23] She contends that the maternal organs are the mother's property and the baby is an unjust claimant to these organs.[24] But this view fails to see that the maternal organs are also the rightful temporary possession of the fetus. They are ordered not only to supporting the life of the mother but also the life of the baby for at least a temporary period of time. It is not always and everywhere true that the mother will certainly die if baby is allowed to "possess the maternal organs."

There are instances where the baby's life can be ended in such situations, not as the set purpose of one's act but as an incidental outcome of one's attempts to save the life of the mother. If fetal use of some maternal organs constitutes a proximate threat to the mother's life, such as if the conceptus lodged in the Fallopian tube, measures could be taken to save the mother that might indirectly threaten the life of the fetus. But this would be different from the killing of the baby that Thomson endorses because the baby is a material threat to the mother.

B. Burdens and Responsible Samaritanism

One of the central arguments made in behalf of the morality of abortion made by Thomson is that the burdens imposed on the mother by the baby warrant abortion in many circumstances. The most serious difficulty with this claim is that making pregnancy a burden that warrants deliberately killing would allow deliberate destruction of innocent human life in many other circumstances that are more burdensome than pregnancy. For example, if the burdens imposed by pregnancy on a woman warrant deliberate killing, it would seem that the burdens imposed by a handicapped child on parents would give even greater justification for abortion. Contrary to this, if a pregnancy does not threaten the life of a woman, its burdens would not be greater than those imposed on a mother over the long term by a handicapped child, and just as we do not permit a mother to kill her child simply because it is handicapped, we should not permit a woman to kill her unborn child simply because she is pregnant.

Thomson argues that the mother has a right to end the life of the child because the rights of the mother prevail as she did not consent to the presence of the child.[25] But if the mother did not consent to the presence of the child, why then did she consent to intercourse? The difficulty with this claim is that the unwanted burdens imposed on the mother are not the result of free decisions or actions of the child. They are more a result of her decision to engage in an act that "risks" pregnancy than they are the result of anything done by the fetus, and it would be unfair to kill the child because of a decision of the mother. Thomson implies that difficulties suffered by the mother are the result of fetal action, but the medical reality seems to be that many of these difficulties are a consequence of the pregnant condition, and the mother and child suffer equally from those difficulties. For if a mother is medically threatened by a pregnancy, the child is equally threatened with death or impairment.

Thomson claims that abortion is permitted because the right of the mother to be free of burdens is violated by the baby.[26] However, if the baby imposes burdens on the mother, it is not by a choice of the fetus, but rather by the mother, and bringing death on the child because of a choice of the mother would be unfair to the fetus. A rapist might intend such harm, and that would give the woman the right to kill a rapist, but such an action would not be justified against an unborn child. Thomson implies that the burdens suffered by a woman are the result of malicious actions of the baby which provide a right to lethal action, but this cannot be universally attributed to the fetus. She seems to be unable to conceive of a situation where the baby could impose unintentional burdens on the mother, without violating her rights—which is what happens in most pregnancies. Her claim is also weakened because she does not compare the burdens of pregnancy with its benefits. For example, what if it was known that the child would receive a fortune which would be put at the disposal of the woman if the child was born? What this points out is that the burdens of pregnancy must be weighed against other benefits before pregnancy can be judged intolerably burdensome.

A further difficulty with claiming that burdens justify abortion is that the burdens of pregnancy increase as the pregnancy develops, which means that the greater the justification for abortion, the fuller a person (to use Thomson's categories) it is who is killed. There are fewer burdens, and hence less justification, for early abortion, but the greater justification for a late abortion is offset by the "fuller personhood" and greater harm done by such an abortion. With an early abortion, there is less harm done because, according to her there is less of a person there, but there are also fewer burdens to bear. Arguing that burdens justify abortion is more complicated than Thomson admits.

Thomson asserts that opposition to abortion is unjustified because it requires a woman to be not just a "minimally decent" or "good" Samaritan to the unborn child, but a "splendid" Samaritan to the child.[27] She contends that most people are only required by justice to be minimally decent Samaritans and only suffer ordinary burdens to protect the life of the unborn, but she holds that the woman is obliged to tolerate extreme burdens for the child.[28] This demand requires the woman take measures above and beyond what is required of others to preserve life to protect the life of the child, and that bearing up under ordinary burdens or trials is not sufficient for a pregnant woman. This misrepresents the requirement to refrain from deliberately lethal acts, for that principle merely contends that all agents, irrespective of their physical proximity to others, must refrain from such choices and actions.

Thomson's theory that burdens make abortion morally permissible is also flawed because it is discriminatory and allows poorer women to have abortions where wealthier women could not because the burden of a pregnancy on a poorer woman would be greater than on wealthier women. She would probably deny this, but the fact is that the wealthy have more means to cope with a pregnancy than do the poor, and this would bias judgments in behalf of abortions for the poor because it is more of a burden on them. She might deny this conclusion, but it seems inescapable.

According to Thomson, the reason why a woman is forbidden to abort is because she is more physically proximate to the child and therefore has greater obligations to save its life.[29] But this misrepresents our obligations to preserve life, for that principle only holds that all agents must refrain from deliberate, free positive choices to end innocent life. Thomson fails to see that the strength of one's duties to refrain from abortion is not based on one's proximity to the agent, but on the obligation to refrain from directly taking life.

Moral judgments concerning abortion do not so much involve questions about burden as they do refraining from taking directly lethal action. But the classical morality never obliged the woman to be deliberately killed to save the life of the child. The mother was never required to submit to all therapeutic actions beneficial to the baby if these actions would threaten her, and she can let the baby die without those treatments. If a woman found that the burdens of raising a child were too great for her, the common morality did not prohibit her from placing the child for adoption so that others more able to sustain the burdens could care for the child, even though it did prohibit her killing the child.

Thomson's analysis of burdens and abortion is unfortunate because it undermines many of the protections that could have been given to the unborn. In other sections of her discussion, she limits the mother's right to abortion, but in admitting that the burdens of pregnancy can justify abortion, she abolishes those protections in practice. The ultimate consequence of this analysis is that she generally makes the rights of the baby contingent on the needs, claims and desires of the mother. Thomson would deny this vigorously, but her theories in fact do deprive fetuses of all rights against a mother who does not consent to their presence or who finds their presence burdensome.

Conclusion

Thomson argues more effectively for the morality of abortion than do most others, but she has asserted so many reasons for permitting abortion and has raised so many questions about the traditional objections to abortion that one must ask if there are any hypothetical instances where she could not morally permit an abortion. Because she holds that (1) excessive burdens can justify abortions; (2) direct killing is not always wrong; (3) abortion is not killing but is withdrawal of nonobligatory maternal support, one must ask if there are any abortions that are clearly immoral. Her criteria for permitting abortion are quite subjective and formal, and as a result one can question if any abortions could be rejected by her as immoral. Her criteria would permit abortion when the mother did not consent to the pregnancy, and this criterion gives justification to abortion-on-demand. She seeks to present herself as only giving justification for abortion in strictly limited circumstances, but her permission for abortion when maternal consent to pregnancy has been withheld allows her to justify all abortions.

NOTES
1. Thomson, Judith Jarvis. "A Defense of Abortion," in Cohen, M., Nagel, T., and Scanlon, T., *The Rights and Wrongs of Abortion,* (Princeton: Princeton University Press, 1974) pp. 3–23; "Rights and Deaths" *Ibid.* pp. 116–128.

2. "A Defense of Abortion," p. 5.

3. "A Defense of Abortion," p. 22. Thomson disingenuously claims that she only supports "disconnecting" the child from the mother and withdrawing maternal support but not the death of the child. It is fantasy to believe that this is merely what happens in abortion, for few abortions result in a baby with viability. Disconnecting and withdrawal of maternal support mean death in reality.

4. *Ibid.* pp. 18–21.

5. *Ibid.* p. 5.

6. *Ibid.* pp. 11–12.

7. *Ibid.* pp. 7–8.

8. "Rights and Deaths," pp. 120–124.

9. *Ibid.*

10. "A Defense of Abortion," p. 16.

11. She does this by comparing the baby to a burglar, "people-seeds," or to one who is attached to a mother after kidnaping and holding her hostage. All of these comparisons imply malicious intent which is imputed to the baby by her comparisons.

12. "A Defense of Abortion," pp. 4–5.

13. She claims that abortion does not mean a right to a dead baby, and that she would not permit the woman to strangle the violinist after she disconnected herself from him, but one wonders if this sort of distinction can be realistically drawn. *Ibid.* p. 22. It is interesting that Thomson does not compare abortion to a hatchet murder or to immersing someone in acid, for there is a closer analogy to these than there is between abortion and withdrawing medical care or treatment.

14. By normal care, what is meant is what the individual would provide for himself or herself if they could, and this ordinarily means food and water, sanitary care and protection from exposure. If such care and treatment is given an unborn child and if positively lethal acts are not inflicted on it in most cases, the child will live indefinitely. See: Grisez, Germain and Boyle, Joseph, *Life and Death With Liberty and Justice*, (Notre Dame: University of Notre Dame Press, 1979) pp. 263, 292.

15. "A Defense of Abortion," pp. 5, 8–9. Thomson here discusses whether killing a baby who is a threat to a mother and whether killing a rapidly growing baby who poses a threat to a woman would be permissible and she agrees that it would be.

16. *Ibid.* p. 22. Thomson speaks only of detaching the violinist from the woman's kidneys which she analogizes to abortion, and this action is analogized to abortion, and is not a terribly fitting analogy.

17. *Ibid.* pp. 14–15.

18. *Ibid.* p. 8. Before the law, she possibly could do this, but it is not clear if this would be morally permissible as the baby is an unintentional aggressor.

19. *Ibid.* p. 8.

20. *Ibid.* pp. 14–15.

21. *Ibid.* p. 15.

22. *Ibid.* pp. 9–10. This comparison does not accurately represent the relationship of the mother to the child, for it would be more apt to say that this relationship is like Smith, who is a fully grown adult, struggling for a blanket with a baby. In a match of physical strength and skills, there is no equality or comparison between the mother and child.

23. *Ibid.* pp. 9–10.

24. *Ibid.* p. 20.

25. "A Defense of Abortion," pp. 11–14. She claims that one has no right to use the organs of one's body unless one gives that right. But is there not something of a conditional grant of use of one's body in sexual relations?

26. *Ibid.* pp. 15–18.
27. *Ibid.* pp. 18–21.
28. *Ibid.* pp. 18–21.
29. *Ibid.* p. 17.

Chapter 11

SELECTIVE TERMINATION: DOING EVIL TO ACHIEVE GOOD?

Sister Renée Mirkes, O.S.F.

It is probably true that almost every medical cure has its undesirable side effects. Drugs which effectively treat human infertility are no exception. As the *Physician's Desk Reference* (1986 ed.) cautions, one of the undesirable effects of a fertility drug treatment involving human menopausal gonadotropin (HMG, trade name: Pergonal) and human chorionic gonadotropin (HCG) is the induction of higher order multifetal pregnancies (or grand multiple gestations), i.e., one mother gestating three or more embryos. Of the

Published in *Ethics & Medics*, 14, 6 (June 1989), pp. 2–4 and 14, 7 (July 1989), pp. 1–2. Revised and printed here with permission.

estimated 20,000 U.S. women who take Pergonal annually, approximately 10% will gestate twins and 1% will gestate a higher number of conceptuses.

The principal drawback of grand multiple gestations is the pregnancy complications it creates for mother and child. Not only is the health and/or life of the mother at substantial risk, but the odds of not bringing the embryos to viability increase in direct proportion to the number of embryos being gestated. The higher the number of gestational sacs, the less likely it is that these preborn babies will ever see light of day.

This reflection will concern itself with an ethical evaluation of the procedure called selective termination which, in cases involving the gestation of triplets or more, is a medical alternative to either aborting the entire pregnancy or trying to bring the pregnancy to term. This procedure, also called selective abortion or selective reduction, is one in which usually all but two of the fetuses are directly aborted in hope that the remaining two will have a chance to grow and develop normally. The question we will address, then, is whether this treatment is an ethically acceptable medical alternative. First, though, to better appreciate the emergency nature of the situation and the moral character of the available medical options, we need to review a real case of grand multiple gestations where for one couple, what is statistically very rare became a reality.[1]

The Schellin Case

For seven years Beth and Dale Schellin were one of an increasing number of couples for whom conception was problematic. For seven years they tried to conceive a child but without success. In May of 1986, after submitting to a regimen of fertility drugs including Pergonal, Beth's pregnancy test proved positive. The Schellins's exhilaration was short-lived, however, when ultrasound revealed that Beth was gestating nine embryos.

The couple was advised to abort all but two fetuses or face the probability of losing the entire pregnancy and her own life as well. The Schellins consented to selective abortion. Shortly thereafter, during the eighth and ninth week of gestation, geneticist-gynecologist Mark I. Evans of Hutzel Hospital, Detroit, using ultrasonic visualization to guide a 20-gauge needle, injected a solution of potassium chloride into the chest cavity of each of the three living fetuses until a heart beat was no longer detectable. A week later, the same procedure was performed on three of the five remaining fetuses. At 35 weeks the two surviving male twins were delivered vaginally.

A Moral Evaluation in Light of Catholic Teaching

Although official Catholic teaching has not addressed the particular issue of selective termination in higher order multifetal pregnancies, the Church is unequivocal in its prohibition of direct abortion under *any* circumstances. Even in conflict cases when tragic consequences (e.g., loss of human lives) might be avoided by doing a morally reprehensible act (e.g., abortion), "it is never lawful, even for the gravest reasons, to do evil that good may come of it" (*Humanae Vitae* #14).

The *Declaration on Procured Abortion* reiterates this teaching. Where weighty reasons such as life of the baby and/or life and health of the mother are at risk, the Church declares that "... none of these reasons can ever objectively confer the right to dispose of another's life even when that life is only beginning" (#14).

Applying this teaching to selective termination, it is clear that the church would consider the procedure morally evil. In other words, it is morally wrong to *directly* abort innocent human life even when doing so may save the life of the mother and her babies. A good end does not justify an evil means.

This principle, that one may not do evil that good may come of it, with its Scriptural roots in Paul's exhortation to the Romans (Roms. 3:8), is true but not self-evident. Unpacking the philosophical presuppositions undergirding this principle demands a clarity regarding the relationship between personal goodness or badness and human free choice as well as the qualitative difference between physical and moral evil.

Emergency situations are effective catalysts; the degrees of goods and evils that are often at stake in the alternative solutions are brought into focus. If a good moral choice is to be made in these cases, we must answer the following: What is the difference between a moral good or evil and a physical good or evil? How do the effects of a moral evil on those who choose it differ from the effects of physical evil on those who endure it?

Physical Evil Vs. Moral Evil

A physical evil is a lack of a physical good, of an integrity or perfection which should be present in the physical make-up of things. In reference to human beings, it implies a lack of physical, psychospiritual perfection or the non-conformity to an anthropological exemplar. For example, a normal human hand has five fingers; the loss or absence of a thumb would constitute a limitation, a physical evil. Pain, blindness, insanity, mutilation, and death (none directly willed as such by the person who suffers them) are physical or ontological evils which threaten the wholeness or integral unity of a living human being.

An important factor in the discussion at hand is this: although the physical, psychospiritual perfection of a human being is threatened (e.g., mutilation, pain) or irrevocably lost (e.g., death), the physical evil is not selected for itself by human choice. Therefore, in the mere endurance or toleration of a physical evil there is no threat to personal moral goodness. It follows, then, that we do not say that a person is good or bad merely because he has four fingers or because he is insane. So, too, in the case of the decision which must be reached in grand multiple gestations, the physical deaths of mother and infants should be averted by every morally acceptable means and lamented if it cannot be avoided; still, the physical evil of death does not, in and of itself, vitiate the person's goodness or his final end, eternal life with God.

Moral evil, on the other hand, unlike physical or ontological evil, involves a disordered human act, i.e., a free, conscious choice on the part of the doer to choose evil. What is freely chosen, by virtue of the nature of a human free act, affects the moral character of the personal agent. The choice to do a physical evil as an end or means not only denies the basic good at stake but limits the goodness of the agent and, thereby, restricts human fulfillment. In other words, human free choice guarantees that the chooser becomes what he chooses. Karl Barth explains the intimate nexus between the human person and free choice when he observed that man "does what he is and is what he does."[2]

If we compare moral evil to physical evil, then, we see that with physical evil the person's moral status is unaffected, and the person who endures it bears no responsibility for the loss which occurs. With the free disordered choice of evil, however, we have quite another case. The moral status of the person is denigrated in direct proportion to the evil which is freely embraced. The constitutive character of a human act necessitates that the person (and community, if others are involved) bears responsibility for the choice. Furthermore, from a Christian perspective, we believe that each person will be judged according to the character of his free actions. In this Christian perspective, to embrace moral evil (sin) is a threat to man's final end, union with God, a God who is all good and with whom only those who are good or who have consistently chosen the good (or repented of the times they have not chosen it) can be united.

In sum, when we apply what we have discussed to the case at hand, the following conclusion can be drawn. The choice to do a moral evil (i.e., to unjustly kill one or more preborn infants) in hope of promoting the physical good of biological life (maternal and prenatal) has greater negative temporal and eternal ramifications then the choice not to do the moral evil with the chance of incurring a physical evil (i.e., the loss of maternal and prenatal lives). Make no mistake: the loss of the physical lives of mother and preborns, if it did occur, would be a great human tragedy indeed, but in that loss, the *final* end, the *ultimate* goal or good of that mother and infants is not jeopardized in the least.

Critiquing the Proportionalist Argument

Dr. Mark Evans, a pioneer in the development and use of selective termination and the doctor in the Schellin case has outlined for the professional medical community an ethical justification for what he acknowledges is a morally controversial procedure.[3] Evans admits that selective termination involves direct killing ("This option did intentionally cause the deaths of six fetuses ... "),[4] but contends that it is justified by the principle of proportionality which must be given priority in lieu of the stark choices which grand multiple gestations require.

The principle (which defines the central characteristic of all proportionalist theories) "is the source of the duty, when taking actions involving risks of harm, to balance risks and benefits so that actions have the greatest chance to cause the least harm and the most benefit to persons directly involved."[5] In other words, in order to make a moral judgment in conflict cases where a single act has both good and evil effects, one must comparatively evaluate the possible benefits and harms consequent to each choice and then choose the alternative action which will promise the most benefit or the least harm.

Proportionalists assert that, in the case of grand multiple gestations where tragic consequences will follow each of the alternative courses of action, to directly kill is a morally good choice by reason of the proportionate or good end of saving life. In other words, choosing the lesser evil of direct killing is the way to prevent the greater evil of losing the entire pregnancy.

There are several compelling arguments which reveal the invalidity of proportionalism. Because space does not allow a complete critique of this moral methodology here, we will only concentrate on two objections: its failure to recognize intrinsically evil acts and its obfuscation of the primary purpose of morality.

According to the principle of proportionality, the morality of an act is no longer determined, as it is traditionally, by its moral object, intention, and circumstances, but by the end—by a proportionate reason or good, i.e., a good which outweighs any accompanying evil or disvalue. If a proportionate good is present, an act that explicit Church teaching considers to be morally reprehensible and never to be done (e.g., direct abortion) can be performed because the consequences of the act (saving maternal and prenatal lives) outweigh the evil of abortion and thus make it morally good.

Proportionalism, then, does not admit of acts which are intrinsically evil such as procured abortion, contraception, and homosexual genital activity. In moral dilemmas, acts which are normally prohibited can be morally acceptable in the presence of a proportionate good.

182

But how can a moral theory which claims to be a coherent one, condone the doing of evil to achieve good? Proportionalism avoids this blatant inconsistency by not specifying an otherwise morally evil act as such but describing it, apart from particular circumstances, as a premoral or ontic evil. Thus, in the situation of grand multiple gestations, the choice to use selective termination would be called a premoral evil. Only if it were used without a proportionate reason (e.g., as a means of sex selection) would it become a moral evil.

Furthermore, according to the proportionalist theory, selective termination is not described in terms of what the agent is really doing but in terms of what the agent hopes to accomplish as a result of that action. Therefore, we can speak about the moral character of an act only after anticipated results are morally evaluated. Selective termination, then, would be morally acceptable if it realizes a greater proportion of good results over evil ones.

Substantial arguments against proportionalism can be raised in defense of the traditional moral theory which recognizes that the morality of an act is determined primarily by the nature of the act, i.e., the moral object, that which the moral agent intends as the *immediate* objective of the act.

First, judging the moral character of an action principally on the basis of hoped-for results is, at best, ambiguous and, at worse, an exercise in futility. Human experience proves how difficult it is to accurately predict the results or consequences that will flow from our actions, especially in the context of moral dilemmic situations.

Second, a proportionalist emphasis on hoped-for beneficial results, which we might call the ulterior purpose or intention, confuses or obfuscates the immediate intention of the agent and what the agent actually will do in the contemplated act. In the case of selective termination, for example, the reality of the action is not accurately described when we define it in terms of the ulterior purpose or intention (saving the pregnancy). It is accurately described, however, when we define it in terms of the immediate intention (to kill one or more human fetal lives). Similarly, the reality of what Dr. Evans accomplished by using selective termination is not clear when his action is described in terms of the ulterior motive, saving the pregnancy. That is only a hoped-for result. But one can say with certainty that what is accomplished or done in the act of selective termination is the killing of six human fetal lives, the immediate intention.

Third, reflection on experience reveals that there are certain kinds of acts like adultery or murder which, whenever they are performed, *always* destroy some basic human good (e.g., fidelity or life) and therefore are an assault on human fulfillment. Common human experience also helps us to grasp the truth of Kant's categorical imperative: " . . . treat humanity in oneself and others as an end and not a means." This maxim reflects the correct understanding which persons of good will are capable of comprehending: every basic human good, each of which is an aspect of humanity or personhood, must be respected in every act. Conversely, any act (e.g., selective termination) which *unjustly* directly denies or destroys a basic human good (e.g., human life) is intrinsically evil and always to be avoided.

These common sense judgments are confirmed by the natural law tradition. Writings such as those of Plato (*Gorgias*[6]) or Aristotle (*Nichomachean Ethics*[7]) conclude that human dignity demands that only acts which show an objective relationship to or respect for human goods are worthy of the human person and will fulfill human beings. Evil choices demean the human person.

Lastly, Catholic moral teaching confirms this insight regarding the nature of good and evil acts. The Ten Commandments of the Old Testament and the two great commandments of the New Testament reveal God's plan for promoting human wellbeing and prohibiting acts which are intrinsically evil, that is, acts which destroy fundamental goods. These norms direct man toward basic human goods and a proper love for self, neighbor, and God.

A second and perhaps even more fundamental flaw in the proportionalist theory of moral decision-making is that it obscures two related aspects of morality which traditional Catholic moral principles do not: human acts have both an objective and a subjective character, and the primary concern of morality is personal existential goodness. Human choice is not only a means to an end outside of itself, a means to effect or realize human goods in the concrete: human choice is also a means to becoming morally good. Human actions have both a transitive and an intransitive effect. When a person acts he not only chooses good or evil he *becomes* increasingly good or evil. Applied to selective termination in higher order multifetal pregnancies, the decision *not* to use selective termination is not only a good choice because it is a choice not to destroy a basic human good but also because, by virtue of being a good choice, it defines the agent as good. Conversely, to the extent one embraces evil in any given act, to that extent is the person deprived of his existential goodness. *Gaudium et Spes* underscores this reality when it states that acts such as abortion, euthanasia, or genocide "degrade (or harm) those who so act more than those who suffer the injury" (#27).

Conclusion

If the proportionalist concern for maximizing good effects despite an evil means is misguided from a moral perspective, what is the correct expectation? The Church is clear: remain faithful to the will of God (i.e., pursue the good and avoid the evil) and let the unforeseeable consequences to God. Actions, not overall consequences, are our primary concern. Our main responsibility as free agents is to become good by doing good. In the case of grand multiple gestations, where there are no morally good means to save the pregnancy, the humanly catastrophic results, though extremely sad, can be seen in their true light. Christian faith teaches us that morally good choices that have tragic consequences involving physical evils are not necessarily catastrophic in light of eternity. What we will be judged on by God is not how many physically good consequences we have effected or how many physical evils we have averted but how we have striven to do moral good and avoid moral evil. We must be committed to doing that which is morally right despite tragic results because God has the ultimate care of the physically good and evil consequences of our acts, and He alone can bring good out of the evil which He permits.

NOTES
1. Dan Chu, et al., "A Dramatic Medical Rescue Saves the Schellin Twins from their Mother's Nightmare Pregnancy," *People*, (May 9, 1988), pp. 51–55.
2. Karl Barth, *Church Dogmatics*, Vol. IV, (Edinburgh: T.& T. Clark, 1936–1977), p. 405.

3. Mark I. Evans, et al., "Selective First-Trimester Termination in Octuplet and Quadruplet Pregnancies: Clinical and Ethical Issues," *Obstetrics and Gynecology,* (March, 1988), pp. 289–96.

4. *Ibid,* p. 292.

5. *Ibid,* p. 295.

6. Plato, *Gorgias,* 469B, 508D.

7. Aristotle, *Nicomachean Ethics,* II, 1107a, 9–18.

PART THREE

FEMINIST ISSUES

Chapter 12

MORAL CHARACTER AND ABORTION

Janet E. Smith

Much ethical theory has recognized that the very importance of the attempt to live an ethical life lies in the fact that in acting the individual forms herself or himself either for the better or for the worse. That is, each and every human act, each act stemming from the deliberate choice of the human agent, determines the type of human being an individual is, or in other words, the kind of moral character that an individual has. Then, in turn, the moral character that one has influences what decisions one makes. For those who share this perspective, one of the foremost questions to be asked by the moral agent in the decision to do an action is: What kind of person will I become if I do this act?

Ethical reasoning of this sort is distinguished from other kinds of ethical inquiry because it focuses on the agent; it is variously known as ethics of the agent, ethics of virtue, or ethics of character. This is not to say that those who are concerned with an ethics of character are not also concerned with other means of determining the rightness or wrongness of an act. An ethics of character can be can be combined with nearly any means of evaluating an action. Yet, for an ethics of character, the question of the effect of an act upon the character of the agent is one of the primary considerations taken into account in evaluating whether or not an action is moral.

Socrates was one of the first to make the effect of an action upon moral character an essential feature of his ethical thought. In the *Gorgias* he argues that "It is better to have harm done to you, than to harm another." He argued that it is better to have another do injustice to you than to do injustice to another because one harms one's own soul through doing injustice; this is a worse harm than any suffering that one may experience at the hands of another. Aristotle, in his *Nicomachean Ethics,* stated the basic premise of an ethics of virtue in these precise terms: "For a given kind of activity produces a corresponding character. This is shown by the way in which people train themselves for any kind of contest or performance: they keep on practicing for it. Thus, only a man who is utterly insensitive can be ignorant of the fact that moral characteristics are formed by actively engaging in particular actions" (1114a).[1] In this view, an individual should avoid telling lies, for instance, not only because it harms the truth, because it harms another who deserves the truth, because it creates distrust in society, but also because in lying, the individual does harm to her or his moral character; lying serves to mold one's character in the direction of being an untrustworthy person. Aristotle also draws upon the analogy of health to explain how one can eventually develop characteristics that may not please one but for which one may be responsible. He notes that much in the same way that one who enjoys good health might gradually become ill through dissolute living, so, too, one might through a series of unjust or selfish acts gradually become an unjust and selfish person (1114a10ff.).

While few who have worked in the area of an ethics of virtue have applied this way of reasoning to specific actions, such a way of reasoning may indeed help us understand more fully why some actions are wrong. Here I shall first apply an ethics of virtue to evaluating adultery, a relatively uncontroversial action, and then I will turn to considering abortion and to evaluating its likely effects on the moral character of women.

An ethics of character assumes that there are some qualities or virtues that are beneficial for most men and women to have. Aristotle, in his study of ethics, relied enormously upon the views of the common man in drawing up the virtues or characteristics that a good person must have. Let us explore the possibility that even in our pluralistic and fragmented and politicized age a list of characteristics that most would laud as appropriate to a good human being could be compiled.

The first task must be the careful choice of words to designate the qualities or characteristics that constitute the goodness of a human being. What qualities would most agree that they would like to possess? Would not at least kindness, generosity, self-reliance, loyalty, commitment, responsibility, reliability, supportiveness, self-determination, sincerity, honesty, good-naturedness, trustworthiness, and self-discipline appear on the list of most people? Do we not also admire those who have reflected upon morality and show a concern for acting morally? We tend to admire those who can articulate and justify their reasons for their behavior and who act in accord with the moral principles they have accepted for themselves. We may observe that not many possess these qualities but we would agree that it would be good to have them. And to the question why people would want to possess these and other beneficial qualities, would not most of us say that having such qualities would enable us to function as we wish to function? That is, if we had these qualities, we would be able to accomplish what we wish to accomplish (given necessary external goods) and to have the relationships we would like to have—that is, we would be good co-workers, good friends, good spouses, and good parents. Do we not think that such individuals will make good moral decisions? We rely upon a just woman to do what is just, a generous man to do what is generous.

How do we judge who possesses these qualities? A common way of doing so is by observing how individuals act. That is, we deem some actions as generous and tend to think that those who consistently perform such actions are generous individuals. Yet, certainly it is not necessarily true that every individual who performs a certain kind of action will acquire the characteristics generally associated with the action, for character is very dependent upon the reasons given for the choice made. We may hold that individuals who perform certain actions tend to do so for typical reasons and before making a judgment we would need to determine if the individual being judged is acting for the typical reasons. The best that we can say is that *it is likely* that individuals who perform certain actions have certain characteristics. (Nonetheless, those who perform bad actions even for good reasons, may suffer some ill effect in their characters; lying for good purposes may still assist one in becoming an adept liar for bad reasons as well). If we can determine an individual's true reasons for making his or her choice, our evaluation would, of course, have greater accuracy. This is important, for it is easy to over-absolutize statements such as "adulterers are untrustworthy"; it is likely that it is so, but not certainly the case that it is so. Nor, of course, does the claim that adulterers are generally certain sorts of individuals entail that those who do not commit adultery are therefore individuals of admirable character. The reasons individuals have for not committing adultery may not be admirable ones (one may fear that one's rich spouse would cancel one's credit cards, for instance). Again, the reasons that one gives for one's action are of decisive importance.

It must also be noted that individuals are not always fully responsible for the moral character that they have. Aristotle repeatedly stresses the importance of a good upbringing for helping one form a good moral character (e.g. 1095b). For instance, individuals who as children have been raised to act responsibly and fairly are much more likely to be responsible and fair adults. Conversely, those who have been spoiled and indulged may grow up to be self-centered and greedy adults; their parents may be greatly responsible for their moral character, but the children are the ones who suffer the effects of being selfish and greedy. Society may be responsible, for instance, for a propensity of its members to be adulterers if there are no disincentives to adultery, approval of it and abundant opportunity for it.

Let us now consider how the choice to commit adultery might reveal and affect one's moral character. While there is a kind of assumption here that adultery is wrong, our foremost concern is not with proving the wrongness of adultery. Rather, our concern is to determine what are the moral characters of those who commit adultery and to answer the question if it is likely or usual for those with admirable moral characters to engage in adultery. If it is true, however, that adulterers can be said to have undesirable moral characteristics and/or that they are forming undesirable moral characters through their choice to commit adultery, this would be taken as an indication at least—though hardly a proof—that adultery is a morally bad action.

For an analysis in accord with an ethics of virtue, answers to the following questions would be useful: What sort of people generally commit adultery? Are they, for instance, honest, temperate, kind, etc.? What sorts of reasons do they give for the actions that they choose? How do they assess their action? Do they understand themselves to be doing something moral or immoral with their choice? Why do adulterers choose to have sex with people other than their spouses? Are their reasons selfish or unselfish ones? Do they seem to speak of their reasons for their choice honestly or do they seem to be rationalizing? What sort of lives have they been leading prior to the action that they choose; are they the sorts of lives that exhibit the characteristics we admire?

Let us suppose that the ethicist might be able to make some generalizations about adulterers. He or she might observe that most who commit adultery are experiencing some difficulties in their marriages. Probably few enter marriage with the intention of committing adultery. They would find such an intention contrary to their commitment to their spouse. Most acts of adultery are most likely the result of a series of dissatisfactions, a series of choices, a series of "separations" from the marital relationship. Yet, given two individuals, both equally dissatisfied with their marriages, one who refuses to engage in adultery and the other who so chooses, the act of adultery by one signifies that he is a different "sort" of person than the other. Thus the individual's response to an opportunity for infidelity would suggest much about the person's character prior to the choice for or against adultery, and, perhaps, also gives some indication of the direction of the person's life after the choice.

It would also be valuable to know how adultery has affected the marriage of the adulterer, his or her relation to his or her children and other family members, his or her relations with co-workers, etc. We would be interested to learn if adulterers drank more, cheated on the job more, were estranged from their families. If we discovered that their lives showed such disarray, we may be able to conclude that these difficulties were connected with and grew out of certain qualities and were reinforced by the decision to commit adultery.

Even those who think it is a moral choice on occasion may well agree that adulterers usually are not the finest of individuals. Indeed, those who think that adultery is a moral choice in some circumstances—unless they are complete nihilists—would still observe that suitable reasons must be given to justify committing adultery. Thus, although some might not feel comfortable saying that all adulterers are liars and unkind and unreliable, most may agree that some true generalizations could be made about adulterers that would lead us to think that in general adultery is not compatible with the moral virtues that we admire. The reaction of the American public to the extra-marital affairs of Jim Bakker and Gary Hart reveal well the wide-spread view that lying predictably accompanies the act of adultery and that adulterers are not to be trusted. Certainly, if someone told us that he or she wanted to be an honest, trustworthy, stable and kind individual with good family relationships, and wanted to know if an adulterous affair would conflict with this goal, we would have little hesitation in advising against adultery.

The judgments that we make about an adulterer's character are made without scientific studies about adulterous individuals. We come to these conclusions, it seems, from the moral lessons of our youth, from novels we have read, from experience with the adulterers we have known. Certainly, we may encounter those who think adulterers are fun-loving, life-embracing, and generous. With those who do not share our analysis of the character of adulterers, we would be interested in comparing the reasons for the differing judgments. But an ethics of character depends upon such judgments. It requires us to draw upon whatever information we have that will help us to judge human character and the effect of human actions upon human character.

There is quite a remarkable amount of information available about women who have had abortions;[2] perhaps no other moral action is as well documented from the perspective of the experience of the agent. The value of reading this material for one who wishes to get an idea of what enters into the abortion decision and the abortion experience is inestimable. Nearly all of this material has been compiled and evaluated by those who find abortion to be morally permissible, and thus, if it is biased in any way, it is biased in the direction of portraying abortion as a good action.[3] Let me acknowledge my position on abortion, for admittedly this may introduce some bias into my interpretation. I consider abortion to be an intrinsically wrong action. Because there is no need to develop a complete argument here, suffice it to say that it is my judgment that abortion involves the taking of an innocent human life. But what I wish to demonstrate here is that abortion does serious harm not only to the unborn child, but to the woman herself, in her formation of her moral character.

One does not need to hold that abortion is intrinsically wrong to see that it may harm a woman's moral character. It is the judgment of this author that by and large many, even those who find abortion morally permissible, would be disturbed by the quality of the moral character of the women having abortions and by the moral reasoning that informs the abortion decision. More precisely, I wish to show that the reasons that many women give for their abortion decisions are not reasons that most would find admirable or acceptable, again, even those who consider abortion morally permissible. The following discussion hopes to show that the choice for abortion is not often, if ever, compatible with the list given above of those qualities that most of us admire and would like to have. Finally, I would also like to note that it is not only women who suffer harm to their moral characters through abortion. If the analysis given here is correct, the men involved, the doctors and the medical staff involved, those advising the women all risk great damage to their moral character.[4] And indeed, the community itself may be most responsible for the harm done, for it permits abortion and has had a role in forming the character of the individuals who perform such actions, and it may suffer through being a community that does not provide for women in need, through not fostering a proper respect for life.[5] The focus here, though, is on the woman for she is most directly involved.

What are the features of the lives of women who have abortions that may be revealing of their moral character? What kinds of reasons do they give for their abortions? Studies give some indication of how some women view their decision to abort. Interviews with women who have had abortions provide a fairly full picture of the lives of women who have abortions and the quality of their abortion decision. They show that women who have abortions are involved in relationships that are not prepared for the eventuality of a child; they show that many, if not most, of the women who abort were pregnant not by "accident," but by some kind of calculated choice; and they also show that many of the women believe that they are taking a human life when they abort. Let us look at some of the evidence that supports these claims.

Upon reading the testimonies of many women who had abortions, Stanley Hauerwas observed,

> . . . I am impressed that in spite of the hundreds of articles published defending or opposed to abortion, the way people decide to have or not to have an abortion rarely seems to involve the issues discussed in those articles. People contemplating abortion do not ask if the fetus has a right to life, or when does life begin, or even if abortion is right or wrong. Rather, the decision seems to turn primarily on the quality of the relationship (or lack of relationship) between the couple.[6]

The quality of the relationship that exists between the couple is, as Hauerwas notes, frequently the key to the abortion decision. The one characteristic that is nearly universal among women deciding to have abortions is that they are engaged in relationships that are not conducive to raising a child. Perhaps it is obvious that most of the women who have abortions are unwed, some of the married women are pregnant by men other than their husbands, and many who are married regularly speak of troubled marriages that they fear cannot sustain a child or another child. Those who are unwed have quite clearly been involved in relationships that, although sexual, were not strong enough to accommodate a child conceived by the sexual union. Since the women having abortions have usually been involved in relationships not designed to accommodate all the responsibilities it may engender, perhaps it is fair to say that they display a significant amount of irresponsibility.

Nor do the relationships in which the women are involved seem to offer them much support as they face their pregnancies. Some women never inform the father of the child of the pregnancy. Those who do tell the male involved do not seem really to involve him and his wishes in the decision-making process, they simply inform him of their decision.[7] That most of the women make their decisions without giving full weight to the view of the male, supports the observation that these were not stable and satisfying relationships—for the sense of mutually sharing one's life and decision seems not to have been present in these relationships.

Moreover, the fact that over half acted without the agreement of the men involved indicates troubled relationships. One researcher, Linda Bird Francke, tells us that in her research almost every relationship between single people broke up either before or after the abortion.[8] Although Francke mentions one study which showed that in marital relationships, the abortion was a positive act, this study was done only six months after the abortion.[9] Most of the statements taken from married women speak of resentment towards the husband. Thus, the relationships of women who have abortions seem characterized by instability, poor communication, and lack of true mutuality. Again, those involved in such relationships seem to be characterized by irresponsibility, and confusion about what they really want—which results in them being dishonest both with themselves and with their partners.

This charge of "irresponsibility" finds support in the contraceptive practices of these women (and the men with whom they are involved), for not only do the women engage in acts that have possible consequences for which they are not prepared but they also do not seem to be willing to take the steps necessary to prevent the occurrence of a situation for which they are not prepared to be responsible. Studies show that the women having abortions are not ignorant of birth control methods; the great majority are experienced contraceptors but, as Zimmerman observed, they display carelessness and indifference in their use of contraception.[10]

Moreover, the failure to use birth control indicates some other characteristics of the women having abortions. There are, of course, many subtle psychological reasons for failing to use contraceptives. Zimmerman reports on the many different reasons that women give: these include such reasons as a break-up in the relationship that seemed to signal that contraceptives would not be needed, a dislike for the physical exam required for the pill, a dislike of the side-effects, inconvenience or difficulty in getting the pills. Zimmerman observes that many unmarried women do not like to think of themselves as sexually active and that using contraceptives conflicts with their preferred self-image.[11] The failure to use birth control is a sign that many women are not comfortable with being sexually active. That is, many of the women are engaged in an activity that, for some reason, they do not wish to admit to themselves. These women seem not to have much self-knowledge, nor do they seem to be self-determining—they seem to be "letting things happen" that, were they reflective and responsible individuals, they may not accept as actions for themselves.

Kristin Luker in an earlier book *Taking Chances: Abortion and the Decision not to Contracept* attempted to discover why, with contraceptives so widely available, so many women, virtually all knowledgeable about contraception, had unwanted pregnancies and abortions. The conclusions of Luker's studies suggest that it is not simple "carelessness" or "irresponsibility" that lead women to have abortions, but that frequently the pregnancies that are aborted are planned or the result of a calculated risk. She begins by dismissing some of the commonly held views about why women get abortions; she denies that they are usually had by panic-stricken youngsters or that they are had by unmarried women who would otherwise have had illegitimate births. She also maintains that statistics do not show that abortion is a last ditch effort used by poor women and "welfare mothers" or that abortion is often sought by women who have more children than they can handle. What she attempts to discern is what *reason* women had for not using contraception although they were contraceptively experienced and knew the risks involved in not using contraception.[12] Luker seeks to substantiate in her study that "unwanted pregnancy is the end result of an informed decision-making process; and more important, that this process is a rational one, in which women use means appropriate to their goals. That pregnancy occurred anyway, for the women in this study, is because most of them were attempting to achieve more diffuse goals than simply preventing pregnancy."[13]

Luker argues that for these women (women who are having non-contraceptive sex, but who are not intending to have babies), using contraceptives has certain "costs" and getting pregnant has certain "benefits." The women make a calculation that the benefits of not using contraception and the benefits of a pregnancy outweigh the risks of getting pregnant and the need to have an abortion. Luker's analysis of the "costs" of using contraception parallels closely that of Zimmerman. She concurs that many women prefer "sponta-neous sex" and do not like thinking of themselves as "sexually ac-tive." She notes that some wondered whether or not they were fertile and thus did not take contraceptives.[14] The "benefits" of a pregnancy for many women were many; pregnancy "proved that one is a woman,"[15] or that one is fertile;[16] it provides an excuse for "forc-ing a definition in the relationship";[17] it forces her parents to deal with her";[18] it is used as a "psychological organizing technique."

In a later chapter Luker analyzes more "contextually" the rea-sons that women have for risk-taking with non-contraceptive sex. Her analysis focuses on pregnancy as a means of forcing marriage in a "depressed marriage market."[19] She insists that she is not suggest-ing that "because women are at a competitive disadvantage in the marriage market that they then go out and become pregnant in or-der to get married; few women are that calculating or naive. On the contrary, . . . when women are at a competitive disadvantage, contra-ceptive risk-taking has a socially induced halo of functionality sur-rounding it, a halo of which women are often only subliminally aware."[20] Ultimately, what she seems to be saying is that women do not calculatingly or naively become pregnant to force marriage, but that "forcing marriage" is one pressure that combines with others to lead a women to risk pregnancy.[21] It is also pertinent to note that almost all of the unmarried women she interviewed had the option to marry (and supposedly to complete the pregnancy) but that none chose this option. Luke attributes this to their unwillingness to get married under such conditions, to the disparity between this kind of marriage and their fantasy marriage, and to their belief that they, not the male, were responsible for the pregnancy, and thus they had no claim on his support.[22]

As noted, Luker argues that these women are rational in their risk-taking, in their not using contraception although they did not in-tend a pregnancy. She maintains that though it is not often an explicit or articulated calculation, that the women weighed the costs of us-ing contraception against the costs and benefits of a pregnancy. One of her examples is of an unmarried woman who did not like using the pill because it made her gain weight. Coupled with this was her wish to force her boyfriend to openly admit his relationship with her to his parents who rejected her, and possibly to force marriage, and thus she decided not to use contraception.[23] Luker considers this a "rational" decision because the woman had determined certain means to achieve her end. Luker further evaluates these decisions as "rational" because the women assigned low "probabilities" to getting pregnant; they thought pregnancy was unlikely to happen to them.[24] Luker compares this to people who smoke and discount the possibility that they might get cancer. Moreover, she notes that those who "get away" with taking risks tend to continue in that behavior; thus, since women can go a long time without getting pregnant, they tend to think they are "safe."[25] Though the aftermath of these decisions—the fact that all the women she interviewed had abortions—led many of the women to characterize their own previous behavior as irrational (an evaluation shared by those doctors, nurses, etc. with whom they came in contact), Luker argues that their decisions were "reasonable " "under the circumstances."[26]

It seems fair to call Luker's evaluation into question. First let it be noted that Luker was not attempting to evaluate the moral character of these women or to assess the morality of their decision to have an abortion. Luker's primary concern was to show that women had *reasons* for not using contraception, reasons that, evaluated in terms of the risks involved, were justifiable. On the basis of this claim, she undertook to argue that more and better access to contraception would not stem unwanted pregnancies; she advised greater access to abortion. Luker, though, stretches to the point of unrecognizability the word "rational." "Rational" more properly refers to behavior that is reflective, based upon clearly articulated judgments in accord with the facts of a situation, and one well-designed to achieve one's end. Luker, in spite of her intentions, depicts these women as taking risks on the basis of ill-defined and unarticulated reasons and pressures, risks that seemed ill-suited to achieve the desired ends. Luker makes no attempt to discern if the women explored other means to the ends that they desired. She never questions, for instance, if it is an intelligent decision for a young woman to get pregnant and have an abortion for the sake of having her family take notice of her, or for the sake of proving her fertility to herself, or for the sake of learning if her boyfriend cares about her.

Furthermore, a usual criterion for a good and rational moral decision (or any decision, for that matter) is that the decision be a fully informed one. Few of the interviews of women having abortions give any indication that the women were fully aware of the size and development of the fetus they were carrying, that they knew the risks to their reproductive capacities or to their emotional health.[27] Many knew little enough about the procedure of abortion itself.

Luker does not write with the purpose of explaining why women have abortions, but her study is most revealing of the reasons why women have abortions. Her study leads this interpreter to judge that these women were not adept at determining how to solve the problems that their lives presented them and that they did not realistically evaluate their relationships and their own expectations for these relationships. Despite Luker's claim to the contrary, I believe that Luker's study supports the claim that many if not most of the women who choose abortion are irresponsible, and to some extent irrational.[28]

Women may get pregnant for a variety of reasons, but the most common reason for having an abortion is that the women are not prepared for the responsibilities of a baby. Again, most are not prepared because they are not married to and not intending to marry the man who impregnated them. It must also be noted that although these women were not prepared to have a child, many reluctantly have abortions. Many state that they felt pressured into having the abortion either because they feared or knew that their parents would reject them, that their boyfriends or husbands would leave them, or because their friends and co-workers thought abortion was the responsible choice for them. This indicates that for many women the decision to abort was only weakly self-determined; they were very much pressured by their situation and their "advisors" to have the abortion. Gilligan, who studied abortion from the perspective of moral development, maintains that women have been socialized not to make choices for themselves, not to take responsibility for their choices.[29] Again, women may not be responsible for the moral characters that they have, but the evidence seems to suggest that the decision to abort is one that women often wish to attribute not to their own values, but to the pressure that others have put upon them. Insofar as making choices in accord with one's own values is indicative of a good moral character, many women who abort seem devoid of this power—whatever the reason for their lacking this power.

One notable recurrent feature found in the interviews of women who have had abortions is the acknowledgement by the women of their belief that they are taking a human life when they have an abortion.[30] Certainly, some claim that they are not taking a life; for instance, a young woman named Chris felt this way: " ... I was talking to the pastor who helped me to get here and he asked me what my conception of life was. And I said, well, I suppose you know just right off the bat the baby is born, you pat it on the back, and it starts breathing. That's life to me. But before then it's nothing. Kind of like a growth."[31] But many others think differently. Consider these statements taken from different sources; seventeen year old Dawn, who decided to have an abortion because she was not emotionally ready to have a baby, admitted, "Well, it's [abortion] killing all the way through, but—um—I'm all mixed up about this. I think it's just killing all the way through."[32] Maria speaks of her second abortion, "This time I hoped the baby was a boy and that I could keep it. My husband and I discussed it and discussed it. We had to convince ourselves to have the abortion. It makes it much harder when you already have a child. You realize it's a wonderful thing to go through a pregnancy and then have a baby dependent on you. This time I couldn't help thinking it was a human being, a living being."[33] Sandra asserts, "I have always thought abortion was a fancy word for murder."[34] Sandra commented on her abortion: "I am saying that abortion is morally wrong, but the situation is right, and I am going to do it."[35] One interviewer, Zimmerman, found that most women who had abortions, prior to their abortion did not approve of abortion except for specific situations—and these situations did not include the situation in which they found themselves. On the basis of her research she observed,

> In summary, the prior abortion attitudes of the women studied here indicate that abortion is considered acceptable only under specific circumstances. The majority of the women would be likely to disapprove an abortion unless the woman had been raped, or unless she had health problems relating to her pregnancy, or unless she were financially unable to take care of a baby. Interestingly, their own abortions did not always fall within these circumstances.... Many of the women claimed that they had approved of abortion but then later qualified that statement

202

by saying, "But I never thought I would have one myself" or "It's the lesser of two evils." None of the women stated their approval without some qualifying remark. The fact that most of these women did not appear to enter into their abortion experience with complete and unqualified approval of abortion is certainly noteworthy.[36]

Zimmerman maintained that the women themselves evaluated their own choice as a form of deviance.[37] Their feeling that they were "treading on thin moral ice" led women to be secretive about their abortions so they would not risk being morally challenged about their abortions.[38]

A pattern seems to emerge here. These testimonies suggest that women who are having abortions are not living in accord with some of the most important values they hold. They themselves frequently, if not usually, characterize abortion and indeed their own decision as taking a human life. Although the women do not generally approve of abortion, they make exceptions for themselves. It seems that the reasons that many women give for their abortion decisions are not reasons that most would find admirable or acceptable, even those who consider abortion morally permissible, even those who are having abortions. If, then, it is a virtue to act in accord with one's principles, many of the women having abortions seem not to have this virtue and are acting in a way that will not advance their possession of it.

The analysis here has been based upon a reading of the testimonies of women who have had abortions, testimony gathered almost exclusively by those who themselves believe abortion to be morally permissible. Most if not all of the interviewers would consider themselves to be feminists. Most believe that through exercising control over their fertility, women who have abortions are acquiring virtues or characteristics once associated only with men. Most of those who subscribe to the values of feminism tend to judge the women who choose abortion to be acquiring some admirable characteristics such as self-assertiveness, rational control over their lives, independence. Still, Sidney Callahan, who considers herself a "pro-life feminist," argues that abortion violates the deeper values of feminism, that is, fosters characteristics that are desirable neither for men nor women.

Callahan's argument has many parts. She states that feminists are dedicated to fighting for the rights of the oppressed; that they are interested in equality and due process and fairness; she maintains that it is inconsistent for feminists, then, to deny the unborn child the right to life, to use the power of technology to kill the innocent and defenseless. She argues that feminists should not adopt the value of individual autonomy with its emphasis on complete control over one's life, a control and autonomy that rejects the responsibilities that come with an unplanned pregnancy. She maintains that being a part of the human family, being a woman, brings with it certain responsibilities that ought to be accepted whether or not freely chosen, whether or not convenient. But what is most important to the thesis here is her observation that there is a general chaos in the lives of many, if not most, of the lives of women who have abortions and a real confusion about the place of sexuality in their lives, about the connection between characteristics that are valuable in one's professional life and in one's personal life. She states:

> ... many pro-choice feminists preach their own double standard. In the world of work and career, women are urged to grow up, to display mature self-discipline and self-control; they are told to persevere in long-term commitments, to cope with unexpected obstacles by learning to tough out the inevitable sufferings and setbacks entailed in life and work. But this mature ethics of commitment and self-discipline, recommended as the only way to progress in the world of work and personal achievement, is discounted in the domain of sexuality.... Responsibly choosing an abortion supposedly ensures that a young woman will take charge of her own life, make her own decisions, and carefully practice contraception. But the social dynamics of a permissive erotic model of sexuality, coupled with permissive laws, work toward repeat abortions. Instead of being empowered by their abortion choices, young women having abortions are confronting the debilitating reality of *not* bringing a baby into the world; not being able to count on a committed male partner; *not* accounting oneself strong enough, or the master of enough resources, to avoid killing the fetus. Young women are hardly going to develop the

self-esteem, self-discipline, and self-confidence necessary to confront a male-dominated society through abortion.[39]

In terms used here, these women do not exhibit much virtue, much moral strength, nor does their choice to abort appear to be an act that will further their virtue or moral strength. A list of moral characteristics was tentatively offered earlier in this paper to provide a base upon which an analysis of action in terms of virtue could proceed. The claim was made that we all would want to have these characteristics and we would want those we associate with to have them, too. The list included kindness, generosity, self-reliance, loyalty, commitment, responsibility, reliability, supportiveness, self-determination, sincerity, honesty, good-naturedness, trustworthiness, and self-discipline. The interviews of women who choose to have abortions indicate that they could not be described in these terms.

Finally let us note, that though there is not a great deal of documentation on how women fare after their abortion, what little evidence there is suggests that it is not an overwhelmingly positive experience.[40] Indeed, nearly one third of abortions are repeat abortions. It would seem that many of these women, at least, return much to the same life that they were leading prior to their abortions. By their own testimony many of the women who were not promiscuous before the abortion become so afterwards; most have difficulty sustaining long term relationships with a male. Most women maintain that relief is the immediate outcome of an abortion though most speak of some depression and confusion afterwards. The conclusions of the psychological studies of those who have had abortions are remarkably mixed. Before the legalization of abortion several studies showed that abortion was traumatic for women. After the legalization of abortion, most studies show that few women suffer little long-term psychological consequences. The validity of these studies has been called into question in terms of their scientific reliability. Certainly the conclusions may also be affected by a bias produced by an ideological commitment to abortion rights.

It is well documented that some women come to regret their abortions and suffer severe trauma after the abortion. They regularly speak of feeling that they were pressured into the abortion. They speak of their confusion at the time of the abortion, their troubled relationships with family and boyfriend; they tell of their suicidal desires, their alienation and loneliness after the abortion. Several groups have been formed to assist women who have come to regret their abortions; Women Exploited by Abortion and Victims of Abortion are both such groups. One author describing women who have had abortions tells that even those who have come to terms with their regret " . . . will tell you that their decision-making skills are damaged, that self-doubt has become the common denominator of their personalities. After all, they made one terrible mistake. When will they stumble into the next?"[41] Women who regret their abortions believe that there are millions of women "out there" who are "broken" and agonizing inside about their abortions, that they are in a state of deep denial about their feelings about their abortions.

Information about the psychological aftermath of abortion should assist us in determining the moral character of women after the abortion. Certainly, some psychological weaknesses or strengths are closely connected with moral character. High self-esteem may assist one in having the confidence and presence of mind to take into account all factors in a situation and to make a good decision. It may enable one to resist undue pressure from others and it may keep one free from debilitating fears that could lead one to act out of cowardice. Indeed, high self-esteem may be connected with how one assesses one's own moral character; those who believe themselves to be morally good may have greater self-esteem. Depression could lead one to be unable to meet one's commitments and obligations and lead to moral failure as a reliable and dependable person. But until the studies done on the psychological aftermath of abortion are standardized and attain a higher degree of reliability, most judgments will continue to be made on the basis of more randomly acquired testimony. This testimony, I submit, suggests that many women exhibit characteristics after their abortion experience that make it difficult for them to advance in moral strength.

An ethics of virtue assesses actions by the type of character that produces and chooses these actions. Abortion, in the eyes of this interpreter, does not fare well as a moral action, according to this analysis. Those seeking to assess the morality of abortion, those seeking to find some ground for discussion and understanding about the morality of abortion, other than the question of a conflict of rights,

206

would do well to ponder what kind of moral judgment goes into choosing an abortion, and what kind of moral character results from an abortion.

NOTES

1. Aristotle, *Nicomachean Ethics* trans. by Martin Ostwald (Indianapolis: 1962) 66.

2. See, Magda Denes, *In Necessity and Sorrow* (New York: 1976); Linda Bird Francke, *The Ambivalence of Abortion,* (New York: 1978); Carol Gilligan, *In a Different Voice* (Cambridge, Mass.: 1982); Nona Lyons, "Two Perspectives: On Self, Relationships, and Morality", *Harvard Educational Review,* 53:2 (1983): 125–145; Judith G. Smetana, *Concepts of Self and Morality* (New York: 1982) and Mary K. Zimmerman, *Passage Through Abortion* (New York: 1977). Some "reinterpreting" of several of these texts cited has been done by James Tunstead Burtchaell, *Rachel Weeping and Other Essays on Abortion* (Kansas City: 1982) 1–60. For a full and up-to-date accounting of the consequences of the decision to abort by one who is opposed to abortion, see the extensive study done by David C. Reardon, *Aborted Women: Silent No More* (Westchester, Illinois: 1987). He interviews only those who regret their abortions, but his findings do not diverge significantly from studies done by those who believe abortion to be moral.

3. I have done a fairly extensive critique of Carol Gilligan's studies of women who have had abortions. This critique attempted to show that her proabortion views skewed her interpretation to interviews of women who had abortions; *International Philosophical Quarterly* 28:1 (March 1988) 31–51.

4. See particularly Magda Denes' work.

5. This is a point powerfully made by Stanley Hauerwas, "Why Abortion is a Religious Issue," and "Abortion: Why the Arguments Fail," chapters 11 and 12 in his *A Community of Character* (Notre Dame: 1981).

6. Ibid, 199.

7. Zimmerman, 136.

8. Francke, 47.

9. Francke, 93.

10. Kristin Luker, *Taking Chances: Abortion and the Decision Not to Contracept* (Berkeley: 1975) cf. Reardon, 8, and see Zimmerman, 77.

11. Zimmerman, 81.

12. Luker, 16.

13. Luker, 32.

14. Luker, 62–63.

15. Luker, 65.

16. Luker, 68.

17. Luker, 70.

18. Luker, 71.

19. Luker, 122.

20. Luker, 122.

21. Luker, 122.

22. Luker, 123.

23. Luker, 83.

24. Luker, 87.

25. Luker, 89.

26. Luker, 79.

27. Reardon, 14 and 16.

28. James Burtchaell has done a comprehensive analysis of a substantial number of interviews of women who have had abortions. He summarizes his conclusions by labelling the abortionists "estranged, submissive, and coherent" (p. 44). He speaks of the estrangement that women having abortions have from their family, of their submission to others and their blaming of others for their decisions, of a conflict or incoherence between the values they purport to hold and those upon which they act. He speaks of these women as "ricocheting through life" (p. 45). His is truly not an unsympathetic portrayal of these women and their decisions; the evidence quite manifestly supports his assessment.

29. Gilligan, 67.

30. Indeed, I believe that there is good evidence that women having abortions generally concede that they are taking a human life, however sorrowfully so. Stanley Hauerwas in his comments on Linda Bird Francke's *The Ambivalence of Abortion* observes that few of the women "claim to have aborted a fetus—they abort a "child" or a "baby" (*A Community of Character*, p. 199). Mary K. Zimmerman calls the issue of "wanting or not wanting a baby" to be the central orienting point for the woman's decision process (p. 110). Burtchaell observes in regard to his reading of Francke's book and Katrina Maxtone-Graham's *Pregnant by Mistake* (1973): "No one among the nearly one hundred persons interviewed addresses the morality of abortion as a serious intellectual issue, or offers a moral defense of having chosen it on grounds other than her or his own feelings. Feelings are invariably the determinant factor, not principles or evidence of facts or even ideas" (p. 28).

31. Denes, 121.

32. Smetana, 75.

33. Francke, 99.

34. Gilligan, 85.

35. Gilligan, 86.

36. Zimmerman, 70.

37. Zimmerman, 72; see also, Reardon, 13.

38. Zimmerman, 72.

39. Sidney Callahan, "Abortion and the Sexual Agenda," *Commonweal* (25 April 1986) 236.

40. For a description of the psychological aftermath of abortion, see Reardon, 115ff.

41. Paula Ervin, *Women Exploited: The Other Victims of Abortion* (Huntington, Indiana; Our Sunday Visitor, Inc.), 16.

Chapter 13

CASSANDRA'S FATE: WHY FEMINISTS OUGHT TO BE PRO-LIFE

Anne M. Maloney

In ancient Greek mythology, Cassandra, a daughter of Priam, was so loved by Apollo that he gave her a great gift: the gift of prophecy. Cassandra did not return Apollo's love, however, and the spurned god was enraged. No gift, once given by the gods, can ever be taken back, and so Apollo could not take away Cassandra's vision of the future. Instead, he cruelly twisted it: yes, Cassandra would always have knowledge of what was inevitably to come, but whensoever she might try to share that knowledge with her fellow human beings, they would disbelieve her. With all of her foresight, Cassandra would be impotent, spurned and laughed at by the very countrymen she would so desperately try to save.[1]

In the late twentieth century, pro-life feminists find themselves in the frustrating and even terrifying situation of Cassandra—seeing so clearly the disastrous consequences of the current abortion ethic, consequences not disastrous just for unborn women, who are aborted in far greater numbers than men, not just for the women who abort, but consequences disastrous for all of society: all women, all children, all men. When pro-life feminists try to point out what awaits us ahead, they are usually ignored, sometimes laughed at, always stripped of their "feminist" label. In this paper, I am going to attempt to show why the mainline feminists' call for abortion rights is in fact a call that, if heeded, will destroy the very women who articulate it, and render impossible the society that they are trying to achieve.

Before proceeding into a discussion of this claim, it would be helpful to define how a few terms are being used. The term "feminist," as it is used in this paper, generally refers to anyone who is dedicated to the ideal that men and women, although possessed of different sexual natures (and thus, as we shall see, of differing ways of relating to reality), have equally valuable and valid contributions to make to the world, and therefore ought to have equality of opportunity. Furthermore, to be a feminist is to be wholly committed to making this world into one wherein both women and men are equally valued and respected.

There are, in this paper (and most certainly in society), two forms of feminism: what I will call mainline feminism, which considers the right to abortion on demand to be an inviolable feminist tenet, and pro-life feminism, which sees abortion on demand as a serious violation of all that feminism ought to uphold. The term "mainline feminism" is used because of the simple fact that the great majority of feminists *are* pro-abortion. Those who call themselves both pro-life and feminist are very few, indeed, and not at all popular, more often than not rejected by both groups with whom they seek to ally themselves. One more term before we proceed: by "pro-life," I refer to the position that human life is intrinsically valuable; in other words, human life ought to "count" in society, regardless of whether it is useful, convenient, or pleasant.

As I mentioned, pro-life feminists often find themselves with few friends in either camp. On one side is much of the pro-life literature, which usually excoriates the "feminists" rather soundly, presenting them as anti-male at best, anti-family at worst, and anti-church at all times. On the other side, mainline feminists react with incredulity, even anger, when pro-life people dare to call themselves feminists. At a "Woman-to-Woman" conference in Milwaukee, Wisconsin, fifteen years ago, Gloria Steinem told the organizers of a Feminists for Life booth to pack up and go home, because they did not belong at a convention dedicated to helping women. What is sorely needed in such a situation is an explanation of why anyone would be both pro-life and feminist, of why, in fact, a correct understanding of feminism *and,* incidentally, of Church teaching, demand that we be both.

The main voices in the feminist movement, writers such as Carol Gilligan and Beverly Harrison, argue on two basic fronts: first, they claim that women have an absolute, fundamental right to abortion because they have a basic right to control their reproductive lives. Without such control, these authors argue, there can never be social equality for women.[2] On the other front, they argue that abortion is proscribed only because we still inhabit a patriarchal society which seeks to elevate men at the expense of women, and anyone who opposes abortion is either a perpetrator or a victim of this patriarchal ideal.[3] Witness the following:

> Many women who espouse the prolife position do so, at least in part, because they have internalized patriarchal values and depend on the sense of identity and worth that comes from having accepted 'woman's place' in society.[4]

Entwined in the mainline feminists' discussion of these points is usually the conviction (a correct one, I think) that men and women approach reality from two different ethical perspectives: that men tend to focus on the principles involved in making choices, whereas women tend to view such choices in terms of the *persons* involved.[5]

Having broadly outlined some basic forms that mainline feminists take in defending abortion on demand, I will now try to point out (1) that the demand for abortion rights as a necessary prerequisite for a woman's reproductive freedom, for a woman's control over her own body, betrays a decidedly patriarchal rather than feminist understanding of both "freedom" and "control"; (2) that whereas our society is, in many ways, constructed on a model that erects and sustains patriarchal values at the expense of feminine values (the Catholic Church, sadly, is sometimes guilty here, if not doctrinally, then in the all too human execution of the truths revealed by Christ), the solution to this patriarchal bias does not lie in an abortion ethic, and in fact, an abortion ethic feeds rather than destroys this bias; and finally, (3) that, while men and women do approach reality from different ethical perspectives, one focused on principles and the other on persons, these are not always conflicting perspectives, and an abortion ethic betrays both of them.

In response, first of all, to the claim that abortion is a necessary right if women are to have control of their bodies and the freedom to determine the course of their own lives, I would like to make several points. First, it seems ironic, and sadly so, that so many feminist writers and thinkers are endorsing and even embracing such a patriarchal definition of *control*. As feminist theologian Anne E. Patrick herself says

> In contrast to the anthropological dualism of the patriarchal paradigm, the feminist paradigm understands reason itself to be embodied, and women and men to be equal partners in the human community. Instead of *control*, the notion of *respect* for all created reality is basic to this [feminist] model, which values the body and the humanity of all women...[6]

Patrick's espousal of respect for "all created reality" rather than control is a point well-taken; however, in calling for abortion rights as the only ultimate guarantee that women can control their own bodies, mainline feminists are viewing a woman's body as a kind of territory to be subdued, interfered with, dominated. This is not a feminist perspective, regardless of how many mainline feminists maintain it. As most feminists will themselves agree (note Patrick, above), the feminine approach to reality has tended to be less confrontational than cooperative; life and nature (including, but not limited to, the female body) are to be *met* rather than subdued, respected rather than subjected to domination. The demand for abortion rights in the name of control speaks volumes: it says that the patriarchal worldview has been right all along, that bodies, es-

212

pecially women's bodies, are undependable, threatening things that need to be dominated and subdued.

Abortion, if it is an act of control, is a violent act of control. When a woman is pregnant, be it six days or six months, her body has become inextricably wedded to the body of another living being; the only way out of that relationship for a women who does not want to be pregnant is a violent one, an act that destroys the fetus and invades the body—and often the mind—of his or her mother.[7] Traditionally, it has always been women who have realized that violence solves nothing and usually begets more violence, that violent solutions often wound the perpetrator as well as the victim. That is why women have historically been opposed to war, to capital punishment, to the rape and destruction of the environment. Why should womens' traditional (and quite wise) abhorrence of violence stop at the threshold of their own bodies?

In the male-dominated world we have all inhabited for the last 2500 years, unfortunately, power (thus, "control") has been accorded only to those strong enough to seize it, or at least demand it. Furthermore, it has historically been those in power who have set the standard for who gets to "count" as persons. For far too many of those 2500 years, it has been men who have been in power, and women who have not "counted." It is, therefore, particularly chilling to read arguments such as those of mainline feminist theologian Marjorie Reilly Maguire, who says that, in order for a fetus to count as valuable, the pregnant woman must *confer* value upon it; as she puts it:

> The personhood [of the fetus] begins when the bearer of life, the mother, makes a covenant of love with the developing life within her to bring it to birth . . . . The moment when personhood begins, then, is the moment when the mother accepts the pregnancy.[8]

The fetus, according to such argumentation, is a person if and only if the pregnant woman decides to invest it with value. How, a pro-life feminist will ask, does this differ from the long entrenched patriarchal ideal that it is the powerful who determine the value of other human life? The mainline feminists, it would seem, need to explain this.

The notions of control and power at work in the abortion ethic, then, are ones that surely ought to give any feminist pause. It is indeed unconscionable that women have, for so many thousands of years, been dominated and victimized by men, whose hold on power was reinforced by the patriarchal structure of society. Thus it is especially disorienting to see the mainline feminists insist that the only road away from such victimization is to victimize, in turn, another group of human beings, and not just any group, either—these completely powerless and voiceless beings are their own offspring. Their very powerlessness makes them the ideal victims; the question which *all* women must ask themselves is whether the path away from victimization really lies in joining the victimizers, whether the road to freedom must really be littered with the dead bodies of their unborn children.

The argument for "control" is so closely wedded to the argument for "freedom" as to be virtually inextricable, so a discussion of how feminists ought to view the notion of control leads quite naturally into a discussion of the idea that abortion rights are the necessary condition for reproductive freedom. In their "March on Washington" in the Spring of 1989, women of all colors and walks of life forcefully proclaimed their commitment to the tenet that women will never be truly free or equal to men until they can walk away from their sexual encounters just as freely as men have always been able to do. The feminists who were *not* marching that day, the pro-life feminists, wonder whether the March on Washington was not a march down the wrong road, a road fraught with danger. All feminists must ask themselves precisely what kind of freedom it is that they want, whether, in marching for the right to abortion as a guarantor of their right to sexual encounters devoid of the possibility of childbirth, they are not unconsciously "buying into" a male-oriented approach to sex and reproduction.

Men and women are different, not just in their biological characteristics, but in their sexual natures as well. There are exceptions, of course, but throughout history, men have traditionally approached sex differently than women have.[9] No one can deny that women have always had a higher biological investment in sexual union; abortion seeks to undo that tie, so that women will have as little a potential investment as men. The question we must ask is

214

whether this is truly what women want. Is the ideal to be pursued a world wherein sex can (and often will be) commitment-free? Is it women who desire uncommitted sex? Desire it so much, in fact, that they willingly seek to damage their own bodies? Leaving abortion aside for just a moment, even most forms of contraception invade the woman's body, *not* the man's—and in more cases than we want to admit, scar and irrevocably damage those bodies. (Even condoms, the one "male" form of contraception, usually ends up being the woman's responsibility—survey after survey shows it is invariably women, not men, who are responsible for purchasing condoms.) The sexual revolution for which abortion on demand is a necessary prerequisite has brought down on women an epidemic of pelvic inflammatory disease, tubal pregnancy, various venereal diseases, AIDS, and infertility. This is a strange sort of freedom for which the mainline feminists fight. And when the various forms of contraception fail (and they all do), do women then want the "freedom" to embrace the ultimate invasion of their bodies and their lives—the abortionist with his vacuum or his knife or his saline-filled syringe?

One of the points on which all feminists agree is that women need to build their self-confidence and self-esteem. In a sexist culture, this can be hard to do. As Carol Heilbrun pointed out in a talk given to the Modern Language Association, a man's traditional experience of selfhood can be summed up in a line from the poet Walt Whitman: "I celebrate myself and sing myself, and what I assume you shall assume," whereas poet Emily Dickinson best sums up how women have, for too long, experienced selfhood: "I'm nobody."[10] Does abortion build a woman's self-esteem?

Here is the response of a woman who had a saline abortion:

Before that needle had entered my abdomen, I had liked myself. Though I may have had my share of problems, I had seen myself as basically a good person. . . . That moment of desperation which had led me to the 'healer's table' had now positioned itself as ruler of my life. I had abandoned myself to despair, and despair was my future. There was no way to stop it. There was no way to put everything back the way it had been. I no longer had any control, any choice. I was powerless. I was weak. I was a murderer.[11]

The point here is not to claim that all women who abort immediately feel like murderers; no doubt, the mainline feminists can produce ample numbers of women who will claim that they felt nothing after their abortions except relief. The point, rather, is to question whether abortion on demand can ever bring about the feminist goal of a society wherein the feminine perspective is valued as much as the male, or whether, in fact, abortion reinforces male-centered patterns of belief and ultimately robs women of their self-confidence and self-esteem.

Anthropologist Margaret Mead has often pointed out the "womb envy" of men in other societies. Nineteenth century German philosopher Friedrich Nietzsche spoke of *ressentiment*—the tendency we human beings have to devalue what we do not ourselves possess, to denigrate any action that we cannot ourselves perform. Given what Mead and Nietzsche tell us, it comes as small surprise that the patriarchal culture of the Western world has always devalued pregnancy and the power to bear children—a power only women have—and have placed far greater value on "work," meaning success in the market place—something men can do.

When mainline feminists acquiesce to the conviction that pregnancy is a form of enslavement and childbearing a burden, they are adding weight to, *not* destroying, the yoke of patriarchy. They are letting men be the arbiters of what is valuable, and fighting hard for the "right" to have their own bodies invaded and their own children destroyed so that they can get it. What feminists, *all* feminists, should be doing, is working to achieve a world in which the power to bear children is viewed as a gift to be protected rather than a burden to be relieved. That means working for fundamental changes in the structure of society, including, but not limited to far greater flexibility in the workplace for both mothers and fathers, better prenatal and postnatal care for impoverished women, and much more stringent enforcement of male responsibility for child support. Such changes would be a true feminization of society. They will occur only when women insist upon them, however, and abortion-on-demand precludes such insistence. When abortion is easily accessible, society no longer has to take pregnancy seriously. Once a women decides to continue a pregnancy, society is under no obligation to help her; it is, after all, *her* choice, *her* responsibility.

216

In militating for the right to abortion-on-demand, mainline feminists are trying to win their game on the same old gameboard—the patriarchal worldview that denigrates what is unique to women as unimportant, trivial, not to be taken seriously. They are accepting wholeheartedly the traditional, male-oriented distrust and dislike of the female body, and embracing a kind of freedom that uses the female body as an object to be invaded, and, if need be, subdued. Feminists who are pro-life see that this can lead only to disaster for women and for their unborn children—yet their voices, so much in the minority, go unheard or unheeded.

Cassandra's fate was to see the future.

And be disbelieved.

NOTES

1. Edith Hamilton, *Mythology*, pp. 202–203.

2. See Beverly Harrison, *Our Right to Choose* (Boston: Beacon, 1983), and Rosalind Pollack Petchesky, *Abortion and Woman's Choice* (Longman, 1984).

3. By "patriarchal" here, I mean the worldview prevalent in Western culture that esteems reason over passion and separates soul from body, elevating one and denigrating the other, a worldview that usually results in the domination of men over women, since women are traditionally taken to represent the passions and the mysteries of the body.

4. Madonna Kolbeschlag, "Abortion and Moral Consensus: Beyond Solomon's Choice," in *Abortion and Catholicism: The American Debate*, eds. Patricia Beattie Jung and Thomas A. Shannon (New York: Crossroads, 1988), p. 122.

5. See, for example, Carol Gilligan's book, *In a Different Voice* (Cambridge: Harvard University Press, 1982).

6. Anne E. Patrick, in *Abortion and Catholicism*, p. 174.

7. This is not to ignore the point, made by Carol A. Tauer and echoed by Anne Patrick, that between 50 and 60% of all embryos abort spontaneously. This fact, while interesting, has nothing to do with the issue of abortion. After all, death happens to 100% of all human beings; this fact is unhelpful in discussing whether all death, that is, killing, is justified. Carol A. Tauer, "Probabilism and the Moral Status of the Early Embryo," in *Abortion and Catholicism*, p. 57, and Patrick, p. 174.

8. Marjorie Reilly Maguire, "Personhood, Covenant, and Abortion," in *Abortion and Catholicism*, p. 109.

9. It is up to the social scientists and geneticists to decide whether these differences result from inherent genetic makeup or social conditioning; the important point for the purposes of this paper is that they exist.

10. I am grateful to Anne Patrick for pointing this out to me. See Patrick, n. 7, in *Abortion and Catholicism*, p. 180.

11. Nancyjo Mann, in David C. Reardon, *Aborted Women: Silent No more* (Westchester, Illinois: Crossway, 1987), xvi.

Chapter 14

ARE WOMEN CONTROLLING THEIR OWN MINDS? THE POWER OF PURITAN AND PLAYBOY MENTALITIES

Mary Rosera Joyce

"About six months after the abortion, I started looking into fetal and baby books, and one book just devastated me. I wanted to bury that book. I went into drinking and severe, severe depression."[1]

Excerpts published in *Women and Choice: A New Beginning* by Mary R. Joyce (St. Cloud, MN: LifeCom, 1986). Reprinted and revised here with permission. An extended quotation published in *The Washington Times*, Washington, D.C. from Nancyjo Mann interviewed by staff writer and columnist Tom Diaz, August 3, 1983 has been reprinted with permission.

This woman's choice to have an abortion, like that of so many others, was not based on informed consent. Her decision was made in the dark. Requiring any woman to know the facts before "the procedure" takes place, has been unconstitutional.

In a 1983 case, and again in a 1986 case, the majority of the U.S. Supreme Court defended the connection—for women only—between darkness and choice, between ignorance and privacy. The majority of the justices seemed to say, "When a woman makes this important decision, the less she knows about it the better. She controls her body best, and with less mental stress, when her mind is out of the way."

This coupling of choice with ignorance (choice abuse) is vividly portrayed by Nancyjo Mann, founder of Women Exploited by Abortion. In her statement to *The Washington Times,* she told about her abortion and the lack of knowledge involved in her choice.

> I went in and asked, "What are you going to do to me?" All he did was look at my stomach and say, "I'm going to take a little fluid out, put a little fluid in, you'll have severe cramps, and expel the fetus."
>
> I said, "Is that all?" He said, "That's all."
>
> It did not sound too bad. But what that doctor described to me was not the truth....
>
> Once they put in the saline, there's no way to reverse it. And for the next hour and a half I felt my daughter thrash around violently while she was being choked, poisoned, burned and suffocated to death. *I didn't know* (emphasis added) any of that was going to happen. And I remember talking to her and I remember telling her I didn't want to do this, I wished she could live. And yet she was dying and I remember her very last kick on her left side. She had no strength left.
>
> I've tried to imagine that kind of death, a pillow put over us, suffocating. In four minutes we'd pass out. We'd have that gift of passing out and then dying. But it took her an hour and a half just to die.
>
> Then I was given an intravenous injection to help stimulate labor and I went into hard labor for 12 hours. And at

5:30 AM on the 31st of October I delivered my daughter whose name is now Charmaine Marie. She was 14 inches long. She weighed over a pound and a half. She had a head of hair and her eyes were opening.

I got to hold her because the nurses didn't make it to the room on time. I delivered my girl myself. They grabbed her out of my hands and threw her, threw her, into a bedpan.[2]

Why did the abortionist deny Nancyjo Mann so much information? Did he believe that women make their best choices in the dark? Did he place any value on the woman's right to know the facts, and to control her own mind? What value did he place, instead, on her cash? How many women would go through with an abortion if they were fully informed about the life they are carrying, about what is involved in the abortion itself, and about the physical and psychological consequences to themselves?

Dr. Eloise Jones, a Toronto psychiatrist, explained why abortion trauma caused her to stop making abortion referrals.

"An abortion has not helped the self-image of any woman I have talked with. I was listening to one recently, who, shortly after an abortion, claimed that it had not affected her and that it was a perfectly justified action. However, I later discovered that she was very frightened lest her teenage daughter discover what she had done, and since the abortion, she has become increasingly tearful, hostile and unresponsive to her husband. In her and in others, I have been presented with psychosomatic illness, sexual frigidity, hatred for a boyfriend or spouse, anxiety, all kinds of neurotic disturbances and some deep depressive reactions.... We are beginning to see the problems of women who had abortions three or four years ago surfacing."[3]

Women who seek professional counseling rarely mention abortion as their presenting complaint. According to Terry Selby (Counseling Associates, Bemidji, Minnesota), a past abortion, in the course of treatment, often shows up as a cause of a woman's problems. Depression, anorexia, suicide attempts, drug abuse, alcoholism, family conflicts, and other disturbances appear on the surface. Beneath the symptoms, however, a past, and sometimes even a forgotten, abortion is often a (the) hidden cause.

Selby says, "The denial continues after the abortion, and is manifest in the woman's unwillingness to talk about it, in her complete repression of her emotions relative to the abortion, and in her selective repression of her memory of the procedure."

A large part of the problem is that women are not informed about the psychological complications of abortion.[4] Nor are they told about the many documented physical complications.[5] Often they *do not know* that women who have abortions suffer, in subsequent pregnancies, more fetal deaths, more premature births, and more delivery complications than those who never had abortions. They do not realize that the feminine, more inward, side of their female nature is deeply violated by abortion, while the masculine, more outward, side might seem, at first, to go unscathed.

A woman who can undergo an abortion without any apparent psychic damage might be able to turn off her conscious mind with sophisticated slogans about freedom of choice. But she cannot turn off her subconscious mind. This part of herself remains in touch with the reality involved. *The subconscious mind is never sophisticated.* Thus, later in life, often during menopause, the deep psychic damage of a long-ago abortion might begin to surface. Dr. James C. Neely, author of *Gender,* says "Repression we now know is more common than not after abortion, and we know that repression sooner or later will surface as psychic complaints."[6]

Regarding the effect of abortion on women, Dr. Howard W. Fisher, a Minneapolis psychiatrist, said that more data is needed, but that the physicians participating in abortion prevent the keeping of records that might contain the data.[7] No one is demanding to know. Nobody wants to know.

Everything you always wanted to know about sex, but don't want to know about abortion is a cultural syndrome. In this mental condition, women are trying to control what they perceive as enemies of their freedom, their own bodies, and making blind choices as if freedom depends on ignorance. In the meantime, men are profiting both sexually and financially. And many women, blinded by choicist rhetoric, continue to look the other way.

What the Rhetoric Buries Alive

If women would listen to pro-abortion rhetoric, they could hear the following:

"My convenience is more important than your life."

"Might makes right."

"Women's bodies are naturally defective because they need so many corrective chemicals and surgeries, even when they are healthy."

"Women need medical personnel, mostly men, to control their uncontrolled bodies for them."

"Women can't be themselves without surgeons to clean up after sex."

"Sex is naturally defective because it causes so many unwanted growths in women's bodies."

"Women's dignity depends on this huge body-count: well over 4,000 each day in this country."

But pro-abortionists say "choice, choice, choice," so much they cannot hear the statements they are really making—all of them heavy downers for women.

Pro-choice females are their own worst chauvinists.

So why are so many women going along with their own belittlement? Are they controlling their own minds? Or is something else controlling their minds for them? New, updated women are clever and assertive about their own autonomy. But are they also wise?

When choices are made in an environment that protects ignorance and encourages denial, the mind that makes the choices is extremely vulnerable. A woman's unknowing mind is easily taken over by a mentality unsuitable to her nature, so that she thinks with that mentality and mistakenly believes she is thinking with her own womanly mind.

A healthy mentality for both women and men has feminine and masculine (inward and outward, being and doing, receptive and productive) qualities with an opposite emphasis in each gender. A woman's mind accents the feminine while including the masculine. Receptivity has a masculine nuance in men, just as masculine qualities have a feminine nuance in women.

Unbalanced by each other, feminine and masculine qualities break down into destructive characteristics. Receptivity, which is active, deteriorates into passivity. Productivity falls from a healthy dominion into a harmful domination or aggression. Extreme masculine or feminine mentalities are unhealthy. Women, as well as men, need to ask themselves what kind of mentality is controlling the way they think.

Puritan and Playboy Mentalities

American culture is shaped by a largely unbalanced masculine mentality that has two basic forms: the puritan and the playboy philosophies of life. The puritan mentality instigated, and still forms, the American character. No other nation on earth was conceived, born, and developed in puritanism. Even the more recent playboy mentality, while strikingly different in some ways, remains basically puritan in its extremely masculine and domineering attitude toward nature.

The original puritan was a principled individualist who believed that he was fallen and depraved by sin, and that all the rest of nature shared this condition. He thought he could manage fallen nature only by force and domination. This domination-mentality eventually moved from puritan suppression of feelings to Victorian repression of feelings.

The playboy, with one exception, agrees that nature should be dominated. This exception is physical sexuality and its psychological preferences. He thinks sex is absolutely good and almost incapable of immoral expression. He also thinks that anything which might interfere with the fun of sex, such as pregnancy and emotional involvement, belongs to defective nature, and must be managed by domination. Instead of controlling his sexual *behavior* like the puritan, the playboy "liberates" his behavior and tries to control its unwanted *consequences* instead. Individualism based on principle becomes, in the playboy mentality, selfism based on preference.

Puritan control of behavior and playboy control of consequences follow from the same inner problem. Neither the puritan nor the playboy knows how to live well with feelings. The puritan hides his feelings, even from himself, because he thinks this will help him control his behavior. The playboy ignores his emotional feelings (especially those of bonding and love), because he thinks these interfere with freely chosen recreational sex. Hiding feelings and ignoring them are not the same. Yet both forms of domination show the same distorted masculine avoidance of feelings. Each, in its own way, says "feelings don't count."

Living well with physical and emotional feelings requires something the puritan and playboy do not recognize in themselves—their inner receptivity. They do not accept this more feminine aspect of their inner life.

Through the feminine part of ourselves (in both women and men), we are able to receive our feelings with awareness and acceptance of what they are. We are able to let them *be* what they are without having to *do* anything about them at all. This ability to receive our feelings is also our capacity to regulate our behavior from within. If we can let ourselves have our sexual, angry, and other feelings without having to do what they suggest, we are really free to act or not to act. We do not feel driven to act. Nor do we feel driven to control ourselves by hiding or ignoring our feelings.

This inner freedom (to act or not to act no matter what we feel) changes the whole meaning of choice. It also changes the meaning of control from careless domination to caring dominion. Instead of suppressing or dominating nature, we regulate it by receiving it deeply, and by freely cooperating with its principles of integrity.

When the masculine part of ourselves is unbalanced, we are not inclined to let anything just be itself. We feel compelled to produce and perform. Both the puritan work-ethic and playboy fun-ethic accentuate performance in this excessive way. Success (in work or in sex) is their measure of self-worth. Simply being oneself causes too much anxiety.

Rarely is an American male today a puritan or a playboy in the total sense. Each one, however, is affected by the mentalities that form the culture in which he lives. To the extent that individual males think and live by these mentalities, they are, partially at least, puritan and (or) playboy in character. And to the degree that American females think and live by the same cultural attitudes, their own minds and lives are controlled by excessively masculine mentalities. Their minds as well as their choices are not really their own.

From Puritan to Playboy

The cultural shift from puritan individualism to playboy selfism probably began in 1900 when Sigmund Freud, reacting against Victorian repression, published his first book. By 1913, Margaret Sanger was beginning to promote birth control. Writers like Shaw, Conrad, and Lawrence were prying open the puritan-Victorian closet. In 1915, some Harvard students known as The Young Intellectuals began reading Freud, Bergson, and Neitzsche. They launched an attack on puritanism and Victorianism by openly promoting an ethic of hedonism, pleasure, and play. These young men were America's first "playboy" advocates of sexual liberation.

Wilhelm Reich, author of *The Sexual Revolution* (1945), and an Austrian psychoanalyst influenced by Freud, rejected Freud's negative version of restraint. Instead of developing the positive, more receptive, version, he simply rejected restraint.

Playboy magazine first appeared in 1953, and soon shifted the sexual revolution into high gear. Recreational sex separated from morality and the family became the selfist preference of the day.

As the playboy mentality emerged in the communications media, "wanted and unwanted" scripts surged around the practice of contraception. At first, abortion was rarely mentioned. But the result of contraceptive failures was not destined to be welcomed with open arms. Pressures to legalize abortion began almost immediately.

Abortion, however, was not as easily accepted as contraception. It met with more resistance in the grassroots population and the legislatures. So the spirit of the sexual revolution, through some of its advocates, was forced to turn to the Courts. This spirit and its advocates had to persuade at least five of the nine Supreme Court Justices to search the farthest reaches of the Constitution, and to find in it the playboy agenda.

The Playboy Mentality and Women's Minds

As feminist cries to "control my own body" soared in the media and rattled the rafters of the republic, the supreme law of the land was forced to yield the desired results. The playboy mentality "pull-

226

ing the strings behind the scene" was urging the tigress to growl and the lioness to roar. The masculine spirit of the times dearly hoped that the feminists would succeed.

After all, a Constitution formed by puritans and deists did not imply, even in its darkest shadows, that sex could be a free-for-all matter. There was no evidence that any political thinker of the 18th century thought that a Constitution should deal with sex. Furthermore, the puritans were opposed to abortion.

But the playboy had to get his playmate and "her" freedom of choice firmly installed in the Constitutional interpretation, otherwise he could not be fully, freely, and legally himself. Somewhere, somehow, some women had to get the message and take a case to Court. Could an appeal for the abortion-choice pass the Constitutional test?

Because cultural pressures can easily creep into Constitutional interpretation, the Justices can slip into *making* law instead of *interpreting* law, thus encroaching on the legislative power of government. The need for wisdom in the interpreters is imperative. Since it requires a wise distinction between the public and private realms, the so-called "right to privacy" has become a special danger zone for the intrusion of legislating judges. The wisdom required to avoid such an intrusion involves an understanding of the human being *as a person,* not just as an individual. A culture so strongly grounded in individualism as our own tends to lack some of this required wisdom.

In spite of individualistic political theory, family life based on religious and cultural traditions flourished in the private realm of American society for almost 200 years. But when the original puritan culture began shifting into the playboy culture the effect on the family became an unprecedented jolt. Using the lever of playboy-playmate sex, the new culture catapulted women out of the private realm of the family into the "privacy" of selfists doing their own thing.

In order to interpret puritan individualism in the light of playboy selfism, the Court needed an appropriate innovation. Individual liberty always existed in tension with social responsibility. But liberty was never before involved in an ethic of pleasure and play. Sexual pleasure separated from commitment—in other words, sexual privatism—was a playboy innovation. *Privatism, a gross exaggera-*

tion of authentic privacy, became the interpreting device applied by the Court to the Constitution.

How did the Court "discover" playboy privatism in a Constitution that was formed without any playboy intentions? As the rhetoric of the "wanted and unwanted child" became increasingly more shrill in the playboy culture, the force of this rhetoric began to be felt in the Court. Finally, as the sexual revolution neared its peak, the playboy mentality, through an individual case, made its first, careful, constitutional move. In the 1965 *Griswold V. Connecticut* decision, a Connecticut law making it a criminal misdemeanor to "use any drug, medicinal article or instrument for the purpose of preventing conception" was struck down. This was the first "privacy" case based on what the Court called a "zone of privacy," meaning the marital bedroom in the private realm of the family.

The newly formed concept of privacy, though not mentioned in the Constitution, appeared to be rooted in the Fourth Amendment's protection against unreasonable searches and seizures. This protection seemed to the Court to include conjugal rights.

On the face of the decision, the Court did not appear to enshrine the right to contraception in the Constitution directly. The Justices were supposedly protecting the family zone of life, as the Constitution is meant to do. But the subsequent judicial impulse clearly opposed the traditional family, and favored radical selfism instead. Only seven years after the first privacy decision sanctioned marital contraception, the 1972 *Eisenstadt V. Baird* decision struck down a Massachusetts law that prohibited the distribution of contraceptives to the unmarried. The family "zone of privacy" was expanded into an individual "right of privacy." Rights previously found within the privacy of marriage were gratuitously extended to the unmarried. The selfism of the playboy culture broke through *Griswold's* vulnerable "zone of privacy" and became, in *Eisenstadt,* outright privatism.

The newly formulated "right to privacy" of the individual was an invention to accommodate the genital activity of the unmarried. The playboy and playmate had gained what was construed to be a constitutional right to separate sex from the family, a separation the puritan would have found unthinkable.

In the case for unmarried sex, Justice William Brennan said, "if the right to privacy means anything, it is the right of the *individual,* married or single, to be free from unwarranted governmental intrusion into matters so fundamentally affecting a person as the decision whether to bear or beget a child." The word "individual" was italicized by Brennan to emphasize that having children is no longer to be regarded as a family matter.

This judgment was a raw judicial intrusion into the privacy of the family, ironically done in the name of privacy. But the *meaning* of privacy had changed so much from one point to the other that it seemed to become two words instead of one. The first meaning referred to the family; the other referred only to the individual. Since the particular individual who ties sex to pregnancy is the female, the next Court decision, the 1973 *Roe V. Wade* abortion decision, was based on the individual privacy of the female.

The outcome of the abortion decision was already implied in the rationale for the previous (1972) defense of contraceptives for the unmarried. In fact, according to John Noonan in his book, *A Private Choice,* the contraception case was decided only after the abortion case had been argued before the Court. He says that the revolutionary rationale in the contraception decision was probably invented as a needed precedent for the subsequent abortion decision.[8] In any event, the 1972 decision favoring contraception for singles was the only true precedent for the abortion decision (Noonan).

Both decisions were based on a society of isolated selfists. Instead of regarding the family as a natural bonding of individuals in a basic social unit to be protected by the State, the Court now implied that the State no longer presupposes, nor protects, the family.

Starting, in 1965, with the intent to protect the privacy of marriage, the Court radicalized privacy so far as to legalize free-choice abortion throughout the full term of pregnancy, and to pit wife against husband and daughter against parents. Four days before the 1976 Bicentennial celebration, in *Planned Parenthood V. Danforth,* the Court denied the father any rights in a woman's abortion decision, and denied the parents of a minor daughter any significant rights in her abortion decision. Finally, *Colautti V. Franklin* (1979) declared that legally prescribed attempts to save the baby's life in an abortion interfered with the abortionist's right to practice. This whole train of rulings solidly installed the playboy mentality in the official interpretation of the Constitution.

Between the 1965 contraception case and the 1973 abortion case, a volcanic kind of logic moved relentlessly toward its conclusion. By 1973, the full force of the playboy culture exploded in what dissenting Justice Byron White called "an improvident and extravagant exercise of the power of judicial review." He also said, "I find nothing in the language or history of the Constitution to suggest the Court's judgment. The Court simply fashions and announces a new constitutional right."[9]

Influenced by the overwhelming impulsiveness of the playboy culture, and the power of its scripts blaring in the media, the Court, too, became impulsive. Acting more on impulse than on judicial wisdom, this eminent branch of government moved to satisfy the playmate's shrill demands for the liberty to "control my own body." Doing so, the Court lost its ability to control its own judicial body. It slipped into an impulsive interpretation of liberty, and read that hapless view into the Constitution's provision for individual freedom. Such a counterfeit right was given by seven of nine men, not directly to men, but to women. This so-called right would not have been given to women, however, unless it directly served male interests of the playboy kind.

A Woman's Permission to Choose

The new "right of privacy" was based on pregnancy management for selfists, not on the dignity of women as persons, nor on the dignity of the family as the basic unit of society. The all-male Court was caught in the mounting pressure of the playboy culture as it broke away from the sexual moralism of the previous culture. The playmate's cries for the legal right to control her own body, sounding like music to playboy ears, found men ready and willing to rally to her cause. The "privacy" decisions boldly served playboy interests by awarding Constitutional protection to the playboy's desire for sex freed from all family responsibilities. These decisions facilitated the playboy culture's formation of the playmate, without whom there could be no fully functioning playboy.

Because sex is bound to pregnancy in the female, the playboy-conditioned Court was compelled to center the separation of sex from the family in the woman's freedom of choice, and further compelled, in subsequent decisions, to separate the woman from her husband, and the dependent daughter from her parents. Isolated from the family, the female now became dependent on the medical profession as a family substitute. The privacy of the woman and her mate in the bedroom was eclipsed by her privacy with her doctor (usually a total stranger who often does not even see her face) in a public abortion facility. The "disease" caused in her body by her male partner could now be legally "corrected" by a professional controller of disease who is willing to serve playboy interests.

The new supremacy of the medical profession over the family in a woman's generative role had to be a Court contrivance. In this judicial scheme, the female's partnership with her husband was transferred to a new partnership with her doctor instead. Based on the new "fetal tissue" theory of pregnancy, a theory peculiar to the playboy mentality, the disease-correcting institution of medicine was allowed to treat the result of a female's copulation with her partner as if it were a growing malignancy whenever it was unwanted.

Something radical happened to degrade a woman's normal, natural, and healthy fertility, and thus to degrade the woman herself. Historically, in tribal cultures, human fertility was so important and mysterious that it was surrounded with magic, religious rituals, and even human sacrifice. In post-tribal civilized cultures, fertility no longer was a magic or religious matter, but still was valued as somehow related to the sacred. In the playboy culture, however, fertility is dissociated from the sacred, and is associated, instead, with disease or malignancy. Fertility is not regarded as a gift of the gods, nor as a gift of God through created nature, but as a *medical problem* to be solved. Human perception of the sacredness of fertility has now given way to the sacredness of contraception, sterilization, and abortion.

None of the above perceptions of human fertility (whether associated with magic and ritual, or with "don't touch" and "don't talk about" Victorian sacredness, or with prescriptions and surgery) treat it as an integral power of a normal human sexuality. Balanced minds (in control of themselves) see human fertility as a natural and healthy power of the whole person. Unbalanced, impulsive, playboy-playmate minds, on the other hand, demand a constitutionally protected prescriber or surgeon to "control" a woman's generative potential for her. She is not recognized as one who is *able* to regulate her fertility by herself.

By lock-stepping the woman with her physician, the Court was not acknowledging her dignity as a person, but was adjusting to something construed as defective in her nature: her inconvenient tendency to produce unwanted "fetal tissue" as a result of her sexual contact with an "infecting" male.

Nor was such a use of medical procedures designed to recognize the physician's dignity as a healer. Doctors who treat normal, healthy physical conditions as if they were deformed are practicing quackery. There are good, noble physicians who recognize better ways of responding to an untimely pregnancy. These ways might not be easy or lucrative. But, as everyone knows, quacks deal in the easy and the lucrative instead of the wise and the true.

Nor was such an adjustment to "depravity" in a woman's nature inspired by a sense of the dignity of the male as a person. The playboy culture's rape of the human generative power in both women and men was motivated by *a profound hopelessness about the human person's ability to regulate sexual expression; it was inspired by a deep sense of sexual helplessness.*

A Man's Inability to Choose

The Court's abortion decisions rendered all males under its jurisdiction legally impotent in their generative role. Even the legal husband was constitutionally relegated to a "child"—male or playboy status, the condition of one who has no direct interest in a playmate's pregnancy potential.

That millions of married men have taken this attack on their generative power with so much lethargic acquiescence shows the mind-binding effect of cultural scripts, and the overwhelming pervasiveness of the playboy mentality. Many of these men would vote against abortion. But their spirit is so decimated by the culture that they have little energy to protest, other than that needed to pull a lever in a voting booth. Only the woman was legally allowed to choose. Her male partner, even if he was the father of a family, had no legal ability to become a father.

This is the price the playboy is all too willing to pay for his ideological control over women's bodies and minds, both in the bedroom and in the public "cleanup" facility. This is the way he wants it to be! And he will continue to fight in the courts, the legislatures, and the media, to keep it that way.

Responsible Choice—A Woman Controls Her Own Mind

When a woman living in a playboy culture is faced with an unplanned pregnancy, her first inclination is to follow her impulses. Everything in the culture encourages impulsive behavior. She need not stop to reflect. She might say to herself, "Here I am pregnant, and I really don't want to be. Now is not the time for me to have a child. It would be irresponsible. So I prefer to have an abortion." Without a second thought, she might call to make the appointment.

If, however, she feels some conflict, and says to herself, "An abortion would go against my principles; I believe it ends a life," her feelings and values would be at odds. Finding her preferences and principles confronting each other, she might choose to confront herself. "If I choose by my feelings and preferences like a selfist, I step into the playboy trap. If I choose by my values and principles *for their own sake*, like a tough individualist, I step into the puritan trap. How can I get beyond this deadlock?"

To Be or Not to Be

Responsible choice is not just a matter of what to *do* in a situation. It is basically, and most importantly, a matter of what to *be*. Responsible choice is basically a question of "What kind of person am I going to *be* in my actions?" Person, not preference or principle, is the starting point.

A woman begins to control her own mind when she moves from doing to being, and asks herself, "Who am I in this situation?" She knows she is pregnant and doesn't want to be. She knows that pregnancy makes her a mother. If she denies that she is already a mother, she makes a statement about her pregnancy and herself. If she thinks she is pregnant with a piece of growing tissue similar to a tumor, she belittles pregnancy and diminishes herself, as the playboy mentality would have her do. But if she thinks she is pregnant with another being of her own kind, her person and her sexuality immediately have more dignity in her own eyes. She might say, "I suppose I *am* a mother whether or not I want to be. Just as I am myself whether or not I want to be. I can only choose what I am or deny it. To be or not to be. What kind of mother am I going to be: one who receives my motherhood and gives birth to my child, or one who denies it and removes what I am carrying? If I choose not to be a mother, I remain a mother. The mother of a dead child is still a mother."

As a woman gains control of her mind in this way, she does not passively, helplessly, let her situation tell her whether or not she is a mother. She does not let her wanting or unwanting tell her who she is. She lets her being inform her mind and her decision. She decides to become *receptive* instead of remaining a passive victim of circumstances. "I choose to receive my being as a mother. I choose to receive my situation and to make the best of it somehow. My situation is not going to tell me that I should not be who I am." When she receives her situation, it becomes a challenge to her being, no longer just an imposition. She can now respond to the challenge according to the kind of person she *really prefers* to be.

In the end, her preference is different than the one with which she started her deliberations. Receptivity deepens her preference. It also brings her into harmony with her principles, not because of her principles, however, but because her being and the being she is carrying. Her principle, "Do not Kill," is less important to her than her real, living self and her real, living child. But this principle is also important because it belongs to her nature as a person. It nudges her to move beyond her first impulsive preference, and to think about her pregnancy, instead of running to an abortionist to get her away from her being because of her situation. Her being, her person, leads her to her true preference in this situation, and brings together into harmony her preferences and principles. Though she might still have some ambivalent feelings, her basic feelings and her values are no longer at odds.

When this woman gains control of her mind, her first impulsive preference, understandable as it might be, is not her final choice. She does not choose according to that impulse, because she receives so much more than her first, reacting impulses. If it were a matter of choosing which pair of shoes to buy, she would have many alternatives and like it that way. She can always throw away a pair of shoes she does not want, but throwing away her child, even in this carrying stage, is a different matter altogether. It is too close to throwing away herself.

When a woman stops to think about the life she is carrying, she can realize that a life can *be* before it can *do*. This life within her is in a state of being with no doing to show for it. The playboy mentality tries to tell her that if there is no functional activity, there is no person, no being. But that is an overly masculine way of identifying being with doing.

The mother experiences the first action of the new life as movement. Then birth. Then crying. This little person cannot do much, cannot talk, walk, take care of feeding and eliminating. Yet the person *is*. Doing is important, in due time, of course. But natural functions emerge from the being who already is.

Even if a woman does not actually think this way, she intuits this way. She knows, even if she does not think. And the feminine, inward, side of her mind knows all of the above about being and its integrity, even if the masculine side writes a book (or two or more) against it.

A woman who tunes into her own intuitive mind, while *receiving* both her feelings and her being's given principles of natural integrity, can free herself from puritan and playboy mentalities that are trying to tell her what to do and how to do it. Her own intuitive mind, with careful reflection, can lead her, instead, to who she is and how she wants to be.

NOTES

1. Paula Ervin, *Women Exploited,* Our Sunday Visitor, Inc., Huntington, Indiana, 1985, p. 42.

2. *The Washington Times,* August 3, 1983, Nancyjo Mann interviewed by staff writer and columnist, Tom Diaz.

3. *The Uncertified Human,* Toronto, September, 1974.

4. See *The Psychological Aspects of Abortion* edited by David Mall and Walter F. Watts, M.D., (Washington, D.C.: University Publications of America, 1979).

5. Ann Saltenberger's book *Every Woman Has a Right to Know the Dangers of Legal Abortion* (Air-Plus Enterprises, 1982) compiles the evidence from medical journals, medical papers, testimony before Senate subcommittees, World Health Organization documents, and findings of investigative reporters.

6. James C. Neely, M.D., *Gender* (New York: Simon and Shuster, 1981), p. 163.
7. Mall and Watts, *op cit,* 50–51.
8. John Noonan, *A Private Choice* (New York: The Free Press, 1979), p. 21.
9. *Roe u Wade,* Mr. Justice White, p. 2.

Chapter 15

THE "FEMINISM" OF AQUINAS' NATURAL LAW: RELATIONSHIPS, LOVE AND NEW LIFE

Mary Hayden

Ever since Carol Gilligan pointed out that the developmental psychology of women has not been properly studied and that the ethical perspective of women is primarily one of care,[1] relationships have been considered central to feminist ethics.[2] Since relationships are fluid with constantly changing requirements, the ethic of care generally seeks to be contextual and to resolve the morality of abortion on an individual basis, i.e. according to whether the abortion would harm or promote valuable personal relationships. Just as an individual's perspective of a loved one cannot be universalized so as to be seen by any and all others, feminism typically holds that moral norms cannot be universalized.[3] Relativity and the endorsement of abortion thus characterize many feminist ethics.[4]

Following Gilligan, the "feminist" ethic of care based upon relationships is usually differentiated from the "masculine" ethic of justice based upon impartiality and rights. Within this ethic of justice, the morality of abortion is determined by specifying whose right dominates, the mother's or the unborn's. Although feminist ethicians have used the ethic of justice to argue that abortions are moral (because the mother's rights are always supreme), it has also been used to argue that abortions are always immoral (because the unborn's right to life overrules any right of the mother not to suffer). This perspective lends itself to such absolute claims because its element of impartiality is easily universalized: it is always the case that superior rights prevail over inferior rights. Now, if Gilligan has correctly distinguished masculine and feminine modes of ethical reasoning, and if any appeal to rights and the norms of justice truly forms a "male" ethics, then natural law arguments about abortion—with their appeals to justice and human rights—would seem irrelevant to women who consider ethical questions in terms of relationships.

But it is not correct to characterize natural law as being dominated by the so-called male perspective—especially the natural law of Thomas Aquinas. For love and its relationships are central to his ethics[5]—so central that he even bases justice upon love. Justice requires that one respect the equality given by one's "humanness."[6] Such respect is not possible unless one cares about equality and such caring is not possible unless the humanness establishing that equality is first loved. Thus, love establishes the possibility of justice and its endurance. It also establishes the obligations of care. This is because the humanness so valued by Thomistic love establishes each and every one of us in a relationship with every other human—a relationship that obligates caring. Thus, since relationships and their obligations are essential to both Aquinas's natural law and the "feminist" ethic of care, Aquinas's natural law not only has a "feminist" perspective but its very basis is relationship and love. Moreover, Aquinas' natural law is an ethic of care that nourishes an ethic of justice. Such is its 'feminism' and such is its single vision that captures the dual perspective that Gilligan describes as mature.[7]

Now, within the feminist boundaries of relationship and the ethic of care must abortion always be treated as morally legitimate?[8] Or, can relationship and love suffice for showing abortion to be immoral? I shall argue that since abortion violates relationship, it is immoral. In order to be successful my argument must show that the relationship between the preborn and mother entails ethical obligations that proscribe abortion.

At first glance it does not seem possible for my argument to succeed, because it is difficult to establish at what point a mother begins to experience her relationship to her preborn child. Indeed, it is likely that various women form this bond at different times. So it seems that abortion must be morally permissible before the mother feels related to her preborn child.

However, the parental relationship is not simply a unidirectional bond extending from parent to child; it also extends from child to parent. After all, it is the existence of a child that makes a man and a woman parents. Thus, it is the relation of origin that establishes a specific man and a specific woman as responsible for a new human being. This relation of origin is never reversible, changeable, or erasable. It is permanent; it always remains regardless of whether the new life is measured in seconds or decades.[9]

This relationship of origin begins at the moment when physiological changes indicate that the self-changing entity is human. And this is the point of conception—as even some pro-abortionists now admit. For from this point onward the fertilized egg takes charge of its own development into a newborn infant.

Now, the relation of origin that establishes the sources of new human life as parents also establishes them as responsible for their offspring. Relationships of origin that entail human dependencies also entail responsibilities and the moral obligation of fulfilling those responsibilities. For to hold otherwise would be to hold that none are responsible for the human dependencies they create. It would be akin to saying that it would be ethical for a pharmacist to refuse to dispense drugs after cornering the market and eliminating all other druggists. But such a refusal would be immoral: one is morally responsible for respecting the humanity of her dependents. Accordingly, morally obligated responsibilities follow from the act of creating the union between a specific sperm and egg. Responsible parents meet the obligations arising from their offsprings' dependencies. They safeguard their own children's health, education, etc. In short, they acknowledge that the relation of origin entails a relation of human dependency that they cannot morally ignore or deny.

But why should the relations of origin and human dependency preclude abortion when a pregnancy is unwanted or due to rape?

According to the "feminism" of Aquinas' natural law, one must fulfill the obligations inherent in one's relationships. For example, since one's humanness relates one to every human being, one is always obligated to respect that humanness by willing good to each and by not harming. No exceptions. This means that once one is in the parental relationships of origin and dependency, one must fulfill the moral obligations inherent in those relationships. Every parent is morally obliged to seek her child's good and to avoid harming her child. If she is unable to care for her child, she is obliged to seek someone who can assume the responsibilities of the parental relationship and care for her child. In some cases, giving one's child up for adoption may be the only moral alternative. But in no case can one justify killing the child. For within the parental relationship, one is morally obliged to act within the boundaries of parenting, i.e. to promote the well-being of one's child and to avoid harming her. For example, if a mother fails to provide for the life of her toddler, it is child abuse: she is violating the moral obligations of parenting. The relationship of parenting always requires that loving care be given to one's offspring. To kill, to willfully deprive another of life is antithetical to parenting, and to love. Abortion violates the parental relationship established by the existence of the preborn. As such it violates the "feminism" of natural law which obliges honoring one's relationships and expressing loving care.

Perhaps one might feel that in certain cases, abortion offers a legitimate way to end a relationship that is "destroying" a woman's life, just as breaking up with a violent boyfriend is legitimate. Is this possible? No, a relationship with a boyfriend is not a relation of origin; it is not irreversible. Rather, its existence essentially requires continual consent. But one's relationship with an in-dwelling fetus does not require continual consent; it is a fact of nature and physiology. This is especially true of the relationship of origin: it spontaneously exists independently of one's choice from the moment of conception. Human choice cannot reverse time and "erase" existence. Killing the preborn does not retroactively prevent their conception, just as killing an adult does not retroactively erase the fact of her existence and the fact that her parents were a particular man and woman. Thus, from the moment that a new human being is conceived, the parental relationship is irreversibly established and its moral obligations are binding. And since abortion is an act directly contrary to the moral obligation of pursuing the health of one's offspring, abortion is immoral—as least as immoral as killing the unwanted boyfriend.

Furthermore, the "feminism" of Aquinas' natural law also condemns abortion as immoral because it is morally imperative to "love neighbors as thyself." This norm obliges loving oneself, i.e. willing good to oneself. It is immoral not to properly love oneself. But the immorality of abortion partially exists in a two-fold failure to love oneself. For abortion negates the humanness of the fetus. This negation and rejection of a fetus's very real humanness negates and rejects one's own humanness. Humanness is the same whether found in a fetus or in an adult. Thus, since abortion involves the refusal to love another's humanness, it also involves the refusal to love oneself. Such refusals denigrate and destroy what is intrinsically valuable. As such, they show hatred of humanity. Indeed, one cannot hate her indwelling offspring and still properly love herself and her neighbors. Does not abortion involve killing the closest neighbor possible, i.e. the neighbor of the womb? Moreover, abortion kills the closest possible likeness to self, that is one's own child. The conceptus is the only thing creatable capable of reflecting one's own full existential range. To abort is to destroy intentionally one's own replicate. Thus, abortion is a failure to love oneself and the self's creative power properly. It sets oneself against nature and its ultimate Creator. Accordingly, abortion involves contempt not only for the preborn child and one's reproductive abilities, but for God. And so, killing the innocent—even if preborn—can never be an act of love.

Therefore, the "feminism" of Aquinas ultimately shows that love answers the question of abortion's morality. Love always honors truth—especially relational truths, such as the dawning of the relationships of origin and human dependency at the moment of conception. Accordingly, love seeks to protect and to cherish the preborn from that moment. Thus, it abhors abortifacient drugs and the abortionist's knife.

NOTES

1. See *In A Different Voice* (Cambridge: Harvard University Press, 1982), particularly p. 159: "Similarly, the standard of moral judgment that informs [women's] assessment of self is a standard of relationship, an ethic of nurturance, responsibility, and care." And, p. 173: "Yet in the different voice of women lies the truth of an ethic of care, the tie between relationship and responsibility,... "

2. See, for example, Nel Noddings, *Caring: A Feminine Approach to Ethics and Moral Education* (Berkeley: University of California Press, 1984).

3. Complete relativity is not characteristic of all feminist ethics. See, for example, *Women and Moral Theory,* eds. Kittay and Meyers (Minneapolis: University of Minnesota Press, 1987).

4. But, feminism does not necessarily support abortion. See Celia Wolf-Devine, "Abortion and the 'Feminine Voice,' " *Public Affairs Quarterly,* Vol. 3, No. 3 (July 1989): 81–97.

5. See his *Summa Theologiae,* I-II, 100, 3 ad 1. This is the crucial text that establishes love as foundation for Aquinas' dissertation, "Love and the First Principles of St. Thomas's Natural Law" (Ann Arbor, Michigan: University Microfilms International, 1988).

6. Aquinas explains that the integral parts of justice preserve equality by proscribing harming others and establish equality by prescribing giving others their due. See *Summa Theologiae* II-II, 79, 1c and ad 2.

7. See pages 166–7 wherein she describes maturity as considering the dualistic frameworks of the ethic of care and the ethic of justice.

8. For important arguments about the morality of abortion that specifically address feminist senses of relationship see Wolf-Devine, *op. cit.* (in footnote 4).

9. I first heard this notion of the unbreakability of the parent-child relationship from Dr. Thomas Sullivan, in a conversation about the nature of marriage.

Chapter 16

LIVING TOGETHER:
BURDENSOME PREGNANCY
AND THE HOSPITABLE SELF

Mary Catherine Sommers

In her article "Abortion and Organ Donation," Patricia Beattie Jung sets out to prove that "Childbearing," like organ donation, "is always in part (if not largely) an act of charity,"[1] where charity comprises supererogatory and discretionary acts, as distinct from acts which are requirements of justice. The analogy is grounded in the notion of "bodily life support," which is of its nature a form of assistance which cannot avoid being invasive and burdensome to the donor.[2] This understanding of both childbearing and organ donation logically entails that every decision about continuing a pregnancy or donating bodily products or organs produces a tragic conflict between self-love and love of others. According to Jung, "neither available option can express human love in its fullness." Therefore, with respect to childbearing "elements of what is authentically human can be expressed *both* in the decision to abort and in the decision to bear the burdensome child."[3]

It is possible, as Dr. Jung herself suggests, to advance a number of disanalogies between organ donation and pregnancy, among them the fact that the preborn is already 'there,' making the refusal to continue pregnancy more like discontinuing bodily life support than declining to provide it, as would be the case if a kidney transplant were refused.[4] In replying to Jung's thesis, I can, nevertheless, accept her analogy. There is a structural similarity between the experience of discovering an unplanned pregnancy and discovering any other situation where there is a need for bodily life support to be extended. It is a morally significant experience because it is the moment at which a good to be desired is first apprehended.

In beginning from this analogy, I assume, as it does, that the preborn has a moral status equivalent to the person requiring an organ transplant. I also assume, along with Jung, that the obligation to extend life support in some sense to one's neighbor is not in question, but specifically *bodily* life support.[5] I propose to question in turn these features of Jung's thesis: 1) that the bodily character of certain forms of life support fundamentally alters the obligation to give life support; 2) that the involvement of women's bodies alters the obligation to give life support in the case of pregnancy; 3) that bodily life support is necessarily charity; 4) that the suffering involved in completing the burdensome pregnancy necessitates that it be an act of charity, since otherwise society or God would be unjust. In addressing these claims I hope as well to suggest a "form of life" within which the obligation to give life support becomes intelligible. I think Hauerwas is correct that arguments against abortion which are abstracted from any substantive commitments about what kind of people we should be, fail.[6] If arguments I offer against Jung's thesis are successful, it is because a life pattern where one must choose between self-love and other-love has little to offer in comparison with one where self-love expresses itself in hospitality.

244

Bodily Life and Bodily Life Support

A woman's right to control her own body is offered by Patricia Beattie Jung and other authors as a value to be weighed in the scale against the preborn's right to life. Two arguments for the existence and protection of the right to control are: 1) that the body is a person's property, and that one's right to its use and disposition should not differ from the rights attached to ownership in general; and 2) that bodily integrity is a foundation of specifically human or moral action and that bodily integrity requires control over one's body.

The first position has a paradigmatic exposition in J. J. Thomson's famous article "A Defense of Abortion." An analysis of Thomson's examples and analogies reveals a consistent theory of property rights and the body as property. This theory holds that the terms of possession, the use, development and disposal of property are unconditionally under the control of the possessor. The body is compared to the house (the archetypal American property, defensible in the myths by the gun-toting patriarch): the house sealed contraceptively against fetal invasion;[7] the house invaded and blown up along with its maternal inhabitant by the fetal invader;[8] the house which, when all is said and done, is owned by the mother.[9] Property rights are *the right par excellence* surpassing all other rights. It is irrelevant for Thomson whether the preborn requires nine minutes use of maternal property, nine months, or the destruction of that property; the issue is the absolute nature of property rights. It may be "greedy, stingy, callous" or even "indecent" for individuals to refuse to share what costs them little with someone with whom they come in contact who is in need, but it is not unjust.[10] The only justice question is who has "clear title" to the property or if the title has been compromised by some degree of voluntary alienation. The image of the "just" boy who "solidly eat[s] his way through the box" of chocolates while his brother, watching, has none, has clear implications for other justice issues as well as for abortion. A finer unconsciously drawn picture of first and third world relations is difficult to imagine.

But it is not obviously unjust to have to use, develop or even disperse one's property in a way one had not planned or foreseen, unless one assumes an absolute theory of ownership. The recognition in common law of right of ways, easements and eminent domain tell against the absolute theory, as do restrictions on the use of force to prevent unauthorized entry, use or destruction of property. Civil rights laws restrict one's discretion in disposing of property or dispensing one's services: owning the pizza parlor does not give me the right to refuse service on the basis of race, religion, or sex; and the same is true of selling one's house or dispensing professional services. More recently, 'stakeholders' in corporations, e.g., employees, customers, "even the community generally" have been recognized to have interests which can be protected, along with those of the shareholders or owners of a corporation.[11]

Why should an unconditional theory of property rights be assumed in defense of abortion unless it is coherent with common understanding of property or is argued to be superior? The requirement of "preplanning" to create obligations towards another with respect to one's property, indeed, seems to have the serious deficiency of ignoring the contingent character of much of human experience. Further, property itself provides space and occasions for contingencies and so for any moral obligations which might arise out of contingencies.

The claim, then, that because a woman's body is her property she has a right to use or dispose of it solely according to her wishes, can only be upheld on the basis of the principle of unconditional ownership of property. This understanding of ownership ignores the legal restrictions placed on ownership from the point of view of the social purposes of property. Ethically considered, the unconditional theory seems to involve a retrogressive consciousness: a return to "a man's home is his castle, to be defended by his gun."

Perhaps it can be argued that the body is a special sort of property or that one does not so much have a body but is "body-ly," or is "embodied." This could create rights to the body which could not be abrogated for any social purpose. The argument, which Jung adapts from Donagan, about the relation between bodily integrity and moral agency, is meant to lead to the existence of these special property rights. "We do not," she says, "hold persons accountable for choices made under undue duress or coercion."[12] This can be explained by the dependence of moral (free, deliberated) action on a condition of bodily integrity or nonviolation. If the possibility of moral agency depends on nonviolation, then this creates a right on the part of the agent to have the body's integrity respected by others and the obligation to accord this respect as well. The right to have one's bodily integrity respected is interpreted by Jung as meaning that no claim can be made upon one's body by another.

If this means that no one has a moral claim upon another if that moral obligation would have to be fulfilled through or by the body of another, it is indefensible. Precisely because I am embodied, there are few moral obligations I can fulfill without engaging the body. For example, if a person or governmental agency has the right to supoena my testimony in a civil or criminal matter, this is usually accompanied by the right to my physical attendance at the proceeding. The same would apply to service on juries and the practice or sequestration, for indeterminate periods. I would not be excused from this duty because of discomfort, inconvenience, or lost opportunities; although ill health or danger to my health would serve as an excuse.

The argument, then, that "bodily life support," like childbearing or organ donation, cannot be a moral requirement because no person can have a claim against the body of another, fails if the nature of the claim is not specified. Perhaps Jung could argue that, while bodily presence could be required where there is a sufficient reason, no claim which involves bodily contact or bodily intimacy or bodily sharing of any kind could be required: no claim against my separateness.

I will not discuss whether such a claim could be justified short of the need to preserve life. It may be argued that a woman struggling onto a bus with two children and a stroller has no claim on anyone's helping hand. But if a small child is about to wander into a busy street, have I not the same obligation to restrain him as the driver of the car has to put on the brakes?

If, for a moment, we take "bodily life support" to mean providing the means of life to another with one's body, it will cover a variety of activities involving the agent in degrees of intimacy with the other person. Carrying a person out of danger, applying pressure to a cut, resuscitating a drowning victim, warming a person with hypothermia, breast-feeding or giving breast-milk to a premature baby, giving blood, bone marrow or bodily tissue or organs: all of these are forms of bodily life support. It is, I think, obscuring the issue to limit bodily life support to "any form of assistance which entails an invasion of the giver's body" as Jung does,[13] since it begs the question of whether invasion is a morally significant factor.

247

Jung seems to argue that the more personal the possession claimed by another's need, the "closer" it gets to us, the more it becomes the matter of charity or gift rather than justice. At the point of invasion, no claim of justice is possible.[14] There are two problems with this line of demarcation: 1) it is not obvious that "inside" one's body is more personal than "outside"; and 2) the argument that the personal character of something would exempt it from claims of justice simply does not work. It would be difficult to claim that anything bodily is more personal than my memory; yet, the most private, incommunicable memory that I have could rightly be claimed by another to save her life. The rape victim, whose body has inarguably been invaded, is morally obligated to testify against her attacker unless she could consistently will that any other woman be so violated.

This framework, therefore, is not useful in determining the nature of moral claims against my body. Let me offer another. There is, J. J. Thomson notwithstanding, a distinction between my body and other kinds of possessions. The body is personal *per se,* and not simply personalized, through acquisition or creation like all other property. Therefore, it cannot ever revert to common usages, nor could I ever, morally, damage or sunder its orientation to my good as a person. Therefore, unlike the food I do not require or the second coat in my closet, my body cannot cease to be "mine," and can only become another's property as well where this does not diminish it as mine personally.

A moral claim which I can only carry out by means of my body is not the same as a claim against my body as an impersonal instrument. The mad scientist of the B-horror film, who extends his life indefinitely with a potion made from the vital organs of young women, has taken their bodies as an impersonal means to his own life. Their right to their own lives is negated. The physician who implants in a Parkinson's victim the tissue of human offspring, who have been killed for that purpose, has denied that the human body is by rights a means to personal life. The physician who transplants the heart of a clinically dead accident victim has not.

Because the very meaning of "organ" implies the ordering of bodily parts to the sustenance of life, any claim against my bodily organs *as such* is an impersonal claim, since it is the claim of one person's life against or in place of another's. I would argue, with

Jung, that "nobody, simply as a human being in need, has a claim" to another's body in this way.[15] It is a claim against his body as *organized* to support his life: this is a claim against personal bodily life as such. A spouse or a child might have such a claim because of commitments which have deepened the orientation of personal bodily life; perhaps one's country as well, when in situations where any one's bodily life is threatened. But these are separate questions.

Certain forms of bodily life support, then, are not matters of justice. But what holds in the case of organ donation, does not hold in the case of the giving of life support through one's bodily products. Resuscitation, warming and breast-feeding are life-supporting acts which employ bodily products and are necessarily intimate. These products are renewable and "exuberant," and so in most cases easily shared and replaced. Claims against me for these products do not constitute claims against my body precisely as organized to support my life. They could, then, be just under the same conditions that any claim for my assistance in maintaining another's life could be just. Since the body is the normal instrument for carrying out my moral obligations, the involvement of my body in the process is *not by itself* a reason for dispensing with a moral obligation. If I have an obligation to use what is at my disposal to prevent the death of another human being, it is irrelevant that what I make use of is my body.

Suppose that a woman is trapped by an earthquake in a cellar with a new-born infant whose mother is dead or is dying from the building's collapse; suppose also that there is both food and drink in the cellar, but only of a kind directly useful to adults. If the child were older, perhaps all the woman would be obligated to do is open cans and mash the contents. But if she were able to breast feed the infant, would not justice require that she do so, given that the food available is useless as a direct means of life?

The Obligation to Give Life Support

Even if we limit our consideration to those moral obligations "which are requisite for a barely human social existence,"[16] the moral minimum, a general positive duty to provide life-sustaining assistance to others, can be shown to exist which does not exempt bodily life support. Simon, Powers, and Gunneman, in discussing corporate social responsibility, argue that the duty to avoid and correct self-caused social harm, the moral minimum, creates a duty to prevent harm not obviously self-caused, under certain conditions. They call this the Kew Gardens Principle, after the location of Kitty Genovese's murder in front of thirty-eight bystanders. The conditions they require are 1) need; 2) capability; 3) proximity; and 4) last resort. They presuppose that in rendering assistance to others one does not imperil oneself or interfere with duties owed to others.[17]

In the case of the woman trapped with the newborn and in the case of the woman "trapped" by pregnancy, the need of inchoate human life to be sustained is clear; that the woman in each case is the last resort for the needy one is also clear. Whatever further means she may require to render life support, without her, it cannot be rendered.

The capability and proximity factors are more problematic. That women, in general, have the physical capacity for nursing and bearing children is inarguable, but it is precisely the relation between capacities (physical or otherwise) and moral obligation that needs clarification. Jung argues that it is precisely because this capacity is feminine that "this burden [of pregnancy] cannot be equitably distributed,"[18] and thus is not morally obligatory. Yet Jung would blame "the robust passerby . . . if he or she fails to save the drowning child by rolling him or her out of the puddle."[19] A "robust" constitution is certainly a characteristic which is relevant to establishing the obligation to render living-saving assistance through bodily means. What is unclear is why having breasts, milk glands, or a womb are not similarly relevant to the starving newborn's or the developing preborn's need for life-support.

If a person has a knack for making money, he or she may justly be required to contribute unequally to financing the public sector through progressive income taxes. A person with professional expertise may be asked to assume the burden of blowing the whistle on an unsound building or hazardous emissions or fraudulent business practices. The fact that not everyone possesses or could possess these capacities does not render their exercise in every situation discretionary. Capacities do not enable us only in the presence of those situations which we anticipate and desire: they simply enable us. This is because putting them into play, exercising and developing

them, is inseparable from opening them up to needs we did not fore-
see. When such a need presents itself, therefore, we could meet the
condition of capacity without having chosen its exercise in this particular situation.

Gender-related capacities like those for childbearing and com-
bat duty do not appear to be exempt from these conditions. It is, perhaps, the politics of these capacities which have created claims for
exemption, rather than anything in the capacities themselves. This
issue cannot be addressed satisfactorily here. But in using abortion
to exempt reproductive capacities from the general consequences of
enablement, women are losing an important historical moment.
Women quite rightly object to being the only segment of society
whose responsibility for life-support to preborn and born offspring
is enforced by law: cooperation in society's reproductive task is
hardly encouraged by the prosecution of young cocaine addicts
whose babies have absorbed drugs in the womb; particularly in conjunction with the lack of a general will to compel fathers to contribute to the support of their children. The Laws of the good city, as
Socrates argues in the *Crito,* should be able to say to the citizen: "We
have given you birth, nurtured you, educated you, we have given you
and all other citizens a share of all the good things we could."[20]
Parenting, then, is a task towards which the resources of a whole society should be turned. But one cannot argue consistently both that
the decision to extend bodily life support to one's offspring is simply
the discretionary use of one's body for a personal project and, that
others, from the father of the child to one's fellow-citizens, are bound
to support this project in various capacities. One could argue that in
a society which, consistent with its individualistic principles, has *de
facto* shifted ultimate responsibility for offspring to those who physically bear them, there is no other way to return to a communal
sense of responsibility unless women abandon or refuse the burden.
The short answer to this is that revolution, like war, has its rules: it
should not be waged on the innocent; Astyanax should not be
thrown off the tower.

Is the fact that a capacity is gender-related relevant at all to its
status in a moral argument? It is, oddly enough, irrelevant to Jung's
argument. If, as she claims, "Nobody, simply as a human being in
need, has a claim to the use of another's body," then the gender of the

body is irrelevant. It should therefore also be irrelevant if one accepts the contrary of her claim, that "Everybody, simply as a human being in need, has some claim to the use of another's body."

It remains to examine the criterion of proximity. Simon, *et al.* understand proximity to be "largely a function of notice: we hold a person blameworthy if he knows of imperilment and does not do what he reasonably can do to remedy the situation."[21] Notice can be actual, where something "comes" to our attention, or constructive, where it is reasonable to expect that we be attentive to it. Now it seems to be true that notice can create proximity where none would normally exist. There is a genre of thriller where the hero, quite by accident, becomes aware of a global plot and, thus, becomes the only person who can save the world from tyranny or annihilation. But given the nearly limitless access that mass media has provided to the needs of others, it may be doubted whether any meaningful concept of proximity can be based on notice. Constructive notice, indeed, is rather based on proximity, "the network of social expectations that flow from notions of civic duty, duties to one's family, and so on."[22]

The question "who is my neighbor?", then, remains the crucial one in determining the obligation to give bodily life support. Susan Nicholson does not think that the rape victim has such an obligation to her offspring, because this is only a relationship of neighborhood.[23] I would hold that proximity or neighborhood is enough of a relationship to obligate, where the other three criteria of need, capacity and last resort have been met.

How, then, is proximity created? Every human being has, at least, an obligation to self-development. Even a moral egoist could concede this much. The project of self-development involves locating, having a place to live, routing one's business, social and recreational activities, acquainting oneself with those persons without whom these activities would not be successful. Locating, therefore, creates a neighborhood. This neighborhood is mapped out by deliberated, substantially free choices, but, at the same time, it creates a field open to collisions which are not desired or anticipated.

But it is arbitrary to limit one's obligations to those desired or contracted for those, in other words, which result directly from the choices which delineate my neighborhood. The proximity to the undesired or unplanned events is self-created, and indispensable to the project of self-development. Proximity is an access to my capacities which I create in the process of realizing my project of self-development. Unless I could argue, like the egoist does, that the field of action or neighborhood is nothing other than the instrument of self-realization, I am bound to be attentive to needs which are manifested within it the, environmental, but especially the personal.

The response made to unforeseen needs can be characterized as reception of the alien, as hospitality. A neighborhood is visited, and the visitors will be expelled, killed, ignored or welcomed. The alien is "out of place" geographically or politically; in the neighborhood which I have created through my attempts at self-realization, the alien is not "on the map" or "in the plan"; he or she crosses *my* path, a path laid out in freedom, but which cannot always be kept free because of inherent instability of human affairs. Hospitality should be extended to the alien because 1) the neighborhood into which he/she has strayed is inseparable from the project of self-development; 2) the imperative to self-development exists for other persons beside oneself and, therefore, one's neighborhood is necessarily a 'cross roads'; 3) the contingency of human life can quickly reverse the role of host to guest. If one is to claim proximity elsewhere—having lost, or being outside of the normal nexus of kinship, friendship, citizenship—one must grant it to the alien through hospitality.

The four criteria which the Kew Gardens Principle lays down for determining when I ought to come to someone's aid can be used to determine obligations to extend hospitality arising from various needs, capacities, etc. We are concerned here only with the need for life support. The four criteria can be specifically reformulated for these cases into a Law of Hospitality: No one can refuse the means of life to those in his/her proximity unless or until alternative means are located, except when refusal will preserve the life of the donor (or the body as organized to support his/her life) or where the means are non-renewable sources of life to the donor or to those to whom the pattern of the donor's life is primarily committed.

Burdensome Pregnancy and the Obligation to Extend Hospitality

We can return now to the problem of assessing the obligation to give bodily life support to the woman trapped in a cellar with a newborn and the woman trapped in a pregnancy she neither anticipated nor desires.

First, I would like to defer discussion of pregnancies resulting from rape and incest, since the creation of proximity in these cases is more complex. In the case of other unplanned pregnancies, proximity results from the exercise of the sexual capacities, chosen as a part of the project of self-development. The partners in the sexual act could intend many different things: good things, sad things, ugly, cruel or just trivial things. Whatever their intentions, whatever they conceive the place of this act (or pattern of acts) to be in their plans for themselves, their intentions do not exhaust the possibilities of the act. One person may intend only the exchange of pleasure, the other may fall in love. The framework of what one expects or plans is *not* the boundary of one's moral responsibility, if the act, as it happens, breaks through those boundaries. The claims of the person who found love where only pleasure was expected or of the unplanned offspring are claims resulting from the voluntary act as it grows into an event, through its encounter with other choices, natural necessities and contingencies. The intention certainly has primary place in the moral formation of the person: if I intend to murder and am frustrated in the execution of it, I, nevertheless, have made myself "murderous"; but if I intend only some rigorous game and end up killing someone, my character can hardly be untouched by my act which has "gone murderous." Further, my duty to correct this harm, while not identical to the murderer's, is certainly clear.

The unintended lover, the unintended offspring, are 'aliens' to the pattern of living laid out by my intentions.[24] They are, then, subject to the enemy-guest ambiguity present in the notion of 'alien' or 'stranger'. Response to the alien resolves the notion of *xenos* into either xenophobia or philoxenia, into hostility or hospitality. Plato, in the *Laws,* recognizes the existence of a contract between the citizen and the alien as well as between citizen and citizen. It is, in fact, more rigorous: "For the alien, being without friends or kinsmen, has the greater claim on pity, human and divine." Sodom has come to symbolize sexual license; its worst crime was to violate hospitality.[25]

The carrying of an 'uninvited' offspring is an act of hospitality, as is all the labor its father, grandparents, or society should expend on the support of mother and child. These are not acts of supererogation, but those demanded of a civilized people; the stranger should neither be killed nor left to perish in his need because we did not know he was coming, or because he is 'out of place.'

Why is such an act not charity? First of all, any good act may be an act of charity, in the Christian sense, if it is done 'for the sake of the Kingdom.' If I take in the stranger because my sharing with her is a foretaste of our permanent shared life in God's presence, this is charity. If I take her in because she is cold and hungry and I have the means to relieve her without significant deprivation to myself, this is hospitality.

Further, hospitality is essentially a response to a temporary state of affairs. The stranger becomes a guest; the guest is expected to pass through. The guest has the 'freedom of the house', but not 'residence.' Even these passing relationships are friendly in Aristotle's sense, since there is some common life. But charity tends to the permanent and the unconditional. Even the friendships celebrated by Plato and Aristotle exhibit these characteristics: friends desire always to be together, they share all things in common. But for these ideal relationships the common ground has to be shared beauty, nobility or virtue. For Christian friendship or *caritas* the ground of the relationship is simply the shared capacity for living with God; there might be no other recognizable similarity between us. An act of charity is, therefore, an affirmation of the permanent and unconditional proximity of all God-destined beings, a proximity which is not even dependent on spatio-temporal relations. Where charity abides there is gratuitous co-habitation, permanent residence and unconditional use.

The parents of the uninvited offspring are morally obligated to sustain him/her only conditionally and temporarily: only what is required for life need be given, only until responsibility can be transferred. It is in the interests of the state, to encourage these parents to receive the child permanently. The 'living together' they must do in justice can become a time in which one or both parents commits to raising the child. But there are numerous acceptable ways for society and the parents to work out their mutual obligation to child support. The legalization of abortion, on the other hand, was a covenant of mutual abandonment.

We can turn now to the special cases of rape and incestuous abuse where, for the mother, at least, proximity to the uninvited offspring is not created in any sense through free choice. Like the woman trapped in the cellar with the newborn, proximity is created through violence; unlike her case, it is through a violation of personhood as well. Unlike all the other cases of claims for bodily life support, the woman who has become pregnant through rape or sexual abuse by a male relative does not 'discover' the need of the other from the pure position of capacity. She is not the 'robust passerby' or the householder with an abundance of food or extra rooms. The need of her offspring for bodily life support is created through her undergoing of abuse and victimization. She is the one left by the roadside, not the one passing by.

Does the woman pregnant through victimization have proximity with her offspring? All sufferers of the same violent act have proximity. They have alike been rendered significantly unfree by either 1) some natural upheaval: a fire, earthquake, flood; or 2) some accident: a sinking ship or plane crash: or worst of all, 3) have been impersonally manipulated to another's ends, like victims of a rapist or terrorist. They all have the task of re-establishing themselves as moral agents, of initiating again their directedness towards self-realization even with diminished means and possibilities. Does the task of each necessarily involve the others, except where this could be judged efficient? Where proximity is no more than common alienation, the capacity to reestablish a 'place to be' may be greater in some than in others. To the degree that they are enabled, these persons become obligated to assume the relation of householder to the others who are more 'displaced.' This is, like all hospitality, temporary and conditional. Nor does the obligation of the victims to help each other relieve other, non-victimized persons of responsibility for the situation.

The woman pregnant through rape or incestuous abuse is different from her offspring as a victim only in being capable of a moral response to their common state. As so enabled, she becomes obligated to 'place' the preborn; to extend hospitality, unless her life is in danger. If the abuse or other factors make her incapable of a moral (deliberated, free) response, then others into whose proximity both victims fall, must see to the needs of both equally. There is, however, no evidence to suggest that aborting restores moral agency.[26]

256

Burdensome Pregnancy and the Suffering of Women

It is inevitable that the question of suffering should arise in conjunction with these cases of pregnancy through victimization. But it is certainly not confined to these pregnancies. One might ask whether any argument which concludes to the obligation to complete burdensome pregnancies can be cogent, since it involves the mothers in pain and inconvenience which cannot be apportioned out to the others who share responsibility for child-support: the father, grandparents, the society as a whole. Is anyone morally obligated to remain in a painful situation which she did not consent to enter, and which others, at least as responsible as she for her predicament, cannot share with her?

First of all, for precisely the same reason that pain cannot in any meaningful sense be shared, it is an unreliable indicator of the just apportionment of burdens between persons. Experiences of pregnancy and birthing are very personal and the balance of pleasure and pain is created by many factors besides one's original attitude to becoming pregnant. Of soldiers in the same unit, some return home to be tortured by nightmares, others to pick up their lives where they left off. The justice of a war needs to be determined in some other fashion.

It might be argued that the inability to share pain among persons is not the issue, but the inability to share the burdens of childbearing between men and women—an inequality which is particularly egregious in the cases of rape and incestuous abuse, where the woman is in no way responsible for becoming pregnant. This structural inequality would then lead to the right of a woman to refuse bodily life support to the uninvited preborn. This seems to be just the reverse side of an obviously faulty argument which was mentioned earlier.[27] If it is mistaken for society *de iure* or *de facto* to assign the full burden of child-bearing to women simply because some part of the process is exclusively feminine, then it is equally wrong to argue from the 'exclusively feminine' part to a woman's right to refuse participation in the process. In both cases the necessary is mistaken for the sufficient. The woman's exclusive enablement to carry and nurture the offspring she has conceived gives a definite but limited responsibility for its birth and subsequent well-being. The failure of those who are co-responsible is a grievous

257

burden on women, the only ones concerned who cannot 'walk away.' But their failures neither reveal a right to abort nor create it.

C. S. Lewis remarks that pain is not much of a philosophical problem unless one introduces a loving and good God into the picture.[28] It is partly to save God from being implicated in the sufferings of women, especially poor, exhausted and victimized women, that M. R. Maguire argues for personhood as conferred by the mother's consent to bring the preborn into the human family. This would relieve God of the responsibility for creating persons from "ugly acts of rape and incest" or for tricking unsuspecting and unprepared women with a surprise pregnancy.[29] Unfortunately this intrusive, voyeuristic god is replaced by an equally unattractive bourgeois god who washes his hands of the sordid aspects of human freedom and watches complacently while the human crises of too many children, too little money, ill health or thwarted dreams are smoothed over by aborting the im-personal offspring.

This invasive deity, at once omnipotent and arbitrary, wherever introduced to determine the boundaries of human freedom, is a straw woman. It is dependent on a one-to-one image of providence, of events as 'happening to me' or 'God doing this to me.' Even the crude peeping-tom or chess master images of providence are not individualistic: there is a 'scene' or a 'configuration on the board.' But the providential character of any event does not result because God is watching or moving the pieces. Providence is first, a 'sending' or an 'opening up' of a field in which human acts, natural necessities and contingencies will intersect to create an event. Providence is also God's measuring presence which gives the creative freedom at work in the event its momentum towards salvation or damnation, its character of 'response.' Providence is certainly personal and teleological. The meaning of an event, though co-created, is ultimately resolvable into each person's movement towards God or away. But it is also essentially social. The burdensome pregnancy, therefore, does not 'happen to' a woman, it 'happens in' a providential opening and it 'happens for' those who co-created the event and those who participate in it. How it shall be 'for them' is a function of their response and the divine measuring.

If we accept St. Augustine's contention that human beings are bound to image God in their action, and only free to do it well or perversely, there will be two 'responses' to the burdensome pregnancy: they will be framed with the same words: "This is my body." One of the variants of this answer emphasizes the personal character of bodily life. This body is 'mine.' The other emphasizes the body as 'presentation,' the means by which the self is introduced into the context of its development, its world. 'Here' is my body. Are both these variants, as P. B. Jung suggest, "authentically human?" Is the choice between them "tragic" because neither reply is complete? The first variant is abstract, committed to no strategy for fulfillment, and is, therefore, unsatisfactory as a moral reply; it is also closed to the possibility of an origin or destiny beyond itself and is consequently unacceptable as a believer's reply.

The second variant, on the contrary, is an affirmation of my concrete presence in a world and before God. It is also an offering, but it is not sacrificial in the sense Jung uses this term.[30] To offer, to put one's self forward, is not to renounce the self in favor of the other, but to take up one's position among others. Nor is it a "voluntary vocation" in her sense, which requires that a stance of not offering, or abstractly affirming control of one's body, is equally authentic.[31] Solidarity is not an attractive option, but a moral necessity. For the Christian, it is the pattern of beatitude: the common life, the common table.

Self-offering is not, certainly, a commitment to crucifixion.[32] The cross is not an explanation, in that sense, of why the Christian woman should complete a burdensome pregnancy. Self-offering on the moral level is an acknowledgement that, as Aristotle argued, justice in its fullest sense is friendly.[33] On the level of Christian love it is a commitment to unconditional proximity; to a life plan in terms of which no other human being is alien. It is possible only because of God's gratuitous provision of a common life between human persons and the divine Trinity, a life only experienced fully in Beatitude.[34] It is the unconditional commitment to bringing about the common life that leads to the cross. When a woman replies 'Here is my body' to the event of the burdensome pregnancy she intends to 'live together' with her offspring because God has offered to 'live together' with them both. But offering oneself in aid of the common life is putting oneself 'in the open.' Since this is a fallen world, self-offering creates exposure to betrayal, violation, agony, even death on a tree. The pregnant woman, Christ-like, may be left alone to bear the full burden, while everyone else has run away or gone into hiding. A society striving for justice and a church working towards the kingdom will not tolerate those who run away from the pregnant woman and the preborn. Their refusal or proximity or neighborhood strikes at the heart of all common life, civil and ecclesial.

NOTES

1. Patricia Beattie Jung, "Abortion and Organ Donation: Christian Reflections on Bodily Life Support," in *Abortion and Catholicism: The American Debate*, N.Y.: Crossroad Publishing Co., 1988, 150; hereafter referred to as "Donation".

2. Ibid., 143.

3. Ibid., 163.

4. Ibid., 145–6.

5. Ibid., 151.

6. Stanley Hauerwas, "Abortion: Why the Arguments Fail," in *A Community of Character,* Notre Dame. Ind.: University of Notre Dame Press, 1981, 214.

7. Judith Jarvis Thomson, "A Defense of Abortion," *Philosophy and Public Affairs,* no. 1 (Fall, 1971) repr. in James P. Sterba, *Morality In Practice,* 2nd ed., Belmont CA: Wadsworth Publishing, 146.

8. Ibid., 143.

9. Ibid.

10. Ibid., 147.

11. Unocal Corporation v. Mesa Petroleum Co. 493 A2d 946. Opinion by Justice J. Moore, Supreme Court of Delaware, sects. 13–14.

12. "Donation," 152.

13. Ibid., 143.

14. Ibid., 151, 153.

15. Ibid., 151.

16. Ibid., 148.

17. John G. Simon, Charles W. Powers, Jon P. Gunnemann, "The Responsibilities of Corporations and their Owners," from *The Ethical Investor: Universities and Corporate Responsibility,* New Haven, Conn: Yale University Press, 1972, repr. in Tom L. Beauchamp and Norman E. Bowie, *Ethical Theory and Business,* 2nd ed., Englewood Cliffs, N.J.: Prentice-Hall, Inc., 1983, 90–92.

18. "Donation," 150.

19. Ibid., 151.

20. *Crito* 51c–d.

21. Simon, Power, Gunneman, 91.

22. Ibid.

23. Susan Nicholson, *Abortion and the Roman Catholic Church,* Knoxville, Tenn.: Religious Ethics, Inc., 1978, 59.

24. The offspring could be absolutely unintended, or unintended in some respect, e.g. as handicapped, as female, etc.

25. *Laws* 729d–730a; on the notion of hospitality v. Jean Danielou, "Exile and Hospitality" in *The Lord of History* Pt. I, trans. by Nigel Abercrombie, London: Longmans & Chicago: Henry Regnery, 1958, 59–71.

26. James T. Burtchaell, C. S. C., "Very Small Fry," in *Rachel Weeping and Other Essays on Abortion,* Kansas City & New York: Andrews and McMeel. Inc., 1982, 68–72.

27. v. supra, 13.

28. C. S. Lewis, *The Problem of Pain,* New York: MacMillan, 1962, c. 1, 24.

29. Marjorie Reiley Maguire, "Personhood, Covenant, and Abortion," in *Abortion and Catholicism: The American Debate,* New York: Crossroad Publishing Co., 1988, 101–120; 107.

30. "Donation," 161–2.

31. Ibid., 162.

32. Ibid., 161–2.

33. *Nicomachean Ethics* VIII, 1, 1155a 28.

34. cf. Thomas Aquinas, *Summa Theologiae* II–II q. 24, a. 1; q. 25, a. 1.

PART FOUR

PLURALISM, DISSENT, AND THE MAGISTERIUM

Chapter 17

ON AN ARGUMENT OF FR. CURRAN'S

J.M. Hubbard

The editors of *Abortion and Catholicism* state that Fr. Curran "provides an argument justifying the possibility of dissent from fallible church teachings."[1] In the following pages this argument will be examined to see what it is and whether it is sound. Fr. Curran considers matters other than dissent in his essay "Public Dissent in the Church," and they will be treated to the extent that they bear on his argument for public dissent. After having set out the argument I shall then try to evaluate it in the light of the teaching of the Church on infallibility.

It should also be noted that Fr. Curran's paper focuses on "pertinent issues and aspects of his present case" and "therefore is bound to serve as an apologetic or defense of his position."[2] In looking at his argument and evaluating it these aspects of Fr. Curran's essay will not be considered, for they do not bear on the argument itself nor need they be taken into consideration in order to evaluate it.

At first glance Fr. Curran's conclusion is surprising because it is unexceptionable. Who could object to the proposition that some noninfallible, authoritative teachings are such that theologians may dissent publicly from them? The teachings of the popes other than Encyclicals, for example, and the opinions of the Roman Congregations not ratified by the pope can be disputed publicly. Yet they are surely authoritative, noninfallible teachings. There is nothing new in this. One suspects that Fr. Curran is not quite correct when he says that "the central point at issue in the controversy is the possibility of public theological dissent from some noninfallible teachings."[3]

When one searches for the premiss for this conclusion his suspicion is confirmed. For the key notion in Fr. Curran's argument is that within the class of authoritative, noninfallible teachings some are more removed than others from the core and central faith realities.[4] The argument is, then, that since such teachings are "somewhat removed from the core and central faith realities" and therefore they can be subject to public dissent by theologians. But the unexpressed premiss, that any teaching somewhat removed from the core and central faith realities is such that a theologian may dissent publicly from it, is problematic to say the least.

First of all there is the very generality of the proposition. Surely it cannot be accepted in all its universality. For obviously a theologian may not dissent from the propositions of physics and chemistry, say. And yet they are (somewhat) removed from the core and central faith realities. (The "somewhat" also raises a problem, but that will be taken up later.) Perhaps, though, the natural sciences are outside the scope of this argument. But what of philosophy? Must one say that theologians may dissent from the truths of natural philosophy or of metaphysics? And are they not (somewhat) removed?

And what of the truths of ethics, for example that the good life consists in virtuous activity? That would seem to be a teaching (somewhat) removed from the core and central faith realities. And this would be so even if one takes faith in the broad sense to include faith and morals. Yet surely a theologian may not deny that this is human happiness.

So the truth of the unexpressed premiss is suspect, and that of course renders the argument unsound. But there is more, and this

266

will lead to the second problem with this premiss: How is one to understand the "somewhat" in it? The claim is that teachings that are somewhat removed from core and central faith realities are such that the theologian may dissent from them. But is this so? To answer this question a brief look at the nature of infallibility is required.

Infallibility is the assistance promised the Church to keep safe and faithfully expound the deposit of faith without error.[5] It is founded on God himself, Uncreated Truth. This assistance is necessary because all created truth is fallible, and so the testimony of created things becomes infallible only when rectified by Uncreated Truth.[6]

To understand this point we shall have to examine the act of faith. The act of divine faith, the supernatural virtue of faith, has as its formal motive God revealing.[7] We assent because God says it is so. His testimony, the witness of Uncreated Truth, is the basis or foundation for the act of divine faith. But how do we know that he says so, and how do we know what he says? To this end he gave us his word: Christ, Scripture and Tradition. However, in his wisdom God decreed that his Son return to him so that man could even more fully participate in the work of redemption. But without an authoritative interpretation scripture and tradition would be a dead letter,[8] and so Christ promised Peter and his successors, and the bishops united to them, an infallible assistance: "He who hears you hears Me,"[9] and "I will be with you until the end of time,"[10] and "the gates of hell will not prevail against you."[11]

The testimony of the Church is not the basis or foundation of the assent of divine faith. God revealing is, as was said. We believe because God has revealed it. However, because Scripture and Tradition are obscure, the testimony of the Church is a necessary condition for the assent of divine faith. The Church points out that God revealed, for example, that Christ is truly human and truly divine. The witness of the Church, then, is a necessary condition for the act of divine faith. It is not, however, the basis or foundation of this act. God revealing is.

One must be careful to distinguish the basis of the act of faith from its necessary condition. It is a bit like the act of thinking. A brain in good working order, so to speak, is a necessary condition for thinking. But thinking is not an act of the brain. So too, the testimony of the Church is a necessary condition for the assent of divine faith.

But the act of supernatural faith is based, not on the testimony of the Church, but on God revealing. This is what it means to say that the formal object or motive of faith is God revealing.

The matter can be put another way. The act of divine faith considered in itself, that is, considered in relation to its formal object or motive, is certain. For its formal object is God revealing, i.e., Truth Itself. However, in relation to us faith is obscure because lacking evidence. Faith is "the argument of things unseen, the substance of things hoped for,"[12] St. Paul says. Because of this lack of evidence we need the testimony of the Church and the Church must be assisted with certainty. For, as Aquinas points out, all human testimony is fallible unless rectified by God. We can say, then, that the Church is assisted in an absolutely infallible way when it acts as a necessary condition for the assent of divine faith. This is the infallibility that Vatican I and Vatican II speak of.

However, theologians agree that the Church is assisted infallibly in another context. Journet calls this divine assistance *prudential infallibility.*[13] This point is crucial for understanding subtleties of the notion of infallibility.

The reason for the distinction stems from the role the Church plays in proposing teachings. It can act simply as a necessary condition for an assent of faith as has been said. The basis of the act of faith is, then, God revealing, and the act of faith is an act of divine faith. The infallible assistance God gives his Church is absolute.

But the Church herself can be the very basis or foundation of an assent of faith. In this case the assent is of ecclesiastical faith or religious faith, as it is called. The difference between the two sorts of faith is founded upon their different bases or formal objects. In divine faith we say, "I believe because God says so." In ecclesiastical faith, we say, "I believe because the Church says so."

In ecclesiastical or religious faith, then, the Church is the immediate or direct basis or foundation of the act of faith. God, however, is the mediate or indirect foundation. For, he assists his church when she proclaims teachings for the sake of our salvation. Furthermore, this assistance can be either infallible or fallible.[14] In either case, however, the assistance will be prudential in nature, not absolute. So, absolute infallibility refers to the assistance the Church has in her role as necessary condition for the assent of divine faith. Prudential assistance refers to the assistance the Church has when she acts as proper basis or foundation for the assent of what is called ecclesiastical or religious faith. This latter assistance can be either infallible or fallible.

The Church is assisted, then, both in her role as necessary condition for an assent of divine faith and in her role as basis for an assent of ecclesiastical faith. In the former instance she always receives an absolute and infallible assistance; in the latter the assistance may be either infallible or fallible—it is always prudential. There are two sorts of infallibility, then, based on the Church's role in relation to an act of faith.[15] When the Church acts as necessary condition pointing out that God has revealed and what he has revealed she is assisted in an absolutely infallible way. When she acts as proper foundation for an assent of faith she is assisted in a prudential way, sometimes infallibly, sometimes fallibly. The fundamental contrast, then, is between an absolutely infallible assistance and a prudential (infallible or fallible) assistance. The notion of infallibility clearly is not a simple one.

When the Church acts simply as a necessary condition for the assent of faith the assistance she is given is absolutely infallible. She points out that God has revealed and what he has revealed. Her definitions are irrevocable and irreformable. She teaches definitively and absolutely. This is what absolute infallibility means. It is this sort of infallibility that was the subject of the definitions of infallibility of Vatican I and Vatican II. There are two sorts of propositions that are proposed by the Church with absolute infallibility. The first are those that are defined as revealed; the second are those defined as irreformable but not as revealed.[16] Examples of the first sort would be the teachings that Mary was full of grace and that she was conceived immaculately. Examples of the second sort would be condemnations of propositions not immediately opposed to doctrines of faith: dogmatic facts, for example that a certain council was ecumenical; the solemn canonization of a saint. As we have seen, Vatican I and Vatican II teach that both the solemn magisterium *and* the ordinary magisterium are assisted in an absolutely infallible manner with regard to these teachings.

How do we, the faithful, recognize this kind of infallible teaching authority? When it is a question of the Solemn or Extraordinary Magisterium (either the Pope alone, or the Pope joined with the bishops in Council) there is seldom any problem. The intention to teach definitively is clear. When it is a question of the ordinary magisterium (the bishops dispersed throughout the world and united to the Pope) Vatican II tells us that, "although the bishops, taken individually, do not enjoy the privilege of infallibility, they do, however, proclaim infallibly the doctrine of Christ on the following conditions; namely, when, even though dispersed throughout the world but preserving for all that amongst themselves and with Peter's successor the bond of communion, in their authoritative teaching concerning matters of faith and morals, they are in agreement that a particular teaching is to be held definitively and absolutely."[17]

There are four conditions, *Lumen Gentium* says, that mark a teaching of the ordinary magisterium as absolutely infallible: (1) the bishops preserve among themselves with the Roman Pontiff the bond of communion; (2) they teach authoritatively; (3) they teach on faith and morals; (4) they are in agreement that a particular teaching is to be held definitively and absolutely. Each of these conditions needs careful consideration, but such attention is not necessary for our purpose. An illustration may be helpful though: the infallibility of the pope prior to the solemn declaration of Vatican I was taught infallibly by the ordinary magisterium; and the Assumption of the Mother of God prior to its solemn definition by Pius XII was also taught infallibly by the ordinary magisterium.

Whenever these four conditions are met one can be sure that the teaching in question has been proposed by the ordinary magisterium in an *absolutely* infallible way. This is not to say that it will always be easy to verify whether these four conditions obtain, but if they do the teaching is proposed infallibly.[18] This, then, is one way the ordinary magisterium teaches infallibly and the conditions by which we can recognize these teachings.

But it is not the only sort of infallible exercise of the Church's teaching authority. As we have seen, when the Church acts as the foundation or basis for an assent of faith—not simply as necessary condition—she can be assisted either infallibly or fallibly. Journet calls this type of divine assistance prudential assistance and speaks of an infallible prudential assistance and a fallible prudential assistance.[19]

It is certain, Journet says, that when the Church acts as the foundation of an assent of faith she has divine assistance. This has been taught constantly by the Church.[20] The assent is not an act of divine faith; rather it is an act of what is called ecclesiastical faith or a religious assent. How do we recognize this type of divine aid and what is its character?

Vatican II describes this religious assent in the following passage and sets out in a general way the conditions for recognizing this degree of divine assistance.

> Bishops who teach in communion with the Roman Pontiff are to be revered by all as witnesses of divine and Catholic truth; the faithful, for their part, are obliged to submit to their bishops' decision, made in the name of Christ, in matters of faith and morals, and to adhere to it with a ready and respectful allegiance of mind. This loyal submission of the will and intellect must be given, in a special way, to the authentic teaching authority of the Roman Pontiff, even when he does not speak *ex cathedra* in such wise, indeed, that this supreme teaching authority be acknowledged with respect, and sincere assent be given to decisions made by him, conformably with his manifest mind and intention, which is made known principally either by the character of the documents in question, or by the frequency with which a certain doctrine is proposed, or by the manner in which the doctrine is formulated.[21]

The "loyal submission of will and intellect" is the religious assent due the Pope or the bishops in communion with the Roman Pontiff when they teach authoritatively on matters of faith or morals even when there is no solemn exercise of the magisterium.

Furthermore, we are told that our assent is to be conformed to the intention of the teaching and that this is to be judged from the character of the document, the frequency of the teaching or the manner of formulation. At one term, then, there will be an infallible prudential assistance that guarantees absolutely the *prudence* of a given teaching. At the other there will be only fallible prudential assistance. How are we to discern these cases and what exactly is our obligation?

We can say that teachings proposed to the whole Church over a long period of time and which the Church constantly repeats and refers to as being taught authoritatively are guaranteed with an infallible prudential assistance.[22] This means that it is impossible for the Church to err against prudence in proposing such a teaching although the teachings themselves are not proposed in an irrevocable and irreformable way. They are not taught definitively and absolutely.

Teachings, however, not proposed to the whole Church or not constantly taught are proposed in a fallible manner. This is not to say that there is no divine assistance at all. It means, rather, that there is no absolute guarantee of the prudence of such teachings, and it may be the case that after further reflection the teaching will be withdrawn, altered or even contradicted.[23]

When the assistance given the magisterium is prudentially infallible the faithful owe a loyal submission of intellect and will. To refuse such interior assent would be to sin against the supernatural virtues of religion, piety and obedience. However, since the infallible *prudential* assistance guarantees absolutely the prudence of the teaching but not its irrevocable or irreformable character it would seem that the faithful can think that the truths proposed could be formulated in some other way. There can be no question of thinking that the opposite of what is proposed could be true but perhaps with development a better formulation of the truth proposed will be found.

When, however, the prudential assistance given the magisterium is only fallible the faithful may think that the opposite of what is proposed can be true. Because the assistance given the Church is fallible one must not think that therefore there is no supernatural assistance at all. Journet is of the opinion that one can even speak, in this case, of an infallible assistance but only in a general and improper sense.[24] By this he means that the general thrust of such teachings safeguards the faith and is prudent, but this or that doctrine may be incorrect. Thus, to use his example, the teachings of the Roman Congregations, when not ratified by the Holy Father, generally are to be considered prudent even though in this or that case what is taught may be incorrect. For this reason it would seem that the faithful owe even to these teachings the "loyal submission of intellect and will" spoken of in *Lumen Gentium 25*. Of course, since

272

there is no irreformable definition, nor even infallible assurance, the faithful can investigate and, with due moderation and respect—for there is even here, after all, supernatural assistance—they can incline to the opposite of what is proposed.[25]

Thus the magisterium is assisted in several ways. First, there is an absolutely infallible assistance. In this case the magisterium teaches in an absolute way that certain doctrines are revealed. Many of these latter teachings become subject of a solemn pronouncement of the magisterium as was the case for the infallibility of the Pope and the Assumption of the Mother of God.

Second, the magisterium is assisted prudentially and that in an infallible way. In this case there can be no error against prudence on the part of the magisterium, although the doctrines proposed in this way may be reformulated. They are not proposed as irrevocable and irreformable. Doctrines proposed to the whole Church throughout the course of history but not taught as definitive and irreformable fall into this category of teachings. The teachings of many papal encyclicals and even of the Roman congregations when explicitly ratified by the Pope would be examples of this.

Third, the magisterium can be assisted prudentially and fallibly. Teachings of this sort do not engage the full authority of the magisterium, are not addressed to the whole Church, and lack the mark of constancy that characterize the previous category of teachings. Nevertheless, as has been noted, it should not be thought that because such teachings are fallible they lack divine assistance. On the contrary, as we have seen, Journet is of the opinion that such teachings can be called infallible in an extended and improper sense. This means that in a general way such teachings are prudent, i.e., that the Church does not act imprudently in proposing them, but that this or that particular teaching may be mistaken.

The faithful, for their part, owe a loyal submission of will and intellect to the magisterium. This allegiance of mind will be absolute when the assistance given the magisterium is absolutely infallible. In this case the truths proposed are guaranteed as revealed, or as irreformable although not defined as revealed. Their guarantee is absolute and definitive. The assent will then be the assent of divine faith; it will be unconditioned because the truths are proposed as irrevocable and irreformable. They are proposed absolutely and definitively. When the Church thus engages her supreme teaching authority, even through the ordinary magisterium, she is assisted by God in an absolutely infallible way.

When, however the magisterium is assisted in a prudential manner the faithful owe loyal submission of will and intellect; that is, religious assent or assent of ecclesiastical faith, conformable with the manifest intent of the magisterium. When that intention is to propose doctrines to the whole Church that have been constantly and repeatedly taught, then the prudential assistance Christ gives his Church is infallible. The religious assent in this case adheres to the absolutely prudential character of the teaching in such a way that it cannot believe it possible that the Church could err against prudence in proposing the teaching. However, the faithful understand that with development, a different, but not opposed, formulation of the teaching is possible since the infallible prudential assistance guarantees the prudence of the teaching but not its irreformable character.

Furthermore, when the ordinary magisterium is aided in a fallible manner the faithful are bound to assent with a loyal allegiance of mind for there is supernatural assistance. One can even say that in a general way such teachings preserve authentic doctrine. But, since the assistance is fallible in nature the faithful can, after due consideration, come to the opinion that this or that particular teaching is mistaken.

We can say, then, that the magisterium is infallible in three very different but related ways. It is absolutely infallible; it is prudentially infallible; and in an improper sense of "infallible" we can even say that it is infallible in a general way.

After this brief and perhaps a bit complicated, but necessary, excursion into the various sorts of infallibility it is time to return to Fr. Curran's argument. The problem is his claim that any proposition that is somewhat removed from core and central faith realities is one that a theologian may publicly dissent from. In view of what has just been said let us examine this claim.

It would seem legitimate to consider the core and central faith realities to be coextensive with teachings proposed with an assistance that is absolutely infallible. If this is correct then the premiss in question is clearly false. For, as we have seen, the magisterium is assisted in a prudential way that is also infallible. This means that the

274

Church, in proposing things to be believed or done cannot err against prudence. This in turn implies that the opposite of these teachings cannot be true. For, if they were, then error against prudence in proposing them would be possible. There may, indeed, be development with respect to the formulation of such teachings, but their opposite cannot be true. Hence, their denial is not possible.

So once again we see that the key assertion in Fr. Curran's argument cannot withstand scrutiny. Furthermore, if one extends the notion of core and central faith realities to include even these latter sort of teachings, then one might wonder whether the class has not now become too large and inclusive to do the duty Fr. Curran would have it do. An examination of this point would, however, take us beyond the intention of the present remarks.

So we may conclude, from these remarks, that Fr. Curran's argument for public theological dissent from some noninfallible teachings is flawed because it depends on a false premise.

NOTES
1. P. B. Jung and T. A. Shannon, eds., *Abortion and Catholicism: The American Debate* (New York: Crossroad Pub. Co., 1988), p. 297.
2. C. Curran, "Public Dissent in the Church," in *op. cit.,* p. 301.
3. *Ibid,* p. 306.
4. *Ibid.* pp. 309, 310.
5. Denz, 1836.
6. Aquinas, *On Truth* 14, 8. "All created truth is defective unless it is rectified by Uncreated Truth. Therefore, assenting on the testimony of men or angels does not infallibly lead to truth unless one considers the testimony of God speaking through them."
7. Aquinas, *Summa Theologiae* 11–11, 1, 1, c.
8. 2 Pet. 3:15–17.
9. Luke 10:16
10. Matt. 28:20
11. Matt. 16:18–19.
12. Heb. 11:1
13. Charles Journet, *The Church of the Incarnate Word* (Tr. A. C. Downes: Sheed and Ward, New York, 1955) Vol. 1, p. 333 and p. 347.
14. See n. 20 below.
15. They are to be considered two *sorts* of assistance, not as species of a genus.
16. Theologians disagree about whether this second kind of proposition is of divine faith or not. Neither Vatican I nor Vatican II settled the matter. All agree, however, that they are infallible. The dispute is not important for our discussion. Cf. Journet, *op. cit.* pp. 342–46.
17. Lumen Gentium 25.

18. An interesting case is discussed by Ford and Grisez, "Contraception and the Infallibility of the Ordinary Magisterium," *Theological Studies* (1978) 258–312.

19. Journet, *op. cit,* 349–50.

20. Op. cit., 349–50

21. Lumen Gentium 25.

22. Journet, *op. cit,* p. 353.

23. *Ibid,* n. 2.

24. *Op. cit,* p. 353.

25. *Ibid*

Chapter 18

ABORTION, MORAL ABSOLUTES, AND DISSENT FROM MAGISTERIAL TEACHING

William E. May

In his Apostolic Exhortation, *Reconciliatio et Poenitentia,* Pope John Paul II spoke of a "doctrine, based on the Decalogue and on the preaching of the Old Testament, and assimilated into the kerygma of the Apostles and belonging to the earliest teaching of the Church, and consistently reaffirmed by her to this day." The doctrine is that "there exist acts which *per se* and in themselves, independently of circumstances, are always seriously wrong by reason of their object."[1] Correspondingly, as the Holy Father noted at another time, "there are moral norms that have a precise content which is immutable and unconditional ... for example, the norm ... which forbids the direct killing of the innocent."[2]

Pope John Paul II clearly teaches, in company with his predecessors, that there are some human acts that are intrinsically wicked, and that corresponding to them are moral absolutes. Moral absolutes are moral norms that identify certain types of action, which are possible objects of choice, as always morally bad, and they specify these types of action without using in their description any morally evaluative terms. Deliberately killing the innocent, having intercourse with someone other than one's spouse, making babies by *in vitro* fertilization, and using contraceptives are examples of types of action specified by norms of this kind. The magisterium of the Church affirms that such absolutes are true, and among the absolutes taught by the magisterium is the norm forbidding direct abortion, an action that the Catholic tradition and the magisterium has consistently condemned as intrinsically wicked.[3] These norms are called "absolute" because they unconditionally and definitively exclude specifiable kinds of human action as morally justifiable objects of choice. Although exceptions to them are logically possible, they are morally excluded. Consequently, these norms are also called "exceptionless."

Many contemporary theologians (hereafter called "revisionists" or "revisionist theologians") reject the doctrine affirmed by Pope John Paul II. They deny that there are any moral absolutes in the sense previously described, and they likewise deny that there are any human acts, describable in morally neutral terms, that are intrinsically wicked. Revisionist theologians likewise claim that Catholics have the right to dissent from authoritative teachings of the magisterium, including the teaching that direct abortion is always an intrinsically wicked act.

In what follows I will first present the views of revisionist theologians on moral absolutes and dissent. I will then show why the thinking of revisionists on both topics is terribly flawed.

Revisionist Theologians on Moral Absolutes and Dissent

1. Revisionist Theologians and Moral Absolutes

Revisionist theologians advance several reasons to support their claim that there are no moral absolutes and no intrinsically evil acts,[4] but two in particular are important. The first is based on the historicity of human existence and the origin of specific moral norms. The second is based on the claim that the fundamental norm of morality is the "preference" principle or principle of "proportionate reason" or "proportionate good."

A. THE HISTORICITY OF HUMAN EXISTENCE

Revisionist theologians—and among them are such well-known and influential figures as Charles E. Curran, Richard A. McCormick, Joseph Fuchs, Louis Janssens, and Bernard Haring[5]—commonly distinguish between "transcendent" human nature and "concrete" human nature. Transcendent human nature is the basis upon which "transcendent" moral principles rest. Among these are such principles as that "one must always act in conformity with love of God and neighbor" and "one must always act in conformity with reason".[6] Revisionist theologians acknowledge that such transcendent moral principles are absolute. Likewise absolute are "formal" moral norms. These affirm what our inner dispositions and attitudes, as human beings, ought to be. Thus it is always and absolutely true that we should be brave, just, temperate, etc.[7] These formal norms are also based on the transcendent aspect of our nature, whereby we are called to a "steadily advancing humanization."[8]

But, revisionist theologians maintain, specific moral norms, such as the one forbidding abortion, are not based on transcendent human nature but rather on "concrete" human nature, which, by reason of its historicity, is subject to far-reaching changes.[9] Revisionists claim that all specific moral norms identify "physical" or "material" or "concrete behavioral" acts, described without any reference to any purposes of the acting subject.[10] They therefore call such specific moral norms—and that forbidding abortion is illustrative—"material" norms, insofar as they are concerned with the material element of human acts. But how do we come to formulate these norms in the first place? How, in other words, do we come to the judgment that, for example, it is wrong to kill innocent persons or to have intercourse with someone who is not one's spouse?

According to revisionists, we come to know these material norms by exercising our intelligence collaboratively with others as we reflect on the meaning of concrete human experiences.[11] Since material norms are known in this way, it follows that they are affected by the historicity of concrete human nature and the ongoing, open-ended character of human experience.

These material norms are not purely subjective and relative. They express an objective truth that corresponds to the actions they proscribe or prescribe as related to the "whole concrete reality of man" and of the particular historical society in which people live.[12] Nonetheless, these norms cannot be absolute in the sense of being universally true propositions about what human beings ought to do in every possible situation. No specific material norm, formulated under specific historical conditions, can be true and applicable universally and unchangeably. In fact, as Fuchs has noted, "a strict behavioral norm, stated as a universal, contains unexpressed conditions and qualifications which as such limit its universality."[13] Precisely because human experience, reflection upon which leads to the formulation of material norms, is itself ongoing and openended, it follows, as another revisionist, Francis Sullivan, says, that

> we can never exclude the possibility that future experiences, hitherto unimagined, might put a moral problem into a new frame of reference which would call for a revision of a norm that, when formulated, could not have taken such new experience into account.[14]

As a result, material norms are "valid for the most part," but exceptions to them are not only logically possible but morally called for in specific conditions.[15] Revisionists grant that some material norms describe actions that for all practical purposes ought never to be freely chosen—for example, raping a retarded child[16] or destroying cities by nuclear bombs[17]—and hence can be regarded as "practical" absolutes or "virtually exceptionless" norms.[18] Nevertheless, because of the historicity of human existence, all material norms must be considered to be in principle open to exceptions in the light of new historical conditions and new human experience.

B. The Preference Principle or Principle of Proportionate Reason

Although not absolute, material norms are intended to guide our choices, to help us distinguish right from wrong actions, and to understand how our actions bear upon human goods and values. Thus, in formulating such norms we must consider how human goods and values will be affected by possible courses of action. Revisionists say that these goods and evils (values and disvalues) are not, of themselves, moral in nature, although they are morally relevant. They are what revisionists call "premoral," "nonmoral," or "ontic" goods and evils, as distinct from moral good and evil, which consists essentially in the goodness or wickedness of the person as a moral being.[19] Thus goods such as life, health, knowledge of the truth, beauty, and friendship are "nonmoral" goods and their privations are "nonmoral" evils. The crucial question is this: how are we to determine, both in developing material norms and in judging which acts are legitimate exceptions to them, which human acts are morally right and which are morally wrong, i.e, which acts promote and enhance these nonmoral goods and values and which do not. We need, in short, a basic moral norm for distinguishing between morally good and morally bad alternatives. But what is this criterion or norm, and how does it relate to the absoluteness of "material" norms?

Revisionists claim that this fundamental moral norm is the "preference" principle or principle of "proportionate reason" or "proportionate good." Bruno Schüller formulates it as follows:

> Any ethical norm whatsoever regarding our dealings and omissions in relation to other men ... can only be a particular application of that more universal norm, "The greater good is to be preferred."[20]

According to this principle it is morally right to intend nonmoral evil, such as the death of an unborn child, if this is required by a "proportionately greater good." Thus Richard A. McCormick says,

> Where a higher good is at stake and the only means to protect it is to choose to do a nonmoral evil, then the will remains properly disposed to the values constitutive of human good. . . . This is to say that the intentionality is good even when the person, reluctantly and regretfully to be sure, intends the nonmoral evil if a truly proportionate reason (i.e., good) for such a choice is present.[21]

281

Since this is *the* basic moral norm, it follows that every "material" norm is open to an exception clause: it is wrong to kill an innocent person, to have intercourse with someone other than one's spouse, etc., *except* when doing so is necessary to achieve a proportionately greater good. Thus direct abortion, on this account, can be morally good, provided it is done for the sake of a proportionately greater good.

2. Revisionist Theologians and Dissent

Revisionist theologians commonly hold that some very general moral principles pertain to the "core of faith." These can be and have been infallibly taught by the magisterium. Among such principles, which are "transcendent" in nature, is the one commanding us to love God and neighbor.[22] However, revisionists maintain, no specific moral norms, i.e., "material" norms, such as those proscribing direct abortion, adultery, etc. have been proposed infallibly by the magisterium.[23] In fact, revisionists commonly argue, such norms simply *cannot* be taught infallibly precisely because they are material norms and hence affected by the historicity of human existence and the ongoing, open-ended character of human experience. Consequently, they are not fit subject matter for infallible teachings.[24]

Since the magisterium cannot propose specific moral norms infallibly, it follows that all such norms taught by the magisterium are authoritative but noninfallible. But, as Charles E. Curran and several associates said in 1969, in the wake of the controversies over *Humanae Vitae*, "it is common teaching in the Church that Catholics may dissent from authoritative, noninfallible teachings of the magisterium when sufficient reasons for doing so exist."[25] This position has since become common among revisionist theologians.[26] To support this position revisionists advance several lines of argument. They maintain, first of all, that the tradition of moral manuals, even prior to Vatican Council II, affirmed the right to internal and private dissent.[27] They contend, secondly, that "loyal dissent" was recognized by Vatican Council II. Here they acknowledge that no specific texts of the Council support their view, but many, like Curran, say that the "ecclesiological atmosphere" of the Council warrants dissent from noninfallible teachings of the magisterium.[28] Still others,

282

like Richard Gula, argue that the Council "implicitly" recognized dissent "in the very process by which it adopted its decrees."[29] They maintain, thirdly, that dissent is warranted by the fact that noninfallibly proposed teachings of the Church have been proved erroneous in the past (e.g., its teaching on religious liberty), and that legitimate dissent is needed if such erroneous teachings are to be discovered and corrected.[30] In addition, they claim that dogma can develop only if the kind of dissent they champion is recognized.[31]

The conclusion to be drawn from these considerations, revisionist theologians argue, is that dissent from authoritative but noninfallible teachings of the magisterium is legitimate.

Critique of Revisionist Position

1. The Revisionist Denial of Moral Absolutes

As has been seen, revisionists seek to support their denial of moral absolutes by two principal lines of reasoning, namely, (1) the historicity of human existence and (2) the demands of the basic moral norm or preference principle (principle of proportionate good). Before offering a critique of these lines of reasoning, however, it is necessary first of all to note how they prejudice matters by their way of describing the moral absolutes whose truth they contest.

As we have seen, revisionists refer to these absolutes as "material" or "concrete behavioral" norms. According to them these norms identify "physical acts" or "material acts," independently of *any* purpose of the agent. Both Catholic theologians today who defend the truth of moral absolutes and those who did so in the past, including St. Thomas Aquinas, offer a much different account of these disputed norms, which they never call "material" or "concrete behavioral" norms. According to these theologians, the human acts identified and morally excluded by such norms are *not* specified independently of any purpose of the acting person. Rather, they are specified, as Pope John Paul II correctly stated in a passage referred to at the very beginning of this paper, by their "object," and by "object" is meant exactly *what the agent chooses,* either as an end *(finis* or *finis remotus*) or as a means (*finis* or *finis proximus*).[32] The tradition affirming moral absolutes holds that such norms do not bear upon acts "in their *natural* species" but rather upon them "in their *moral* species."[33] The "form," the "intelligibility" of such acts is not given by their nature as physical events in abstraction from the agent's understanding and willing, but from their intelligibly chosen objects.[34] For example, the same material or physical act (the "natural" species of the act), namely, sexual intercourse, can be, by reason of its "object"—that is, by reason of the form or intelligibility it has as understood and willed by the acting person— either a marital act, an act of incest, an act of adultery, or an act of fornication.[35]

Consequently, the account given by revisionist theologians of specific moral norms, including the disputed moral absolutes, is skewed from the beginning by their insistence that such norms are "material" and that they identify the "physical" or "material" or "concrete behavioral" aspects of human acts independently of *any* purposes of the acting subject.

A. The Argument from the Historicity of Human Existence

It is, of course, true that morality is in some ways relative to contingent historical and social reality. Thus societies, like individuals, make choices that both generate and limit moral responsibilities; new alternatives become available as societies develop and new scientific and technological discoveries are made; and moral insight is often blocked by cultural biases and opened by changed conditions or new "horizons."[36] But from this it in no way follows that *all* specific moral norms are relative to changing historical and social conditions. Revisionists themselves seek to avoid a radical historical relativism by appealing to the "transcendent" standard of a "steadily advancing 'humanization' " or to the self-realization of persons and of the communities in which they live.[37] But, as Germain Grisez has noted, this vague standard lacks the content "needed to determine what should and should not count as morally determinative when one fills the formal concept of human self-realization with the whole concrete reality of persons in society and their world."[38]

The argument that the open-ended, ongoing character of human existence and experience excludes the possibility of universally and permanently true specific moral norms is undoubtedly sound with respect to *some* moral norms, for after all, not all moral norms are absolute. This argument assumes that an action can be morally evaluated only as a totality (which includes all the circumstances and ends considered in relationship to all the nonmoral but morally relevant goods and bads involved in that totality) for the purpose of identifying the behavior that will foster human self-realization and self-development.[39] But this assumption simply does not stand up under scrutiny. It is true that, for an action to be judged morally good, it must be evaluated in its totality—*bonum ex integra causa.* But, for an action to be judged morally bad, it suffices that any element in the act is known to be bad or contrary to reason—*malum ex quocumque defectu.* Once an action has been properly identified as, for instance, an act of rape, one need not delay judgment about its morality until one knows why the rapist is choosing to rape, who the victim is, in what century or millennium it occurs, etc. One can, on the basis of relevant moral principles, declare at once that it is simply the sort of act that a human person ought not freely choose to do.

Revisionists claim that "material" norms are based on "concrete" human nature, which is subject to radical change, as opposed to "transcendent" human nature, and that consequently no specific moral norms based on concrete human nature can be universally and irreversibly true.[40] Those making this claim, however, never clearly explain what "concrete," as opposed to "transcendent," human nature means. They do not show how fundamental human goods, such as life itself, health, knowledge of the truth, friendship, etc. might cease to be good for human persons, nor do they show how their claim about radical human change is compatible with the unity of the human race or our solidarity in Christ.

From all this we can see the terrible flaws in the argument from historicity when it is advanced to support the denial of moral absolutes.

B. THE ARGUMENT BASED ON THE PREFERENCE PRINCIPLE

According to revisionists, the basic moral norm is the preference principle or principle of proportionate reason (or good). This principle requires that moral judgments be made on the basis of a comparative evaluation of the "nonmoral" goods and evils promised by the various alternatives, and the alternative promising the greater balance of nonmoral good over nonmoral evil is the one that ought to be chosen. According to this principle it is morally right deliberately to intend a non-moral evil, such as the death of an unborn child, for the sake of a proportionately greater nonmoral good.

This principle seems, initially, to make some sense. Indeed, to most revisionists it seems self-evidently true. According to this principle we are to choose the alternative promising the greater balance of good over evil. If the principle is not true, it seems to follow that we ought to choose the alternative promising the greater balance of evil over good; but this is absurd. McCormick is one revisionist who stresses the absurdity of denying this principle. He states the principle negatively to show how it is used in "conflict" situations in which evil inevitably results, no matter what we choose to do. He writes:

> The rule of Christian reason, if we are to be governed by the *ordo bonorum,* is to choose the lesser evil. This general statement, it would seem, is beyond debate, for the only alternative is that in conflict situations we should choose the greater evil, which is patently absurd.[41]

The initial appeal of this principle, however, rests on the ambiguity of the word "good." The morally upright person naturally seeks to do the greater good, in the sense of what is morally good. But the revisionist "principle" assumes that it is possible to determine, prior to choice, which among various options is *morally* good by balancing or measuring or commensurating the various nonmoral goods and evils in these different options. The problem here, as Germain Grisez, John Finnis, and Joseph Boyle have shown,[42] is that there is no unambiguous or homogeneous measure according to which the goods in question (goods such as life itself, knowledge of the truth, appreciation of beauty, friendship, justice, peace) can be compared with one another or according to which individual instances of such goods (e.g., the life of Mary Jones and the life of Peter Smith) can be weighed or measured or commensurated. Although none of these goods is absolute—only God or the *Summum Bonum* is the absolute good—each is truly a priceless good of human persons and as such a good to be prized, not priced, a good participating in the incalculable goodness of the human person. To attempt to weigh or balance them against each other, to commensurate them, is like trying to compare the number 87 with the length of this line _____ . One simply cannot do so. One, could, if they could be reduced to some common denominator, as one can compare the number 87 with the length of this line _____ , if one compares these items by means of a common denominator such as centimeters or inches or miles, scales adopted not by discovering a truth but by an arbitrary act of the will. But the goods involved in human choices are not reducible to some common denominator. They are simply different and incomparable goods of human persons. Thus the basic presupposition upon which the "preference" principle is based is false. One cannot determine, in a nonarbitrary way, which human goods are greater and which are lesser. They are all incomparably good, irreducible aspects or dimensions of human flourishing and well-being.[43] And the same is true of individual instances of the different goods of human persons.

Most revisionists have simply ignored this criticism, and those who have attempted to respond to it have failed to meet it adequately. This can be seen by looking at the response given to this criticism by McCormick. McCormick has been forced to admit that it is impossible, in the strict sense, to "commensurate" goods of different categories "against" each other. But he now says that, "while the basic goods are not commensurable (one against the other), they are clearly associated." He then claims that it is possible, by considering these goods in their association or interrelationship, to judge that the choice to destroy an instance of one good in present circumstances will not undermine that good, and that destroying or impeding it here and now is necessary in order to foster the flourishing of related goods.[44]

This response is clearly inadequate. It amounts to saying that, although there is no nonarbitrary way to commensurate goods, we somehow succeed in doing so by "relating" or "associating" them. McCormick himself admits as much, for he speaks of assessing the greater good as a "prudent bet" and of commensurating in "fear and trembling" by *adopting* a hierarchy of goods.[45] By saying this he is admitting that the commensuration required by the "preference" principle is accomplished by an act of choice. But the alleged *principle* was advanced in order to determine, *prior* to choice, which possibilities are morally good and which are morally bad. McCormick now says that in order to commensurate goods, which one must do if one is to judge which alternative promises the greater proportion of good or evil, we must first *adopt* a hierarchy of goods and make prudent bets. He fails to realize, apparently, that this response is an acknowledgement that the alleged "preference" principle is not a principle but rather the assertion of one's preferences.[46]

Another telling argument against the "preference" principle is advanced by Bartholomew Kiely, who observes that this principle fails to take seriously the reflexive or immanent consequences of human acts as self-determining choices.[47] We make ourselves to be the persons we are by the actions we freely choose to do. In choosing to do evil—and revisionists urge us to *do evil for the sake of a proportionately greater good*—we make ourselves *to be* evildoers. This is something that revisionist theologians simply do not take seriously.

For these reasons—and others can be added[48]—we can see that the alleged preference principle or principle of proportionate reason is spurious. Thus denial of moral absolutes on the basis of its demands is unwarranted.

2. Revisionists and Dissent

Before offering a critique of the revisionist account of dissent, some introductory comments on the magisterium itself will be helpful.

Catholic faith holds that the authority to speak in the name of Christ, which was entrusted in the apostolic Church to the Apostles under the leadership of St. Peter, has been invested, by the authority of Christ Himself, in the college of bishops under the headship of the Pope, the Bishop of Rome.[49] It thus possesses a magisterium or teaching authority, and to it is entrusted the mission of preserving faithfully the saving *truths* that Christ has communicated to the Church. This magisterium is concerned with truths of both faith and morals. Thus it teaches in Christ's name both truths that must be believed—such as those concerning the nature of God, His inner triune life, the mystery of the union of the divine and the human in the one person of Christ, and the like—*and* truths that must be lived, that is, moral truths, the truths to which human choices and actions must be conformed if they are to be compatible with the life that Christians have received as adopted children of God, as living members of Christ's body and temples of the Holy Spirit (cf. 1 Jn; 1 Co 6). Moreover, the magisterium, in order to carry out its mission properly, has the competence and the authority to declare and confirm truths of the natural moral order.[50]

The magisterium invested in the college of bishops under the headship of the pope *always* teaches with the authority of Christ. At times it proposes matters, whether of faith or morals, infallibly, i.e., with the assurance that what it proposes is absolutely irreformable and a matter to be held definitively by the faithful. At other times it proposes matters of faith and morals authoritatively *and as true,* but not in such a way that the matter proposed is to be regarded as absolutely irreformable. Nonetheless, whatever the magisterium teaches in this second way is something that the faithful, including the pope, bishops, ordinary laypeople, *and theologians* are to accept as true with a "religious submission of mind and will."[51]

With these preliminary comments on the magisterium in mind, it is now opportune to note that the magisterium can teach *infallibly* on matters of faith *and morals* in one of two ways. First, a matter of faith or morals can be solemnly defined as such either by an ecumenical council or by the pope when, "as the supreme shepherd and teacher of the faithful . . . he proclaims by a definitive act some doctrine of faith or morals."[52] This way of teaching infallibly is called the *extraordinary* exercise of the magisterium.

Secondly, and it is most important to recognize this, the magisterium teaches infallibly on matters of faith *and morals* in the *ordinary,* day-to-day execution of its pastoral mission so long as specific conditions are met. The Dogmatic Constitution on the Church of Vatican Council II clearly spelled out these conditions when it said:

> Although the bishops, taken individually, do not enjoy the privilege of infallibility, they do, however, proclaim the doctrine of Christ infallibly on the following conditions: namely, when, even though dispersed throughout the entire world but preserving for all that among themselves and

with Peter's successor the bond of communion, in their authoritative teaching concerning matters of faith or morals, they are in agreement that a particular teaching is to be held definitively and absolutely.[53]

What the Fathers of Vatican II add to this passage is also most important to keep in mind, for they immediately continue, "This is still more clearly the case when, assembled in an ecumenical council, they are, for the universal Church, teachers of and judges in matters of faith and morals, whose judgments must be adhered to with the loyal and obedient *assent of faith*."[54]

Revisionist theologians, who deny that any specific moral teachings of the Church have been proposed infallibly, simply ignore the relevance of this important passage. In the minds of many theologians (and of the faithful) the core of Catholic moral teaching, as summarized in the Ten Commandments *as these have been understood traditionally within the Church* and as set forth in such sources as *The Roman Catechism,* which was mandated by the Council of Trent and used universally throughout the world to instruct the faithful for centuries,[55] has been taught infallibly: We are not to kill the innocent; we are not to fornicate or commit adultery; we are not to steal; we are not to perjure ourselves.

Note that the Fathers of Vatican II, after affirming that matters of faith and morals can be taught infallibly in the ordinary, day-to-day exercise of the magisterium by bishops in union with one another and with the pope, insisted that this is even more the case when the bishops, assembled in an ecumenical council, explicitly pass judgment on questions as teachers of the universal Church. In the light of this clear teaching it is instructive to examine key statements of Vatican Council II about *specific moral issues.* Thus the Council Fathers branded abortion and infanticide as "abominable crimes"[56] and insisted that

the varieties of crime [against human life and human persons] are numerous: *all* offenses against life itself, such as murder, genocide, *abortion,* euthanasia, and willful self-destruction ... are criminal; they poison civilization; and they debase their perpetrators more than their victims and militate against the honor of the creator.[57]

In sum, it seems clear to me and to many others that the core of Catholic moral teaching has been proposed infallibly by the magisterium according to the criteria set forth at Vatican Council II. Nor is this surprising. That central moral teachings, such as those forbidding the direct killing of the innocent (as in abortion), are infallibly taught was the common view of theologians prior to Vatican Council II, as the following citation from Karl Rahner, writing just before Vatican Council II began, makes clear:

The Church teaches these commandments [the Ten Commandments] with divine authority exactly as she teaches the other "truths of the faith," ... [at times] through her ordinary magisterium, that is, in the normal teaching of the faith to the faithful in schools, sermons, and all the other kinds of instruction. In the nature of the case this will be the normal way in which moral norms are taught, and definitions of the Pope and general council the exception; but it is binding on the faithful in conscience just as the teaching through the extraordinary magisterium is.... *It is therefore quite untrue that only those moral norms for which there is a solemn definition ... are binding in the faith on the Christian as revealed by God.... When the whole Church in her everyday teaching does in fact teach a moral rule everywhere in the world as a commandment of God, she is preserved from error by the assistance of the Holy Ghost, and this rule is therefore really the will of God and is binding on the faithful in conscience.*[58]

In light of what has been said thus far, I submit that the claim of revisionist theologians that the magisterium cannot and has not taught any specific moral norms infallibly is spurious. To the contrary, evidence sustains the judgment that the core of Catholic moral teaching has been proposed infallibly according to the criteria set forth at Vatican Council II and that this moral teaching is to be given the assent of divine faith.

The claim by revisionists that the faithful are free to dissent from noninfallibly but authoritatively proposed magisterial teachings whenever "sufficient reasons for doing so exist" is also spurious. Theologians prior to Vatican Council II did not, contrary to the claims made by revisionists, justify dissent. In fact, the term "dissent" was not even used by them. They did recognize that one might, on occasions, "withhold assent" from noninfallibly proposed teachings, but "withholding assent" is a far cry from "dissenting."[59]

Moreover, Vatican Council II in no way justifies dissent in the sense understood by revisionist theologians. So true is this that many revisionist theologians, such as McCormick, frankly admit as much and now fault the ecclesiology found in such documents of Vatican Council II as *Lumen Gentium.*[60] The other lines of argumentation used by revisionist theologians to support their claim that Catholics are free to dissent from authoritative but noninfallibly proposed teachings whenever there are seemingly good reasons for doing so have been shown by Grisez and others to be seriously defective.[61]

The kind of dissent championed by revisionist theologians does not take seriously the reason why Christ invested the magisterium with the authority to teach in His name, namely, to assure His people of sound guidance in matters of faith and morals. The magisterium has the responsibility to care for the souls of the faithful—a very weighty responsibility, one that can be carried out properly only with divine assistance. Revisionist theologians, by instructing the faithful that they are free to set aside the teachings of the magisterium whenever they can find sufficient reasons for doing so, are usurping the pastoral office of the bishops under the headship of Christ. The faithful ought never to "believe" theologians—they should look at their arguments to see whether they are sound. But they ought to believe their bishops and the Holy Father, for their bishops and the Holy Father have been given by divine authority an office in the Church, one of leading the faithful to Christ.

The failure of revisionist theologians even to consider seriously the possibility that the core of Catholic moral teaching has been proposed infallibly is indicative of their failure to support their claims. With St. Thomas, I believe that we ought rather to believe the Roman Pontiff, when he is speaking on matters of faith and morals, than any theologian, however erudite.[62] For the Roman Pontiff is Peter's successor, and it was to Peter that our Lord entrusted the task of feeding His sheep with saving truth.

Both reason and faith support the truth that it is always morally wrong directly to kill innocent human beings, as is done in abortion.

Attempts by revisionist theologians to deny this truth rest on specious arguments.

NOTES

1. Pope John Paul II, *Reconciliatio et Poenitentia*, n. 17.

2. Pope John Paul II, "Discourse to International Congress of Moral Theology," 10 April 1986, in *Persona, Verita e Morale* (Rome: Citta Nuova Editrice, 1987), p. 16.

3. From the very beginning Christian writers vehemently condemned abortion as absolutely immoral. Important early witness is provided by the *Didache*, a second century document, and by the Fathers of both East and West. Representative texts from these sources are given by Germain Grisez, *Abortion: The Myths, the Realities, and the Arguments* (New York: Corpus, 1970), pp. 137–149. During this century abortion has been unequivocally condemned by Popes Pius XI, Pius XII, John XXIII, Paul VI, and John Paul II. John Paul II has addressed the moral evil of abortion in countless discourses and in such documents as his Apostolic Exhortation, *Familiaris Consortio*, n. 30. Vatican Council II called abortion an "abominable crime" (*Gaudium et Spes*, n. 51). In 1974 the Congregation for the Doctrine of the Faith issues a *Declaration on Procured Abortion*. This important document noted the teaching of the *Didache* on the grave evil of abortion and then went on to say: "In the course of history the Fathers of the Church, her pastors and her doctors have taught the same doctrine—the various opinions on the infusion of the spiritual soul did not cast doubt on the illicitness of abortion. It is true that in the Middle Ages, when the opinion was generally held that the spiritual soul was not present until after the first few weeks, a distinction was made in the evaluation of the sin and gravity of penal sanctions. In resolving cases, approved authors were more lenient with regard to that early stage. *But it was never denied at that time that procured abortion, even during the first days, was objectively a grave sin. This condemnation was in fact unanimous*" (nn. 6–7).

4. Revisionists also seek to support their denial of moral absolutes by appealing to the "totality" of the human act, to the teaching of St. Thomas, and to selected texts from Vatican Council II. An analysis and critique of these appeals of revisionists is provided in my Pere Marquette Theology Lecture for 1989, *Moral Absolutes: Catholic Tradition, Current Trends, and the Truth* (Milwaukee: Marquette University Press, 1989). Here I simply wish to note that appeals by revisionists to the teaching of St. Thomas and to the teaching of Vatican II are completely specious. On the thought of St. Thomas see my essay, "Aquinas and Janssens on the Moral Meaning of Human Acts," *Thomist* 48 (1984) 566–606, and Servais Pinckaers, OP, *Ce qu'on ne peut jamais faire: La question des actes intrinsèquement mauvais. Histoire et discussion* (Fribourg: Editions Universitaires; Paris: Editions du Cerf, 1986).

5. In addition to these well-known authors, revisionist thought has been championed by many others who have popularized it in the United States. Two texts on fundamental moral theology, intended primarily for seminarians, espouse revisionism, namely, Timothy E. O'Connell, *Principles for a Catholic Morality* (New York: Seabury, 1978), and the recent work of Richard A. Gula, *Reason Informed by Faith: Foundations of Catholic Morality* (New York: Paulist, 1989). The revisionist view as applied to sexual morality has been set forth by Anthony Kosnik et al., *Human Sexuality: New Directions in American Catholic Theology* (New York: Paulist, 1977) and Philip S. Keane, *Sexual Morality: A Catholic Perspective* (New York: Paulist, 1978).

6. O'Connell, *Principles for a Catholic Morality*, pp. 157–158.

7. Louis Janssens, "Norms and Priorities in a Love Ethic," *Louvain Studies* 6 (1977) 207; O'Connell, *Principles*, pp. 158–159; Gula, *Reason Informed by Faith*, pp. 286–289.

8. Josef Fuchs, *Personal Responsibility and Christian Morality* (Washington: Georgetown University Press, 1983), p. 142.

9. Ibid., pp. 132–133.

10. Ibid., p. 191; Fuchs, *Christian Ethics in a Secular Arena* (Washington: Georgetown University Press, 1984), p. 74; Janssens, "Norms and Priorities in a Love Ethic," 210, 216; Gula, *Reason Informed by Faith*, pp. 289–295.

11. Francis Sullivan, *Magisterium: Teaching Authority in the Church* (New York: Paulist, 1983), pp. 150–151. Sullivan says that this is the view of Charles Curran, Franz Bockle, Josef Fuchs, Bernard Haring, and many others.

12. Fuchs, *Personal Responsibility and Christian Morality*, p. 133.

13. Ibid., p. 124.

14. Sullivan, *Magisterium*, pp. 151–152; Fuchs, *Personal Responsibility and Christian Morality*, p. 140.

15. Fuchs, *Personal Responsibility and Christian Morality*, p. 142.

16. Daniel Maguire, *Death by Choice* (New York: Doubleday, 1974), p. 99; Janssens, "Norms and Priorities in a Love Ethic," 217.

17. O'Connell, *Principles*, p. 162.

18. Fuchs, *Personal Responsibility and Christian Morality*, pp. 141–142; Janssens, "Norms and Priorities in a Love Ethic," 217–218.

19. "Premoral" is the term preferred by Fuchs; "nonmoral" is that preferred by Richard McCormick and Bruno Schuller; "ontic" is that preferred by Janssens.

20. Bruno Schuller, "What Ethical Principles Are Universally Valid?" *Theology Digest* 19 (March 1971) 24.

21. Richard McCormick, "Ambiguity in Moral Choice" (his Pere Marquette Theology Lecture for 1973), as reprinted in *Doing Evil to Achieve Good*, ed. Richard A. McCormick and Paul Ramsey (Chicago: Loyola University Press, 1978), p. 39.

22. E.g., Gula, *Reason Informed by Faith*, p. 158, p. 209.

23. Charles E. Curran et al., *Dissent in and for the Church: Theologians and Humanae Vitae* (New York: Sheed & Ward, Inc., 1969), p. 26; Curran, *"Humanae Vitae: Ten Years Later,"* Commonweal 105 (July 7, 1978) 429; Maguire, "Morality and the Magisterium," *Cross Currents* 18 (Winter, 1968) 41–65.

24. Curran, *Dissent*, p. 26; see Sullivan, *Magisterium*, pp. 150–151.

25. Curran, *Dissent*, p. 26.

26. E.g., see Gula, *Reason Informed by Faith*, pp. 209–212.

27. Curran, *Dissent*, p. 14; Gula, *Reason Informed by Faith*, p. 208.

28. Curran, *Dissent*, p. 124.

29. Gula, *Reason Informed by Faith*, p. 208.

30. E.g., Bruno Schuller, "Remarks on the Authentic Teaching of the Magisterium of the Church," *Readings in Moral Theology # 3. Morality and the Magisterium*, ed. Charles E. Curran and Richard A. McCormick (New York: Paulist, 1982), pp. 29–30.

31. McCormick, "Teaching Role of the Magisterium and of Theologians," *Proceedings of the Catholic Theological Society of America Convention* 24 (1969) 244–245.

32. Thomas Aquinas, *In II Sent.*, d. 40, q. un. a. 1, ad 4; *In IV Sent.*, d. 16, q. 3, a. 1b, ad 2; *Summa Theologiae*, 1–2, 1, 3, ad 3. See Karl Hoermann, "Das Objekt als Quelle der Sittlichkeit," in *The Ethics of St. Thomas Aquinas*, ed. Leo Elders (Vatican City: Libreria Editrice Vaticana, 1984), pp. 122–123, 126–128; Martin Rhonheimer, *Der Natur als Grundlage der Moral* (Innsbruck and Vienna: Tyrolia Verlag, 1987), p. 95; Theo Belmans, *Le sens objectif de l'agir humain* (Vatican City: Libreria Editrice Vaticana, 1980), pp. 214–216.

33. Thomas Aquinas, *Summa Theologiae*, 1–2, 20, 2; *In II Sent.*, d. 40, q. un., a. 2.

34. For texts from St. Thomas with commentary, see Patrick Lee, "The Permanence of the Ten Commandments," *Theological Studies* 42 (1981) 431–432; Belmans, *Le sens*, pp. 62, 109–119, 124, 162, 237; Rhonheimer, *Der Natur als Grundlage*, pp. 91–99, 317–345, 367–374.

35. Thomas Aquinas, *In II Sent.*, d. 40, q. 1, a. 1, ad 4; *Summa Theologiae*, 1–2, 1, 3, ad 3.

36. On this see Germain Grisez, "Moral Absolutes: A Critique of the View of Josef Fuchs," *Anthropos: Rivista di Studi sulla Persona e la Famiglia* (now called *Anthropotes*) 1 (1985) 170.

37. Fuchs, *Personal Responsibility and Christian Morality*, p. 129.

38. Grisez, "Moral Absolutes," 172.

39. Fuchs, "Naturrecht oder naturalistischer Fehlschluss?" *Stimmen der Zeit* 29 (1988) 409, 420–422; Fuchs, *Christian Ethics in a Secular Arena*, p. 75; McCormick, *Notes on Moral Theology 1965–1980* (Lanham, MD: University Press of America, 1980), pp. 710–711.

40. Sullivan, *Magisterium*, p. 152; Karl Rahner, "Basic Observations on the Subject of the Changeable and Unchangeable Factors in the Church," *Theological Investigations*, Vol. 14 (New York: Herder & Herder, 1976), pp. 14–15.

41. McCormick, "Ambiguity in Moral Choice," as reprinted in *Doing Evil to Achieve Good*, p. 38.

42. Germain Grisez, "Against Consequentialism," *American Journal of Jurisprudence* 23 (1978) 21–72; Grisez, *The Way of the Lord Jesus*, Vol. 1, *Christian Moral Principles* (Chicago: Franciscan Herald Press, 1983), pp. 141–172; John Finnis, *Natural Law and Natural Rights* (Oxford and New York: Oxford University Press, The Clarendon Press, 1980), pp. 118–125; Finnis, *Fundamentals of Ethics* (Washington, DC: Georgetown University Press, 1983), pp. 86–105; John Finnis, Joseph M. Boyle, Jr., and Germain Grisez, *Nuclear Deterrence, Morality, and Realism* (Oxford and New York: Oxford University Press, 1987), pp. 254–261.

43. In *Nuclear Deterrence, Morality, and Realism* Finnis, Boyle, and Grisez show how the revisionist principle is incompatible with free choice. They note that this principle requires that "two conditions be met: (i) that a morally significant choice be made and (ii) that the person making it be able to identify one option as offering unqualifiedly greater good or lesser evil. But these two conditions are incompatible, and in requiring that they be met simultaneously consequentialism is incoherent" (p. 254). As they show, choice is possible only when there are two or more alternatives. But an alternative exists only when the good it promises is not available in other possibilities. Thus if condition (ii) is met, condition (i) cannot be, and vice versa.

44. McCormick, "A Commentary on the Commentaries," in *Doing Evil to Achieve Good*, p. 227; cf. pp. 251–253.

45. Ibid.

46. McCormick's response is subjected to devastating criticism by Finnis, *Fundamentals of Ethics*, pp. 99–105, and by Grisez, *Christian Moral Principles*, pp. 161–164.

47. Bartholomew Kiely, S.J., "The Impracticality of Proportionalism," *Gregorianum* 66 (1985) 656–666.

48. For other critiques of the proportionalism of revisionists, cf. the works of Pinckaers, Belmans, Lee, and Rhonheimer cited previously in notes 4, 32, and 34.

49. Vatican Council II, *Dei Verbum*, nn. 8, 10; *Lumen Gentium*, n. 20.

50. Vatican Council II, *Dignitatis Humanae*, n. 14.

51. Vatican Council II, *Lumen Gentium*, n. 25.

52. Ibid.

53. Ibid.

54. Ibid.

55. The *Roman Catechism*, popularly called *The Catechism of the Council of Trent*, was mandated by the Council of Trent and was in use throughout the Catholic world from the end of the sixteenth century until the middle of the twentieth. One section of this catechism was devoted to the Ten Commandments, and it teaches unambiguously that all killing of the innocent, all adultery and fornication, and all perjury are always wrong and gravely sinful if freely chosen. This work was approved by all the bishops of the Catholic world and by the pope.

56. Vatican Council II, *Gaudium et Spes*, n. 51.

57. Ibid., n. 27.

58. Karl Rahner, *Nature and Grace: Dilemmas in the Modern Church* (New York: Sheed & Ward, Inc., 1963), pp. 51–52. Rahner, after the Council, became a revisionist theologian. Yet nothing in the Council would lead one to revise anything he says in this passage. Nor did Rahner himself ever explicitly disown what he said here.

59. A list of these manualists is provided by Curran in *Dissent*, p. 14. A study of them shows that they did not even speak of dissent, but merely acknowledged that one might, on occasions, withhold assent form noninfallibly proposed teachings.

60. Thus McCormick acknowledges that appeal to the text of *Lumen Gentium*, n. 25 in no way can justify dissent but rather seems to exclude it. He then says that "it is widely, even if quietly, admitted in the theological community that this paragraph represents a very dated and very discussable notion of the Church's teaching office." In other words, he says that the theological community (= revisionist community) does not regard this text of the Council as an instance of good theology! Cf. his *Notes on Moral Theology 1965–1980*, p. 667.

61. Grisez, *Christian Moral Principles*, pp. 871–916.

62. St. Thomas Aquinas, *Quodlibet* IX, 8, corp., in *Quaestiones Quodlibetales*, ed. R. Spiazzi (Rome: Marietti, 1949), p. 94: "We must abide rather by the pope's judgment than by the opinion of any theologian, however well versed he may be in divine Scriptures."

PART FIVE

CHURCH, PUBLIC POLICY, AND THE LAW

Chapter 19

WHAT'S IN AN ASSERTION?

Dennis Q. McInerny

One of the most commonly heard assertions of the part of those who do not want to condemn abortion unqualifiedly goes something like this: "I am personally opposed to abortion, but I honor a woman's right to have an abortion." An alternate version, if the speaker is a woman, would be: "I myself would never have an abortion, but I acknowledge that there are certain circumstances in which a woman would be justified in having an abortion." Other forms of the assertion might be spelled out, which would vary in one particular or another from the two versions just cited, but they would offer nothing radically new as far as the substance of what is being communicated is concerned.

However precisely it might be worded in any given instance by any particular person, the assertion in question has certain basic and invariable formal features, and it is to these that I want first to turn my attention. For one thing, the assertion, regarded grammatically, is a complex sentence, which is to say that it is composed of more than one clause. In this case we are dealing with two clauses. In the first the speaker makes the claim that he is personally opposed to abortion; in the second he claims that he approves of the fact that abortions are actually performed. The second thing to note about the formal character of the assertion is that it is commonly expressed in the indicative mood. This grammatical feature can be translated into logical terminology, roughly, by saying that the assertion is made up of two categorical propositions. Sometimes there is an exception to this pattern, in instances where a speaker will state the first clause categorically ("I am personally opposed to abortion") but express the second clause in the subjunctive mood ("but there may be occasions in which abortion is permissible"). Finally, and moving now away from strictly formal considerations, the contents of the two clauses is such that a contrast is established between them, as indicated by the conjunctive "but." The syntactical pattern of the assertion might be loosely described as the "yes—but" pattern. A statement is made, then another statement is appended to it whose semantic effect is to qualify substantially the force of the initial statement.

That will suffice for an analysis of the general characteristics of the assertion. In this essay I will be concerned not so much with how the assertion is structured as with what it says. My thesis is simple. I contend that the assertion, based upon an understanding which follows from a reasonable construal of its meaning, shows itself to be incoherent. The main task of the essay, then, will be to demonstrate this thesis. A point concerning procedure. For the sake of convenience, and I hope stylistic simplicity as well, I shall throughout the essay refer to the assertion that I am explaining simply as "the assertion."

Before getting "inside" the assertion, it might be best to say a few words about the social context from which it most commonly emerges. I then want to comment on what I perceive to be the rhetorical weight that the assertion usually carries in our society. Earlier I had identified the assertion as one which is often heard from people "who do not want to condemn abortion unqualifiedly." That will do as a broad description of the attitude of those who use the assertion. But we can be more specific about the matter. There are at least three categories of people who are likely to make the assertion. (1) Those who are active advocates and promoters of abortion on demand, and who see abortion, for whatever reasons, as a good for society. (2) Those who are genuinely ambivalent about the subject of abortion, and whose use of the assertion is a sincere expression of their ambivalence. (3) Those who may or may not be genuinely ambivalent about abortion, but who take the stand expressed by the assertion primarily as a matter of expedience.

People in the first category use the assertion to disguise their true feelings concerning abortion, and for them the incoherence of the assertion would most probably be irrelevant. Presumably, the exposure of its incoherence would not inhibit their continued use of the assertion. If words are employed to cloak rather than to reveal one's meaning, then the communicative capacity of the words, objectively considered, is an issue of no great moment. But to use words to cloak one's true meaning is a purposeful act. What conjectures might be made about purposes in this instance?

I suspect that what principally is at stake here is public relations. The explicit, unqualified avowal of an uncompromising advocacy of abortion is not likely to be received favorably by the American public. And pro-abortionists know this. If then the pro-abortionist wants to gain a hearing for his views he must not state them forthrightly. He must clothe them in very carefully chosen language. Interestingly, and perhaps ironically, the last thing that the pro-abortionist wants to do is to reveal himself clearly in public as a pro-abortionist. It is bad form in the sense of being bad politics. It is incumbent upon him, if he is to be rhetorically effective, to traffic in verbal circumlocutions, such as the yes—but variety, in his public pronouncements. We can see a more comprehensive example of the rhetorical strategy employed by pro-abortionists in the habitual manner they have of identifying themselves as "pro-choice." That this is a vacuous designation has nothing to do with its rhetorical effectiveness. As Plato pointed out on several occasions, rhetorical effectiveness is not dependent upon semantic accuracy, or even coherence. It is possible to move masses by speaking gibberish. Though the phrase says nothing by dint of the fact that it says too much (being "pro-choice" is comparable to being "pro-thought"), it nonetheless carries considerable impact with those who are so swayed by its enchanting quality of vague affirmation that they are disinclined to stop and consider it closely and thereby discover what it is really worth. To claim that one is pro-choice is ostensibly to put oneself immediately and securely on the side of the angels. After all, who would want to put himself in the silly position of being against choice? But we need only push the matter just that far and ask that kind of obvious question in order to let the cat out of the bag. The vacuousness of the rallying cry is revealed. There is no such thing as choice pure and simple. Put differently, choice is not an act without content and context. We never just choose, period. We always choose to do, or to refrain from doing, something. Choices have subject matter, in other words, and the quality of the choice is intimately bound up with the quality of the subject matter with which the choice is concerned. With all these elementary but critical considerations in mind, we see that no rational creature declares himself to be pro-choice unreservedly. Choices are specific acts, and before anyone associates himself approvingly with any given choice he would want to know with what the choice was concerned. Such information is anything but incidental. The simple question before him in this: Is it a good choice or a bad choice? "Before I built a wall," Robert Frost once wrote, "I'd ask to know/ What I was walling in or walling out." If the choice is to clothe the naked or visit the sick, then the rational man is pro-choice. If the choice is to mug an old man in Central Park or kill a baby in a womb, then he is definitely anti-choice.

The rhetorical strategy employed by pro-abortionists today is not unlike that employed by pro-slavery advocates in this country in the 19th century. In the 1840's not even the most fervent proponent of slavery would make an explicit public admission of his position. That would work against the very cause he was attempting to further. So, by a deft rhetorical sleight of hand he invested himself with an acceptable, and no doubt subjectively comforting, positive image by telling the world that what he was chiefly concerned with was states rights. For public consumption, he was not against slavery (indeed, he would even want to leave the impression that that was almost a side issue); rather, he was for the hallowed rights of states to determine for themselves the kind of control they wanted to exercise over their own bodies politic. By appealing to an ambiguous but lofty sounding standard, suddenly one's position attains a dignified status, almost a kind of nobility. And so today in this country the pro-

302

abortionists never identify themselves as such. By operating under the aegis of "pro-choice," all the while invidiously referring to their opponents as "anti-choice," they strive mightly to be perceived in the public eye as far-seeing citizens who have taken the moral high ground in the debate over abortion, while their hapless antagonists can do no better than wander about in the dark vales of unproductive negativism. And, needless to say, they have the full support of the mass media in sustaining this charade.

As to the other two categories of people who use the assertion, I would like to suppose that, for them, the assertion's being shown to be incoherent would have some relevance. The hope would be that, once they see the assertion to be incoherent, they would cease to have recourse to it. However, I think we might have to say that that is more likely to be the case with respect to those for whom the assertion is a sincere expression of ambivalence over the subject of abortion. As for those in the third category, those who use the assertion primarily as a matter of expedience, the matter is more difficult to determine. Let us examine this category a little more closely. Here we are dealing with people who by and large do not use language in a deliberate effort to cloak their meaning. By and large, their intention is first and foremost to make their view on the subject of abortion as appealing to as wide and as diverse a public as possible. We are not speaking here of people who have no fixed views on any subject, and will say whatever they imagine their audience wants to hear just to be accepted by that audience. No, these people do have set views on any number of important issues, and, specifically, on abortion, but they do not want the fact that they hold particular views on this or any other subject to have a negative effect upon the public. Most of the people to be found in this third category are elected officials, or people in public life who consider it crucial to the maintenance of the security of their position that they be seen continuously in a favorable light. They are keenly aware of the fact that abortion is a volatile and divisive issue. They also know that those who tend to be either strongly for or strongly against abortion tend as well to be politically active. Instead of appealing exclusively to one faction or the other, their tactic is to try to appeal to both, while at the same time attempting to maintain as positive an image as possible for the benefit of the population at large.

What can be said about the actual rhetorical impact of the assertion? At first blush, and in terms of what I would identify as a superficial response to it, its rhetorical impact could be said to be decisively positive. The assertion leaves the impression that the one who makes it is, on the one hand, taking a definite stand on a difficult issue, and that can count for courage—a virtue to which the public usually attaches a high value. On the other hand, the speaker can be perceived as one who is broad-minded and modest enough so as not to presume that his views on abortion should become the single standard by which public policy concerning the matter ought to be guided. He is perceived as at once convinced but cautious, a magnanimous man and—the sine qua non for any contemporary American politician who wants to make a go of it—a man of compassion. He is not one who is about to commit the unpardonable social sin of imposing his personal views on others. The assertion that one is personally opposed to abortion but not opposed to the practice of abortion in one's society carries faint resonances of Voltaire's expansive expression of willingness to defend to the death the right of anyone to propound views which Voltaire himself considered to be totally wrong-headed, and thus is thoroughly suffused with a well-nigh irresistible flavor of quintessential liberality. At least to those who systematically refrain from going beyond the surfaces of things.

But if one does go beyond the surfaces of things, one is, at the very least, invariably made uncomfortable at hearing this assertion, especially if it proceeds form the mouth of a politician. Furthermore, the careful calculation of the true semantic import of the assertion has just the oppositive effect, rhetorically, from what follows from a superficial response to it. It is seen as a typical political ploy, an effort to temporize, to fence straddle, effectively to evade an issue while giving the appearance of confronting it bravely. Conscientious Catholic voters who hear Catholic politicians make the assertion feel frustrated and even betrayed, for they know that these politicians are not assuming an authentically Catholic position. As a result, their reaction to the assertion tends in the final analysis to be negative. On the other hand, it is an open question whether or not Catholic politicians who make the assertion actually succeed in wooing the pro-choice constituency with whom often enough they are quite clearly trying to ingratiate themselves. The advocates of abortion are just as likely to be as suspicious of temporizing Catholic politicians as are

Catholics themselves, and for pretty much the same reason. Those on either side of a fence necessarily view a fence straddler from different perspectives; but both are looking at a fence straddler, someone who is not definitely on their side.

Those general consideration out of the way, we can now turn our attention to a more specific analysis of the assertion. When I say that the assertion is incoherent, what I mean is that it is logically at war with itself; it is self-contradictory. We have a complex sentence, composed of two propositions, and what is asserted by one proposition is incompatible with what is asserted by the other. In order to see, concretely, how this is so, we must first arrive at a reliable determination of what each proposition says, of what each means.

"I am personally opposed to abortion." The first clause of the assertion requires some translation. It is very important to determine the semantic heft of the phrase "personally opposed to." What does that mean? First, let us note the peculiar function of the qualifier "personally." It seems evident that the purpose behind the speaker's making that word a part, and a critical part, of the assertion is to insure that his audience fully appreciates that the domain of the first clause is not only quite different from, but also separated off from, the domain of the second clause. The first clause deals with the private domain; the second clause deals with the public domain. The speaker wants us to understand that while he as an individual, a private citizen, holds certain views on the subject of abortion, views which he has every right to hold, those views, because they are personal, are not to be taken to have any bearing on the public domain. The peculiar meaning of "personal views" here is that they do not have, and should not have, any carry-over effect with respect to the public domain. Thus understood, personal views are, apparently, those whose implementation, to the extent that they are implemented at all, is restricted to the subjective world of the one who is expressing them. Personal views are not to be regarded as proper criteria for the formulation of public policy.

Despite the heavy rhetorical weight that the adverb "personally" is being asked to bear here, it really adds nothing substantial to the central import of the first clause. If I say "I personally believe," or "I personally feel," or "I am personally opposed to," I am saying nothing substantially different from simply "I believe," or "I feel," or "I am opposed to." The "personally" is a stylistic excess and a logical redundancy. If I hold something to be true, the very fact that it is I who am doing the holding makes it a personal experience. My views are personal views, not in the sense that I alone hold them, but in the sense that at least I am holding them.

With this in mind, we can ask if what is implied by the assertion that one should not attempt to implement one's personal views in the public arena—is it at all tenable? Without too much reflection, we can see that the answer to the question is clearly negative. In the first place, not only is it simply a matter of record that people's personal views are continually and ubiquitously being implemented in the public realm, it is quite impossible to imagine how it could be otherwise. And to suggest that it is appropriate that there be some sort of prohibition against such implementation is, at the very least, rather odd. To the contrary, we would want to urge that if anyone's personal views on whatever subject are worthy, that is, sound and potentially efficacious, then he should be encouraged toward putting those views into effect in such a way that contributes to the common good. Furthermore, if one truly believes that his "personal views" have no bearing on the public realm, then why does he express them publicly. Given that belief, such expression would be an exercise in futility.

We know it to be an every day occurrence in the world of American politics that elected representatives, for example, are always assiduously at work in the effort to insure that their "personal views"—whether those views pertain to the budget, to taxes, to foreign policy, to disarmament, to whatever—will eventually, in some degree or another, have an effect upon American society. To suppose that it could or should be otherwise is simply not to understand the nature of politics, or for that matter of human societal relationships in general. And, indeed, if an elected representative were not trying actively to realize his personal views, we could justifiably conclude that he was not living up to his responsibilities. Now, with respect to their potential for implementation, there is no difference between one's views on taxes and one's views on abortion. Given the intrinsic worthiness of the views and the contribution they could make to the common good, there should be no a priori prohibition against the implementation of one set or the other.

It is at this point that an objection is likely to be raised to the effect that in fact there is a difference between one's views on taxes and one's views on abortion. The objection usually takes two forms. It is sometime said that abortion is a private matter, and therefore any attempt on the part of the state to prevent a woman from exercising an assumed right to an abortion is a violation of an assumed right to privacy. Immediately we can see that what is being appealed to here is a narrowly defined and tightly circumscribed notion of privacy. The so-called right to an abortion must be rejected out of hand, and without equivocation, for there can be no right to take the life of an innocent human being. Whether or not there is a constitutional guarantee to a right to privacy is, to say the very least, an arguable issue, but it need not detain us here. What bears noting is that those who make this objection are really not concerned with protecting the integrity of an individual's private domain against any and all intrusions on the part of government. They are not against government intervention pure and simple, but only against certain kinds of government intervention, e.g., of the sort that would curb the practice of abortion on demand. We all know that in our own country, prior to the Roe versus Wade decision, every state in the union had laws which in some way or another regulated abortion. The pro-abortionists, in retrospect, look upon those laws as representing an infringement upon a right of privacy. It is important to recognize that with Row versus Wade we did not see an end to government intervention with respect to abortion; we saw a new kind of government intervention. On this occasion, there were no concerns expressed by pro-abortionists about violation of the right to privacy. Concern for a supposed right of privacy, then, is highly selective. We have yet to hear pro-abortionists worry publicly over any right of privacy that might apply to the unborn child.

The second form of the objection is a bit more subtle. Here the point is made that, given the sacrosanct separation of church and state in this country, no single citizen should have the temerity to try to impose his religious views on others. Practically speaking, what is usually understood to count as an act of imposing one's religious views on others is the attempt to have those views realized in the form of public policy. For example, if I, as a Seven Day Adventist, attempted to effect legislation in my state that would make Saturday a non-workday, a day on which no commercial transactions would be allowed, then I would be dutifully accused of trying to impose my religious views on my fellow citizens. Now, undeniably, there is

307

much which is commendable in the doctrine of the separation of the church and state, and there is little doubt but that by and large it has served our country well. But we must be very wary of how that doctrine is appealed to, under what circumstances, and by whom. Specifically, it is most necessary to be aware of how pro-abortionists appeal to that doctrine, and what are their purposes for doing so.

The first thing we must notice is that the pro-abortionists' use of the doctrine of the separation of church and state, like so much else that makes up their rhetorical strategy, is oblique and ambiguity-bound. Seldom if ever is the meaning of the doctrine itself precisely delineated, so things become only more complicated by the pro-abortionists' manner of constantly referring to a criterion whose contours are from the very beginning exasperatingly obscure. Secondly, pro-abortionists are guided by the unwarranted assumption that views on abortion are somehow religious views.

When the pro-abortionist accuses the Catholic of wanting to impose his religious views on others, we are dealing with a charge that carries with it rather specialized, almost exotic, import. Once that import is discerned, the problematic nature of the charge is made evident. The Catholic sees abortion as the willful killing of an innocent human being, that is to say, as an intrinsically evil act, and therefore the type of act that should not be countenanced by our society or by any other society. Abortion is a form of murder, and like every other form of murder it should be prohibited by civil law. The pro-abortionist responds by saying—or at least he seems to want to be saying—that this Catholic position is a purely religious point of view and consequently, in deference to the separation of church and state, it should not be admissible in the debate over abortion.

But is this point of view a purely religious one? More specifically, is the anti-abortion stand only a Catholic position? While it must be admitted that a Catholic's understanding of the nature of abortion is informed by his religious faith, it is not exclusively dependent upon that faith. A Catholic, or anyone else, can arrive at an appreciation of the intrinsic evil of abortion through the exercise of natural reason alone. We have dramatic evidence of this in the case of Dr. Bernard Nathanson, who has come to see the evil of abortion, but who is not, if my knowledge is correct, a religious believer at all. That the anti-abortion position is not an exclusively Catholic one is manifest enough by the number of people from other Christian bodies, most notably the Lutherans, who have with great energy and determination made it their cause.

The closer we look at the pro-abortionists' strained concern for the separation of church and state, the more we are tempted to conclude that their concern smacks of the disingenuous. The Catholic position cited above is peremptorily thrown out of court by pro-abortionists because it is said to be religiously motivated. In contrast to this, it is interesting to reflect on the warm reception invariably given by pro-abortionists to those Catholics who claim that there is an "alternate" Catholic position on abortion, a position which, *mirabile dictu*, is identical to that subscribed to by those who march under the pro-choice banner. Now, two rather significant things need our special attention here. The first is that these "pro-choice" Catholics make much of their identity as Catholics; indeed, they take pains to insure that the public is aware of their peculiar religious affiliation. Secondly, it is just that religious, specifically Catholic, identity that the pro-abortionists seem to find especially attractive about this group.

And this creates a problem for the consistency of the pro-abortionists position. On what basis do they find Catholic pro-choice types such a welcome addition to their camp? Presumably it is because these people have arrived at their views on abortion precisely as Catholics, and have been guided in doing so by peculiarly religious values. But if that is the case, on what basis should those views be worthy of consideration in the debate over abortion? Are not those views religious views? Are not then those who hold them, and announce to the world that they hold them, attempting to impose their religious views upon the American public?

Clearly, the pro-abortionists are tying to have it both ways in this matter. The answers they would give to the questions posed above would undoubtedly all be negative. The appeal to the separation of church and state is a red herring, a rather inept attempt to distract attention away from what the pro-abortionists are actually up to. As it turns out, ideas that conflict with their presuppositions are branded as "religious views," and summarily dismissed. On the other hand, ideas that come from virtually the same context as what they call "religious views" somehow end up as not being so, and the reason for this, of course, is that those ideas are compatible with their position.

Let us return to the first clause in the assertion. In light of the foregoing discussion we can now say that the expression "I am personally opposed to abortion" is tantamount to saying "I am opposed to abortion." And now we must ask, What does it mean to say that one is opposed to abortion? A trivial meaning of "being opposed to" can be quickly dispensed of if we make the assumption right at the outset that abortion is regarded, by all parties concerned, as a very serious matter. This assumption can be properly made, I think, and the effect of it is to avoid interpreting "I am opposed to" as synonymous with flaccid statements such as "I do not like," or "I am displeased with," or "I would prefer not to be associated with." If the object of one's opposition is itself a very serious matter, I think we are then justified in supposing that there is a very serious quality to one's opposition, taken in itself. Why, under normal circumstances, is any rational creature opposed to anything? Because, at the least, and even if only vaguely, he perceives that there is something about the object he is opposed to which is not quite right. At the most, and presumably with great clarity, he sees the object in starkly negative terms. He regards it as something obviously wrong, or, more seriously, as simply evil. Now, here I am assuming that anyone who would make the public claim that he is opposed to abortion, given the universally acknowledged seriousness of abortion, does so because he thinks abortion to be wrong, to be a clear evil. If this seems too careless an assumption to make, perhaps it would seem otherwise if we ask, Why would anyone publicly announce his opposition to something which he regards as innocuous? We do not publicly state our opposition to matters to which we are indifferent, but to those we assess negatively. We approve the good and oppose the bad. The other possibility, that me might oppose what we think to be good, would be clearly irrational.

It seems that we have arrived at a reasonable understanding of the meaning of the first clause of the assertion. The speaker is saying, in essence, that he regards abortion as something that is wrong. As soon as that is made clear, we see that there is a fundamental incompatibility between what the first clause says and what the second clause says. Let us turn our attention now to that second clause. Its basic idea is usually expressed in the words cited earlier: "but I honor a woman's right to have an abortion." To this statement sometimes various qualifying elaborations are added; for example, the speaker might refer to certain circumstances which he thinks justify a woman's having an abortion. On occasion the basic idea of the second clause is stated less boldly: "but regretfully abortions are sometimes necessary and therefore should be permitted." Whatever the exact wording of the second clause, the underlying message that is being communicated by it is that the act which the speaker perceives to be wrong, i.e., abortion, should nonetheless be permitted in his society. More specifically, the message is that government should not impose any restricting limitations on abortion. Abortion should be pervasively permitted in our society, and for a large variety of reasons.

Having before us now what each of the clauses in the assertion is saying, their fundamental incompatibility is apparent. We are listening to someone who asserts that a certain act is wrong, yet he wants people in his society to be able freely to perform that act. But one might say, Is that so incongruous a circumstance? Realistically, do not we all admit that it is impossible to extirpate all evil from any society, and that in some societies at certain times it might be better to allow certain evils to take place because any attempt to eliminate them may bring about yet greater evils? We do admit as much, but the pertinent question is this: Is abortion that kind of allowable evil? And the answer to the question is No. There are certain evils that are so heinous that they are never allowable, and abortion is one of them, no matter what "benefits" would supposedly accrue from its being permitted. That is the first point that needs to be made. The second is that the person who makes the assertion, as a matter of practical fact, is not simply acceding to a situation in which abortion is minimally allowable in his society, as if it were something that happens only rarely and under the most peculiar of circumstances. The assertion has to be understood in terms of the social context in which it is actually being made. So, someone who makes this assertion in the United States of America today accedes to a situation in which abortion is not simply allowed, it is actively, even militantly, promoted. We are not dealing with a sometime thing, a desperate last resort. Abortions are performed to the dolorous tune of 1.5 million per year. Abortion is a pervasive practice; it is a part, an infamous part, of the American way of life. Someone who makes the assertion, then, is assuming a highly problematical stance. On the one hand he is plainly asserting that he believes abortion to be wrong. On the other hand, he is saying in effect that a society in which there is promiscuous commission of that wrong is a society to which not only can he manage to accommodate himself, it is one of which he positively approves. This, I would submit, represents a morally incoherent position.

The moral incoherence of the position might be brought into greater relief if we were to replace, in the assertion, the term "abortion" for one or another term denoting a commonly acknowledged moral evil. What, for example, if we were to substitute the word "rape," or "racism," for "abortion." If someone were to say, in our hearing, "I am personally opposed to rape," or, "I am personally opposed to racism," would we not be fairly dumbfounded to hear a "but" following those claims? More likely than not, we would not be very sympathetic to anything following the "but." The critical issue at hand is this: if an act is consciously and conscientiously acknowledged to be morally evil, then, if one is going to say more about the subject as it relates to the practical order, the only rational thing to add are your ideas as to how that evil might at every turn and at all costs be eliminated from the society of which you are a member. There is really only one recourse for those who sincerely acknowledge a certain kind of activity to be evil. They must, obviously, refrain from engaging in that activity themselves. But they must also work toward the creation of a society in which no one engages in that activity, for what might very well be at stake is the health, perhaps even the very existence, of the society itself.

Chapter 20

PRO-CHOICE

The Reverend Ronald D. Lawler, O.F.M. Cap.

Freedom is dear to us. Hence it is often a winning strategy to speak broadly in favor of choice, to tell people they have a right to decide for themselves. In the abortion controversy, those who use the expression "pro-choice" to represent the side that wishes abortion to be legitimate have a powerful verbal advantage.

Still, to be in favor of expanding choice is certainly not to be in favor of legitimizing every kind of choice. Pro-choice people must put severe limits on the kinds of choice they advocate. They do not, for example, argue that parents should be allowed to choose to slay their older children when they get impossibly difficult, or that spouses should have the right to slay each other on days when that seems attractive. Usually, indeed, pro-choice people do not like to say too plainly what sorts of choice they favor: they like to think they are in favor of choice in general, forgetting how dreadful some choices are, like choosing to kill the innocent.

But those who describe their position as pro-choice in the present abortion controversy generally hold positions like the following. (1) People should be allowed to *choose* the course of their own lives. If they could not decide for themselves whether they are to become parents, with all that means, they are subjected to alien determination of their existence. Laws should not require them to live in ways that they are utterly opposed to. (2) They argue that, since people have a right to run their own lives (a point that pro-life people will broadly agree with), they certainly have a right to do things that will effectively enable them to get control of their lives, things like aborting their children. Hence it is misleading to attempt to argue too closely about just what sort of act abortion is. If it is an effective and sometimes needed way to vindicate an important right, it has to be a right of women. If an end is good, the most effective means of reaching the end are good also. (3) They believe they have the right to *choose* or *decide* for themselves (in the face of fierce controversies) what abortion is, to determine by their own wills (attending to how various alternatives serve the goods to which they claim an unqualified right) what moral arguments are relevant and true, and hence by their own choice to settle decisively whether abortion may properly be chosen.

Where Pro-life and Pro-choice People Should Agree

Many of the goals praised by pro-choice people are such that even pro-life people can be, and should be, heartily in favor of them. The desire for "reproductive freedom," when it is moderate in scope, can be expressed in ways that a Church as much opposed to abortion as the Catholic Church supports their ends.

For example, the Church is clearly on record as defending the view that people should not be pressured to having children when they do not want them. It is not the business of the state, or of any other outsiders, to tell people what vocation in life they should choose, whether they should become spouses and parents, or how many children they should have. This is a matter for spouses to determine for themselves (see Vatican II, *The Church in the Modern*

314

World, n. 50). The Church is by no means in favor of forcing or pressuring people to have children they do not want to have—assuming that the children do not yet exist. It would be hard to hide the fact that the Catholic Church is opposed to terminating the lives of children who already are.

Don't force your morality on me! Pro-life people can well agree with pro-choice people that in this pluralistic and freedom-loving society, one group should not have the right to enforce its peculiar morality on others.

Laws should be established to defend the rights and the liberties of people, but not to canonize one set of morality, and make others conform to that. To virtually all it is obvious that where there are many competing sets of morality, the law cannot possibly enforce all of them. Neither should any citizen in a pluralistic and free society like ours be legally obliged to follow a set of values and moral directives he or she does not believe in.

Nor should a common morality be enforced by law. Even when it is not a question of escaping the dubious moral systems of people we do not agree with, it is not the business of the state to enforce all moral directives. The Catholic Church, though she has stern moral directives, herself professes to believe that people's moral lives should be lived freely. It is true that we have no absolute right to do evil kinds of deeds. But if it is merely a question of doing something intemperate or lustful (which does not harm or do injustice to others—and intemperate acts can be also unjust), it is not the business of the state to seek to require people to be good. People should be good freely; forcing or pressuring adults to live in ways they are determined not to live will not make for a peaceable kingdom.

Even if people want to do things that we all agree and know to be wicked, we should not ordinarily want to force people to be good. No one can become virtuous without freely choosing to be virtuous: and force impedes that. (Note how the Catholic Church, in the Vatican II *Decree on Religious Liberty*, n. 2, points out that people who wish to be bad, and even abuse the right to run their own lives, should not be forced to act virtuously. The case considered here is that of the person who sinfully abuses religiously liberty; he is not to be compelled to do what is right.) Even when we have clear obligations not to act in certain ways, the obligation is normally one to *freely* abstain from such deeds. A society that likes to force people to be good makes it impossible for the best human things: people freely doing what is good.

Contraception. The Catholic Church teaches that the moral law is a "natural law," that all human beings are in principle capable of learning for themselves whether various kinds of acts are morally good or bad kinds of acts. She professes to believe also that God has graciously given to the human race other ways of being certain of the truth of these intelligible moral principles through the special kind of knowing that comes through faith. She believes that God is really a Teacher of mankind, and that in certain exceptional ways he has enabled us to confirm important moral directives that intelligence itself can discern. What intelligence itself is capable of knowing about moral directives can be known even more surely in the light of intelligent faith as a word of God. Both intelligence and faith lead the faithful Catholic to the conviction that some of the means one might use for the legitimate end of controlling one's life (such as contraception and direct abortion) are always immoral means of pursuing that end. But the Church does believe or teach that the state has the right or duty to enforce all the rules of morality. Its basic task is to create a just order in which the common good can be pursued: it should enforce what justice requires, but not all that morality requires. The state should enforce justice, and keep people from killing one another, and even from killing very young human beings. But the state's role is not to enforce moral virtues like chastity, when no real matter of justice is concerned. The state should not be the enforcer of contraception morality. (Here we speak of the kinds of contraception that prevent life from coming to be: barrier methods or anti-ovulation methods, that keep conception from occurring. Practices that do not prevent conception, but kill the newly conceived very early in their lives—as the typical "contraceptive" pill sometimes does—are not really contraceptive but abortifacient.)

Protection of human rights. Precisely in societies that care about the freedoms and the rights of persons, the state should not permit every kind of choice. The coercive power of the state should stand in the defense not of every moral ideal, but of justice. Hence the people who wish to defend choice seldom argue that it is right to defend freedom of choice about slavery or segregation. People should not be allowed to choose to act unjustly in a world that wishes all to be free, and to be able to exercise their rights without hindrance. For if tyrants are told that they should choose for themselves whether or not to have slaves, or bigoted segregationists are told to decide for themselves whether they will let minorities eat in public restaurants or live in choice neighborhoods, the expansion of one person's choice is granted at the price of brutal unfairness to others. One person's liberty to do as he chooses ends when there is a question of choosing to do what assaults the rights of another.

Where Pro-choice and Pro-life People Differ

Pro-choice partisans in the abortion controversy agree with pro-life people (when they happen to think about the matter) that one should not be free to choose to harm the rights of another. But they claim that abortion offends no one's rights. They assert firmly, and (as we shall see) claim to have every right to assert this: that the fetus is not and should not be considered a person.

But the mother is a person: and she has a right to shape the course of her own life. But she cannot do this effectively, if she is not given the right to abort. A pregnant adolescent, a young woman whose career hopes would be dashed if she had to bring a child to term and care for it, a raped woman or one made pregnant by incest, indeed any woman pregnant with a child and whose life would (in her own firm judgment) be ruined by having this child, has rights that transcend those of the biological mass in her womb that is not yet a child. Women, pro-choice people say, have a right to shape their own lives, and so choose acts like abortion that are at times necessary for them if they are to freely guide their own lives.

Pro-life people, on the other hand, insist that the small living realities in women's wombs, with the tiny little faces and fingers and hearts of six-week old and older fetuses, and indeed even young human entities conceived and growing in the womb toward full maturity, are human being *like us*, only younger and weaker; and that no one has the right to choose to kill them. Of course, virtually no one denies that people have a right to fight death: to take medical treatments they need, even if, in a side effect really not chosen, they know that the child may die as a result of efforts to save the mother. No one argues for killing mothers to save babies, or for any other reason.

317

This sharp difference, noted and argued in many of the essays of this book, reflects another dimension of the pro-choice position. The pro-choice advocate seldom wishes to debate directly the question of what abortion really is, and whether it is really wrong. Rather, they prefer to argue that people have a right, in the controversies of our time, not only to choose what they will do, but to *choose what the truth is.* They may decide for themselves what the facts are, what abortion is, and what human rights are or are not involved. This is a *peculiar* position, and deserves especially careful reflection.

What Is Abortion?

What is abortion? Just what do abortive acts do? In an abortion, does one end the life of a human being, and a human person, who is already in existence? Or does abortion keep a human being from coming into existence? Once Planned Parenthood literature nicely distinguished contraception from abortion by stating that in birth control one keeps a child from coming into being; in abortion one slays a child that has already begun to be. Now that they have gone into the abortion business in a large way they do not talk about such things any more. And, indeed, most pro-choice people don't like to argue about what abortion in fact is. They prefer (as we shall see) to defend the right to hold the views they hold, and with them the right to do the things they choose to do to make the lives of those they especially care for more pleasant.

Some pro-abortion people frankly admit that a human life begins at conception, and continues uninterruptedly and in a continuous path until death. Some do not even wish to make a facile distinction between "persons" and "human beings," as if only some human beings have rights, while other human beings (lacking some trait or other that they pretend to be of decisive importance) do not have rights, and so may be labeled "non-persons" and slain if the interests of others demand it. Often those who admit that abortion involves slaying young human beings argue insistently that the Judeo-Christian morality (reflected in our Declaration of Independence and in most statements of the Rights of Man) is simply wrong in saying that human beings have inalienable rights and that we should vindicate the right to kill some people to make life for most

318

people better. Those who remember Nazism generally do not like such arguments and they have little common popularity, so such arguments are not much pressed in campaigns to win political favor for pro-choice.

Ultimate Pro-choice: Choosing for Myself What Is Real

Pro-choice people don't much like debates on whether or not a fetus is a human being. The argument that it is just an undifferentiated mass of cells gets little scientific support; the fetuses of abortion age commonly have very human-looking faces and hands and hearts.

But there is a freedom-type argument they like to use. In the fierce debates of our times, they argue, no one has the right to impose his theories on another. Many intelligent people are convinced that fetuses are so *unlike us* that they really cannot count as human beings and persons. If anyone wishes to accept their similarities to us as signs they are persons, let them: each may choose as he or she wishes. But it is only a personal choice, and it ought not be imposed by law on others. We have a right to decide for ourselves whether or not fetuses are human beings. *I have a right to decide for myself whether the thing I am about to destroy is or is not a human being.*

Do Only Some Human Beings Have Inalienable Rights?

Many sophisticated intellectuals, who have adopted life styles for which abortion is an important convenience and defense, do not wish to be urged to consider the patterns of their thinking in this matter. In all other rights debates in Western history, a very different course of thinking from that advocated by pro-choice people was triumphant, and was saluted by the overwhelming majority as demanded by the requirements of human freedom and of human rights.

In every debate about human rights, each side protested that it was on the side of rights and liberty: but each side argued thus in distinctive ways. The abolitionist argued that to enslave minorities was outrageous: for they are our brothers and sisters, they are *like us;* we must not treat them as things. The slave-holder argued that the abolitionist was the tyrant. A whole way of life demanded slavery; there were good people who argued that the slave people were very *unlike us.* The passion of their arguments compensated for its logical flaws. ("Slave people are not like us"; "their whole inner life is utterly different"; "they need to be and probably want to be slaves, since they could not compete as free citizens against the more sophisticated whites." Compare this with more modern arguments that unborn human beings would prefer being aborted to being born unwanted.) But the prime point was: when we consider letting each do as he chooses, we mean that those adults who want slaves, or do not want them, have the right to choose. The one who is disenfranchised, the slave, does not count as a person in this formula.

When some European-Americans wished to defend their interests against the Native Americans, they felt it would be disastrous to count Indians as *like us.* Obviously they are very unlike us! They are savages, beasts! Perhaps we may be pro-choice: those who are too tender to kill Indians should move to other places; but those who have the courage to do what needs to be done to protect what we need to do must not be impeded. Do not impose your morality on me! I have a right to decide whether, in the relevant sense, Blacks or Indians have rights. Not every biological human being is one who has rights.

Understandable Errors and Intolerable Arrogance

When in any age different groups differ sharply in questions about basic human rights, a serious crisis is at hand. It is hard to exaggerate the depth of such questions. Is slavery, which so many find essential for defending a loved style of life, actually unjust, inhuman, cruelty to persons? Must Indians be accorded the rights native to Europeans? The claim is a frightening one, and the defenses of what are not seen as dreadfully wrong views are in some ways understandable. It takes time for society to catch with a common vision what is first seen only by perhaps a small minority, but grows, and ultimately is seen by all. The defenders of institutions that abuse human rights could conceivably be innocent, because so many social forces often incline them almost irresistibly.

It is understandable, when a loud voice cries out that the rights of a whole class of human beings are being crushed, that those who loved other ways should first argue against the pretended prophet. Sometimes prophets are proved false. But what is not tolerable, is that, in the face of such voices, those who would be profiting from the injustice to others (if it is an injustice) refuse to face serious challenges, and simply insist: we have a right to *decide* for ourselves. And we decide that our side is right. We do not recognize any duty to examine the arguments that might convict us of grave injustice. We *decide* that those who challenge us are wrong, and we are unwilling to face seriously any evidence that might convict us of error. We are pro-choice: we defend the right to choose for ourselves what is true in this matter, and deny the duty to search with our whole hearts for the truth.

Logically this is in error, and morally it is bankrupt. People cannot *choose* the truth of things. Either the reality slain in an abortion is a human being, and a person, or it is not. Crucially important things are at stake.

Human Rights and Abortion

In a society like ours, which likes to hold that it is built on the principle that all human beings are equal before the law, and that every human being has inalienable rights, some duties are inescapable. We cannot coherently ward off claims that we are treating some human beings unjustly by saying simply: we don't count them as real humans, and we are not willing to look at the evidence. We have *chosen* to stand on this position: they are *not* like us. When we will not even seriously debate the matter, but exclude candidates for personality by arbitrary choices, we give up the very foundations of the vision that our own rights are built upon.

Some may think it hysterical to claim that young fetuses are human beings like us, and have a right to live. It may seem exaggerated to cry out that 1,500,000 innocent human beings are killed every year by abortion. But as more and more intelligent people are seen to be convinced (as the "fanatical" abolitionists and anti-segregationists were joined by more and more prophets), it becomes essential to think honestly and openly. "What really is the truth of things? Could we have made a mistake as tragic as our fathers made in similar debates?" To err in such debates is tragic; but to be unwilling to face the debates honestly is wicked. Pro-choice is perhaps the basest of all alternatives, when it means: we have *decided* for ourselves that this is the truth, and claims that we are participating in mass murder we will not even consider.

Is Pro-choice Really Pro-abortion?

Some are indignant at the claim that a pro-choice stance is a pro-abortion stance. What we wish, pious editorialists sometimes cry out, is not abortion or anti-abortion, but restoring to people the right to choose for themselves. So personal a question is not to be decided by legislatures and courts, but by the women whose lives are at stake in the issue. Let each decide as her own heart directs.

However, this is a confused claim. First of all, When one says that the abortion debate is obscure, and each woman should decide for herself about abortion, one does not in fact believe that the debate is obscure. For in taking a stand, he or she has already *decided* that unborn babies have no inalienable rights. To affirm dogmatically that each individual has a right to decide to kill fetuses is to decide that they are not persons, that pro-life people are all wrong.

Here we are speaking about the standing of the helpless before the powerful. Once it was considered a powerful argument: let each person or state decide whether slavery is permissible. People argued for slavery and against it. They did not persuade each other, so some wanted each to do as he would choose, as he thinks best. In our day, of course, everyone knows that such a suggestion is unthinkable: if slaves are persons like us, they must be treated as persons; and if there are reasons to think they are persons (and even reasons to think they are not), then the solution of this question is the first order of civic business. We can survive as a society of free persons with many trials; we cannot survive as a society of the free if we do not passionately care for the truth in this matter, if we do not seek that truth about such matters with all our hearts. We cannot honorably remain in the state of being unsure whether we are enslaving or killing many of our brothers and sisters.

322

Are Catholic Pro-choice People
The Basest of Pro-abortionists?

By "Catholic" we here mean a believing Catholic. We mean the Catholic who professes indeed to believe personally that what the Church teaches about abortion is true: that the living being killed in an abortion is a person, and has really the right to life. But, while he really believes this is so, he has no desire to impose his views on others. So he will fight for funding for abortions if his constituents want it; he will oppose legal defenses for the lives he believes sacred, but others do not.

The question we raise in this section is a global, not a personal, question. It does not pretend to penetrate each heart, and determine its sincerity. It is rather about the pattern of thinking: if one were clear-headed and realized what he or she were doing, would the Catholic pro-choice advocate be especially base?

Most pro-abortionists (i.e., people who believe that abortion should be treated as a legally and morally acceptable option) seem seriously to believe that a fetus is certainly not a person. They may be unwilling to debate the case clearly; but, however artfully, they have reached a conviction: in abortions, the mothers are persons, but the fetuses are not. We are not engaged in killing human beings, and we would never do that. Those who accuse us of this are barbarians (like Mother Theresa). If it were killing babies, true human persons like us, we would never do it.

But the Catholic politician who professes to be a believer and to be pro-abortion politically has another position. He refuses to believe that the 1,500,000 who are killed by abortion every year in this country are, as the Church teaches, certainly to be counted human persons. He professes to count them as such himself. But he adds: pardon me if I help in the slaughter of these little ones who are human like me: for political and constitutional considerations require it of me that I help the butchers slay them.

Not many tyrants and genocidists have said things like that.

Chapter 21

OPERATION RESCUE

Charles E. Rice

Charles H. Langston, son of a Revolutionary War[1] soldier and himself described as "part Negro," was convicted in a U.S. District Court in Ohio in 1859 for violation of federal law in his rescue of John Price, an alleged fugitive slave. Because of "mitigating circumstances," Langston was sentenced only to 20 days' imprisonment and to pay a $100 fine and $872.70 costs. In his speech before sentencing, Langston said (as reported in the trial record):

Published in *The Wanderer*, January 19, 1989, p. 6. Reprinted here with permission.

"The law under which I am arraigned is an unjust one, one made to crush the colored man, and one that outrages every feeling of humanity, as well as every rule of right.... I stand here to say that I will do all I can, for any man thus seized and held, though the inevitable penalty of six months' imprisonment and $1,000 fine for each offense hang over me! We have all a common humanity and you all would do that; your manhood would require it; and no matter what the laws might be, you would honor yourself for doing it, while your friends and your children to all generations would honor you for doing it, and every good and honest man would say you have done *right!* (Great and prolonged applause, in spite of the efforts of the Court and Marshal.) (Finkelman, ed., *Slavery, Race and the American Legal System, 1700–1872: Fugitive Slaves and American Courts* (1988), vol. 4, pp. 11, 17–18).

There are parallels between the movement to rescue slaves and the movement to rescue unborn babies today. Charles Langston and Randall Terry are admirable, heroic figures. Slaves were regarded then as nonpersons and so are the unborn today. The rescuers in both cases appealed to the higher law. No federal judge ever refused to enforce the fugitive slave law on the ground that it was unjust; nor has any appellate court recognized that abortion rescuers have a privilege to save unborn children from execution. The Underground Railroad and other efforts to rescue slaves were widely criticized at that time. Operation Rescue, of course, has drawn criticism from the pro-abortion camp. But it has also drawn censure from pro-life sources as well. Clergy were prominent in the slave rescue movement. Operation Rescue is supported by prominent clerics, including Rev. Jerry Falwell. And numerous clergymen have submitted to arrest as part of Operation Rescue, including Roman Catholic Bishop Austin Vaughan of New York and Anglican Catholic Bishop O. Mote of Denver, among others.

The Abolitionist movement, including its rescue efforts, was a significant factor in causing the Civil War and the freeing of slaves. It is appropriate to ask what, if anything, is the role of the abortion rescue movement in the overall pro-life effort.

326

Saving Babies' Lives

"I am willing to be arrested for breaking a law," said one rescue participant, "because I'm obeying a higher law, the law of God. We are saving human lives" (William Calvin, quoted in *The Rescuer,* July-August, 1988, p. 2). Randall E. Terry, founder of Operation Rescue (P.O. Box 1180, Binghamton, N.Y., 13902), spelled out the characteristics of the rescue movement:

> "To state our position concisely: Rescue missions are saving babies and mothers today in such a way that stimulates political change tomorrow.... Our people have all got to commit to nonviolence both in word and in deed. We have shown our commitments to that very clearly. It's a kind of passive resistance. We go limp—there is no violence, no yelling. The rescues are very peaceful, very prayerful....
>
> "I believe the most pressing and immediate goal is saving the lives of babies. We also want to change public opinion to prevent abortion....
>
> "Going to jail is probably the best statement we can make at this time. We've had over 1,000 people go to jail in the past three months. This is probably the best thing that has ever happened to the pro-life movement, because it gives credibility to our word. People see us and they say, my goodness these people are willing to sacrifice their freedoms as they stand up for these babies and mothers. So it makes us more credible, it draws other people further into the movement, willing to make more sacrifices, and it makes the people who are going to jail come out very courageous. It makes them a force to be reckoned with against the child-killing industry. The system has given them its best shot and they're still not afraid....
>
> "The (legal) risks are there, but they're not that great when people move in unison. Thomas Jefferson said in the Declaration of Independence that the government receives its just powers from the consent of the governed. When we no longer consent, the government no longer has the power to enforce the child killing industry. So if masses of

people rise up, it's over for the abortionists. The jails can't hold us, the courts can't prosecute us. It would become a *de facto* end to child killing in this country. And then the laws will change to coincide with the reality of the situation, which is that nobody can have their child killed. . . .

"Our short-term goal is to end the killings *now;* our long-term goal is to end the child killing permanently by a constitutional amendment" *(The New American,* Nov. 7th, 1988, p. 19, emphasis in original).

"Anarchy and Chaos"

The rescuers may be nonviolent—they "are very peaceful, very prayerful"—but they use forcible tactics. The force of bodies, chains, locks, cement blocks, etc., is used to deny access to the abortuary. They are nonviolent only in the sense that the participants do not shoot, punch, kick, bite, throw things, or otherwise engage in active aggression. The tactics are, however, forcible and they are aggressive. When a rescuer fastens himself with a kryptonite lock and chain to a concrete block in the doorway of an abortuary, so that he cannot be moved, he is a forcible aggressor in any reasonable sense of the word even though he does not hit the policeman who tries to dissuade or move him. These "nonviolent" rescues, in violation of trespass laws, are clearly forcible. But that does not make them wrong.

Some Protestant and other pro-life sources have challenged the legitimacy of any effort to prevent abortion that involves the violation of civil law. Rev. Charles Stanley of Atlanta's First Baptist Church, advocates "all lawful means of protesting abortion," but he opposes Operation Rescue on the ground that it is likely to lead to "anarchy and chaos." The Christian is justified in disobeying the civil magistrate," says Presbyterian Pastor Grover E. Gunn III, of Carrollton, Miss., "only when his obeying the civil magistrate's law necessarily involves his disobeying God's law" (Grover E. Gunn III, *Operation Rescue: An Ethical Evaluation, The Counsel of Chalcedon,* December, 1988, p. 22).

As Judge Robert A. Hamack, of Seattle Municipal Court, said in arguing against Operation Rescue on biblical grounds, "No government agency or person or any private person was moving to command (the rescuers) to commit an offense against God's law. . . . There was, in the Renton (abortion sit-in) case, no act by the government (at any level) to compel or coerce any woman to submit to an abortion. . . . Reference by the promoters of "Operation Rescue" and their demonstrations to Nazi Germany is analytically unsound. In Germany the government was actively moving against the physically infirm, the mentally retarded, and the defective, and ethnically against the Jews and other ethnic groups, violating the law of God. . .

"They were being rounded up and citizens like you and me were asked to identify our neighbors. We were being coerced and compelled to participate in violating God's law.

"In the Renton case the government . . . had only declared it would not punish those seeking, obtaining, or performing abortions. Yes, the women and the physicians were going to commit a sin. What Scripture gives me the authority to commit a crime against those women or those doctors, or to break the peace of an ordered society—that society wherein God has ordained and instituted civil government for the preservation of order between citizens and between citizens and their governments?

"God knows we all have wept for this holocaust. But, no emotional posture can authorize us to violate the civil law by direct rebellion against the civil government, or by the direct commission of crimes against our neighbors for their sin" *(Chalcedon Report,* January, 1989, pp. 15, 17–18).

A Perversion of Law

These criticisms are quoted at length because they question the legitimacy not only of Operation Rescue but also of the basic concept and of the unjust (and therefore void) law. St. Thomas Aquinas explained that we are morally obliged to obey a just law. But if a human law "deflects from the law of nature," it is unjust and "is no longer law but a perversion of law." St. Thomas explains that a law may be unjust in two ways:

"First, by being *contrary to human good...*either in respect of the end, as when an authority imposes on his subjects burdensome laws, conducive, not to the common good, but rather to his own cupidity or vainglory; or in respect of the author, as when a man makes a law that goes beyond the power committed to him; or in respect of the form, as when burdens are imposed unequally on the community, although with a view of the common good. The like are acts of violence rather than laws; because as Augustine says *(De Lib. Arb.* i.5), a law that is not just, seems to be no law at all. Wherefore *such laws do not bind in conscience, except perhaps in order to avoid scandal or disturbance,* for which cause a man should even yield his right. . . .

"Secondly, laws may be unjust through being *opposed to the divine good:* Such are the laws of tyrants inducing to idolatry or to anything else contrary to the divine law; and *laws of this kind must nowise be observed,* because, as stated in *Acts v* 29, we ought to obey God rather than men" *(Summa Theologiae,* I, II, Q. 96, Art. 4, emphasis added).

Every abortion is the killing of an innocent human being; it is, in the moral though not in the legal sense, a murder. *Roe v Wade,* which defined the unborn child as a nonperson subject to execution at the discretion of others, is an unjust law and therefore void. Contrary to Judge Hamack, the analogy to Nazi Germany is correct. The Nazis defined Jews and other target groups as nonpersons. The essential evil of the Nazi program was not that it compelled the killers to kill; incidentally, no psychiatrist was ever compelled to participate in the Nazi euthanasia program—they volunteered. Nor did that evil lie in the fact that German citizens were required to identify targets for extermination. Rather, the essential evil was that the Nazi program defined its targets as nonpersons and subjected them to execution at the discretion of others, which is what the Supreme Court does with unborn children. *Roe v Wade* is a void law.

A Prudential Judgment

The abortion rescuers, however, violate the laws prohibiting trespass which themselves are neutral and just laws. But when those trespass laws are applied to prevent the rescue of the unborn, they are unjust, not inherently but as applied in that case. They do not compel the would-be rescuers to do anything. But they prevent them from interfering with the execution of the unborn; they forbid the exercise of the natural right to defend another person who is under unjust attack. The trespass laws in that context would seem to fall into St. Thomas' category of laws "contrary to human good ... which do not bind in conscience, except perhaps in order to avoid scandal or disturbance."

Contrary to the Protestant views quoted above, there is no absolute moral injunction against violating such a law. Rather, the decision whether to obstruct the abortuary in violation of trespass laws is a prudential judgment as to whether it is the most effective way to prevent the murder of the innocent. In this light, the abortion rescue is a legitimate option. "Operation Rescue," said Atlanta's Archbishop Eugene A. Marino, "is one very dramatic and courageous effort to confront the reality of abortion in the community" *(The Wanderer,* Oct. 13th, 1988, p. 8, col. 6).

The rescuers are engaged, not in protest or demonstration, but in actual rescue. In fact, the rescuers ought to be regarded as not even violating the civil law. If you were walking down the street and saw a mugging in progress, you would have a legal as well as a moral right to intervene forcefully to protect the victim. You might even have a moral duty to intervene forcefully, although you would have no legal duty to do so. If you did intervene, you would have a legal as well as a moral right even to take action that causes the death of the mugger if that was apparently the only way to save the life of his victim. If you saw not a mugging on the street but an attack in progress inside a house so as to be visible from the street, you would have a legal as well as a moral right to commit what would otherwise be a trespass in order to enter that house to save the victim.

The common law or statutory defense of necessity or justification includes the privilege to defend a third person from attack. In *Roe v Wade,* however, the Supreme Court ruled that the unborn child, whether or not he is a human being, is not a person at any time before birth. The Court declined to decide when human life begins but the ruling is the same in effect as a ruling that an admitted human being is a nonperson. You have to be a "person" to be protected by the Constitution with respect to your rights to life and to the equal protection of the laws. The unborn child, as a nonperson, is therefore not protected by the Constitution. The necessity defense, however, is not limited to the protection or rescue of "persons"; it applies to the protection or rescue of all human beings as well as to animals and other property. The Supreme Court, of course, did not—and could not—change the reality that the unborn child is a human being from the moment of conception. The result is a schizophrenic conflict of entitlements: the mother is entitled, by Supreme Court decree, to kill her child; other persons are entitled to rescue a human being in danger, which the unborn child is.

The necessity defense, in the opinion of this writer, ought to apply to the abortion rescue situation, so that the rescuers would be held not even to violate the civil law. The Supreme Court has not ruled on the necessity issue. But state and federal appellate courts have uniformly denied the necessity defense to pro-life trespassers and rescuers in the abortion context. Pro-life lawyers should continue to press the necessity issue. No one, however, should base his decision to join the rescue movement on any expectation that the courts will relent and will allow the rescuers the protection of the necessity defense.

The Most Effective Way

As noted above, some critics of the rescue movement overstate their objection by denying absolutely any right to disobey trespass laws. At the other extreme, some rescue advocates argue that participation in rescues is a moral duty. If the civil law compelled a physician to perform an abortion, it would be what St. Thomas described as a law that is "unjust through being opposed to the divine good: Such are the laws of tyrants inducing to idolatry or to anything else contrary to the divine law; and laws of this kind must nowise be observed. . . . " *(Summa Theologiae,* I, II, Q. 96, Art. 4). The physician would be morally bound to refuse to perform the abortion even at the cost of his own life. But neither *Roe v Wade* nor a trespass law compels the would-be rescuer to do anything wrong. Some rescue proponents argue that there is a moral duty to prevent abortions by obstruction of the premises or by other forms of "nonviolent" physical forces. Granted, that when one knows of an impending murder, one is morally obliged to do what one effectively can do to stop it. The usual response would be to call the police to stop the murder.

The problem is that murder by abortion is legalized. Therefore one has to try something else. But it can hardly be said that there is a moral duty to use force to interfere if one's judgment is that the use of that force is not the most effective way to prevent the killings. There can be no moral duty to interfere forcibly apart from the prior affirmative resolution of the prudential question of whether that interference is the most effective way to save the lives of the intended victims.

The pro-life movement should seek to prevent the killing of individual unborn children here and now. And it should work toward a restoration of constitutional protection to all human beings. The most effective tactic to achieve the first goal is not the rescue but the legal, peaceful prayer vigil combined with sidewalk counseling and referral to pregnancy help centers. At some abortuaries such counseling is difficult because the entrance to the abortuary is separated from the public sidewalk by a privately owned parking lot; the counselors therefore have no immediate access to the women entering the abortuary. In some cases legal action might be advisable to seek a declaratory judgment that the parking lot is a type of public forum and therefore accessible to the counselors, especially where the abortuary is in a building with numerous tenants all of whom are served by the one parking lot. The outcome of such legal action may be unsatisfactory. Pro-life advocacy at abortuaries is one form of speech about which the courts do not appear to be too excited or protective. The difficulties encountered in performing effective sidewalk counseling in some situations apparently have provided impetus for rescues and other forms of disruptive tactics.

Nevertheless, even allowing for the difficulties, the exercise of First Amendment rights in legal, peaceful prayer, and sidewalk counseling is generally a much more effective way of saving lives at the abortuary than is the rescue. The rescuers might close the abortuary for the day. They might be able to point to women who were dissuaded from abortion; but so can the sidewalk counselors. And the rescuers are soon gone. The next day, the abortuary is back in business and the rescuers are in jail or otherwise embroiled in legal proceedings. And the cancelled abortion appointments can be rescheduled. But the sidewalk counselors can continue their efforts every day.

Informed Consent

The abortion industry has adopted an attrition tactic of wearing down the rescuers movement by tort damage suits, private actions under RICO (The Racketeer Influenced and Corrupt Organizations Act), and other forms of litigation as well as criminal prosecution. RICO, enacted in 1970, has been aptly described as "the most sweeping and draconian federal criminal statute ever drafted" *(Insight,* Dec. 26th, 1988, p. 42).

The abortion industry's legal offensive against the rescue movement has hardly begun. As it picks up steam, it will be likely to monopolize an increasing share of the energy and resources of the pro-life movement. The leaders of the rescue movement are counting on massive numbers of pro-life people who will be willing to be arrested; they hope to clog the legal system, thereby preventing enforcement of trespass laws against abortion rescuers. When that clogging is accomplished, they believe, abortions will cease because the abortuaries will be blocked by rescuers whose numbers will have practically immunized them from prosecution.

For the rescue movement to succeed it must enlist a substantial number of people who are willing to be arrested not just once but many times. In the not-so-long run, it is likely that such repeat rescuers will be taken out of circulation by criminal and civil proceedings. Often, otherwise uninvolved pro-lifers will decide to participate in a rescue; it may be the only one they will ever take part in and their decision is commendable. But it is not unfair to ask what is the deterrent effect on future pro-life activity by such one-time rescuers when they face the "morning after" of prosecution and, more significant, civil litigation.

Except for a few situations, there is no indication that clogging of the courts will occur on the scale anticipated; nor is there any indication that tort actions and other civil suits will be prevented by the numbers of the rescuers involved. And injunctions can sweep broadly and be used to immobilize ordinary rescuers as well as leaders by subjecting them to contempt proceedings. Those who choose to make a habitual practice of rescues, as well as those who participate occasionally, should be respected in their decision and admired for their conviction.

Full information as to the potential legal entanglements should be given to those who are encouraged to participate in rescues, however. Their consent should be fully informed as to all the circumstances including the likelihood that sidewalk counseling is the most effective tactic for saving the lives of babies scheduled for execution at the abortuary on that day and on the succeeding days. If a volunteer were to ask me what he could most effectively do, I would strongly counsel him to participate in a legal Rosary vigil with sidewalk counseling rather than in a forcible rescue. But those who choose to participate in rescues are entitled to respect and especially to aid in their legal defense.

Whether to engage in forcible rescues is a matter of prudential choice. The rescue is a legitimate option. But if the rescue effort dominates the pro-life movement and if a clear distinction is not maintained between the rescue movement and the nonforceful, prayerful sidewalk counseling and pregnancy help movement, those latter essential efforts could well be destroyed in the legal backlash against the rescue movement.

A Symptom of Deeper Problems

In sum, the rescue movement is a legitimate tactical option. But it raises other issues more fundamental than the tactical. Some critics reject the rescue effort as a secular, political movement that distracts from the essential task of religious conversion. "Too many pro-life people," says Rev. Rousas J. Rushdoony, "seem to believe that we will be saved from abortion slaughter by laws, or else by civil disobedience. Both are forms of *works salvation.* The solution is Jesus Christ, not congressional action or civil disobedience" *(The Counsel of Chalcedon,* December, 1988, p. 2, emphasis in original).

And Presbyterian Rev. Jeffrey J. Meyers, of Huntsville, Ala., claims that "rescues may save a few lives, but they will not restore God's order in our society" *(The Counsel of Chalcedon,* December, 1988, p. 20). Pastor Meyers concludes, "I don't think rescues are biblical or prudent.... In fact, even if they are successful and civil magistrates do respond, Christians will have been trained to lean upon civil and political measures to effect change in society."

335

Objections of this sort are serious because abortion is not itself the problem. Rather, abortion is a symptom of deeper problems for which the only solution is a reconversion of the American people to love God and respect for His law. The rescue movement has the evidently unintended effect of isolating abortion (and only surgical abortion at that) and treating it as itself the problem, to be solved by the secular techniques of power politics, consensus building, etc. To some extent it is unclear at this stage what the rescue movement is all about. But if that movement has an identity crisis, it is a reflection of the larger identity crisis of the pro-life movement as a whole.

In truth the main objective of the pro-life movement has to be the reconversion of the American people to faith and trust in God. *Roe v. Wade* is merely one inevitable symptom of a disintegration of the social and legal order that has been three centuries in the making. In an apt phrase, Fr. Francis Canavan, S.J., described "the present stage of Western culture" as "the fag end of the Enlightenment" *(Catholic Eye,* Dec. 10th, 1987, p. 2). The Enlightenment, including Hobbes, Locke, Rousseau, and others, rejected the Church, revealed religion in general, the objective moral law and the capacity of the intellect to know truth. Man himself became the autonomous arbiter of right and wrong, that is, he made himself god.

Legalized abortion is merely one manifestation of this trend. It is fruitless to try to restore legal protection for the right to life without confronting this root problem of faith. In this real sense, abortion is inescapably a religious issue. All pro-life tactics, whether rescues or others, should be measured by whether they advance or inhibit the needed restoration of faith.

Loss of Faith

The contraceptive mentality is today the leading manifestation of loss of faith in God and in His Providence. It is also the decisive pro-life issue. Most pro-life groups tiptoe around the contraception question but any "pro-life" effort that temporizes on contraception will be ultimately futile. Legalized abortions in this country are usually estimated at about 1.3 to 1.5 million a year. This figure, however, does not include early abortions caused by the intrauterine device and some so-called contraceptive pills. Such early abortions have

336

been estimated at between 6.4 and 8.8 million each year in this country. (See John Kippley, *Birth Control and Christian Discipleship,* Couple to Couple League, Box 111184, Cincinnati, O., 45211, 1985.) It is clear that the abortion of the fairly near future will be truly a private matter. And when the abortifacient is used in the very early stages of pregnancy, the woman can spare herself the knowledge with certainty that she killed her child. The only practicable legal prohibition on abortifacient pills will be through licensing. But there is no hope of building sufficient support for such restraints as long as the contraceptive mentality remains dominant. And the dominance of that mentality is a product of loss of faith rather than of faulty political tactics. In the abortifacient era, it will be more important than ever to restore spiritual conviction and to emphasize the determining evil of contraception.

It is fair to say that the rescue movement tends to focus on abortuaries and surgical abortions as if they were the whole problem. "So if masses of people rise up," says Randall Terry, "it's over for the abortionists. The jails can't hold us, the courts can't prosecute us. It would become a de facto end to child killing in this country. And then the laws will change to coincide with the reality of the situation, which is that nobody can have their child killed." This scenario misses the point that most unborn babies are killed privately by pills or abortifacient devices. You cannot stop those killings without confronting the contraceptive mentality. And you cannot overcome that mentality by clogging courts, but only by unclogging hearts and minds through prayer. The major drawback in an overemphasis on abortion rescues is that it would distract attention from the need to deal with the underlying problem of faith, in the context of the contraceptive ethic.

The Law of God

Until the Anglican Lambeth Conference did so in 1930, no Christian denomination had ever taught that contraception could ever be objectively right under any circumstances. As various Popes have stated, contraception is wrong because it is the willful separation of the unitive and procreative aspects of sex. The evil involved was described in more basic terms by Pope John Paul II in his audience of Sept. 17th, 1983:

"When therefore, through contraception, married couples remove from the exercise of their conjugal sexuality its potential procreative capacity, they claim a power which belongs solely to God: The power to decide, *in a final analysis,* the coming into existence of a human person. They assume the qualification not of being co-operators in God's creative power, but the ultimate depositaries of the source of human life" (emphasis in original).

Through secularism, we have denied the subjection of the human law to the law of God; through relativism, we have denied objective morality and our capacity to know what is right and wrong; and through contraception, we have made ourselves the arbiters of the beginning of life. We ought not to be surprised at the results:

EUTHANASIA—If, through contraception, we claim the power to decide when life begins, it is no surprise that we claim the power to decide when it shall end;

ABORTION—A dramatic separation of sex from life, abortion is prenatal euthanasia and an inevitable alternate form of birth control in a contraceptive society;

PORNOGRAPHY—This involves not only the separation of sex from life but, like contraception, the reduction of sex to self-gratification. In the process, woman becomes an object as she is in contraception which is, in its essence, a noncommunicative exercise in mutual masturbation.

PROMISCUITY—In the natural order of things, sex is reserved for marriage because sex has something to do with babies and the natural law dictates that children be raised in a monogamous marriage. But if, through contraception, we claim the power to decide whether sex will have anything to do with reproduction, why should we have to reserve sex for marriage?

DIVORCE—In the natural order, marriage should be permanent because sex is inherently related to reproduction and it is according to nature that children should be raised in a home with parents permanently married to each other. But if it is wholly our decision whether sex will have any relation to reproduction, why should marriage have to be permanent?

IN VITRO FERTILIZATION—This is taking the procreative without the unitive, while contraception is the reverse. And the creation of life in a laboratory dish is a dramatic example of man as the "arbiter" of life.

HOMOSEXUAL ACTIVITY—The contraceptive society cannot deny legitimacy to this without denying itself. If it is entirely man's decision whether sex will have any relation to reproduction, if no one can really know what is right and if God's law is excluded, then the objections to allowing Freddy and Harry to get married are reduced to the aesthetic and arbitrary.

To focus the pro-life movement primarily on a constitutional amendment to prohibit abortion is to miss the point. Though such an amendment is an essential objective, it will be achieved only as a result of a reconversion of the American people. That reconversion has to be the main pro-life objective, as stated above by some Protestant critics of Operation Rescue. Contrary to those critics, however, the primacy of the spiritual goal does not automatically exclude rescues. Those rescues depend for their legitimacy on a prudential judgment as to whether they promote both objectives of the pro-life movement—to save lives and to advance the conversion of America.

Contrasts in Courage

Operation Rescue is a reproach to the passive pro-life movement and to the nation at large. The predominantly Protestant character of Operation Rescue is also a reproach to the Catholic Bishops. On Feb. 13th, 1973, the Administrative Committee of the National Conference of Catholic Bishops condemned *Roe v. Wade* and urged "legal and constitutional conformity to the basic truth that the unborn child is a 'person' in every sense of the term from conception." On March 7th, 1974, Cardinals Krol, Manning, Cody, and Medeiros testified before the Senate Sub-committee on Constitutional Amendments. They insisted on the full restoration of personhood to the unborn child with respect to his right to life and they rejected the constitutional amendment proposed by Sen. James L. Buckley (R., N.Y.) which would have allowed abortion "in an emergency when a reasonable medical certainty exists that continuation of the pregnancy will cause the death of the mother." The Bishops soon abandoned that forthright stand. They supported the states' rights Hatch Amendment, and they now promote the "seamless garment" approach which tends to discount the abortion issue. The Bishops have downplayed their responsibility to the unborn child and they favor instead the agendas of feminoids, pacifists, and the homosexual lobby. The contrast between the courage of the rescuers and their own timidity is not flattering to the Bishops.

The rescue movement, however, despite its spiritual motivations, is still essentially a political movement in its tactics and in its proximate and remote objectives. It tends to regard abortion as the problem and its prohibition by constitutional amendment as the ultimate solution. But as a political movement it will tend to compromise. Operation Rescue has already compromised with its own rhetoric in its limitation of itself to "nonviolent" means. They are willing to intervene only to save those babies they can save without the use of "violence." But this is inconsistent with their rhetoric. If there is an absolute biblical injunction to rescue, as they say there is, where does it say or imply in Scripture that it must be done only to the extent that the rescue can be accomplished by "nonviolent" means, passive resistance, going limp, etc.? The rescuers are willing to intervene, up to a point, to deny the woman access to the abortionist. Yet when the woman is escorted past them in the passageway, on her way to the killing chamber, they do not stop her. The objective of saving lives is subordinated to an insistence on pacifist tactics left over from the 1960s.

A more logical position was taken by the bombers and arsonists. If saving lives is really the objective, as it is, and if abortion really is murder, as it is, one answer would seem to be to shoot the abortionist, or at least blow up or burn his abortuary. There are numerous prudential and more basic reasons why such action must not be taken. But at least the four young people who blew up three Pensacola abortuaries on Christmas Day, 1984, lived up to their rhetoric. The rescue movement mobilizes the troops with heroic rhetoric and then the mountain brings forth the mouse, i.e., "going limp." The political character of the rescue movement is seen in this contrast between its rhetoric and its tactics. It chooses the means which will appeal to the public, to build a consensus to stop abortion. But it will

340

be a consensus founded on frustration with disturbance and other secular political grounds.

A Prayer Crusade

The Operation Rescue leaders analogize their movement to the civil rights crusades of the 1960s. The point is well taken, but it is a point of caution rather than of reassurance. Archbishop Eugene A. Marino of Atlanta said that, at the time of the civil rights movement in the 1960s, "There was a general acceptance that what blacks and other minorities had to endure was manifestly wrong. Even in the white community of the South there was a feeling that this wasn't right. By contrast, Operation Rescue is not generally accepted on the notion that abortion is fundamentally evil and wrong. Perhaps many people have this conviction under a layer of apathy. Operation Rescue appears to be based on the hope that this conviction exists and can be roused into action" *(The Wanderer,* Oct. 13th, 1988, p. 8, col. 6). The civil rights marches of the 1960s exhibited many ministers, priests, and nuns. But, whatever its moral origins, it became essentially a political movement. As such, it was vulnerable to compromise. And what has it given us? An abandonment of principle, leading to, among other things, a new system of racial compulsion involving quotas, express and implied.

The main thrust of the rescue movement is secular, political action supported by prayer. On the contrary, the only chance to restore respect for life lies in the opposite approach, not secular action supported by prayer, but rather a prayer crusade supported by secular action, including political as well as counseling and pregnancy help efforts, arising from that prayer and based on inflexible principle. There is no intrinsic reason why rescues could not be a tactic in support of this approach. Operation Rescue is a sacrificial effort to awaken the American people from their tolerance of abortion. While it is not the essence of the pro-life movement, it merits respect and its participants must be defended in court on every legitimate ground, including the argument that the neutral laws that shield murder factories from interference are unjust when so applied. While the rescue movement has its problems, at least its participants are doing something.

As Bishop Austin Vaughan said:

"The things that are decided by governments are not always right. We can't go along, passively accepting them. It's a horror that our law authorizes abortion. In a sense, it's like living in the Roman Empire when Christians were faced, even with death, in trying to live their faith. We are faced with the same kind of situation.

"The biggest threat to our country, faced with this, is complacency and toleration. The longer you live with something bad alongside of you, you get used to it. I don't mean you accept it, but you no longer get excited. We can't afford to have that happen. That's an enormous disaster. Not just for the babies who are killed, not just for the people doing the killing, it's an enormous disaster for all of us. Our standards of what is important and vital wind up being eroded more and more as times goes on. That's the main reason I am here. Nothing much is happening to change the situation; this disaster gets worse the longer it lasts.

"Some feel this kind of protest [direct action rescues] is not effective, but in a sense, to me, it's almost the only show in town!

"I would like to see more peaceful alternatives, but with the political situation, for example, where abortion is not even an issue, something has to happen to get us off the dime" *(The Rescuer,* June, 1988, p. 4).

Peaceful Prayer and Speech

The rescue movement calls us to re-examine, not only *Roe v Wade,* but ourselves. We have no option as to whether we will fight the evil of which the abortion power is a symptom. And the rescues remind us that we are obliged to do something at the scene of the crime. The most effective, on-site, life-saving tactic is the legal, peaceful prayer vigil with sidewalk counseling and referral to pregnancy help centers. These activities, legally conducted on sidewalks or other public property, must be increased. Clergy of all denominations should be encouraged to participate.

Moreover, prayer and informational picketing on the sidewalks in the neighborhoods of abortionists can be an effective, peaceful way of reminding his neighbors of what the abortionist does for a living. Such picketing is apparently protected under the First Amendment, subject to some restrictions which should be checked with an attorney before undertaking it.

The First Amendment protects our right to use the sidewalks and other public property, in a reasonable, nonobstructive manner, to pray and to speak. Operation Rescue has focused national attention on abortion as no other tactic has. The opportunity should be used to increase the numbers of those engaged in the on-site prayer vigils and counseling activity which is protected by the First Amendment. The police, city attorney, etc., should be notified in advance that what is going on is not disruption but peaceful prayer and speech. If the authorities impose unreasonable restrictions, legal action should be taken to vindicate the First Amendment right. (Free Speech Advocates, New Hope, Ky., 44052, a project of Catholics United for Life, provides free, effective representation to sidewalk counselors and other pro-life activists.)

Even if the abortuary is situated behind a private parking lot so that close access to the mothers is not practicable, the prayer vigil should be held and help should be offered. The importance of this is underlined by the experience one college student related to me. She was pregnant and her boyfriend, in the finest tradition of the 1980s, talked her into having an abortion in another city. She was in the abortuary, she filled out the papers, and then her name was called. In her mind she suddenly pictured the little Franciscan nun (in a habit) who was standing on the sidewalk praying the Rosary as the girl entered the abortuary. She thought of that nun who was praying for her and she immediately left the place. She had the baby, placed him for adoption, and is now a very happy, settled young lady. She left the abortuary without ever saying a word to that nun. And that nun probably went home and thought she hadn't done much that day. But God responds to prayer as He knows best.

A Wonder Weapon

Prayer is not a last resort, to be used only when nothing else works. God is in charge. "All power in Heaven and on earth has been

343

given to me" *(Matt.* 28:18). If we really believe that, we ought to put our reliance on Him. And the most effective onsite weapon at aborturies is the Rosary. It is time for us to come out of the bomb shelters and to advocate the Rosary as the prayer of the pro-life movement. The Rosary is a wonder weapon. As at the battle of Lepanto in 1571, it can sink ships.

"In this field," said Pope John Paul II to the Italian Pro-Life Movement, "since it goes beyond human forces, do not fail to invoke the protection of the Blessed Virgin, Mary Most Holy" (Address, Jan. 25th, 1986).

There may be some who hate the Church more than they hate abortion. But as Methodist Rev. J. Neville Ward wrote, the Rosary is an "inexhaustible source of help in the spiritual life" (Ward, *Five for Sorrow, Ten for Joy,* (1973), p. 10). For those who cannot go to the aborturies, let them pray openly in the churches. As Mark Drogin of Catholics United for Life put it: "We hope that this public prayer in the parishes will be a strong foundation for those who are able to be more active. We believe that the most effective response to the public tragedy of abortion is for us to pray the Rosary in front of the abortion chambers where the innocent babies are being slaughtered. We call this prayer and counseling at the aborturies 'sidewalk counseling.' We have been doing it for years and we have saved a great number of babies who were scheduled for abortion." (For more information, contact Catholics United for Life, New Hope, Ky., 40052.)

We began this essay with a statement by Charles H. Langston, a rescuer of persons from slavery. Appropriately, we conclude with a comment by John Cardinal O'Connor on Bishop Austin Vaughan, a rescuer of persons from death:

> "Our Bishop Vaughan is going to jail. For trying to rescue babies from death and their mothers from tragic memories. No gold medal. No ticker-tape parade. Jail. For two days. . . . "
>
> + + +
>
> "The people who risk jail in Operation Rescue believe that preborn babies are precisely that—babies, real, live human persons. They also believe that a great number of mothers who have their preborn babies destroyed will suf-

344

fer shattering guilt and soul-wrenching memories for years to come. They don't hate the young girls or women who go to abortion clinics. They love them and want to protect them from their own foolishness and from the propaganda that has lured them to have an abortion. . . . "

+   +   +

"As my Auxiliary, Bishop Vaughan sees to it meticulously that Operation Rescue does not prevent his carrying out his duties here in the Archdiocese of New York. He needn't worry, if he has to miss a Sunday Mass or a Confirmation ceremony because he's in jail, I'll be proud to fill in. Who knows? One day he may have to do the same for me. For the same reason."

Chapter 22

ABORTION: A CATHOLIC CASE FOR NONVIOLENT INTERVENTION

James G. Hanink

I

How are we to measure the justice of a society?

The Catholic tradition, rooted in Scripture, answers that the first test of the justice of a people is how it treats the weakest of its members. In our society the weakest and most vulnerable are surely the preborn. And how do we treat them? More often than any group among us, they become victims of homicide.

In this essay I assume that the nearly unanimous verdict of Catholic theologians and philosophers with respect to abortion is right: direct abortion is an intentional taking of an innocent human life; as such, it is a grave moral wrong. Vatican Council II, accordingly, speaks of abortion as an infamy and rejects it as "opposed to life itself."[1] My purpose, given this assumption, is to address the question of how Catholics (and others who similarly reject abortion) might best respond to abortion in our current cultural context. I give special attention to a program of nonviolent direct action.

Indeed, it is the character of this American culture of ours, and the extent to which abortion is now entrenched within it, that leads me to encourage disciplined direct action. Here, a pair of statistics, if they do not paralyze us, offer a useful measure of the *status quo.* Since Roe *v* Wade in 1973, we Americans have legally aborted some 24 million preborn human beings.[2] This figure translates into over 4,000 abortions each day.

Our abortion culture insists, however, that the killing of the unborn be kept as invisible as possible, the better to be dismissed as imaginary. A simple contrast illustrates the point. We all recognize the role that graphic television coverage played in our questioning the tragic conflict in Vietnam. Yet when the pictures or the bodies of the aborted are brought forward, every effort is made to suggest that to do is obscene. Not only pictures are prohibited; words are carefully screened. "Fetus," which is suitably clinical, becomes mandatory. Of course, even careful editors doze. A recent story on cocaine addiction and pregnant mothers offers a striking example. The writer presents the mother, who at first rejects her pregnancy, as asking, "How do I get rid of a baby?" When acquaintances mention primitive abortion methods, she reflects, "But, why suffer so much just to kill a child?"[3]

II

Perhaps because abortion is so culturally entrenched, some think that Catholics ought not, at least at the present, lobby to overturn Roe *v* Wade or otherwise endeavor legally to restrict abortion. This line of argument takes various forms and is suggested by New York's Governor Mario Cuomo. The Reverend Richard McBrien, while he does not affirm this position, seems quite taken by the notion that "when the church cannot convince even its own members that something is a sin, it cannot run to the state to have it made a crime."[4]

Broadly construed, the argument is roughly as follows. On the one hand, abortion is a grave wrong. Catholics should be clear about this and carefully explain why to their co-religionists—and to their fellow citizens, should the latter be willing to listen. On the other hand, it is evident that the Catholic rejection of direct abortion, in any case whatever, is not widely shared. Reliable polls tell us, even if our own experience does not, that most Americans believe that abortion is sometimes morally legitimate. A still greater majority believe that the decision whether or not to abort should, by law, be left to the pregnant woman. Since this is the majority view in what we all admit is a highly pluralistic society, our commitment to a democratic polity suggests that we not attempt to translate our moral judgments into binding legal prohibitions.

Amid such reflections, one might even encounter an appeal to the legacy of John Courtney Murray, S.J. Consider, for example, Murray's observation that, unlike the moral law, civil law "looks only to the public order of society; it touches only external acts, and regards only values that are formally social."[5] We are sometimes instructed, too, that St. Thomas Aquinas warns us not to confuse morality and law. Indeed, Aquinas taught that the civil law "does not lay upon the multitude of imperfect people the burdens of those who are already virtuous, namely, that they should abstain from all evil. Otherwise the imperfect ones, being unable to bear such precepts, would break out into yet greater evils . . . "[6]

The burden of this line of reasoning seems to be that in legal matters Catholics ought to accommodate themselves to the democratic consensus, one that involves a multitude of the imperfect. Since the existing consensus supports (increasingly?) legal abortion, Catholics ought to tread lightly in trying to overturn the *status quo*. We especially ought not rock the boat, some add, if doing so seems to penalize poor women whose access to abortion depends on state funding.

Let's call this general line of thought the "consensus position." It urges us to tailor our stand on legal abortion to what we can safely suppose the consensus of Americans supports. Both with respect to some of its presuppositions and to what it claims of its own right, the consensus position is, in my view, altogether bankrupt. Let's begin by noting its dubious assumptions and then look more closely at the position itself.

A first presupposition is that most Americans believe that abortion is sometimes, indeed often, morally legitimate. There are, of course, polls and conflicting polls. But few commentators seem to have paid enough attention to a recent *Los Angeles Times* poll which found that 57% of those surveyed agreed with the proposition that "abortion is murder." (Indeed, a fourth of the people who generally favored legal abortion themselves view it as murder.)[7]

A second presupposition is that St. Thomas and John Courtney Murray, S.J., can be enlisted in support of the consensus view. Neither addressed the question of whether Catholics ought to accept abortion as legal. But neither can be plausibly read even to hint that the common good, which it is the purpose of the law to promote, is compatible with the deliberate killing of the innocent. Nor would they agree that we honor the poor by allocating special monies for them to destroy their unborn babies. Surely, the deliberate killing of the innocent, even if hidden behind abortuary walls, is an "external act" that violates "values that are formally social," to use Murray's language.[8]

A third suspect presupposition, though it is more tacit and tentative, is that the American consensus on abortion (whatever it is) has a certain coherence and consistency. Yet one hardly needs to be a political scientist to recognize that on a given issue, whether abortion or gun control or the death penalty, a particular opinion can be reached on the basis of very different premises and that what amounts to a *de facto* consensus is often shifting and contradictory. One can challenge the latest consensus, at any rate, without challenging democracy. Even then, however great a friend democracy is, justice is a greater friend still.

But, let's move now from the presuppositions of a generalized consensus view to a specific consensus argument. In this schematic version, it might find few existing sponsors. Its influence, however, is pervasive. The consensus argument, then, is as follows:

(P1) There is no consensus in American society that abortion is immoral.

(P2) There is no consensus in American society supporting the legal prohibition of abortion.

(P3) If there is no consensus against a moral evil and no consensus supporting its prohibition, then—

especially in a democracy—Catholics ought not to contest the legal protection of the moral evil at issue.

(C) Therefore, Catholics ought not to contest the legal protection of abortion.

In this argument, "contest" refers to the standard range of lobbying efforts and the support of legislation that would challenge the supposed *status quo* consensus, as determined by Roe *v* Wade. I have already, in effect, disputed the truth of (P1) and (P2). Note that, in doing so, I have not contradicted my claim that abortion is culturally entrenched in our society. For it is quite possible—indeed, I think that it is actually so—that abortion has become culturally entrenched because it has the support of powerful groups within the society even though it does not have the support of a bare majority of the American people. At its best, our political democracy is limited. Our cultural and economic democracy is still more limited.

Nonetheless, I reject the consensus argument chiefly because I think it is untenable. Let us, then, for the sake of a deeper criticism of the consensus argument, temporarily waive any objections to (P1) and (P2) and look instead to (P3).

Why do I dispute (P3)?

It is not that (P3) is entirely implausible. Suppose that the moral evil in question is, say, habitual cutting and sarcastic comments directed at one's neighbors. Should we legally prohibit this practice? By no means. There is a moral evil at issue; but, by itself, the evil is not sufficiently grave.

Or suppose we consider the failure to join in public worship. Again, legal sanction is out of place. The evil is grave; but in this case it does not involve a direct attack on the common good. What is meant by the common good? Broadly understood, the common good is the whole array of material preconditions for the basic goods of human flourishing, together with those goods.[9] But (P3), while plausible with reference to the above cases, is far too permissive if left unqualified. As formulated, it precludes the contesting of racist and sexist laws in a society which has not yet reached a consensus view against racism and sexism. (Has our society, even now, reached a stable consensus in these matters?) But Catholics, to their credit, contested Jim Crow Laws. We were right to do so, even when a societal consensus supported racist laws, because racism is a grave moral wrong that violates human rights. As such, it inescapably attacks the common good. To violate a human right is to attack some basic good, a constituent of human flourishing. Racist laws violate the goods of civic friendship and justice. They, therefore, compromise the common good.

And what is the case with a legal system that allows and protects abortion? Life itself is a basic good without which all other basic goods are denied. So abortion attacks, in one sense, the most fundamental of human rights. Hence, abortion attacks the common good.

Catholic social thought, as it has properly developed in the years leading to and following from Vatican II, shows a strong predilection for democracy. Nonetheless, it can happen that a democracy supports what objectively attacks the common good. (The practice of euthanasia in The Netherlands, where it has gained a *de facto* legality, is a relevant example). While democratic processes are to be supported insofar as they do not directly attack the common good, justice requires that Catholics—always in accord with prudence—intervene to safeguard human rights. Such intervention might involve no more than changing a supposed democratic consensus for legal abortion. But it might *also* involve a wide range of efforts, legal and technically otherwise, to circumvent that consensus until it changes. But in any case (P3), as it stands and unqualified, fails to recognize this moral imperative to safeguard human rights. Hence, we must reject (P3). It follows that we also reject the consensus argument, whatever our estimation of it in (P1) and (P2).

III

The next question, of course, is just how Catholics ought to contest abortion's current legal status. The answer is that we ought to proceed at several levels, including the political-legislative level, the educational level, and the pastoral level.

Certainly the *Webster* decision shows the importance of political efforts. The Supreme Court would not have reached the decision it did had not its newest appointments been made by a president who opposed abortion. Moreover, now that states have a wider leeway to restrict abortion, our political representatives in the state legislatures come to play an extremely important role. Whether at a state or federal level, Catholic legislators ought to take a visible initiative. In this regard, Archbishop Roger Mahony has spoken decisively:

> ... Catholic officeholders—Democrats and Republicans, liberals and conservatives—have a *positive moral obligation* to work for an America that is hospitable to the stranger, the alien, and the weak; to work for an America in which the abortion liberty has been repealed, in our culture and in our laws; to work for an America in which the community, with compassion and care, helps meet the needs of all those involved in an unplanned or unwanted pregnancy.[10]

Nonetheless politics remains the art of the possible. It is often an exceedingly blunt instrument. If we endorse a consistent ethic of life, such as Archbishop Mahony's statement advances, contemporary American politics, only too often, gives us precious few options. A candidate who would support the common good by restricting abortion often compromises the common good by gutting programs that meet the basic material needs of the poor and the sick. The reverse is equally prevalent. A candidate who might help raise significant numbers of people out of poverty is blind to the malice of abortion. We must, of course, continue to function—and wisely—at the political level. But we should not expect overmuch from our current political leaders.

And what of the educational and pastoral levels? If we are to be a Church, we must serve our members, and those outside our fellowship, as teachers and pastors. Especially must we serve those women whom poverty and isolation make most vulnerable to the pressures of an abortion culture. Too few of us take our share of responsibility for women who face crisis pregnancies. Too few of us minister to women already exploited by abortion. That so many Catholics have restored to abortion shows us how much deeper and stronger our educational and pastoral endeavors must become.

And yet we can hardly suppose that such efforts will, themselves, end abortion. We cannot forget the thousands of abortions, all legal, that are performed each day. While we renew and develop our pastoral and educational responses to abortion, the slaughter of the innocents continues. What else might we do?

IV

So far, in discussing whether and how Catholics ought to contest legal abortion, we have addressed only "legal" tactics. I turn now to the response of nonviolent direct action. In proposing such action, let's understand that it incorporates acts of civil disobedience—or what is typically perceived by the judiciary as such. I attach this qualification because there is a strong argument to be made that, say, attempts to blockade abortuaries or to dismantle the instruments of abortion (for example, suction machines) do not, in fact, violate criminal law because they fall under the defense of necessity. That is, such acts are carried out to save lives, and so are not in fact prohibited by laws against trespassing or interfering with private property. Unfortunately, this defense has not won judicial recognition.

Let me next clarify the meaning of "nonviolent direct action" and "civil disobedience." We might, for a start, point to certain paradigm cases. Gandhi's *satyagraha* campaigns in India or Martin Luther King, Jr.'s sit-in campaigns in the early 1960's, offer excellent examples. Still, formal definitions are in order. "Nonviolent direct action" refers to any protest or intervention that, without the use of violence, i.e., the forceful violation of another's right, contests the practice of an institution or state. Ordinarily, nonviolent direct action is civilly disobedient in that it publicly violates a law but does not attempt to escape the sanction for having done so. It is important to note that one can consistently support nonviolent action that is civilly disobedient *and* argue that one always has an obligation to obey the law. The classical Catholic contention already expressed by Augustine, that law which is not just seems to be no law at all, allows us to say that justifiable civil disobedience does not violate a true law but only its simulacrum.[11]

The foundation of Augustine's point is that we must first obey God.[12] All law ultimately derives its authority from God. But, any "law" that would, in effect, have us disobey God is not genuine law. Scripture often illustrates this very point. An apt example, for our purposes, is the Hebrew midwives rejecting the Pharaoh's order to kill the male infants in their charge.[13] The most powerful of such cases is, however, Christ's violation, upon the Father's raising him up, of Pilate's order that the burial tomb be sealed![14]

But how is it that Catholics might contest legal abortion by non-violent direct action? Just what do I propose?

Happily, the examples of what I have in mind are increasingly familiar. (They would be more so were they fully and accurately reported in the media). What is broadly referred to as "Operation Rescue" provides the best example. The standard nonviolent direct action which Operation Rescue (OR) carries out is the blockading of abortuary doors so that no one seeking an abortion or intending to carry out an abortion can enter. This blockade action is "illegal" in that it violates trespass laws and, in many cases, violates injunctions expressly enjoining such blockades. The blockades, in addition to stopping abortion for as long as they can be maintained, win time for OR counselors to speak with women seeking abortion. OR blockades are nonviolent in that they do not violate anyone's moral rights. No one has the moral right intentionally to kill an innocent human being.

An initial question about OR is whether it is effective. Its potential effectiveness is enormous. When hundreds and even thousands of rescuers unite, abortuaries can be closed down for whole days. In fact, this much has already been frequently achieved. Even when police arrest rescuers, the arresting process can often take several hours. During such long periods, counselors are sometimes able to convince women seeking abortion to change their minds. In this summer, OR has already saved identifiable human lives. This, by itself, is a priceless accomplishment.

In addition, while the visible results are less clear, widespread OR actions play a critical educational role. They make it inescapably plain to the abortion culture that many of its most responsible citizens challenge the state's complicity in the destruction of the innocent. A silent holocaust is no longer silent when, day after day and week after week, thousands of citizens risk jail in order physically to contest the practice of abortion.

But, important as the effectiveness question is, there are "deeper" and more searching questions to raise about OR—though such questions, in their own way, bear on the movement's ultimate efficacy. The deeper questions which I want initially to consider touch on the spirit of OR. What motivates rescuers? What makes them think that they can achieve the short term goal of saving lives and the long range goal of the legal prohibition of abortion?

OR is, above all, a prayerful appeal to Christians (and to all people of good will) to repent for the sin of complacency. Again and again, the Prophets called God's Chosen People to repentance. Christians in America are no better. The abortion holocaust simply could not continue in the face of unified Christian resistance. Nor could the practice of slavery have been maintained against such opposition. So OR asks us to look first to ourselves and to pray for a change of heart. Our hope is in *metanoia.*

But, like faith, prayer without works—in this case, pro-life action—is dead. OR does *not* claim that all Christians have an obligation to practice civil disobedience against abortion. But it does insist that an active involvement against abortion, given the circumstances of one's life, is not some special charism. It is a shared Christian duty, as are the corporal works of mercy.

Joan Andrews, a long-time rescuer who suffered years of imprisonment for her actions, makes this point clearly.

> I think the greatest problem we have faced in the prolife movement has been the view that this work is a separate entity from the Church, the Christian community and from one's basic Christian duty. Surely, this duty is based on fundamental Christian love and justice, and is imperative to all Christians living amidst the holocaust.[15]

Justice is not optional. It is essential to the Christian life. To make this inescapably clear and to draw on the only source that can insure effectiveness, OR actions are always carried out in a context of shared and public prayer.

Another deeper question about OR is its sense of the "signs of the times." If one is effectively to challenge a culture, one needs a grasp of how that culture functions. And when a practice is culturally entrenched, as abortion is, one must be able to read a culture in order to find an avenue for its penetration. Has OR done this?

The answer to this query is not yet clear. What is apparent is that OR has given an enormous stimulus to the broader prolife movement. It is also clear that nonviolent action has a striking pedagogical capacity. It is public; it encourages widespread participation. Insofar as it is civilly disobedient, it draws the judicial system into the increasingly uncontainable debate over abortion. It also, in many respects, evades the media's systematic denigration of the moral significance of abortion. When thousands and thousands of people practice disciplined nonviolence, in an open attitude of prayer and repentance, those who have eyes cannot but see.

There are, then, cogent reasons for increased Catholic participation in nonviolent "rescue" interventions against abortion. But the case for nonviolent direct action is incomplete unless we consider at least a pair of important objections to it.

V

Often, the most serious objections to a position come not from its foes but from its friends, friends who nonetheless see it as, in the end, inadequate. The criticisms to which I now turn have such a provenance. (See Professor Charles Rice's contribution to this volume).

The first criticism is that OR too narrowly focuses on surgical abortion. Its usual strategy is the blockading of abortuary doors. But a great many abortions are caused by what are marketed as contraceptive drugs or devices (for example, certain abortafacient "birth control" pills and, of course, intrauterine devices). Such abortions are not reported and so do not figure in the statistics for abortion cited earlier. But, the future promises the further and more deliberate privatization of abortion. We need, in this country, only wait for the inevitable marketing of France's RU–486. The objection, then, is that OR is silent with respect to the contraceptive mentality so intimately linked with abortion. On this account, it might very well restrict our attention to an overly limited range of abortions.

This is an important objection. But I think it can be readily met, especially with increased Catholic participation in OR. Some in the rescue movement have already publicly and sharply opposed contraception. The more that Catholics faithful to the magisterium's teaching against contraception join in OR actions, the clearer will the movement's voice against contraception become. In the meantime, it is unfair to fault OR for beginning with what is more obviously anti-life and then moving to what is, for so many, far more difficult to see as a distorted response to the good of life.

And what of the emphasis on surgical abortion, given the predictable marketing of RU–486 in this country? We would do well to recognize the striking flexibility of nonviolent direct action. If such a drug as RU–486 is to be marketed in the United States, it doubtless will be manufactured here as well. The location of its manufacture would inevitably become known. But then comparable interventions will be carried out at the locations of its manufacture and distribution. Whatever experience we gain now from OR will be to our advantage should such a future come to pass.

The second criticism is that abortion itself is simply a symptom of a progressively secularized society. Insofar as OR leads us into what amounts to a merely political activism, we will, at best, be spitting in the wind. In some ways, this criticism is mistaken at its core. Many Christians—and many Catholics—support legal abortion. It is not always clear that they are "secularized," however complete their moral folly is. Moreover, it is trivializing abortion to call it a symptom of anything. It is *already* blasphemous to abort what is made in God's image.

But, beyond these counters to this second objection, those who have participated in the rescue movement know that it is a deeply religious response to abortion. OR recognizes that those who build the city—who struggle for a just society in which the weakest can come to birth—labor in vain unless they labor with the Lord.

I have sketched, at least, a Catholic case for direct nonviolent intervention against abortion. Such a case takes into account the entrenched position of child-killing in our culture. It rejects the consensus argument that cautions against any aggressive challenge to the *status quo*. At the same time, it recognizes the ongoing role of political, educational and pastoral responses to legal abortion.

But the case for nonviolent intervention is, of course, only *described* in such an enterprise as mine. The case for such action is *made* in the lives of Catholics who give substance to their beliefs. Joan Andrews sees this plainly when she writes:

> ... we will not be able to halt the killing, even if we were to win a High Court reversal of Roe and Doe and even were we to gain a Human Life Amendment, until and unless our

people stop the killing physically with their own bodies . . .
if this is not made clear, if we do not make the protection of
children a fact by the obvious means we have always had at
hand—our own bodies, our own lives—then abortion will
continue barely abated once it's made illegal. It will simply
go "underground" . . . [16]

Philosophical analysis is sometimes essential and always welcome. But ethical analysis—the exercise of *practical* reason—
becomes our own only when we act on it.

NOTES

1. *Pastoral Constitution on the Church in the Modern World,* no. 27.

2. The National Right to Life Committee, drawing on U.S. Government figures, reports that from 1973 through 1988 there were some 22 million legal reported abortions.

3. See "Hooked and Pregnant: A Time Bomb," by Barry Bearak, *Los Angeles Times,* Aug. 22, 1989, p. 1.

4. See his "Religion and Politics in America: A Catholic Reflection," Casassa Conference, Loyola Marymount University, 1988.

5. John Courtney Murray, S.J. *We Hold These Truths* (Sheed and Ward: New York, 1960), p. 166.

6. *Summa Theologiae,* I–II, quest. 96, art. 2.

7. See "Most Americans Think Abortion Is Immoral," by George Skelton, *Los Angeles Times,* March 19, 1989, p. 1.

8. Though Murray did reject the Connecticut birth control statute struck down by the *Griswold* decision, he also wrote "The real area where the coercions of law might, and ought to, be applied, at least to control an evil—namely, the contraceptive industry—is quite over-looked." See *We Hold These Truths,* p. 157.

9. For an analysis of the role of basic goods in human flourishing, see Germain Grisez's monumental study *The Way of the Lord Jesus: Christian Moral Principles* (Franciscan Herald Press: Chicago, 1983). Grisez's approach to natural law informs my own thinking.

10. See "A Policy Statement," *The Tidings,* June 1, 1989.

11. *De Lib. Arb.* i.5.

12. *Acts* 4:19.

13. *Exodus* 1:15–21.

14. Richard Mouw first called this point to my attention.

15. See *You Reject Them, You Reject Me: The Prison Letters of Joan Andrews,* ed. by Richard Cowden-Guido (Trinity Communications: Manassas, Virginia, 1988), p. 148.

16. *Ibid,* p. 166.